# Unlocking
# Internet Information
# Server©

Joel Millecan          Thomas Dawkins

Justin Higgins         Michael Rice

Paul Tso               Sean Mathias

**New
Riders**

New Riders Publishing, Indianapolis, Indiana

# Unlocking Internet Information Server

By Joel Millecan, Justin Higgins, and Paul Tso
With contributions by: Thomas Dawkins, Michael Blair, Michael Rice, Sean Mathias, Leon Salvail, Jeff Rowe, and William Weinman

Published by:
New Riders Publishing
201 West 103rd Street
Indianapolis, IN 46290 USA

Printed in the United States of America 1 2 3 4 5 6 7 8 9 0

**Library of Congress Cataloging-in-Publication Data**

```
***CIP data available upon request***
```

## Warning and Disclaimer

This book is designed to provide information about Microsoft's Internet Information Server. Every effort has been made to make this book as complete and as accurate as possible, but no warranty or fitness is implied.

The information is provided on an "as is" basis. The authors and New Riders Publishing shall have neither liability nor responsibility to any person or entity with respect to any loss or damages arising from the information contained in this book or from the use of the disks or programs that may accompany it.

| | |
|---|---|
| **Publisher** | Don Fowley |
| **Publishing Manager** | Julie Fairweather |
| **Marketing Manager** | Mary Foote |
| **Managing Editor** | Carla Hall |

**Product Development Specialist**
Julie Fairweather

**Acquisitions Editors**
Pete Bitar
Jeff Durham

**Senior Editor**
Sarah Kearns

**Development Editor**
Christopher Cleveland

**Copy Editors**
Cliff Shubs
Greg Pearson

**Technical Editor**
Chris Boucher

**Associate Marketing Manager**
Tamara Apple

**Acquisitions Coordinator**
Tracy Turgeson

**Administrative Coordinator**
Karen Opal

**Cover Designer**
Sandra Schroeder

**Cover Production**
Aren Howell

**Book Designer**
Sandra Schroeder

**Production Manager**
Kelly D. Dobbs

**Production Team Supervisor**
Laurie Casey

**Graphics Image Specialists**
Daniel Harris
Clint Lahnen

**Production Analyst**
Jason Hand

**Production Team**
Heather Butler
Kim Cofer
Terrie Deemer
Beth Rago
Scott Tullis
Megan Wade
Christy Wagner

**Indexer**
Chris Barrick

# About the Authors

**Joel Millecan** has been involved in the growth of the computer industry since learning Basic programming in 1971. He currently specializes in Network and Telecommunication Systems, with a strong focus on Windows NT, Novell Netware, and various UNIX Operating Systems. Joel considers the task of keeping pace with the rapid growth of technology, both hardware and software, an enjoyable responsibility.

**Justin Higgins** began working with the Internet in 1992 on a community Internet service in the Washington, D.C. area. He developed an interest in UNIX and Internet servers soon after that. Justin is currently a webdeveloper at digitalNation, Inc., an Internet Service and Presence Provider in Alexandria, VA. Among other things, he created and maintains the One-Stop Windows 95 Site (http://www.win95.com), the One-Stop Windows NT Site (http://www.windows-nt.com) and WinExpo '96 (http://www.WinExpo.com). He can be contacted via e-mail at jhiggins@dn.net.

**Paul Tso** is an independent consultant specializing in Windows NT networking. He has implemented large scale network security and Internet-related projects. He lectures in computer networking courses at New York University, Information Technology Institute. Paul Tso has a B.A. in Computer Science from Hunter College, C.U.N.Y. He is a certified NetWare Engineer and a Microsoft Certified Systems Engineer. On his weekends, he serves as a 1st Lieutenant signal officer in the U.S. Army Reserves.

**Thomas L. Dawkins** has a broad background from his 14 years in the computing industry. His VAX\VMS, UNIX and NT systems and network administration experiences has given him the expertise to consult and teach in these areas. Thomas is currently working for Sof Teach Corp. in Denver, Colorado. In his spare time, he climbs and hikes in the Rocky Mountains.

**Sean Mathias** is a Windows NT network engineer and has implemented Windows NT networks into critical care environments of leading hospitals and integrated them with diverse network architectures. Currently he is the network architect at Online Interactive where he is providing the insight and direction for their capacity and growth planning while designing a high degree of security, redundancy, and fault-tolerance into their information systems infrastructure. He lectures to various learning institutions and technology groups as requested. As time permits, he enjoys hiking, biking and golf.

**Michael Rice** is a software engineer with Science Applications International Corporation. He has developed large real-time computer simulation models for the Air Force on various platforms including VMS and Unix. He specializes in development of network software for Windows NT, with a special focus on Internet protocols. Mr. Rice has a B.S. in Computer Science from the University of Colorado, with additional training in real-time software systems.

## Trademark Acknowledgments

All terms mentioned in this book that are known to be trademarks or service marks have been appropriately capitalized. New Riders Publishing cannot attest to the accuracy of this information. Use of a term in this book should not be regarded as affecting the validity of any trademark or service mark. Internet Information Server is a registered trademark Microsoft.

## Acknowledgments

**Justin Higgins:** I would like to thank Christopher Cleveland and Pete Bitar at New Riders for helping me to get my part of the book together. I'd also like to thank Brian Gill at Studio B for all his help and support. Finally, I'd like to thank Bruce Waldack and everyone at digitalNation.

**Joel Millecan:** One of the more pleasurable aspects of being an author is having the opportunity to thank others involved with the evolution and culmination of the project. I want to thank Christopher Cleveland and Pete Bitar of New Riders, for their exemplary support, and for initially bringing me aboard the project. Special thanks to Michael Blair, for his participation and assistance. I also want to acknowledge the technical excellence and creativity of the Microsoft programmers and developers. Without them, this book would not have been possible.

**Paul Tso:** I wished to express my thanks to the wonderful staff at New Riders (especially Christopher Cleveland and Jeff Durham) for their patience and guidance in this project. I would like to dedicate this book to coffee, cappucino, and Coke for helping me through the late nights.

**Thomas Dawkins:** I would like to dedicate my work on this book to my parents, Albert and Mary Joan Dawkins, for giving me the direction to do the right things and to all my new friends in Colorado who have been there to support me in all my endeavors. Special thanks go out to my great friend, mentor, and boss Terri Olson, for giving me the many opportunities to enrich my life and profession.

**Michael Rice:** This is dedicated to my parents, Mike and Paula. For my father who gave me my start in software engineering and continues to be a source of inspiration. For my wonderful mother who not only put up with all of the late nights at the computer while I was in high school and college, but even made me coffee and snacks at 3:00 a.m. I would like to acknowledge my employer, SAIC, for allowing me to keep an extremely flexible schedule to accommodate my personal software development efforts.

# Contents at a Glance

# Part VI: Advanced Internet Information Server Tasks

# Table of Contents

## 3  Planning Server Connectivity

# Part II:  TCP/IP and Internet Protocols

## 4  Introduction to TCP/IP

## 5 TCP/IP Routing

## 6 IPng

# Part III: Configuring Internet Information Server Publishing Services

## 7 Configuring the WWW Publishing Service

## 8  Multihoming: Creating Multiple Domains

## 9  Configuring the FTP Publishing Service

## 10 Configuring the Gopher Publishing Service

## Part IV: Managing Internet Information Server

## 11 Monitoring Server Activity and Performance

## 12 Site Administration Utilities

## Part V: Internet Information Server Security

### 13 Server Security Basics

## 14 Security Utilities and Testing

# Part VI:   Advanced Internet Information Server Tasks

## 15 CGI Basics

# 16 Database Interfaces

## 17 Introduction to Database Connectivity with Microsoft SQL Server and Oracle CGI Scripting

# 18 ISAPI

# Index                                                  579

# Chapter 1

# Introducing Microsoft Internet Information Server

Microsoft Internet Information Server is one of the newest members of the Microsoft BackOffice Suite of Server applications. Internet Information Server (IIS) provides services for hosting an Internet or Intranet information repository on the Windows NT platform.

First, let's define our terminology. The term *Internet* is used to refer to the independent, global TCP/IP network that has exploded in popularity over recent years. The *Internet* is loosely connected with little regulation and no specific owner.

*Intranet* refers to a private TCP/IP-enabled network, usually owned by the organization using it and regulated in use and content for distributing pertinent information relating to the organization or its industry to be used internally.

For the purposes of this book, *Internet* and *Intranet* will be used interchangeably to refer to a TCP/IP-enabled network unless otherwise specified.

# Brief History of the Internet

The global *Internet* that has rapidly grown in popularity over the last several years originally began as a research project funded and sponsored by the Department of Defense in 1973. This project was originally termed *DARPANET (Defense Advanced Research Projects Agency Network)* and was implemented as a research program to investigate techniques and technologies for interlinking packet networks of various kinds.

The goal of this project was to develop protocols that would facilitate the linking of geographically dispersed and diverse packet networks for improved communications.

In 1986, the U.S. National Science Foundation formed a similar network, called NSFNET, to improve communications between a large number of researchers. During this time, several other similar networks were developed around the world. Eventually all of these were connected to produce what is known today as the global *Internet.*

Over a period of time, the originators of these networks (primarily the DOD, NSF, NASA, and DOE) abandoned or relinquished control of these networks, and maintenance and administration was assumed by loosely organized groups to form what are now known as the "governing" bodies of the Internet. Although there truly is no "owner" or single authority for the Internet, these governing bodies are accepted almost unanimously around the world and are necessary for the continuation of this growing phenomenon. Without some sort of guidance and direction, this effort would quickly deteriorate and cease to exist.

The primary bodies of the Internet are as follows:

➤ Internet Society (ISOC): Anyone may become a voting member of the Internet Society, which consists of people who continue to work toward furthering the Internet effort and reaching even the most geographically remote areas

➤ Internet Engineering Task Force (IETF): The protocol engineering and development arm of the Internet, elected by and from the ISOC membership

➤ Internet Engineering Steering Group (IESG): A subset of the IETF focused on identifying Internet issues and providing direction for the growth of the Internet

➤ Internet Assigned Numbers Authority (IANA): The central coordinator for the assignment of unique parameter values for Internet protocols

➤ Internet Network Information Center (InterNIC): Administers and provides directory, database, and registration services for IP address space and TCP/IP domain names

The most compelling reasons for the recent growth of the Internet are its global nature, extending to most every corner of the world, and that the protocols it is built upon (TCP/IP) enable internetworking heterogeneous networks over a variety of communications mediums.

Of the various protocols implemented from the TCP/IP protocol suite, the three most popular and commonly used are FTP, HTTP, and Gopher. This leads us to the topic at hand—Microsoft Internet Information Server—an application that provides these services on the Windows NT platform.

# Internet Information Server

With the explosive growth of the "Internet" concept, the demand for server applications capable of providing these services has also grown dramatically. At this point, all the major network players such as Microsoft, Novell, IBM and many new Internet companies have rushed to provide these services for their customers.

Three of the primary uses of the Internet, in addition to electronic mail, are document publishing, file transfer and exchange, and information searching and retrieval. As stated previously, many companies have brought server applications to market to enable these technologies on diverse platforms other than Unix (the original platform of the Internet). One such server application is Microsoft Internet Information Server (IIS), part of the Microsoft BackOffice suite of server applications.

Microsoft Internet Information Server provides native Windows NT services to provide the previously mentioned Internet functionality. Specifically, IIS comprises of the following services:

➤ World Wide Web publishing services (HTTP) for document publishing

➤ FTP publishing services for file transfers

➤ Gopher publishing services for information indexing, searching, and retrieval.

# Features and Components of Internet Information Server

In Internet Information Server, Microsoft has bundled these key components of Internet computing into one single package, which tightly integrates into the Windows NT operating environment, thereby reaping the benefits of a scaleable and secure server platform.

# HTTP, FTP, and Gopher Services

The HTTP, FTP, and Gopher services in Microsoft Internet Information Server are tightly integrated with the Windows NT environment; in fact, they are native networking components of Windows NT Workstation and Server 4.0.

HTTP (HyperText Transfer Protocol), or WWW services as they are referred to with IIS, along with FTP and Gopher services are native components of the Windows NT 4.0 architecture. The user is given the option of installing these services during the network setup portion of Windows NT 4.0 installation. These services can also be installed at a later time using the Internet setup icon on the desktop (conveniently provided by the Windows NT setup program).

Because of this integration, the three publishing services are able to fully exploit the architecture of Windows NT. They can take advantage of the symmetrical multiprocessing (SMP) capabilities of Windows NT, utilize the tight security native to Windows NT, and operate as true, 32-bit multithreaded applications.

One of the most compelling reasons to use Windows NT as an *Internet* server platform is its 32-bit architecture, native support for SMP (Symmetrical Multiprocessing), multithreading, and strict security policies. By supporting robust and fault-tolerant systems, the threat of downtime or system overload is effectively removed, providing an *Internet* information store that will always be available and able to serve your customers and the public at large.

These services also run as native Windows NT services, which means that they run as fully functional operating system components in the background. Services can be configured to run in a specific security context (say an account with sufficient rights to perform all necessary *Internet* functions, but restricted from any other operating system services or functions) or use the local system security context. What this boils down to is that IIS's services can be configured to have only the security permissions needed to perform their function, subsequently eliminating many potential security risks. If the security context for a service is configured properly, an errant script will be unable to cause significant damage to the system or provide access to unauthorized system components or files.

Services can also be stopped, started, and paused independently of the rest of the system. This means it is never necessary to take the server offline and reboot when changes are made to the Internet server components. Additionally, services can be configured to start automatically on system startup, thus preventing the need to manually initialize the service should the system go down and reboot.

# Additional Services and Features of Windows NT

Microsoft, with its emerging Internet-centric focus, has included several other services that facilitate the use of Windows NT as an Internet server platform, as well as modifying some existing services and functionality of Windows NT to support Internet computing.

## Peer Web Services

Microsoft Windows NT Workstation 4.0 now offers *Peer Web Services*. Effectively, these are Internet services designed for small, departmental intranets. These provide an excellent mechanism for information sharing among a relatively small group of users, such as online policies and procedures, or Web-based help desk requests. Like IIS, Peer Web Services are native to Windows NT Workstation 4.0, yielding the same benefits as IIS that were previously mentioned.

# DNS Services

Windows NT Server 4.0 also offers a *Domain Name Server (DNS)* service. The DNS service translates user-friendly names such as *www.microsoft.com* to the IP network address (in this case, 198.105.232.7) that computers and networks use to find the appropriate host and service. This is a new feature to Windows NT Server 4.0 that enhances the Windows NT platform for Internet services.

# Key Manager Utility

The Key Manager Utility component of Internet Information Server is a security mechanism that provides data encryption, server authentication, and message integrity over a TCP/IP connection using *Secure Socket Layers (SSL)*. SSL is a key-based authentication and security implementation that further extends the native security of Windows NT to the protocol data level.

# Performance Monitor and Counters

Counters have been added to *Performance Monitor*, which is the Windows NT utility for monitoring virtually every aspect of systems resource usage for IIS. Counters enable the system administrator to monitor the performance of the server, determine potential bottlenecks, and make optimization and expansion decisions without having to guess where the weak point may be.

Internet Information Server is truly an integrated component of Windows NT, exploiting the advanced functionality, robustness and security to provide the fastest, most secure Internet server available.

# Scripting

In addition to providing traditional Internet services, Microsoft has improved them in many ways. In traditional HTTP servers (for document publishing), it is common to embed scripts in

HTML pages to provide interaction or added functionality to the user. This is typically implemented through the use of what are known as CGI (Common Gateway Interface) scripts. The drawback of these scripts is that each time they are invoked, they create new processes and execute independently of each other, needlessly wasting system resources. For active Internet sites that sustain thousands and sometimes millions of accesses (hits) a day, this can become cumbersome or overwhelming to the server. Microsoft has implemented this feature differently through the use of DLL files, which load themselves into memory once when the server starts and handle all requests without creating a new process each time, which conserves server resources. This is referred to as the Internet Server Application Programming Interface (ISAPI), a programming standard provided by Microsoft.

## Remote Administration

Microsoft Internet Information Server, like all other Microsoft BackOffice components, supports remote administration from client workstations. Provided the users have appropriate network rights, they can install only the server administration component on their local workstations. This enables users to administer the Internet Information Server services remotely. In fact, all IIS services on the network can be administered from a single remote console.

This functionality is extremely useful and important for networks with multiple Internet Information Servers that are geographically separated or widely dispersed across the enterprise from the person responsible for administration and maintenance. This capability is provided through an easy-to-use management interface, shown in figure 1.1.

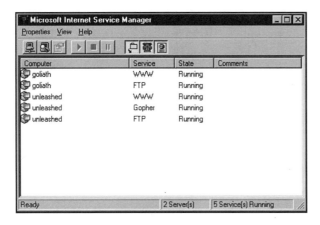

**Figure 1.1:**

The Internet Information Server management console.

From the Internet Server Manager, all available services on the network can be administered centrally. Services can be stopped, started, and reconfigured from the Internet Server Manager. The processes that cannot be carried out from the Internet Server Manager include the following:

➤ Installation of servers and services on the network

➤ Removal of servers and services on the network

➤ Maintaining and updating Internet site content.

Microsoft does, however, make a tool to remotely update and author Web content—Microsoft FrontPage.

# Customization and Extensibility

All of the services within Internet Information Server are easily customized and configured through a graphical interface. The administrator can quickly set the connection timeout value for disconnecting idle sessions, the maximum number of allowable concurrent connections, and the security context that remote users will operate under (usually a guest equivalent with highly restricted access).

IIS's publishing services can be configured to allow three different security configurations:

➤ Anonymous users and users with special privileges (using usernames and passwords)

➤ Only anonymous users

➤ Only privileged users (users with usernames and passwords for the given server)

## Virtual Servers

All services can be configured to host multiple "virtual servers." Virtual servers enable the implementation of multiple HTTP, FTP, or Gopher servers on a single system without resorting to using multiple instances of the application or nonstandard TCP/IP ports.

The addition or creation of virtual servers is fairly simple and straightforward. The following lists the basic steps necessary:

➤ Add one or more IP addresses to the Windows NT network configuration using Control Panel, Network

➤ From the Internet Service Manager, choose the service you wish to create a virtual server for, select Properties, Service Properties, and then choose Add from the Directories tab

➤ Specify the root directory for the virtual server (shown in figure 1.2), check the Virtual Server box, and provide the IP address you previously added to the system

You now have a second virtual server running on the same system as your primary server. To simplify access to the site for your users you can create an alias for the service on your DNS server (such as www.foobar.net). Creating virtual servers and aliases will be discussed in Chapter 8, "Multihoming: Creating Multiple Domains."

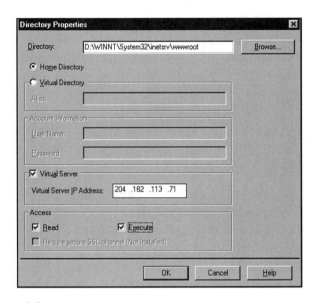

**Figure 1.2:**
The directories and virtual server configuration dialog box.

Effectively, virtual servers provide the capability to locate and run *winnt.bhs.com* (IP address 206.17.91.10) and *backoffice.bhs.com* (IP address 206.17.91.210) from a single server, with the appearance of being two individual Internet servers to the outside world.

This is a useful feature to many organizations that may have multiple Internet domain names (microsoft.com, msn.com, and so on) or that operate under several trade names and want to be accessible to all of their potential customers. Another common usage of multiple servers or Internet sites is to provide specific information for various divisions of a company (internet.microsoft.com, windows.microsoft.com, and so on).

# Configuring HTTP Servers

The HTTP server provides an option to enable a default document for when a remote user attempts to access an URL (Uniform Resource Locator) by generic address, such as

**www.prosolve.com**. Entering a generic address will locate the server; however, there needs to be a default document that pops up for the user. When a user types in the generic address, what is actually accessed and returned is *www.prosolve.com/default.htm*.

The HTTP server also has the capability to enable directory browsing that provides the user with a hypertext listing of the directory structure, subsequently enabling the user to traverse and browse the directory tree to access files.

Directory browsing can be an effective method of providing a "document warehouse," providing descriptive directories that contain pertinent documents related to a given subject. Publishing in this manner makes much more efficient use of server resources and network bandwidth because each document is not automatically displayed—only the specific document requested by the client must be passed over the network.

## Configuring Gopher Servers

The Gopher publishing service is fairly simple and straightforward. As mentioned earlier, Gopher is primarily an information indexing search and retrieval service. The Gopher publishing service is designed specifically for document and keyword searching and indexing. Although the HTTP and FTP publishing services can also provide this functionality (to a limited degree), the Gopher service is optimized to handle searches and queries for information.

The IIS Gopher service also enables name and e-mail specification for the service administrator. This is primarily for remote users to send comments or problems to a responsible person at a given organization.

## Monitoring FTP Server Activity

The FTP publishing service provides a utility for the service administrator to view the current FTP sessions, as shown in figure 1.3.

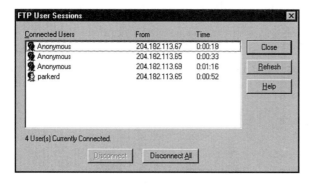

**Figure 1.3:**
The Current Sessions utility of the FTP server service.

From here, the administrator can view the currently connected users, the IP address they are connected from, and the amount of time they have been connected. This feature has proven useful for monitoring specific users who are connected to the server and for disconnecting users who, for some reason, should not be connected to the server.

Each user shown is also represented by one of two icons. The head or torso icon represents a user who is connected with a valid username and password; a head with a question mark in it represents an anonymous user. From here, the administrator can also disconnect a specific user or all users with the push of a button.

# Configuring FTP Servers

The FTP publishing service enables administrators to specify informational messages to be displayed to users upon their arrival and departure from the FTP server. The FTP service also enables administrators to specify a message to be displayed when the maximum number of connections has been established. The directory output style can be configured to emulate MS-DOS or UNIX style. Also, each FTP server or virtual server can be configured for read and/or write access.

By design, all of these services are fully compatible with remote client software. By virtue of the protocol used, the client-side operating system is irrelevant, provided a seamless integration between client and server for information exchange is used.

# Logging Options and Access Restrictions

Each of IIS's publishing services provides options for logging activity on the servers. Activity can be logged to a text file or to an ODBC-compliant database through an ODBC database source.

ODBC (Open Database Connectivity) is a standard (developed by Microsoft) for interfacing and exchanging information with a database system. ODBC greatly simplifies establishing a connection to a database and the passing of information between a client application and a database system. Supported databases are said to be ODBC-compliant, meaning they adhere to or support the ODBC specification.

When logging on to an ODBC database, there must be a system data source name (DSN) configured on the host system for the ODBC database to reference. Create a System DSN on the server system that references the database to be logged to. Provide the necessary information in the SQL/ODBC log configuration field and all activity information will be logged to the specified data source where it can be parsed (searched for information that meets a specific criteria, similar to *queried*) and used to create customizable reports. Please note, IIS includes a SQL script to create the necessary table to output the log information in a database. The script name is *logtemp.sql*. This script is very useful for projecting growth and analyzing the effectiveness of an Internet site—an extremely important feature in a time when more and more commercial organizations are hosting an Internet presence.

For text file logging, there are options to create a new log daily, weekly, or monthly, or when the file reaches a specified size.

Finally, IIS enables administrators to restrict access to servers and services based on IP address or by setting a bandwidth usage ceiling. Specific IP addresses or address ranges can be explicitly granted or denied access to a server or service. This is an excellent feature for two specific reasons:

➤ If this is a corporate intranet, access can be restricted to only IP addresses within your organization.

➤ If you have a situation where a user is trying to gain unauthorized access to your systems, you can deny access to his IP address or address range.

The maximum network use can be restricted on a system by specifying the maximum amount of bandwidth available to Internet services. This can be useful on a corporate *Intranet* where everyone shares a 4, 10, or 16Mbps network segment and bandwidth is at a premium.

# Summary

Microsoft Internet Information Server is an integrated Windows NT service, providing unparalleled performance and stability in an Internet server application. By loading only a single instance of the program, multiple servers and virtual servers can be supported. Scripts can be implemented as DLL files that only need to be loaded to the server once to process all requests rather than executing separate instances of a CGI script each time. These factors help to provide a higher overall performance over other Internet server suites.

Additionally, by exploiting the native security and TCP/IP components of Windows NT, IIS is able to achieve stability and security unmatched by any other server.

Here is a brief overview of the components and features of IIS:

➤ WWW, FTP, and Gopher publishing services that are integrated components of the underlying operating system

➤ Easy to use management interface for centrally administering all publishing services on a network

➤ Multiple levels of security and authentication options

➤ Ability to support multiple virtual servers on a single server system

➤ Options to log server activity to a text file or an ODBC-compliant database system

➤ Provisions for restricting access to publishing services by IP address and restricting network bandwidth usage

➤ Optimized method of loading and executing scripts

➤ Tight integration with Windows NT that provides advanced security, fault tolerance, and scalability

To enhance the functionality of Microsoft's Internet Information Server, consider looking into the following associated and complementary products for use with IIS:

➤ FrontPage: Microsoft's remote Web authoring and content management product.

➤ SQL Server/Access: Mircosoft's enterprise and workgroup databases (respectively). Both are ODBC-compliant and capable of acting as a repository for IIS logs and interacting with IIS.

➤ Internet Assistant: Add-on for Microsoft Office applications that can be used for HTML (Web document) authoring or converting Microsoft Office files to HTML files.

# Part I

## Internet Information Server Preliminary Issues

# Chapter 2

# Configuring Windows NT Server

The Microsoft Internet Information Server (IIS) is tightly integrated within Windows NT Server to provide an efficient, reliable, scaleable, and secure platform for access to the Internet. Without a secure environment, business critical data is unprotected, which leaves an open door for users who could access systems to maliciously corrupt or delete data or an operating system. To ensure an optimal level of security, the Microsoft Internet Information Server uses the security features of Windows NT Server to manage individual user and group access to the server. NT Server uses the Windows NT Access Control Lists (ACLs) to ensure that users only get access to the files that they have permission to access.

The Microsoft Internet Information Server can also utilize the services, utilities, and tools provided by Windows NT Server. For instance, an administrator might load Microsoft SQL Server to log server statistics provided by NT Server and put these statistics in a database for analysis. The Windows NT Event Log is a utility that an administrator would use to keep track of security, to access information, and help troubleshoot problems in the system. An administrator will use the Remote Access Service (RAS) to provide Internet Information Server resources to remote workstations.

Windows NT Server utilizes protected memory, which protects a 32-bit application from crashing when other applications on the system crash, and uses its micro-kernel architecture to provide a reliable platform for your Web server to avoid crashes. Built into NT Server are also some advanced fault tolerance software tools to provide redundancy in a data recovery process. Software RAID (Redundant Array of Inexpensive Disks) is used to provide fault tolerance in an NT environment if hardware RAID is unavailable. Disk mirroring (RAID level 1) and disk duplexing provide redundant data by writing the data to another physical device while the data is being written to the orginal device. *Disk duplexing* is when the other physical device is on a separate controller—this provides not only redundancy in data but also hardware controllers. Striping with parity (RAID level 5) is another software implementation of fault tolerance that distributes parity information across all the disks that are involved in the stripe set. The parity information is key to this type of fault tolerance—without it the data cannot be regenerated. Striping without parity (RAID level 0) is also supported but is not considered fault tolerant.

## NT Server Configuration

Before loading Internet Information Server, it is best to make sure that NT server complies with the minimum configuration standards to install and utilize the Internet Information Server. If your NT server does not comply with the minimum configuration parameters that Microsoft has suggested, be aware that if there are other programs or services that are being used on this NT server, additional resources might be needed: hard disk space, memory, processor upgrade, or additional processor. These resources are interdependent and should be monitored regularly, using the Performance Monitor application, to ensure optimal system performance.

The minimum configurations to use the Internet Information Server are discussed in the following sections as they pertain to specific resources.

# Hardware

Having the appropriate hardware is about as important as having the correct operating system. If Internet Information Server does not have the correct hardware resources, it might not load during installation or the software performance would be reduced greatly. Currently, Microsoft recommends the following hardware requirements for the Internet Information Server:

➤ 50 MHz 80486 or higher CPU (a Pentium® 90 or above is recommended)

➤ Minimum of 16 MB of RAM (32 to 64 MB of RAM is recommended)

➤ Minimum of 50 MB of free hard disk space

➤ Mouse

➤ Network Adapter Card, Modem, ISDN or T1 connection for intranet and/or Internet access

➤ VGA, SVGA, or XVGA display adapter and monitor

➤ CD-ROM drive, 3.5-inch 1.44 MB floppy disk drive

The Network cards for your intranet should be a 32-bit card to provide the best throughput for your users to access IIS. It is recommended to use a network card that is in the NT Hardware Compatibility List (HCL). Not abiding by selecting approved vendors could limit your support from Microsoft. The HCL can be downloaded from the Microsoft Web site at **http://www.microsoft.com**.

The 32-bit cards provide 1.14 MB throughput, whereas a 16-bit card provides 740 KB. If you are planning to use more than one network card, to segment your network and use your NT server as a router, use the custom install to be able to configure both the cards at one time. The IRQ and an I/O port address are configurable parameters that can be configured via a switch on the network card or can be configured via software. It is important to know what these settings are when installing NT. If these settings are wrong, the system might not get access to your intranet.

For modem access it is best to use the fastest available modem for the best throughput (28,800 baud). The capacity of an ISDN line is 64Kbps (or 128Kbps if two channels are used) and the capacity of a T1 line is 1.54 megabits per second. Modems are the cheaper solution for access; ISDN is higher and may not be available in most areas. T1 lines are very expensive and are a direct access to a provider. T1 access needs to be configured through the provider.

Many local area networks now take advantage of new technology, such as concentrators, hubs, switches, or FastEthernet media, which is capable of delivering data on the order of 10-100 megabits per second.

## Software

Internet Information Server software requirements also need to be met to provide a supported operating system platform. Microsoft might not provide support to systems that do not meet the software requirements, so it is important to install and configure the following software:

➤ Microsoft Windows NT Server 4.0

➤ TCP/IP protocol

➤ Optional DHCP, WINS, and DNS

➤ A drive using the NTFS file system

If DHCP, WINS, and DNS are going to be installed on the same server, additional hard disk space and memory will be needed.

Dynamic Host Configuration Protocol (DHCP) is used to lease IP addresses to client computers. DHCP helps ease the configuration of the client computers and prevents network errors that can occur if a duplicate IP address is on the network.

Windows Internet Naming Service (WINS) helps to resolve NetBIOS computer names in a TCP/IP environment. WINS will dynamically associate the NetBIOS computer name with the computer IP address when the system is first booted. If another computer wants to access resources on a WINS-enabled computer, the WINS Server handles the resolution of the IP address of the computer.

Domain Name Service (DNS) provides the naming structure that all TCP/IP nodes will use on the Internet.

# The NTFS File System

Microsoft NT Server supports four different file systems:

➤  NT File System (NTFS)

➤  High Performance File System (HPFS)

➤  File Allocation Table (FAT)

➤  CD-ROM File System (CDFS)

Only the NTFS file system provides a secure and reliable environment for Internet Information Server and is required for an Internet Information Server installation. NTFS utilizes hot-fixing or what some call Sector Sparing. This functionality automatically moves data from a bad disk sector to another disk sector that is not damaged. A clean sector is provided for the data to be written to by the disk heads. Hot-fixing is only supported on SCSI and fault-tolerant devices.

In combination with NT's Security Account Manager, NTFS builds a secure file system that cannot be accessed unless both the user and password have been validated by the Security Account Manager. Users will not be able to access an NTFS partition by rebooting the machine with a DOS boot disk due to the security that is enabled in an NTFS partition. Be aware that there are some new shareware utilities that can access an NT system even if the system partition is NTFS. When a user implements these utilities, it could expose the system to outside threats.

For users to be given permission to access a file, the administrator will set some type of permissions on the file for the user to read or update the file. This file permission access is controlled by the Access Control List (ACL). Every resource that a user can access through NT has an ACL associated with it. The ACL is checked when a user tries to access that resource. If the ACL has the user permissions set to no access, then the user will not get access to the resource. Each user that accesses a resource must be validated by the system and get access to a resource via the ACL.

The NTFS partition is not restricted by the 8.3 filenames. It supports long filenames that can have up to 256 characters in the name including spaces and punctuation.

Example: My First Home_Page.HTML

NTFS also provides aliases for long filenames so that a DOS or a Windows 3.1 system can recognize the file.

Example: My_First.HTM

The example would be an alias for the long filename that is shown above.

An NTFS partition can be created during the install process or an administrator can convert an existing FAT or HPFS file system by using the following command line syntax:

```
CONVERT c: /fs:NTFS
```

The system will reboot with the partition marked for conversion. The next reboot will take some time to complete due to the conversion process. This should take no more than 10 minutes for the last reboot.

# TCP/IP

Microsoft supports the following networking protocols:

➤ NetBEUI (NetBIOS Extended User Interface)

➤ NWLink (IPX/SPX Internet Packet Exchange/Sequenced Packet Exchange)

➤ DLC (Datalink Control)

➤ TCP/IP (Transmission Control Protocol/Internet Protocol)

Microsoft changed the default protocol on NT from NWLink (IPX/SPX) to TCP/IP when version 3.51 was released. This change was due to Microsoft's new direction to make all applications Internet-accessible. TCP/IP and NWLink are fully routable protocols, which means that the packet that these protocols use can be delivered through a network router to be delivered to another subnet on the intranet.

TCP/IP is the protocol for the Internet and is considered the glue for a heterogeneous environment. The Internet has many types of systems that communicate with each other; VAX/VMS, UNIX, and DOS to name a few. These systems cannot communicate without a standard, mature, and nonproprietary protocol such as TCP/IP.

TCP/IP is very easy to install, but proper configuration is important and takes a lot of planning to implement in a computing environment. There are two ways in which to install TCP/IP: manually, or by using DHCP (Dynamic Host Configuration Protocol). It is best to have an understanding of how to configure the systems manually to fully understand how to configure the system with DHCP.

TCP/IP uses a 32-bit addressing scheme to communicate with other systems. These addresses are not hard coded in your computer or other system devices due to different subnet configuration parameters in each company. Each device has to be configured with TCP/IP addresses to communicate and pass data back and forth on a TCP/IP network. This is done with a configuration utility that most TCP/IP stacks include in their version of TCP/IP.

There are several TCP/IP parameters that can be manually configured on the NT Server at the time of installation or anytime after NT has been loaded. Additional information might be needed if there is a WINS Server or DNS Server available. If any of the information is incorrect in configuring TCP/IP, serious network problems might arise. For instance, you might not be able to PING another system on a different network. This is probably due to the subnet mask being incorrect or having a duplicate IP address on the network.

The following information is needed to configure TCP/IP during the installation of NT Server:

➤ Host Address: The IP address of the computer

➤ Subnet Mask: The address used to verify that a destination machine, one that is trying to be accessed, is on the current subnet by comparing the IP address of the remote system and the subnet mask

➤ Default Gateway: The address of an existing router that the system needs to access to get outside of its subnet

These addresses can be changed at any time after the system has started under Network Properties and TCP/IP protocol. If an IP address for another system has been entered in the Host Address area, the TCP/IP protocol will not start and a duplicate IP address error will occur in the Event Viewer. Duplicate IP addresses could cause a machine to be unable to access other subnets.

If the NT Server has been configured to use the Dynamic Host Configuration Protocol (DHCP), the automatic way of configuring TCP/IP, then the user does not need to enter the configuration information for the IP address, subnet mask, or default gateway. The DHCP Server will lease a server or any computer an IP address and provide the subnet mask and default gateway information. DHCP reduces the probability of mistyped configuration information that could cause network problems and result in an administrator having to configure every machine manually.

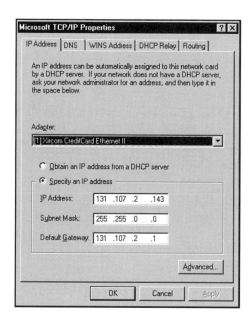

### Figure 2.1:
Manual configuration of TCP/IP.

To configure the computer system to get its IP address from an existing DHCP server, check the DHCP box during the install. DHCP configuration can also be configured later when a DHCP server is available. This is located in Network Properties, under the TCP/IP properties.

Whether you are providing access to the Internet or an intraoffice intranet, TCP/IP must be loaded before loading IIS. The Internet Information Server uses this information to build its services. The DNS Service must also be configured for external Internet access.

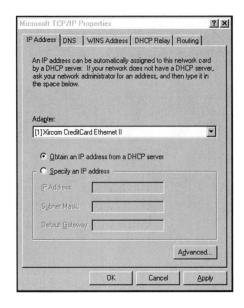

**Figure 2.2:**
DHCP configuration of TCP/IP.

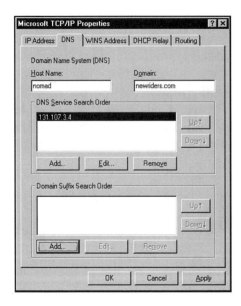

**Figure 2.3:**
Configuring DNS.

# Domain Planning with the Internet Information Server

There are many configuration scenarios IIS can exploit in the NT environment. These configurations are based solely on trust relationships and the roles that the NT Servers are playing in each of the domains. A domain is a lot like a workgroup, but it utilizes a server for logon validation to get access to network resources.

Before we go into the different scenarios, it is best to have an understanding of the roles that NT Servers play and to understand trust relationships.

## NT Server Roles

During the installation of the NT Server software, you will be asked to assign the role that the server will play in your enterprise. The server can be configured to fit into one of three roles:

➤ Primary Domain Controller

➤ Backup Domain Controller

➤ Server

### Configuring NT Server as a Primary Domain Controller

If the server will be acting as the Primary Domain Controller, you will be asked during the install to provide the computer and domain. This will create the domain that the Primary Domain Controller will be a member of.

The Primary Domain Controller originates the domain information during installation and builds the Security Account Manager Database that is replicated to the Backup Domain Controllers.

The Primary Domain Controller has a large role in computer browsing. It is configured, by default, as the Domain Master Browser. The Domain Master Browser browses other domains to get an updated browse list for computers that are requesting a browse list inside of its domain. There is only one Domain Master Browser per domain.

The Primary Domain Controller is also responsible for validating users so that they can access resources and can have responsibilities that pertain to other services loaded, such as Directory Replication.

## Configuring NT Server as a Backup Domain Controller

When installing the NT Server software as the Backup Domain Controller, the install will ask you for the computer's name existing domain name, and will prompt you for the administrator's account and password. This will associate the Backup Domain Controller with an established domain. The Backup Domain Controller gets a copy of the domain information and the Security Account Manager Database, which is a database of users added to the domain, from the Primary Domain Controller. The replication of the Security Account Manager Database occurs automatically when the Backup Domain Controller becomes a part of an existing domain.

The Backup Domain Controller will also receive a domain browse list to distribute to computers asking for a browse list. The Backup Domain Controller can be configured as a Master Browser or a Backup Browser in the browsing strategy. The Master Browser answers the request for a browse list and provides computers with an updated browse list. The Master Browser will also do an inventory of the computers on the subnet and pass this computer list to the Domain Master Browser to compile the full computer browse list. If a Master Browser or the Domain Master Browser goes offline, an election process occurs automatically to promote a Backup Browser to that browser level.

The Backup Domain Controller is also responsible for account validation and can have other responsibilities that relate to services that are loaded such as Replication, DHCP, WINS, and DNS just to name a few. The Backup Domain Controller provides redundancy in the domain environment. If the Primary Domain Controller was to go offline, the Backup Domain Controller could be promoted to take the responsibilities of the Primary Domain Controller.

## Configuring NT Server as a Server

When loading NT Server software as a server, you will only be asked for the computer name. No association to the domain will occur. A server does not receive a copy of the domain information and a copy of the Security Account Manager Database from the Primary Domain Controller. Because of this, it is not involved in the validation process.

An NT Server is considered a separate entity to a domain. It has its own Security Account Database, but can join a domain and share a part of the domain's Security Account Manager Database (global groups). The NT Server has a lower role in the browsing strategy and does not have the overhead that the Primary and Backup Domain Controllers have validating users, browsing, and replicating.

## Trust Relationships

A trust is a communication link between two domains where one domain honors the requests of users of another domain, trusting the other domain to validate the logons of its own users. The domain that is providing the validation is called an Account Domain or Trusted Domain. The other domain is called a Resource Domain or Trusting Domain. A domain strategy that includes trust relationships provides room for growth and organization. For instance, a company might have a single domain where all resources and user accounts reside. As the company grows and departments require some autonomy, a resource domain could be added with a trust to the domain with the accounts. This is what is called the Master Domain model. (See figure 2.6.)

In the Resource Domain, the administrator might put NT Servers that are used primarily for an application or service like IIS, SQL Server, WINS, DHCP, or DNS to name a few. Trust relationships provide the ability for a user account to access all resource domains that have a trust to the account domain where the user was validated.

# IIS with a Backup Domain Controller Scenario

The first scenario is based on a configuration that a dedicated NT server is not possible due to budget, resources, or other constraints. In this configuration, IIS is placed on a Backup Domain Controller. The Backup Domain Controller should be a machine that has a lot of system resources in order to handle the number of people accessing the IIS, providing user validation and browsing. This scenario could be used for a small environment to provide intranet access.

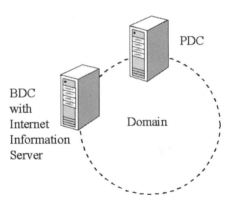

**Figure 2.4:**
IIS on a BDC Scenario.

# IIS with a Dedicated System Scenario

The next scenario shows a dedicated NT server for IIS inside of the domain. This scenario is best for mid-size to small environments that can utilize a dedicated system for IIS. There will be no system overhead for browsing, user validation, or replication. The system will be fully dedicated to the Internet Information Server and its services.

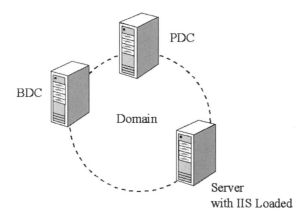

**Figure 2.5:**
IIS Dedicated System Scenario.

# IIS with a Trusted Configuration Scenario

The best configuration environment for IIS is shown in figure 2.6. This configuration provides the flexibility for growth and organization. The Internet Information Server is placed in a dedicated resource domain that has a trust relationship to an account domain for the validation of users. This scenario would be applicable in a large to mid-level environment where the resources need to be grouped accordingly. For instance, a company might want to utilize more than one Internet Information Server. These servers might be owned by different departments in the company and have different administrators. Using this Master Domain model, the company's enterprise can grow and still keep all resources organized accordingly.

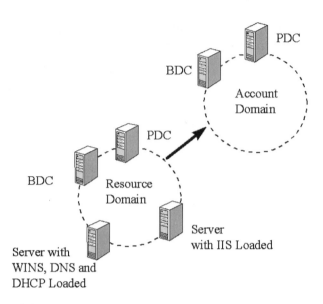

**Figure 2.6:**
IIS Trusted Configuration Scenario.

## Summary

Hopefully, this chapter has given you some general insight to configuring Windows NT Server as a server. This is a fundamental process for ensuring a solid foundation to configure it further as an Internet server.

# Chapter 3

# Planning Server Connectivity

Connectivity can have many different meanings. Connectivity can be as simple as two people joining together to develop and share ideas. When discussing connectivity and computers, the general definition in the past has been the development of links between processing power and users. The connections have changed to accomodate improved connection methods and changed work methods and environments. Connectivity is no longer contained at the LAN level, but has grown to include WAN connectivity for a large number of users through the Internet. This chapter examines the impulse behind connectivity to the Internet with the specific purpose of determining and obtaining the proper level of connectivity for World Wide Web (WWW) information provision.

This chapter contains a basic discussion of the potential reasons for connecting to the Internet. Obviously, not everyone needs an Internet connection. This book is for companies who have identified a specific need that the Internet can help them address: information distribution. With the advent of the WWW, and the resulting explosion of commercial Internet activity, an increasing need exists for companies to promote themselves and provide information to the growing consumer base on the Internet. In general, the information is being provided through WWW sites, either private or commercial. This chapter examines the factors that determine Internet connectivity needs and the providers of Internet connectivity, and briefly touches on the future trends in connectivity.

Although the Internet can be a useful tool and information and entertainment source, it is not required for everyone.

Many businesses want to "get connected" to the Internet without any particular reason. Although the Internet can serve to increase the communicative abilities of a company, this connectivity has a cost, both in financial and human resource terms. The days of connectivity for all enterprises will come, but that time is a few years away yet. Staying on the cutting edge can be beneficial and give a company a leg up on their competition, but the "bleeding edge" can be costly.

## The World Wide Web, or the "New" Internet

When the Internet was first envisioned, the creators were concerned about the security and reliability of communications. Soon after the first set of connections were established, users quickly discovered that the Internet could easily be used to exchange information and collaborate on projects. Even so, Internet usage grew slowly, being mainly contained in larger organizations and universities. The major change came with the development of the *World Wide Web* (WWW) project by CERN, a Switzerland-based organization for physicists, in 1990 (official launch date).

Working from the idea of hypertext as developed by Ted Nelson of Stanford Research Institute (SRI) in the 1960s, the CERN group developed an implementation of a markup language named *HyperText Markup Language* (HTML). The concept behind this language was to provide a mechanism for organizing data and information for collaboration between physicists. Because this collaboration occurred on a global basis, the CERN Institute developed a language that could be used over the Internet, and at the same time made the specification public. Between 1990 and 1992, the WWW grew slowly, with servers and text-based browsers being developed (and made available for free—the first of which were developed by CERN itself).

The change in the Web's growth came with the development of a graphical WWW browser (a client program that enables the user to view HTML in a standard manner). In 1992, Marc Andreessen was working on an information collaboration project for the National Center for Supercomputing Applications (NCSA). Aware of the project developed by CERN, he worked to develop a Web browser that used the same specification, but incorporated the use of a graphical interface for use with Graphical User Interface (GUI) systems. This first graphical browser included the capability to view text and graphics, as well as to launch other programs for the utilization of sound and high-resolution graphics ("helper applications," as they have become known).

With the advent of the first graphical browser, the WWW blossomed. The capability to publish information worldwide with very little cost caught the attention of users and businesses. The potential for graphics, sound, and video methods of portraying information created an explosion of users and providers. At the same time, Web browsers have continued to develop and progress, including more and more features (currently,the most popular browser is Netscape by Netscape, Inc.). Today, some of the most exciting developments for the WWW include Virtual Reality Markup Language (VRML), Java (a scripting/programming tool that allows applications to be embedded in HTML code), and narrow-casting audio and video.

Narrow-casting audio and video in the context of the Internet is the use of specialized software to provide real time audio and video services via the WWW. Since this software only sends the information to those who request it, this is often reffered to as narrow-castion. The name stems from the contrasts between this distribution method and that of broadcasting, which sends all information to all users at all times (like cable TV).

The development of graphical and specialized uses for the WWW not only has provided for the rapid growth of the Internet, but also has created the need for greater connectivity. Because of the possible applications of the WWW, the need for bandwidth and Internet connectivity is based on the following three major factors:

➤ The information you provide

➤ The reason to provide the information

➤ To whom you provide the information

## Information: The Determining Factor

The type of information you provide for your clients is one-third of the equation that determines whether or not, and to what degree, you need to be connected to the Internet. If you are providing basic textual information applicable to only a small set of users, then your needs will be modest. Large quantities of useful high-bandwidth information increase your needs greatly, by increasing the trafic to your site, in terms of the number of clients and volume of information that your site serves. The first task of any potential WWW site manager is to determine what type of information to provide, how often to update the information, and to what level to maintain historical data.

# Types of Data Provided

Early in the planning process, a prospective WWW site manager must determine what type of information his or her site will carry. In general terms, this information can be broken down into three main categories:

➤ Text

➤ Graphics

➤ Time-based multimedia (sound and video)

Each category is discussed in the following sections to create a more detailed picture of the bandwidth implications of these data types.

## Text

Text is the simplest of all the information contained on the WWW and is the base for the entire Web. No matter how fancy and interactive the WWW becomes, the basic means of distributing information is text. As browsers, and the HTML standard, are modified to include more formatting functionality, the use of text will become even more popular. In no other form can vast volumes of information be contained and distributed with such a small bandwidth requirement.

A well-designed page of text in HTML format might consist of as much as 3 to 4 KB of data, for example. This book could be contained in a set of HTML documents (with hyperlink references throughout the document) consisting of 400 (pages) $\times$ 4 KB = 1,600 KB (or 1.6 MB). A video file 30 seconds long compressed using a lossy compression (a high efficiency method of compression that discards data not required for optimal human viewing via monitors) method also might take 1.6 MB of space.

In this example, the 400 pages of text would provide a much greater level of information, but unfortunately, given the human desire for color, sound, and motion, the Web site probably would not be well utilized. Although content is important in a WWW site, the truth is that presentation and usability are just as important. One of the best methods of increasing the usability of information is to incorporate graphics into your Web pages.

## Graphics

Graphics in WWW pages can increase the visibility of a site and enable you to create better designed pages (currently HTML provides very limited formatting capabilities, although this is changing with the revisions to the standard). Simple headers can give a consistent look to your pages, and with the addition of CGI-scripting, images can become maps to other HTML documents.

Although the added functionality of the images can increase interest in your page, the cost of these images is the additional bandwidth they require to be transmitted. A simple logo banner across the top of a page can greatly increase the size and consequently the bandwidth cost of a page. Take an image 4.5" by 1" in diameter. This image before compression contains $4.5 \times 1 \times 72 \times 72$ bytes of information, or approximately 28 KB. Even after compression using GIF format (one of the formats generally used for images not requiring picture-like colors), this image could still be as large as 20 KB. As a result, for every image this size used in a Web page, the bandwidth requirements could increase by a factor of five to seven. Consequently, a text-based WWW site that required a 28.8 connection may require an ISDN connection if graphics are used instead of text.

Putting all WWW information into graphical format is not cost-effective. This book digitized into graphics takes up as much as 75 MB of space on a server (7" by 6" $\times$ 72 bits per inch $\times$ 72 bits per inch $\times$ 400 pages). As a result, a WWW site manager has to decide how much information to store as graphics and how much to maintain as text. As well as static text and graphics, the site manager can use a third type of information: time- or motion-based information.

## Time-Based Multimedia

No matter where you turn today, you hear talk about *multimedia*. Generally this term refers to the integration of sound and video with the everyday text and graphics of our published world. Due to the digital nature of WWW information distribution, these types of information can be incorporated into the WWW. In fact, the incorporation of this information happens today.

Unfortunately for a Web site manager, the use of these formats of information can be very bandwidth-intensive. A 30-second video clip compressed with an advanced compression routine, such as the AVI format (a common Windows-based video compression format), can take as much as 3 MB of space and bandwidth. Video broadcasts via the Internet are based on compression routines that are lossy (data is actually lost in the process) and work on the basis that the human brain is able to provide the missing steps in the pattern. Even so, video conferencing via the Internet is limited to 10 frames per second on ISDN-level bandwidth.

Like the information that you provide on your WWW site, the time between updates also plays a role in determining your connectivity needs.

# Time between Updates and Historical Data Caches

A second major factor in determining your bandwidth requirements is the degree that your site provides updated information, and the amount of *data caching* (maintenance of historical data over a period of time) that you provide. Because the WWW, and most browsers, provide information caching, information that has not changed is not reloaded across the Internet. The limitations of caching, the degree that you change your site, and the level of historical data that you store have heavy impacts on the bandwidth requirements of your site.

## Changing Information

Although information on the WWW is easy to manipulate and update, changing information is one of the main sources of bandwidth usage. Changing information increases your site's bandwidth in two ways. First, the information that changes is reloaded by browsers and individual WWW users on a regular basis so that users are able to maintain data integrity (that is, their data continues to match the data supplied by your site).

Although a number of organizations are providing data caching for entire organizations through proxy servers (the CERN server in proxy mode supports this function), this data caching does not reduce demand on a server that has changing information. Every time the site is queried, even through a proxy, the information about that site is verified to not have been altered. If the site has been changed, or the server is unable to verify, the information is reloaded.

## Maintaining Historical Data

Not only does updating information add to your bandwidth by increasing the traffic to your site, but so does the maintenance of historical data. You have to decide whether to maintain old data after new data is added to the site. The maintenance of stored historical data increases dramatically the amount of bandwidth used by each new client for your site because instead of accessing only new information, any added client may download both the new and old information.

You can find an example of this situation at any number of Webzine sites. A *Webzine site* is any site that provides an online magazine functionality. Although any such site wants to provide some past issues online rather than only introduce new issues, each old issue adds potential bandwidth requirements for new clients. When logging on to a site that includes 12 back issues of an online magazine, you  have the opportunity to download all 12 issues. If the number of issues stored continues indefinitely, the bandwidth requirements would also increase. (The increase in bandwidth assumes that the data being maintained retains its value as time elapses and is still requested by clients.)

# Why You Provide the Information on Your Site

The second of the three determining factors for providing information via the WWW, and for the way your activities impact your connectivity requirements, is the *why* of your information equation. Generally, WWW information is provided for one of three reasons:

➤ As information about your enterprise for future benefit (such as advertising information for a company, or a demo of your current software)

➤ As information of a direct benefit to the client (generally provided as a commercial service or to reduce costs)

➤ As a general public service

## Company Information

By far the most prolific use of the WWW by enterprises is the publishing of company advertising in an electronic format. This information can be presented in a number of possible methods, but generally reflects current printed literature with a few of the benefits of hypertext incorporated. As a result, the number of people that visit the site is limited to at least vaguely interested clients; therefore, the number of clients and the direct cost of bandwidth is low. Although employing this style of advertising helps keep costs down, it also limits the benefit of the site. After all, no one can force clients to visit the site, a fundamental difference from television and the Internet. As a result, many sites combine this functionality with the second reason for service provision: information that provides direct benefit to the clients.

# Direct Benefit Information

The following are the two basic types of information that provide a direct benefit to the client:

➤ Cost-elimination services

➤ Commercial services

In both cases, the goal is to provide information that the client needs in some way. This information has the purpose of generating more traffic to the site or generating revenue to offset site costs.

The first situation—eliminating costs while providing information the client needs—is a common aspect of computer-oriented sites. Most major software companies have WWW sites that are used to distribute bug fixes and demos, and provide additional documentation for their software products. Not only are these sites of great use to clients, the services also decrease distribution and production costs.

The second method of direct benefit services is to provide a service for which great demand exists, but to charge a fee for the service. In general, the site must provide a service that is of great value to users and is easy to access. In other words, the service's collection methods must be based on a simple method, either credit card (securely transferred) or a prepayment registration. An example of this type of WWW site is the Canadian Open Bidding Service (OBS). The OBS provides bidding information to companies about possible contracts with the federal government. Access to the service is controlled via passwords, and the fees are fairly steep considering the cost of transferring files electronically. Even so, the service is well used because of the high potential gain for the clients.

# Public Service

Unlike the OBS, there are a number of sites that exist simply as a public service and charge no fee. These include a number of information sites by private individuals and vary in size from a simple page to a complete index of the WWW. Key examples are the WWW search engines (as an example, check out New Riders' WWW Yellow Pages at **http://www.mcp.com/newriders/ wwwyp**). Generally, these search engines are free to users and to the companies and organizations listed within. The sites operate on the principle that the publicity the search engine draws provides the traffic needed to sell advertising banners on search results pages. Companies pay fees to advertise their site or product to the millions of searching clients.

# Targeting Your Clients?

The third of the three factors that determine your connectivity needs is the "who" of your clients. Depending on the type of information you provide, your clientele can change, and different clientele will use your site in different ways. In general, your site will attract one of two types of clients: the professional looking for specific information, and the surfer just checking out the site.

## The Professional

When referring to the concept of the professional WWW client, I am not talking about a business professional necessarily, nor any class of people in general, but only about the way in which these clients use the Internet. The professionals know what they are doing, and generally come to your site for a reason: you have the information they want. As a result, the professional tends to jump right to the area of information required and download only what is needed. The result of professional users for a well-designed site is the elimination of redundant downloading of information, consequently reducing bandwidth usage. Typically, sites that provide information that has a specific purpose, such as software bug fixes, attract this type of client.

## The Surfer

Unlike the professional, the surfer has no true purpose in his or her Web activity other than the exploration of the WWW. As a result, the surfer is attracted to sites that are cross-linked in many places, provide an interesting variety of information, or keep up with the latest new WWW fad (or a few old standbys such as image archives). In general, surfers use a haphazard approach to site access, which generally results in a deeper and more random penetration of your site. The surfer might download that 3 MB video clip of your cat just because the clip is there.

## Providers of Connectivity

After considering the type of, reasons for, and clients of your information to determine whether you have a connection need, and your bandwidth requirements, a WWW site manager must next examine the options for Internet connectivity. This section discusses general service providers and the benefits each type of provider brings to the business.

In general, the Internet services you require as a WWW information provider are split into two types: bandwidth usage over the Internet in general, and local loop service to the bandwidth provider.

## Internet Service Providers (ISPs)

Although the Internet is a collection of interconnected networks that no single company owns, the main backbones of bandwidth are owned by a number of larger providers. These providers in turn sell access to their backbones to smaller providers, who in turn resell the bandwidth again. The whole food chain of bandwidth is based on the principle that not all users use all their bandwidth at once. The policy of oversubscribing bandwidth is similar to an airline overbooking flights. As a result, a number of minor lags can develop in networks, although because communications are so slow at the local link level (limited to modem speed), clients are not truly affected.

Internet access providers are divided into the following two main types:

➤   Dedicated Internet access providers

➤   Commercial network services that provide a platform for access to the Internet

The difference between the two is that dedicated Internet providers provide your site with a direct link to the Internet, whereas commercial network services provide a home for your home page, site, or server.

Although commercial networks such as America Online, CompuServe, and others provide an alternative for client access to the Internet, they do not provide the access required for WWW site development. Therefore, "commercial providers" in this chapter refers to the Internet Service Providers that provide commercial services such as home page/site hosting along with design, markup, and promotional services.

# Dedicated Internet Service Providers

*Internet Service Providers* (ISPs) that provide dedicated Internet access come in many different sizes and types. The key to choosing a provider is to identify the types of service providers that can accommodate dedicated connections, and some issues that influence the quality of the service provided. ISPs can be divided into the following two main designations:

➤   Local providers

➤   Regional or national providers

## Local Providers

Local providers provide access to a variety of clients in a relatively local area. In general, local providers gain network access from larger regional or national providers. Because local ISPs resell bandwidth acquired from national providers, their price-to-bandwidth ratio is likely to be higher than that of the national providers. In theory, the use of a local provider should always be rejected. In practice, however, local service providers can fulfill the valuable role of providing technical expertise in your WWW site. Depending on the ISP you choose, the service might include the provision of routers, installation, and other technical services. These services might cost you more than just purchasing bandwidth, but if your organization does not have the technical expertise required to set up the site, then the cost may be worthwhile. Again, the extra level of bureaucracy of a local provider is costly, but the smaller size and personal attention can be beneficial.

## Regional or National Providers

With the recent increase in Internet popularity due in large part to the WWW, the market for bandwidth has become more competitive as larger companies acquire or create regional or national service providers. The market for national service provision currently is dominated by the backbone companies and other large corporations. In the case of the backbone companies, or infrastructure maintainers (Sprint, MCI, ANS, and so on) access is provided through commercial companies that have spun off the parent (Sprintlink and so on).

Although these national infrastructure providers also sell bandwidth, the account size required is very large. Because few companies need full T1 or T3 access, there is little demand for these providers. Also, smaller accounts have less influence with larger national providers because they contribute little to the profit of the larger companies (any single account is unimportant to the larger provider because it manages so many). As a result, even though using a large national provider eliminates the extra layer of bureaucracy and (possibly) cost of a local provider, you can lose some of the personal touch and fringe available from a smaller ISP.

# Commercial Providers

Commercial providers are companies that provide commercial services for WWW sites in addition to providing the simple pipe to the site. Instead of only selling bandwidth to a client, the provider provides one of two types of services:

➤  Housing services

➤  Parking services

## Housing Services

Generally speaking, the provision of housing services is better suited for a smaller WWW site of an enterprise that does not require strong control over their site. The service can be as simple as a place to have a home page (technically can be a small site of a couple of pages), or as complex as a full-blown site including scripts and online databases. The key to a good housing service consists of the following:

➤  Site Access

➤  Technical Support

Because your site is part of the active WWW server run by the service provider, your site access is limited to what the provider allows. Generally, scripts have to be approved by the systems administrator prior to installation, and changes to HTML also might have to be performed by the service provider's HTML staff.

Because the rules for access can vary, shop around to find the provider that best suits your needs. A service provider should be willing to allow you unlimited shell access to your files (in a private directory). Do not accept a limited number of changes to your files per period, because you could end up paying hidden markup charges. Try to find a provider that allows you to choose your own HTML authors, or even perform the markup yourself.

The provider should be willing to set up a virtual CGI-bin directory for your organization. The presence of this directory simplifies the task of adding and removing scripts for your site. If the service provider is unwilling to provide CGI-bin access, then it should institute a standard method of script checking that enables you to know exactly when your script is installed. The existence of such a procedure ensures that both groups know their obligations, and enables you to better schedule necessary changes to your site.

Even though having access to your site enables you to perform your own maintenance and upgrades, the service provider also should be able to provide you with technical services. If a provider is unable to supply CGI-bin, markup, and backup services then reconsider your choice. Most of these services are required by the provider to maintain its site, and although fees for such services can be expected, failure to provide the services should concern most managers. Lack of technical support may indicate a lack of trained personnel and, therefore, available backup resources in the event of a network crisis.

## Parking Services

Parking services simply refers to allowing the placement of your server (generally one host) on the local area network (LAN) of the ISP. After it is configured properly, the host will be accessible from throughout the Internet. The LAN connection should be high speed (at least Ethernet speeds), and your server configuration and uses should be determined by you. The three main issues with a server park are:

➤   access to the physical server,

➤   dial-up or dedicated access to the server for maintenance, and bandwidth charges.

Any server park agreement should contain some provision for site access to your server. In general, access during normal business hours should be free and unrestricted. The caveat is that limiting access to simplify the maintenance of the server is understandable—organizations should not expect an office with their server park. During off hours and weekends, emergency access should be available. Such access undoubtedly is limited in scope and a number of providers charge a time-based fee. Use the privilege sparingly, or your welcome will be worn out.

Although physical access sometimes is necessary, you can perform most work on a server remotely using a telnet or rlogin service. To accomplish this, a server park must provide you with one of the two following access methods:

➤ Dial-up

➤ Dedicated modem link

The charge for a dial-up link should be included in your server park fees because it limits the amount of physical tinkering you have to do on the server. Dedicated link fees should be limited to the telephone company line and the bandwidth you use over the link. The company already charges you for bandwidth used by your server (see the following section on "Telephone Companies and the Local Loop"), therefore the dedicated connection band-width can be routed through your server for the cost of the local loop.

The bandwidth your server uses depends on the type of site you have; however, you should at least be provided with a flat amount of bandwidth per month, with clearly defined prices for extra bandwidth. The fees charged should be no higher than those fees charged for WWW housing services. Also ask to see the rates charged by your ISP's bandwidth provider. If the profit margin on the fees you pay is too high (more than 50 percent), either switch providers or renegotiate the deal. Service providers that are unwilling to provide these figures should be avoided. If the provider has flat fees for bandwidth, ask how the current fees were determined. If the provider refuses or the calculations are not convincing, move. The provider is the single most important link for your site, and if trust cannot be established, then the relationship will fail.

# Telephone Companies and the Local Loop

After you arrange for service provision in terms of bandwidth access, you must still look to your local telephone company for the local loop between you and your ISP. Whereas the telcos also can provide bandwidth, your ISP cannot provide you with the local loop (unless you happen to have an office next door). The type of loop you require depends on the type and size of service you are using. The main types are local lines, ISDN lines, and dedicated switched services.

## Local Lines

At a bare minimum, your local telelephone company provides any telephone lines you need for your service. The lines can be for simple dial-up access to a server in a server park, or for a dedicated SL/IP or PPP connection. In either case, the service is limited to 28.8 kbps because of modem technology. Due to the slow speed of such modem connections, the usefulness for basic line services is minimal.

Consider the possibility that your telephone company does not allow dedicated use of regular telephone services. As a result, the company could dump your line periodically. For a management circuit between your office and a server park, this would not cause a big problem; but if your line is your WWW site's only connection to the Internet, any interruption is devastating.

## ISDN Services

*Integrated Services Digital Network,* or ISDN, provides a more robust method of closing the local loop between you and your service provider. The ISDN service generally consists of two 64 kbps data channels and one 16 kbps control channel. As a result, ISDN can provide you with a larger local loop pipe down which to send your data. Again, be careful about the "camping" policies of the telephone company (camping is the telephone company term for using a line as a dedicated circuit when it is not licensed for such use).

## Switched Services

Although ISDN provides an alternative method for providing the local loop, the tried and tested method is to lease a switched circuit from the local telephone company. The simple explanation is that the telephone company provides the requisite number of switched pairs of copper wire to equal your bandwidth needs (each pair can carry 64 kbps fully duplexed). Because these circuits are dedicated to your organization, the telephone company expects (and allows) full utilization. The drawback to switched circuits is that their installation and monthly charges can be expensive.

# Future Internet Connectivity Options

Current methods of obtaining bandwidth and local loops depend on the telephone companies and ISPs (ultimately the network or national backbone companies), however a couple of trends look promising for future provision. One is a general technological infrastructure upgrading occurring through the introduction of optical cabling at the local loop level. As well, the introduction of Internet services by satellite and cable companies could lead to savings on Internet access.

## Optical Cabling

As long as the communications infrastructure of an area is based on older copper lines, the costs of Internet access include a fairly large local loop charge. As more telephone companies and cable companies begin installing optical cabling into developments, the cost for high bandwidth access will fall. The falling costs will result from an infrastructure capable of carrying the higher bandwidth without an increase in the number of lines required.

Whereas copper lines can carry 64 kbps per pair using existing technology, optical cables can carry an unknown quantity. According to Nicholas Negroponte in *Being Digital*, we literally do not know how many bits per second we can send down a fiber.

Recent research results indicate that we are close to being able to deliver 1,000 billion bits per second. This means that a fiber the size of a human hair can deliver every issue of the *Wall Street Journal* in less than one second—roughly two thousand times faster than the theoretical maximum of twisted pair (Nicholas Negroponte, *Being Digital*, Alfred A. Knopf, New York, 1995, p. 23).

Also, optical cabling has recently become cheaper to install and maintain than traditional copper wires. As a result, the telephone and cable companies are moving to replace aging infrastructure with optical cabling. As the infrastructure is upgraded, so will be the capability to transmit data from a local loop to an ISP. If anything, bandwidth costs will fall rather than climb. The question is when—the near complete replacement of the infrastructure could take as long as 20 years.

## Satellite Internet Access

Satellite technology is just beginning to move into Internet provision, however most consumers are familiar with the concept of satellite TV. In fact, the smaller mini-satellite disks for satellite TV are basically the same ones used for satellite Internet. The satellite Internet has some major problems as a connectivity solution for WWW sites, but the service might be useful in certain circumstances.

## Cable Modem Internet Access

Cable modem connections deserve a brief mention here as a technology that has great potential for future expansion. Other than the telephone companies, the cable modem companies and broadcasters have one of the few infrastructures capable of providing high levels of throughput for data transmissions. The current infrastructure can carry approximately 500 kbps fully duplexed.

The problem with cable access lies with the switching technology currently in place. As a result of the historical uses of switches in broadcasting, the switches in place are one way, making the upstream bandwidth much smaller than the downstream bandwidth. The cable companies aim to upgrade the switching infrastructure, and in the near future, the changes might result in a viable option for Internet local loop and bandwidth services.

# Summary

Now that you have some idea of the bandwidth requirements of your WWW site, and the various bandwidth factors influencing your bandwidth choices, you are in a better position to assess your WWW needs.

# Part II

# TCP/IP and Internet Protocols

# Chapter 4

# Introduction to TCP/IP

TCP/IP is a family of protocols used for computer communications. The letters stand for *Transmission Control Protocol/Internet Protocol*, but other than in the press, the full name rarely is used. TCP and IP are both individual protocols that can be discussed separately, but they are not the only two protocols used in the family. Often a TCP/IP user does not use the TCP protocol itself, but some other protocol from the family. To talk about using TCP/IP in this situation is still proper, however, because the name applies generically to the use of any protocol in the TCP/IP family. Because TCP/IP was developed by the Department of Defense, the protocol family is sometimes called *The DoD Suite*, but does not have a classical "marketing" name as does Apple's AppleTalk suite of protocols.

Protocols usually are grouped into "families" (sometimes called *suites* or *stacks*). Which protocols are grouped together is usually determined by the protocols' implementors. Many protocol families are developed by commercial organizations; for example, AppleTalk is a family of protocols developed by Apple Computers. Each protocol in a family supports a particular network capability. No protocol is of much use on its own and requires the use of other protocols in its family. In some ways, protocol families are like a set of golf clubs; each club is used for a particular purpose, and no one club can be used to play an entire game. Usually a golfer purchases all the clubs in a set from the same vendor. Just as each vendor might offer a slightly different set of clubs, network protocol families try to solve the same network problems with a slightly different set of protocols, but many are similar from family to family.

The TCP/IP protocol family includes protocols such as *Internet Protocol* (IP), *Address Resolution Protocol* (ARP), *Internet Control Message Protocol* (ICMP), *User Datagram Protocol* (UDP), *Transport Control Protocol* (TCP), *Routing Information Protocol* (RIP), Telnet, *Simple Mail Transfer Protocol* (SMTP), *Domain Name System* (DNS), and numerous others. Keeping all the acronyms straight can be difficult, especially because some are reused by other protocols (for example, the Novell, or IPX, family has a RIP protocol different from the TCP/IP family RIP protocol). An understanding of all the protocols in a particular family is not a prerequisite to knowing how a network basically works. This chapter concentrates on the IP and ARP protocols (mentioning the RIP and ICMP protocols briefly). This focus, coupled with a minimal discussion of a particular link protocol (Ethernet is used for the examples in this chapter), illustrates how a TCP/IP network causes data to flow smoothly across an internet.

# Understanding TCP/IP: Six Questions

In TCP/IP, all protocols are transported across an IP internet, encapsulated in IP packets. IP is a *routable protocol*, which means that two nodes that communicate using IP do not need to be connected to the same physical wire. To have a basic understanding of how information travels across a routed network, it is only necessary to understand the answers to the following six questions:

1.  What is the format of an address in this protocol?

2.  How do devices get an address?

3. How is the address mapped onto a physical address?

4. How does an end node find a router?

5. How do routers learn the topology of the network?

6. How do users find services on the network?

The rest of this chapter answers these questions and illustrates by example how these answers tie together to explain how information flows across a TCP/IP-based network.

# Understanding Basic Network Concepts

Before answering the preceding questions (or possibly even before understanding what they are asking), you must know the meanings of some terms and concepts discussed in this chapter.

# Addressing

The central concept of networking is *addressing*. In networking, the *address* of a device is its unique identification. Network addresses are usually numerical and have a standard, well-defined format (each defined in its specification document). All devices on a network need to be given a unique identifier that conforms to a standard format. This identifier is the device's address. In routed networks, the address has at least two pieces: a *network* (or *area*) piece and a *node* (or *host*) piece.

In this chapter, *network* refers to a set of machines connected to the same physical wire (or set of wires connected only by bridges and repeaters). *Internet* means one or more networks connected by routers. The word *internet* (lowercase *i*) is not to be confused with the *Internet* (uppercase *I*). The Internet is a specific internet that connects millions of computers worldwide and is becoming predominant in the press and elsewhere.

If two devices on an internet have addresses with the same network number, they are located on the same network and thus on the same wire. Devices on the same wire can communicate directly with each other by using their data link layer protocol (that is, Ethernet). The examples in this chapter use Ethernet as the medium connecting the devices. Although some particulars might differ, the concepts are the same if the networks are built on Token Ring, *Fiber Distributed Data Interface* (FDDI), or many other common physical media.

Correct addressing of devices on a network requires that every device connected to the same network (wire) be configured with the same network number. Also, every device with the same network number must have a different node (or host) number from every other device with the same network number. Finally, every network in an internet must have a unique network number. To rephrase, every network on an internet must have a unique network number, and every node on a network must have a unique node number within that network. This rule ensures that no two devices on an internet ever have the same network *and* node number and therefore have a unique address within the internet.

In addition to a unique address for every device on an internet, special addresses often are used to address multiple nodes simultaneously. These addresses are called *broadcast* or *multicast* addresses.

The following discussion references two different types of addresses—network layer addresses and *Media Access Control* (MAC) layer addresses. These two address types are completely independent of each other. The network layer addresses are all IP addresses. These addresses are used to communicate between nodes across an IP internetwork. The MAC addresses are used to communicate from node to node on the same wire and often are built right into the communications card (for example, the Ethernet card). MAC addresses are the lowest level addresses and are the means by which all information is ultimately transferred from device to device.

# Packets

On most networks, such as TCP/IP networks, the information sent is broken down into pieces called *packets* (or *datagrams*) for two main reasons: resource sharing and error detection and correction. On networks that have more than two computers (for example, Ethernet or Token Ring), the medium connecting the devices is shared. If any two devices are communicating, no other devices can communicate at the same time. A network works like a party line in that respect. If two devices want to share a very large amount of information, it is unfair for them to become the sole users of the network for a long period of time; other devices might have urgent information to transfer to other parties. If the large block of information is broken into many small blocks, each of these can be sent individually, enabling other devices to interweave their own messages between the packets of the extended conversation. As long as each piece is individually addressed to the intended destination and contains enough information for the receiver to piece it back together, the fact that it is broken into pieces does not matter.

The other main use of packets is for error detection and correction. Networks are ultimately made up of wires (or radio waves or light beams) that are prone to interference, which can corrupt a signal sent across them. Dealing with corrupted messages is a big part of networking; in fact, most of the complexity in networking involves dealing with the what-if-something-gets-corrupted scenarios. Many error detection and correction techniques are based on *checksums*; when a sender transmits information (as bytes of data), a running total adding up all the bytes sent is kept and then transmitted at the end of the data transmission. The receiver computes the total of the data received and compares it to the total transmitted. If a difference exists between the total bytes received and the total bytes computed, then the data or the total is corrupted. The sender is asked to retransmit the data. This version is much simpler than what really happens, but is sufficient to illustrate the concept.

If the medium on which the transmission takes place has an average error rate of one bit in one million (that is, for every one million bits sent, one is corrupted on average), then there is a practical upper limit to the amount of data that can be sent in one transmission. Imagine that ten million bits are sent. Normally a transmission of this size contains ten errors, the checksum is wrong, and the sender is asked to retransmit. The retransmission size is the same as the original transmission, so it contains on average ten errors again. The only way to break out of this loop is to break the data into smaller pieces, each with its own checksum, that can be retransmitted individually.

## Protocols

Each of these packets is a stream of bytes. For true communication to occur, these bytes must have meaning associated with them. This meaning is provided by the protocol specification. A *protocol* is a set of rules that defines two things—the format of the packets and the semantics of their use.

Most packets have a format that includes a header and a body. The *header* often includes information such as a source and destination address, the length of the packet, and some type indicator so that the receiver knows how to decode the body. The *body* can be raw data (for example, a piece of a file or an e-mail message), or it can contain another packet that has its own format defined by its own specification. Packet formats usually are depicted in a specification by a rectangular picture that gives the order, size, and names of the pieces of information that make up the packet. Figure 4.1 is an example of an Ethernet frame.

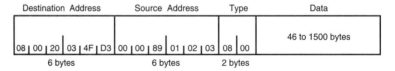

**Figure 4.1:**

An Ethernet frame.

You must know more than the format of a packet to understand the protocol. You also must know when to send which packets and what to do when they are received. Many protocols have very simple formats, but their use is very complicated. Imagine teaching a non-English speaker to behave as an English-speaking receptionist. The "packet formats" might be as follows:

"Hello, this is company X."

"How may I direct your call?"

"Please hold."

"Good-bye."

"That line is busy, may I take a message?"

"That person does not work here."

The "protocol" for answering the phone needs to include when to say each of these phrases, how to look up an extension in the company phone book, what to say if the party being called is not in, how to take a message, what to do with the message after taking it, what to do with a wrong number, and so on.

A protocol specification specifies the format of the information exchanged (the packets) and the correct sequencing of that information as well as the additional actions (logging, mail delivery, table updates, and so on) that might be required. Just as the receptionist described earlier was only trained to direct incoming calls (and not answer tech support questions), each protocol has a specific set of functions with which it is designed to deal.

In the TCP/IP world, most protocol specifications are available online as *Requests For Comment* (RFCs). These specifications tend to be very technical in nature and are directed at engineers who intend to implement these protocols. One site (of many) on the Internet that makes the RFCs available for anonymous ftp is **ftp.internic.net.** An index is available at that site in the file /rfc/ rfc-index.txt.

# Routers and End Nodes

Routed networks have two classes of devices: end nodes and routers (see fig. 4.2). *End nodes* are the devices with which users interact—workstations and PCs, printers, file servers, and so on. *Routers* are devices that connect networks. Routers have the responsibility to know how the whole network is connected and how to move information from one part of the network to another. They shield end nodes from needing to know much about the network so that the end nodes can spend their time doing user tasks. Routers are connected to two or more networks. Every device on a particular network must have the same network number as every other device on that network, and every network must have a different network number. Thus routers must have a separate address for every network to which they are connected. Routers are very much the "post offices" of the network. End nodes send information they don't know how to deliver to the local router, and the router takes care of getting it to its final destination. Sometimes a device such as a file server also is a router, for example, when that end node is connected to more than one network and is running software that enables it to route information between those networks. Routing is often a CPU-intensive chore and can significantly impact the performance of a machine doing tasks other than routing. For this reason, most routers are dedicated machines.

Routers are introduced to networks for several reasons. Routers enable more devices to ultimately be interconnected because they extend the address space available by having multiple network numbers. Routers help overcome physical limitations of the medium by connecting multiple cables.

The most common reason for using a router is to maintain political isolation. Routers enable two groups of machines to communicate with each other while remaining physically isolated, which is especially important when the two groups are controlled by different organizations. Many routers have filtering functions that enable the network administrator to strictly control who uses and what is used on the network. Problems that occur on one network do not necessarily disrupt other networks.

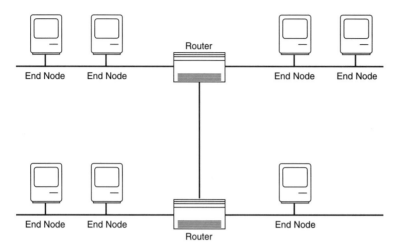

**Figure 4.2:**

Routers and end nodes in a network.

# End Node Network Send and Receive Behavior

When a node on a TCP/IP network has an IP packet to send to another node, it follows a simple algorithm to decide how to proceed. The sending node compares the network portion of the destination address with the network portion of its own address. If the two networks are the same, it implies that the two nodes are on the same wire—either directly connected to the same cable or on cables separated only by repeaters or bridges (see fig. 4.3). In this case, the two nodes can communicate directly using the data link layer (for example, Ethernet). The sending node uses ARP to discover the destination node's MAC layer address and encapsulate the IP packet in a data link layer frame to be delivered directly to the destination node.

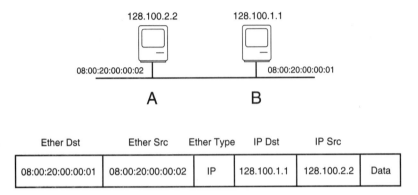

| Ether Dst | Ether Src | Ether Type | IP Dst | IP Src | |
|---|---|---|---|---|---|
| 08:00:20:00:00:01 | 08:00:20:00:00:02 | IP | 128.100.1.1 | 128.100.2.2 | Data |

**Figure 4.3:**
Two end nodes communicating on the same network.

If the network portions are different, the two nodes are separated by at least one router, which implies that the sending node cannot deliver the packet without using a router as an intermediary. The packet is encapsulated in a data link layer frame addressed to the MAC address of a router on the same wire (if no router is on the wire, then that particular network is isolated and cannot send IP packets to other networks). The router delivers the IP packet to the remote network.

When an end node receives an IP packet, it compares the destination address in the IP packet to its own address and to the IP broadcast address with which it is configured. If the destination address matches either of these addresses, the end node accepts the packet and processes it further. The way it is processed depends on which subprotocol of IP it is. If the destination address does not match, the packet is dropped (ignored), as shown in the following end-node algorithm:

```
Receive

if((dst addr == my addr) or (dst addr == broadcast)){
   process packet
}
else{
    drop (ignore) packet
}
```

```
Send
if(dst net = my net){
  deliver (may need to "ARP")
}
else{
    send to router
}
```

# Router Send and Receive Behavior

When a node is functioning as a router and it receives an IP
packet, it examines the destination IP address in the packet and
compares it to its own IP address. If the addresses are the same or
the destination IP address is the IP broadcast address, the packet
is processed as it would be for an end node. Unlike an end node, a
router does not automatically drop packets that are received but
not addressed to it. These are packets that end nodes on the
network are sending to the router to be forwarded to other
networks (see fig. 4.4). All routers maintain routing tables that
indicate how to reach other networks. The router compares the
network portion of the destination address with each network in
its routing table. If the router cannot find the destination network
in its routing table, it checks for a default route (typically listed as
a route to 0.0.0.0). If it does not find a default route, the packet is
dropped (and an ICMP destination unreachable message is sent
to the source IP address in the dropped packet).

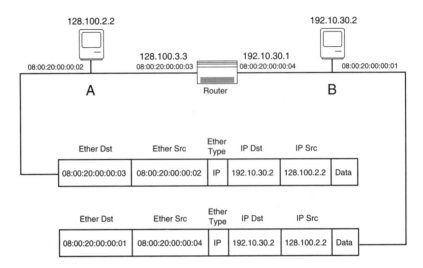

**Figure 4.4:**

Two end nodes communicating on different networks.

When a matching route to a network is found (or a default route
exists), the router checks the distance to the remote network. If
the distance is listed as 0, the network is directly connected to the
router. In this case, the router sends an ARP request for the
destination IP address and encapsulates the IP packet in a data
link layer frame addressed to the MAC address of the destination
returned in the ARP response. If the distance is greater than 0, the
packet must travel through at least one more router. In this case,
the router uses the next router field from this route and sends an
ARP request for that router, encapsulating the IP packet in a data
link layer frame addressed to the MAC address of the next router.
This way, an IP packet travels across an internet, maintaining the
same source and destination IP addresses the entire time, but
having the source and destination MAC addresses change for
each hop. The algorithm a router uses when receiving a packet is
as follows:

```
Receive
if((dst addr == my addr) or (dst addr == broadcast)){
    process packet
}
```

```
else if(dst net is directly connected){
   deliver (may need to "ARP")
}
else if(dst net in table){
   deliver to next router
}
else{
   drop (ignore) packet
}
```

# Examining the Format of an IP Address

For any routable protocol to be efficiently routable, the address must have two parts. TCP/IP addresses have two components—a *network component* and a *host* (or *node*) component. Addresses used with TCP/IP are four-byte (32-bit) quantities called simply *IP addresses* (not TCP/IP addresses) (see fig. 4.5). These addresses are written in *standard dot notation*, which means that each byte is written as a decimal number separated by dots (the period character)—for example, 192.37.54.23 (pronounced "192 dot 37 dot 54 dot 23"). Because each piece of the IP address is 1 byte, its value must be between 0 and 255 inclusive—for example, the IP address 125.300.47.89 could not be a legal IP address because 300 is greater than 255 and would not fit in a single byte.

| Bits | 0 | 4 | 8 | 16 | 19 | 24 | 31 |
|------|---|---|---|----|----|----|----|
| | VERS | LEN | TYPE OF SERVICE | TOTAL LENGTH | | | |
| | IDENT | | | FLAGS | FRAGMENT OFFSET | | |
| | TIME | | PROTO | HEADER CHECKSUM | | | |
| | SOURCE IP ADDRESS | | | | | | |
| | DESTINATION IP ADDRESS | | | | | | |
| | OPTIONS | | | | | PADDING | |
| | DATA | | | | | | |
| | . . . | | | | | | |

### Figuro 4.6:

Format of an IP address.

IP addresses are composed of a network portion and a host portion. The split is not as simple as the first two bytes being the network portion and the last two being the host portion. The designers of the TCP/IP protocols were concerned that they not limit the size of potential networks too severely, so they opted for a graduated method of network and host division. If the split was to be two bytes for each, no network could have more than $2^{16}$ hosts on it. Also, smaller networks would waste much of the address space by using only a fraction of the available nodes on any given network.

To provide for efficient address use, IP addresses are divided into *classes*. The three most important classes of networks are A, B, and C. IP addresses are split into these classes according to the first few bits of the address (or the value of the first byte, if you don't like working in binary), as in figure 4.6.

An IP network is customarily referred to as an IP address whose host portion consists of all zeroes—for example, 10.0.0.0 or 128.37.0.0 or 200.23.45.0. For example, 137.103.210.2 is a class B address that has a network portion of 137.103 and a host portion of 210.2. This network, the 137.103.0.0 network, can have up to two bytes worth ($2^{16}$) of hosts on it—all of which must share the exact same first two bytes 137.103 and must have unique host portions.

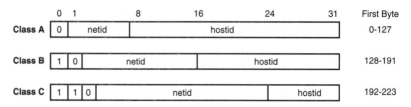

### Figure 4.6:
The three classes of IP addresses.

# Assigning IP Addresses to TCP/IP Devices

IP addresses can be assigned in a number of ways. If an organization wants to build a TCP/IP internetwork that never will be connected to any other TCP/IP network outside the organization, then it is acceptable to pick any class A, B, or C network number that allows an appropriate number of hosts on it. This method is rather short-sighted, because much of the benefit of having a TCP/IP network is the capability to connect to the outside world and share resources beyond those in the organization—for example, connecting to the Internet. A better strategy is to contact the InterNIC's registration services at Network Solutions, Inc. and request an officially assigned network number. The InterNIC ensures that the network number assigned to each applicant is globally unique. All the host ids on that network are free to be assigned as the assignee sees fit.

Sometimes when an organization connects to the Internet through another organization (for example, a commercial service provider or a university), that second organization provides the network number. In addition, many larger organizations have internal network administrators in charge of assigning IP addresses to individual users within the company.

When an IP network number has been acquired from an internal network administrator, service provider, or the InterNIC, it is possible to start assigning specific host IP addresses from that network to individual devices. Usually an organization keeps records of which IP addresses are assigned already and has some method of distributing the unused IP addresses to individuals who need to configure new IP devices. IP addresses must be configured into devices with the same network number as all other devices on the same wire but with a unique host portion. If two or more devices have the same IP address, they will not work reliably and will present a very difficult situation to debug.

Most IP devices require manual configuration. The person installing the device must obtain a unique and correct IP address and type it in to some configuration program or console, usually along with other information such as IP broadcast address, subnet mask, and default gateway address.

Some sites support dynamic configuration of IP devices. Protocols such as *Boot Protocol* (BOOTP) and *Dynamic Host Configuration Protocol* (DHCP) enable the use of centralized servers to hand out unique IP addresses and other configuration information on an as-needed basis. At the time of this writing, this sort of configuration is not a mature enough technology to find widespread use.

# Mapping IP Addresses to MAC Addresses

Ultimately, all computer communication takes place by moving data from node to node over some form of link such as Ethernet, Token Ring, FDDI, and the *Point-to-Point Protocol* (PPP). Many links support attaching more than two nodes and therefore require that all data sent over them be addressed to a specific destination to be delivered correctly. These addresses have nothing to do with IP addresses; they are completely separate and in addition to IP addresses. These addresses are MAC addresses— sometimes called *physical, hardware,* or *link addresses.* Unlike IP addresses that are assigned, most MAC layer addresses are built into the hardware by the manufacturer of the device or *network interface card* (NIC).

On an Ethernet network, every device on the network has a built-in Ethernet address. This address is a six-byte quantity usually written using hexadecimal numbers with a colon separating the bytes—for example, 08:00:20:0A:8C:6D. Ethernet addresses are assigned by the *Institute of Electrical and Electronics Engineers* (IEEE) and are unique among all Ethernet devices. No two devices should ever have the same Ethernet address (manufacturing errors do occur on occasion). The Ethernet address is divided into two parts; the first three bytes constitute the *vendor code*. Each vendor of Ethernet equipment obtains a unique vendor code from the IEEE. Every piece of equipment supporting Ethernet made by that vendor is programmed with an Ethernet address that begins with that vendor code. In the preceding example, the vendor code 08:00:20 corresponds to Sun Microsystems; every Ethernet device manufactured by Sun begins with those three bytes (see fig. 4.7). The vendor is responsible for making sure that every Ethernet device it manufactures has the same first three bytes (vendor code) and a different remaining three bytes to guarantee that every Ethernet device in the world has a unique address built in.

If every Ethernet device already has a unique address, why are IP addresses necessary? First of all, not every device has Ethernet support; IP addresses enable devices that connect to fiber and Token Ring and serial lines to use IP without having to get an Ethernet address. Second, Ethernet addresses are organized by equipment vendor rather than by owner organization. To come up with an efficient routing scheme based on who made the equipment rather than on where it is located would be impossible. IP addresses are assigned based on a network topology, not on who manufactures the device. Finally, and most important, is that devices can be more easily moved or repaired when an extra level of addressing exists. If an Ethernet card breaks, it can be replaced without getting a new IP address. If an IP node is moved from one network to another, it can be given a new IP address without getting a new Ethernet card.

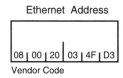

Ethernet Address

Vendor Code

## Figure 4.7:

A typical Ethernet address including a vendor code

Network hardware communicates only with other network hardware (for example, two Ethernet cards on two network devices). This network hardware often uses an addressing system that is not friendly to humans, but is convenient for the hardware itself. Users and services on networks communicate with other users and services. These services are easier to access if they are addressed in a way that makes sense to people. Addressing that is easy for humans to understand, however, is not always easy for hardware to manage. To solve this problem, a method of mapping user-level addresses to hardware is needed.

Ethernet addresses are long and cryptic and not meant to be regularly dealt with by users. To provide a mechanism for nodes to determine each other's hardware addresses without intervention from the user is possible. For TCP/IP, this mechanism is ARP. When an IP node wants to communicate with another node with the same network number, it assumes that having the same network number implies that the destination is on the same wire. On an Ethernet, for example, the source Ethernet card can directly communicate with the destination Ethernet card if it knows the Ethernet address. To determine the Ethernet address of a node on the same wire, the sending device sends an ARP request to the Ethernet broadcast address (see fig. 4.8). This address is a special address that all Ethernet cards are configured to listen to (it consists of six bytes of all ones, written in hex as FF:FF:FF:FF:FF:FF). Setting the destination Ethernet address to this value and sending an Ethernet packet causes every device on the Ethernet to accept the packet as if it were addressed specifically to it. It is the Ethernet equivalent of the U.S. postal address "Occupant."

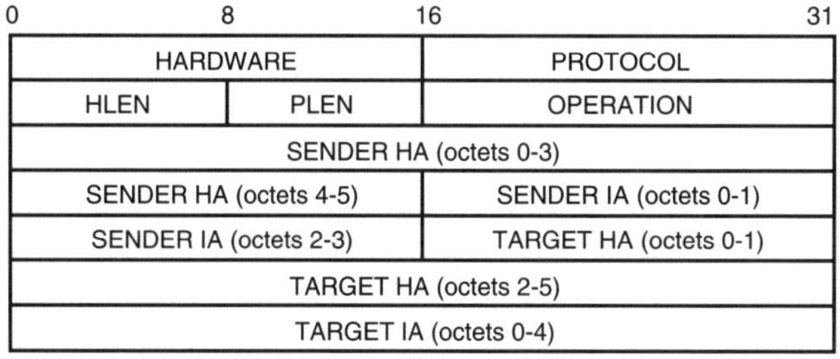

| 0 | 8 | 16 | 31 |
|---|---|---|---|

| HARDWARE | | PROTOCOL | |
|---|---|---|---|
| HLEN | PLEN | OPERATION | |
| SENDER HA (octets 0-3) | | | |
| SENDER HA (octets 4-5) | | SENDER IA (octets 0-1) | |
| SENDER IA (octets 2-3) | | TARGET HA (octets 0-1) | |
| TARGET HA (octets 2-5) | | | |
| TARGET IA (octets 0-4) | | | |

## Figure 4.8:

The format of an ARP packet.

An ARP request asks every node on the wire what the Ethernet address is for a particular IP address. The ARP request contains (among other things) the sender's source IP address and Ethernet address as well as the IP address with which the sender wants to communicate. Every Ethernet device on the network accepts this packet and, if the receiving device supports IP, recognizes that it is an ARP request. The receiving device then compares its configured IP address to the IP address being looked for. If an exact match occurs, the receiving device sends an ARP response back to the sender (through the Ethernet address in the ARP request, not as a broadcast) containing its Ethernet address. The sender can then encapsulate the IP packet it wants to send in an Ethernet packet with a destination Ethernet address as specified in the ARP response.

Why doesn't the sending node simply broadcast every packet it sends? On a large or busy network, this would require every node to be interrupted to process every packet on the network to determine whether the packet was destined for it. This interruption would be very inefficient and would slow down the network considerably. To make sure that broadcasts are minimized, nodes on broadcast networks requiring the use of ARP maintain a list of IP addresses and the Ethernet addresses that correspond to them (determined by previous ARP requests). This list is called the *ARP cache* and is updated whenever an ARP response is received. A node needing to send many IP packets to the same destination sends an ARP request the first time it tries to contact the node and records the Ethernet address it receives in the ARP response. Subsequent IP packets use the Ethernet address in the cache instead of sending another ARP request. Each entry in the cache is kept for some amount of time decided by the implementor of the TCP/IP software in use. This timeout might be as little as 30 seconds or as much as several hours or even be configurable. The shorter the time, the more broadcast ARP requests there are. But if the time is too long, then a node that changes its Ethernet address (because the Ethernet card was replaced, for example) cannot be contacted until the entry is updated.

# Examining How End Nodes Find a Router

To send a packet to a node on another network, an end node requires the aid of a router. If two nodes on the same network want to communicate, they can do so directly by encapsulating their IP datagrams in link level frames (for example, Ethernet frames) and sending them to each other. This procedure works because nodes on the same network are attached to the same wire (separated only by cable, repeaters, and bridges). When a destination is on another network, it is on another wire and can't be reached directly. The end node encapsulates the IP datagram in a link level frame destined for a router. The router then determines where to send the packet next. Because a router is needed to contact a node on another network, it is necessary for the router to be on the same network as the source node (otherwise the source node would need a router to reach the router!). Routers behave much like a post office for U.S. mail. If you want to deliver a message to someone very close (for example, next door), you would most likely deliver the message yourself. But if the destination is unfamiliar or is far away, you would deliver the message to the nearest post office. The post office would deliver the message for you if the message is for a local address serviced by that post office; otherwise, it looks up which post office should deal with it next. The letter might pass through a number of post offices before being delivered.

To deliver a packet to a node on a different network, a source node sends the unmodified IP packet to the local router by encapsulating it in a link level packet addressed to the router's MAC address. If the link level is Ethernet, the source node needs to know the Ethernet address of the local router. For reasons given previously, nodes should not deal with Ethernet addresses directly; therefore, TCP/IP end nodes need to know how to obtain the Ethernet address of a router. By using the ARP protocol, an end node that knows the IP address of a router can obtain the Ethernet address. TCP/IP end nodes need to be manually configured with the address of at least one router (usually called a *default gateway*). Some TCP/IP implementations enable the router's address to be obtained dynamically by "eavesdropping" on the routers' conversations. In this case, the node is configured to "listen" to a particular routing protocol such as RIP.

# How Routers Learn the Network Topology

For routers to fulfill their role as "post office" of the network, they need to know which networks are reachable and how to get to them. To accomplish this, routers store information about the topology of the network. This topology is usually stored as a *routing table* that lists each known network, tells how "far" away the network is, and indicates which router is the next one to send a packet to reach a network not directly connected (see table 4.1 and fig. 4.9).

**Table 4.1    A Routing Table for a Three-Router Network**

| Network | Distance | Next Router |
|---|---|---|
| **Router 1** | | |
| 1 | 0 | — |
| 2 | 0 | — |
| 3 | 1 | 222.222.222.2 |

*continues*

| **Table 4.1** | **Continued** | |
|---|---|---|
| **Network** | **Distance** | **Next Router** |
| **Router 1** | | |
| 4 | 1 | 222.222.222.2 |
| 5 | 2 | 222.222.222.2 |
| 6 | 0 | — |
| **Router 2** | | |
| 1 | 1 | 222.222.222.1 |
| 2 | 1 | 222.222.222.1 |
| 3 | 0 | — |
| 4 | 0 | — |
| 5 | 1 | 200.15.22.3 |
| 6 | 0 | — |
| **Router 3** | | |
| 1 | 2 | 200.15.22.1 |
| 2 | 2 | 200.15.22.1 |
| 3 | 1 | 200.15.22.1 |
| 4 | 0 | — |
| 5 | 0 | — |
| 6 | 1 | 200.15.22.1 |

The *cost* of a network can be declared in many ways (depending on whose network you look at), but is most often simply a count of how many routers a packet must go through to reach a network. The cost to a network is often called the *distance* or *number of hops* to a network.

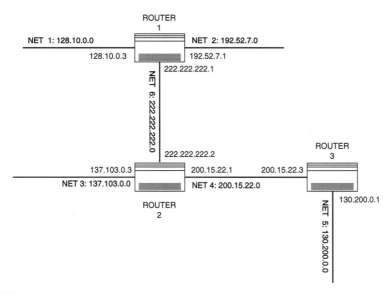

**Figure 4.9:**

A network with three routers.

A cost of zero means that the specified network is directly connected to the router. Packets destined for such a network can be
delivered from the router to the final destination by encapsulating the datagram in a data link layer frame (for example,
Ethernet) by sending an ARP request for the node. For this
reason, the next router field for directly connected networks is
meaningless.

When the cost is non-zero, the network in question is not directly
connected and requires routing through at least one more router.
In this case, the routing table indicates which router is the next
one to send to. The router sends an ARP request for this "next
hop" router and encapsulates the datagram in a data link layer
packet addressed to the MAC address of the next router. When
this router receives the packet, it checks its routing table and
determines if the packet can be delivered locally or needs to be
routed to yet another router.

If the destination network (or default network) does not appear in the routing table, then the packet cannot be delivered and is dropped (ignored). This could happen for a variety of reasons, including the following:

➤ The sending node was mistaken or misconfigured

➤ The router was misconfigured and does not know about the network

➤ All routes to that network are no longer operating (a router farther along the path to the network went down)

Usually when a packet is dropped due to the lack of a route, the router sends an ICMP Destination Unreachable message to the source, which should cause the node to log a message informing the user that data is not getting through.

Routing tables are set up in routers by two means: manual configuration and dynamic acquisition. (Sometimes a combination of both methods is used.) Manual configuration is the most straightforward method, but the least robust in the face of a changing network, and also can be impossible to maintain in a very large network. When *manual configuration* is used, the person installing the router is responsible for typing in the various fields for the routing table—telling the router which networks are reachable, how far away they are, and which routers should be used to reach them.

*Dynamic acquisition* of routing tables is achieved by means of one or more routing protocols. In TCP/IP, the most commonly used routing protocol is RIP (not to be confused with the IPX routing protocol of the same name). *RIP* is a simple protocol that enables routers to tell each other what networks they know about and how far away they are. With this information, each router can assemble a table of every network on an internet, enabling packets to be sent from any network to any other network, which could mean excessively large routing tables if the network were attached to a worldwide network such as the Internet. Therefore, provisions are made to "clump" many networks together in a default route represented by the IP address 0.0.0.0. Routers advertising connectivity to network 0.0.0.0 are saying, "If you don't see the network number anywhere else, send the packet to me."

RIP updates are broadcast by every router on every network every 30 seconds. Because these updates can impact network performance considerably on very large or slow networks, more efficient (in bandwidth, at least) protocols are being developed. *Open Shortest Path First* (OSPF) is a routing protocol becoming popular. OSPF provides a number of benefits to large networks, such as less traffic and faster "flooding" of information regarding changes to the network, but at the expense of a more complex algorithm (implying the need for more memory) to implement. Other protocols are used by routers to learn dynamically the topology of the network and advertise changes in that topology. The mechanics of each one is different, but the general purpose of binding the network together is the same.

# Finding and Using Services

In the end, the purpose of all this encapsulating and routing is to provide users access to services. Users are interested in terminal emulation, printing, file sharing, and e-mail; they're not concerned with how these services are created.

Services require support to make them easy to find and use. Most people are not very good at dealing with numbers even if they have sensible structures like IP addresses (never mind Ethernet addresses), for example. People like to deal with names that are like words (if not words themselves). The command Telnet server is far easier to remember than telnet 192.34.50.3, for example.

Most services in the TCP/IP world are found through well-known names. Such services are found published in books, in company documents, or by word-of-mouth from the system administrator to users. You can access services if you know the name of the device that provides the service and what program to use to access it. FTP the file printers.txt from server.company.com might be the directions to access the file that describes the names of all the printers you can use. A user would type **ftp server.company.com**; log in; and type **get printers.txt** to access the file.

IP packets cannot be addressed to a name; they require a four-byte IP address. Much like ARP is used to map an IP address to a hardware address, a service name can be mapped to an IP address in a number of ways. The simplest way is to maintain files that contain the name and IP addresses of devices of interest. This file is often called the *hosts file* because in UNIX it is found in the file /etc/hosts, and many IP implementations for other platforms have maintained the convention of calling the file hosts. This solution is simple, but not efficient on large networks. To maintain an up-to-date file on every single IP device can be difficult.

Usually a network administrator configures one or more servers to maintain a network-accessible database of name-to-IP mappings. Two commonly used methods are the *Domain Name System* (DNS) and Sun's *Network Information System* (NIS). Maintaining such a database requires that one or more machines be designated as "keepers of the database," and all other machines send requests to these servers to have a name converted into an IP address or vice versa. A network-accessible database of name-to-IP mappings is easy to maintain on a large network and requires little per-device configuration (only needing to know which machine to go to for lookups).

## TCP and UDP

*Transmission Control Protocol* (TCP) and *User Datagram Protocol* (UDP) travel encapsulated in IP packets to provide access to particular programs (services) running on remote network devices.

Throughout this chapter the discussion of TCP/IP has revolved entirely around IP. IP addresses enable data to be addressed to a particular node on an internet. After the data arrives, some mechanism is needed to enable the proper service within the device to receive the data. The data might be e-mail or a file or part of a print job. To direct the data to the appropriate program, another level of addressing is needed. Each service available on a node is accessed through a unique address called a *port* (sometimes also referred to as a *socket*). Ports are identified by a simple decimal number. For example, port 25 is the SMTP address. These numbers are contained in the TCP and UDP headers of TCP and UDP packets, which are encapsulated within IP packets (see figs. 4.10 and 4.11).

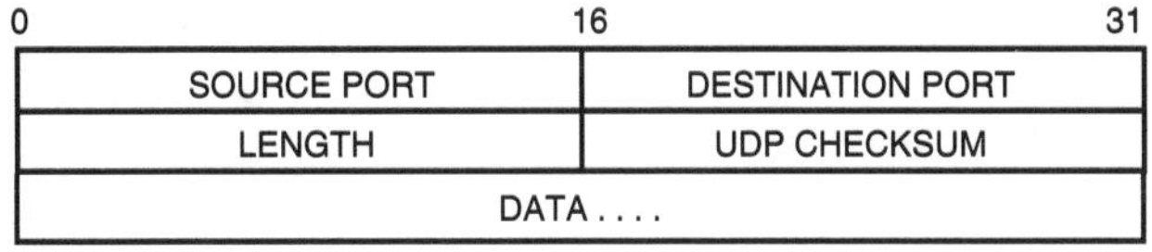

| 0 | 16 | 31 |
|---|---|---|
| SOURCE PORT | DESTINATION PORT | |
| LENGTH | UDP CHECKSUM | |
| DATA . . . . | | |

**Figure 4.10:**
Format of a UDP packet.

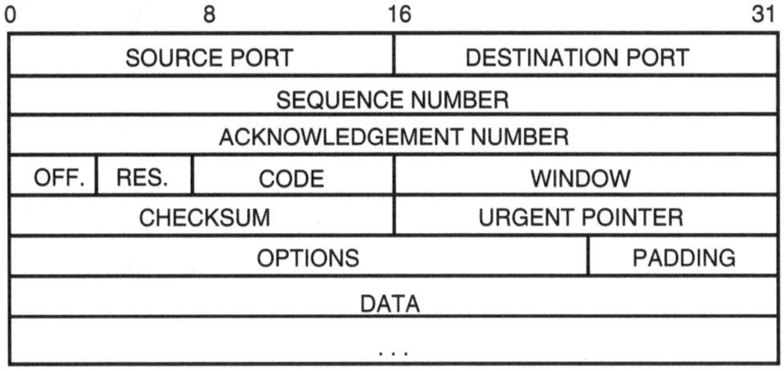

| 0 | 8 | 16 | 31 |
|---|---|---|---|
| SOURCE PORT | | DESTINATION PORT | |
| SEQUENCE NUMBER | | | |
| ACKNOWLEDGEMENT NUMBER | | | |
| OFF. | RES. | CODE | WINDOW |
| CHECKSUM | | URGENT POINTER | |
| OPTIONS | | | PADDING |
| DATA | | | |
| . . . | | | |

**Figure 4.11:**
Format of a TCP packet.

To understand the difference between UDP and TCP, you must know what is meant by datagram versus stream-oriented protocols, and what is meant by reliable versus unreliable protocols.

A *datagram-based protocol* is one that imposes a maximum size on the amount of data that can be sent in a single transmission. Ethernet, IP, and UDP are all datagram-based protocols. An upper limit to how much data can be sent in a single transmission exists. This type of protocol is analogous to sending a normal letter through the U.S. Postal Service. A single stamp limits the amount of "data" you can send at one time.

TCP is a *stream-oriented protocol*. A user of a TCP-based protocol does not need to worry about the maximum size of a transmission. TCP breaks the transmission into smaller sizes, retransmitting lost pieces, reordering data delivered out of order, and filtering out any extras that might occur due to faulty retransmissions. This type of transmission is analogous to a commercial freight carrier that can deliver as much "data" as the customer wants. The overhead necessary to support TCP is proportionally higher than that of UDP. An application that uses TCP requires more memory and more bandwidth to ensure that the transmission is completed properly.

The other factor that differentiates UDP from TCP is reliability. UDP is an *unreliable* or *best-effort* protocol. This definition does not mean that reliable data transfer cannot happen if based on UDP, but that the UDP protocol itself does not handle reliable data transfer. An application using UDP is responsible for implementing retransmissions, duplicate filtering, and so on, itself. If a UDP packet is lost or corrupted in transmission, it must be noticed by the application sending the data, which is again analogous to the U.S. Postal Service for normal mail. If the post office loses a letter, the letter is gone. They do not store a copy of it and "retransmit" it. Ethernet and IP also are best-effort protocols.

By pushing the overhead needed for reliability into an application, it is possible to make a reliable protocol or application that uses UDP. Sun Microsystems has implemented an entire file system—NFS—on top of UDP. NFS uses a less efficient set of algorithms than TCP to implement reliability, but the overhead is far less. UDP is appropriate for networks in which an application like NFS is used because the level of loss and corruption on a LAN is usually very low.

TCP is a *reliable protocol*. This definition does not mean that TCP guarantees delivery of the data it sends, but that TCP delivers the data if at all possible and reports back to the application if the data cannot be delivered (for example, if the destination node crashed). This reliability requires a great deal of overhead compared to UDP. Overhead is incurred to provide this service efficiently. TCP fragments and reassembles the data stream (so that the data can fit in datagram-based IP packets), retransmits lost packets, filters out duplicates caused by hasty retransmissions, handles flow control between computers of different speeds, and maintains *windows* (packets sent ahead that don't wait for an acknowledgment). If the network connectivity is preserved during the transmission, the data arrives in order and uncorrupted. If the connectivity is lost (the receiving program or machine crashed or an intermediate router went down), that fact is reported to the application using TCP.

Applications that invoke *sessions* usually use TCP to transfer data. These applications usually require the user to log in or connect before data can be moved. Applications that claim to be *stateless* are usually built on UDP, such as NFS.

Applications and protocols that use UDP include the following:

➤  NFS

➤  RIP

➤  *Trivial File Transfer Protocol* (TFTP)

➤  *Simple Network Management Protocol* (SNMP)

Applications and protocols that use TCP are as follows:

➤  FTP

➤  Telnet

➤  SMTP

# Summary

This chapter covered the basic concepts of TCP/IP and how members of the TCP/IP protocol family interplay to enable users to access services across an internet. Basic network concepts applicable to any protocol family—such as packets, protocols, addressing, routers, and end nodes—were covered. These general concepts were then applied to the specifics of the TCP/IP protocols. The formats of IP, UDP, and TCP packets were explained, as well as how ARP is used to enable IP addresses to be mapped to MAC addresses. Lastly, UDP and TCP were shown to be the means of addressing individual services within a network device whereas IP is the means of addressing specific devices on an internet.

# Chapter 5

# TCP/IP Routing

Just as stand-alone computers have readily become relics of the past, so too now are stand-alone networks. What was once simply a LAN must now become part of a WAN or MAN. Faced with the requirements to connect to wider geographical locations and more users, administrators have quickly had to embrace bridges, routers, and gateways.

This chapter examines routing on the TCP/IP protocol, how it is implemented, why it is implemented, and what you need to know to implement it.

## Examining the OSI Model

Every technology has its own jargon; computer networks are no exception. No matter what the protocol is—TCP/IP or NetWare—the basic underlying concepts are the same. Today they all start with the *Open Systems Interconnection model*, more commonly referred to as the *OSI model*.

Because of the existence of numerous types of computer operating systems, the OSI model was developed in 1977 by the *International Standards Organization* (ISO) to promote multivendor interoperability.

The OSI model itself does not specify any communication protocols. Instead it provides guidelines for communication tasks. It divides the complex communication process into smaller, more simple, subtasks. This way, the issues become more manageable, and each subtask can be optimized individually. The model is divided into seven layers as shown in figure 5.1. Note that the layers are numbered from the bottom up.

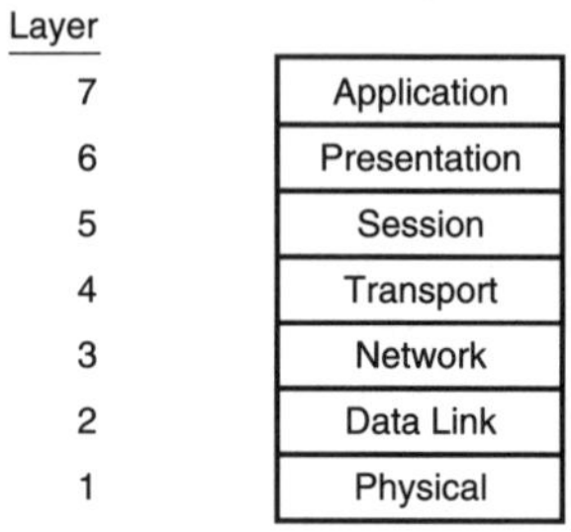

| Layer | |
|:---:|:---|
| 7 | Application |
| 6 | Presentation |
| 5 | Session |
| 4 | Transport |
| 3 | Network |
| 2 | Data Link |
| 1 | Physical |

**Figure 5.1:**

The OSI model.

Each layer is assigned a specific task. Also, each layer provides services to the layer above it and uses the services of the layer directly beneath it. For example, the network layer uses services from the data link layer and provides services to the transport layer.

In the context of this chapter, it is important to explain the services provided by the first three layers of the OSI model:

➤ The *physical* layer (layer 1) provides the physical connection between a computer system and the network wiring. It specifies cable pin assignments, voltage on the wire, and so on. The data unit at this layer is called a *bit*.

➤ The *data link* layer (layer 2) provides the packaging and unpackaging of data for transmission. The data unit at this layer is called a *frame*. A frame represents the data structure (much like a database record template).

➤ The *network* layer (layer 3) provides routing of data through the network. The data unit as this layer is called a *datagram*.

The TCP/IP protocol suite was developed before the OSI model was defined and is based mostly on the U. S. Department of Defense's own networking model, known as the *DoD model*. The DoD Model also is known as the *Internet model*. The DoD is discussed in the next section.

# Examining the DoD Model

In the mid-60s, the U.S. Department of Defense defined its own networking model. The DoD model, which defines only four layers, is much simpler than the OSI model. Figure 5.2 compares the DoD model to the newer OSI model.

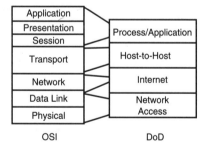

**Figure 5.2:**

A comparison of the OSI and DoD models.

Although the DoD model predates the OSI model by some ten years, a comparison between the two can still be made:

➤ The *process/application* layer in the DoD model maps to the top three layers of the OSI model.

➤ The *host-to-host* layer in the DoD model maps to OSI's transport layer.

➤ The DoD *internet* layer corresponds to the network layer in OSI.

➤ The *network access* layer in the DoD model maps to the bottom two layers in the OSI model.

Associated with each layer is one or more protocols that specify how certain networking functions behave. The Internet/Network layer protocols for TCP/IP are discussed in a later section. The next section examines the internetworking devices associated with the first three layers of the OSI model (the first two layers in the DoD model)—physical, data link, and network.

# Internetworking Devices

The basis for all TCP/IP routing decisions is a table of routing information maintained by the stack and routing protocols. The routing table is one of the most frequently accessed structures in the TCP/IP stack; on a busy host this can be hundreds of accesses in a second. The TCP/IP netstat command can be used to view the contents of the routing table. The following table illustrates the output from the netstat -r command used to display information stored in the routing table.

| destination | router | refcnt | use | flags | snmp metric | intrf |
|---|---|---|---|---|---|---|
| 132.1.16.0 | 132.1.16.3 | 1 | 63 | U | -1 | lan0 |
| 132.1.16.5 | 132.1.16.4 | 0 | 22 | U | -1 | ppp0 |
| 127.0.0.1 | 127.0.0.1 | 1 | 0 | UH | -1 | lo0 |
| default | 132.1.16.1 | 2 | 1351 | UG | 1 | lan0 |

Each entry in the table contains a destination and router (sometimes referred to as an IP gateway) address pair. For a given destination address, the router address indicates the host to which an IP datagram should be forwarded to reach that destination. The following minitable should help alleviate confusion about what a router does.

The flags in the table can have the following values:

| Flag | Description |
| --- | --- |
| D | The route was created via a redirect message. |
| G | The route is to a gateway/router. |
| H | The route is to a host. If this flag is not set, the route is to a network or subnetwork. |
| M | The route has been changed by a redirect message. |
| U | The route is currently up. |
| <null> | If this flag is not set, then the destination can be reached directly. |

A few comments are in order regarding the routing flags. If the G flag is not set, then the destination can be reached directly, that is, the host has both the IP address and the physical or link layer address of the final destination workstation. The net result is that the IP datagram can be sent simply by encapsulating it in the physical network frame.

For indirect routes (G flag set), the IP address corresponds to that of the final destination workstation and the link layer address is the physical address of the gateway. The *Address Resolution Protocol* (ARP), an integral part of the TCP/IP stack, maintains a cache of local IP address and link layer address pairs to facilitate the translation of IP addresses to link layer addresses.

The *Simple Network Management Protocol* (SNMP) metric indicates the desirability of a given route; a positive metric indicates a more preferred route. The intrf field indicates the interface (transport type and unit number) that the route is associated with. Possible interfaces include lan<n> (Token Ring; IEEE 802.5), le<n> (Ethernet; IEEE 802.3), sl<n> (*Serial Line Internet Protocol* or SLIP), ppp<n> (*Point-to-Point Protocol* or PPP), and lo<n> (the Loopback interface). The terminal string <n> represents the interface unit number. Note that the actual name assigned to an interface is vendor specific and varies from system to system.

This section defines the terms *repeater, bridge, router, gateway,* and *brouter* and their functions. It is important to understand how each of these devices functions so that you can make an informed decision when it comes to time for you to either connect your network with another, or segment your existing network into smaller networks to improve performance.

# Repeaters

When electrical signals traverse a medium, they attenuate (or fade) as a function of distance traveled. The longer the distance a signal travels, the lower the signal comes out at the other end. This shortcoming can be overcome with the use of a repeater. A *repeater* simply reconditions the incoming signal and retransmits it—in other words, it can be used to extend distance. Therefore, it works at the physical layer of the OSI model.

Because a repeater simply "passes on" the signals it receives, it performs no error checking. Therefore, any errors (such as CRC in Ethernet) are passed from one segment to another.

Repeaters cannot be used to connect segments of different topologies, such as Ethernet and Token Ring. However, repeaters can be used to connect segments of the same topology with different media, such as Ethernet fiber to coax Ethernet.

A repeater, such as an Ethernet multiport repeater, also can act as a signal splitter.

A repeater does not slow down your network because it performs no filtering. A repeater is transparent to protocols; however, because a device is involved, you can expect minute delays (one to two seconds).

# Bridges

A *bridge* is usually used to separate traffic on a busy network. A bridge keeps track of the hardware addresses of devices for each network to which it is directly connected. The bridge examines the hardware destination address of the frame and, based on its tables, decides if the frame should be forwarded or not. If the frame needs to be forwarded, a new frame is generated.

A bridge is a *store-and-forward* device; it does not pass the original signal to the destination segment.

Consider figure 5.3. When Earth sends a frame to Jupiter, the bridge knows that (based on its internal tables) Jupiter is on the same segment (Segment A) as Earth; no frame is forwarded to the segment on the right (Segment B). However, if Earth sends a frame to Saturn, the bridge, knowing Saturn is not on the same segment as Earth, forwards the frame.

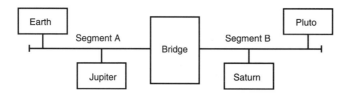

### Figure 5.3:
A briged network.

Because the bridge has access to information at the frame level, it "operates" at the data link layer of the OSI model (see fig. 5.4).

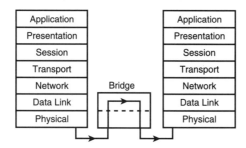

### Figure 5.4:
A bridge in reference to the OSI model.

Like repeaters, bridges are transparent to protocols. Because the bridge "operates" at the data link layer, it also can perform physical layer functions. Therefore, you can use a bridge to extend the distance of a segment.

Unlike repeaters, bridges do not propagate errors from one segment to another.

The four types of bridges available today are as follows:

➤ **Transparent bridge.** The *transparent bridge* is the most common type of bridge. It does not care about the protocols on the wire. A transparent bridge also is known as the *learning bridge* because it "learns" about the hardware addresses of the devices to which it is directly attached. It also is referred to as *spanning tree bridge* because of the spanning tree algorithm (IEEE 802.1D) it uses to manage paths between segments with redundant bridges.

➤ **Source routing (SR).** The *source routing bridge* (SR) is popular in IBM Token-Ring environments. IBM uses source routing to determine whether a frame needs to cross a bridge based on ring number information within the frame.

➤ **Source route transparent (SRT).** The *source route transparent bridge* (SRT) is a combination of a transparent and a source routing bridge. It "source routes" if the data frame has the SR information, or "bridges transparently" it if does not.

➤ **Translational bridge.** Some manufacturers produce *translational bridges* that connect Ethernet to Token Ring. An example is IBM's 8209 bridge.

In general, a bridge connects segments of similar topology such as Token Ring to Token Ring. They also can connect segments of the same topology with different media (much like a repeater).

If bridges are connected through a WAN link, they are known as *remote bridges*.

Some bridges have security features that you can define—by
hardware address or protocol type—as to whether frames are
passed to a certain destination address. This feature enables you
to filter traffic that might be destined for a specific server.

A workstation accessing resources across a bridge has slightly slower
performance than a workstation accessing resources across a repeater
because a bridge performs more functions than a repeater.

# Routers

A *router* can determine the best route between two or more
networks. A router has access to the network (software) address
information, which means it operates at the network layer of the
OSI model (see fig. 5.5). Because it needs to access the network
address information, it is very protocol-specific. When a router
encounters a datagram with a protocol it does not support, the
datagram is dropped.

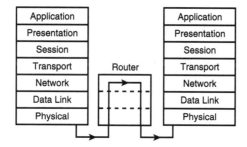

## Figure 5.5:
A router in reference to the OSI model.

For example, if one of your networks has TCP/IP and NetWare
traffic, and your router only supports TCP/IP (or only TCP/IP
routing is switched on), no NetWare traffic will ever leave that
segment. Therefore traffic is confined to a local segment.

A router is a much more intelligent device than a bridge; it can make decisions on selecting the best route for a datagram to reach its destination. This path can change depending on a number of factors, such as availability of link, traffic level, and others. A bridge, on the other hand, simply decides whether a frame needs to be passed on.

Routers do not pass errors from one network to another.

Because a router works at the network layer, it has no information about the topology (the frame information is stripped off by the data link layer). As a result, you can use a router to connect segments of different topologies.

Routers usually have some built-in filtering capability. The filtering is based on upper-layer protocols. For example, you can set up the filter table such that users cannot see certain servers across a given router. This type of filtering is much more powerful than filtering done with bridges.

A workstation accessing resources across a router has a slower performance than a workstation accessing resources across a bridge, which in turn is slower than when a repeater is involved. A router performs more complex functions than a bridge or repeater, resulting in slower workstation performance.

Traditionally in the IP world, routers were called gateways because they were the "gateway" to the outside world. However, with the accepted definition of the OSI model and standardization of internetworking terms within the industry, gateways are now called routers. Be careful, however, when reading some of the RFCs because the term "gateway" is still used liberally. Do not confuse that with the "OSI definition" of gateway as discussed in a following section.

A router connected to two or more physical networks has two or more IP addresses. In rare instances a TCP/IP host has two or more physical connections. Such a host is called a *multi-homed host*. If a multi-homed hosts's routing table is configured properly, it can function as a router.

# Brouters

A *brouter* (bridging router) is a device that first routes the protocols it understands. Tailing that, it attempts to bridge the traffic.

Certain protocols (such as NetBIOS) cannot be routed because they have no network information. If you need to pass these protocols together with, for example, TCP/IP traffic, you need to use a brouter for your network.

In most cases, hardware-based routers, such as 3COM, Cisco, and Wellfleet are capable of being a brouter. Software-based ones, such as Novell's Multiprotocol Router, cannot (even though Novell's MPR 2.11+ supports Token Ring SR bridging).

Check your router documentation; not all hardware routers can function as brouters.

# Gateways

A *gateway* is a device that translates between two different protocols and sometimes topologies. For example, a gateway is needed to translate between TCP/IP over Ethernet to SNA over Token Ring.

Gateways tend to be upper-layer-protocol specific, as is the e-mail protocol, for example. Therefore, if you need to exchange both e-mail and printing traffic between two hosts, two separate gateways may be needed.

Because a gateway translates most, if not all, protocol layers, it covers the entire seven layers of the OSI model.

# Deciding Which Device to Use

Oftentimes, you need to modify your current network—expand, improve performance, or add new services, for example. How can the different internetworking devices discussed in the preceding sections help? What should you use when? Look at the following two simple case studies and apply what you learned in the preceding sections.

## Case Study 1

You are given a task to extend the distance of your current Ethernet coax (10BASE2) network to include another floor of the building. What device should you use?

Before you answer, ask yourself the following questions:

➤ How long is the existing network?

➤ Is traffic an issue right now? Will it be an issue with the additional distance?

➤ Is there more than one protocol on the wire? Do you need to separate them?

If the current network is within the distance specification of 10BASE2 Ethernet, and the addition of the new segment does not exceed that, you can use a repeater to extend the distance. This is the lowest cost solution.

If the addition of the new segment exceeds the 10BASE2 distance limitation, you need at least a bridge to extend the distance because the bridge has (at least) two network cards, and the other side of a bridge is considered a new network (as far as cabling goes, not protocol). Of course, you can use a router here, but it is more expensive.

A router needs to look at the software address "buried" deep within a frame; therefore, it has to do more work to get at the information. A bridge only needs to look at the hardware address, which is near the beginning of the frame, requiring less work. Therefore, as a rule of thumb, a bridge can forward data much faster than a router. A repeater does not look at any "data"; therefore, it is faster than a bridge.

In reference to the second question, if traffic is a consideration, then a bridge should be used even if distance is not an issue. A bridge keeps traffic local and only passes frames to the other side when required.

If (data link layer) broadcast traffic (frames addressed to all devices on a network) is an issue, a bridge is not a good internetworking device to use. By definition, a broadcast address is not "local"; therefore, broadcast traffic always propagates across a bridge. In such cases, use a router.

Use a router if multiple protocols are on the wire. A router helps you isolate the protocols, if desired. It also helps you reduce the amount of broadcast traffic as well as manage multiple paths.

## Case Study 2

Today some sites do not want multiple protocols on the wire for various reasons. In such an instance a gateway serves as an ideal solution. Consider the sample network in figure 5.6.

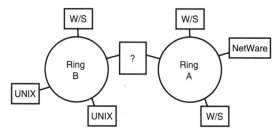

### Figure 5.6:
A sample network for Case Study 2.

This network contains two (Token) rings. The users on Ring A are Novell NetWare users with a NetWare server on the local ring. The UNIX servers are located on Ring B; some UNIX users also are on Ring B. Users on Ring A need to access a custom application on the UNIX servers on Ring B, but the network management folks don't want NetWare traffic on Ring B or TCP/IP traffic on Ring A. What is the best solution?

If both TCP/IP and NetWare traffic is allowed on the rings, the solution is quite straightforward: load dual protocol stacks on the workstations on Ring A and put in either a bridge or a router to connect the two rings. Multiple protocols, however, are not permitted on the ring, which leaves only one solution: an IPX-TCP/IP gateway.

The workstations on Ring A will speak IPX (NetWare) to the gateway; the gateway will convert from IPX to TCP/IP and put them out on Ring B. Two examples of such a gateway are NOV*IX for NetWare (NLM-based) from Firefox, Inc. (408-321-8344; 800-230-6090) and Catapult (OS/2-based) from Ipswitch (617-246-1150).

Now that you know the difference between repeaters, bridges, routers, and gateways, take a look at the various routing protocols associated with TCP/IP.

# IP Routing Protocols

Initially, a router only knows about the networks or subnets to which it is directly connected. It learns about other networks by two means: static routes and routing protocols.

A *static route* is a path in a router's routing table that is manually configured by a network administrator. For each network or host destination, the network administrator configures the next hop router and the cost associated with the route. This information is never changed, even if a portion of the path becomes unavailable. For example, in figure 5.7, a static route is configured for Router 1 so that to reach Network C, it must use Router 2.

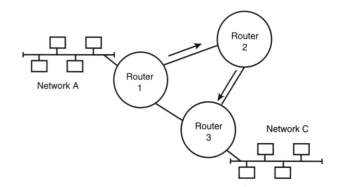

**Figure 5.7:**
A static route example.

Should the path between Routers 1 and 2 or between Routers 2 and 3 go down, Router 1 cannot reach Router 3 through an alternate path until it is manually reconfigured.

This is not a problem if the connectivity between Network A and Network C is not critical, because it will take some time before Router 1 can be reconfigured. However, this option is not viable if the link is important or automated path reconfiguration is desired. In such a case, a routing protocol is required so that routers can exchange path information automatically and update any route changes dynamically.

A number of different routing protocols are used in the TCP/IP world. They are not compatible with each other, though. Therefore, to resolve IP routing problems it is essential that you understand them.

The four routing protocols discussed in some detail in later sections are as follows:

➤ *Routing Information Protocol* (RIP)

➤ *Open Shortest Path First* (OSPF)

➤ *Interior Gateway Routing Protocol* (IGRP)

➤ *Internet Control Message Protocol* (ICMP)

This chapter does not explain all the details of each of these protocols because you can easily refer to the *Request For Comments* (RFCs)—documents that detail the protocol—for such information. The information presented here, however, gives you a working understanding of each of the protocols.

Before learning about the individual routing protocols, however, you must understand the classification of routing protocols used today.

# Classification of Routing Protocols

When dealing with internet routing, routing protocols are divided into different "classes"—*interior routing protocols* and *exterior routing protocols*.

*Interior routing protocols*, sometimes known as *interior gateway protocols* (IGPs), are generally used within an autonomous system to dynamically determine the best route to each network or subnet. An *autonomous system* (AS) is a group of routers that share information through the same routing protocol. Each autonomous system is assigned a unique identification number by the Network Information Center. The AS number is used by some routing protocols to control the exchange of routing information.

Exterior routing protocols, sometimes known as *interdomain routing protocols*, are used to exchange routing information between different autonomous systems.

Depending on the algorithm used to determine routes, cost of paths, and so on, routing protocols are further classified as either *distance-vector routing protocols* or *link state routing protocols*.

In *distance-vector routing protocols*, each router keeps a routing table of its perspective of the network. For example, as shown in figure 5.8, Router 1 sees that Networks A and B are one hop away (connected to directly), whereas Network C is two hops away. However, Router 2 sees Networks B and C as one hop away, and Network A as two hops away. The two routers "see" the network differently.

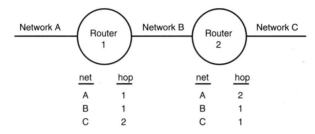

## Figure 5.8:

A sample network consisting of two routers and three network segments and its corresponding routing tables.

The distance-vector protocol is sometimes known as the *Ford-Fulkerson routing algorithm*, named after the inventors of the algorithm (L.R. Ford, Jr. and D.R. Fulkerson, *Flows in Networks*, Princeton University Press, 1962). The distance-vector protocol also is sometimes referred to as the Bellman-Ford algorithm because it was based on the Bellman Equation (R.E. Bellman, Dynamic Programming, Princeton University Press, 1957).

Each router takes the routing information passed to it, adds one hop to the route (to account for its own presence), and passes the updated information to the next router in line. In essence, distance-vector routing protocols use "secondhand" information from their neighbors.

Distance-vector routing protocols select the "best route" based on a *metric* ("some" unit of measurement). The metric used is different based on the actual protocol. One drawback of distance-vector routing protocols is that when routers send updates, they send entire routing tables. To keep the information up-to-date, the updates are *broadcast* at regular, fixed intervals.

The opposite of distance-vector routing protocols are link state routing protocols. With a link state routing protocol, a router calculates a "tree" of the entire network with itself as the root (see fig. 5.9).

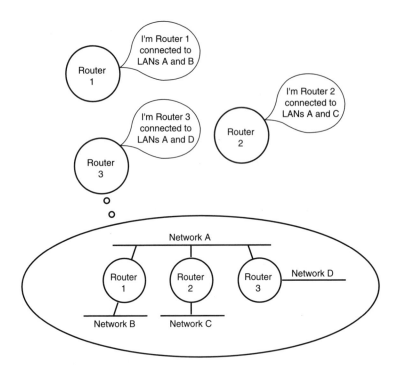

**Figure 5.9:**

Network layout as "seen" by Router 3 using link state protocols.

In this example, Router 3 constructs a network layout based on the route information received *directly* from the other routers. Under link state, each router distributes information about its directly connected networks and their associated metrics only.

The routers only include the best path derived by the metric to other nodes (routers). When a router detects changes in the state of its direct link (for example, a link comes up or goes down), the router distributes (broadcasts) the change to all other routers through a process called *flooding*. Flooding updates every router's database because it only sends state change information (hence the name link state).

In general, these flooding packets are very small and are sent infrequently. They contribute very little to the overall broadcast traffic unless routes change often.

The following sections examine the individual routing protocols.

# Routing Information Protocol (RIP)

The *Routing Information Protocol* (RIP; RFC 1508/1388) was first introduced in 1988. RIP is a *distance-vector* routing protocol as discussed earlier.

Because distance-vector routing protocols have regular, fixed update intervals, RIP's update is sent every 30 seconds.

For readers familiar with Novell's protocols, do not confuse this RIP with the RIP used by NetWare. Although they bear the same name and perform a similar function, NetWare RIPs are sent once every 60 seconds.

Therefore, in an environment in which you have both NetWare and TCP/IP, you will have RIP broadcasts from both protocols.

If a route is learned through RIP update messages, and then a subsequent update message does not refresh this route within 180 seconds (six update cycles), the route is assumed to be unreachable and is removed from the routing table.

RIP is probably the most common routing protocol used today because it is easy to implement. RIP has some serious limitations, however. For example, RIP data carry no subnet mask information, which limits RIP to advertise only network information (no subnet information), or requires RIP routers to make assumptions about the subnet mask. The latter makes it very vendor-implementation-specific and often causes interoperability problems.

If you are experiencing routing problems, check the routing tables of the routers involved and see if RIP is enabled. Some network administrators who want to cut down on the amount of broadcast traffic on their network disable RIP on the routers and use static routes instead.

Some routers enable you to adjust the RIP update timer to reduce broadcasts. If you do this, check that all other routers are configured similarly. Otherwise, you might see routes "come and go" on certain routers, resulting in intermittent routing problems.

For RIP, hop count is used as the metric. In figure 5.8, Router 1 "sees" that Network C is farther away than Network A or B because Network C has a metric (hop count) of two, whereas the others have a metric of one. If Router 1 learns (from another router not shown in the figure) of another path to Network B with, say, two hops, it discards that new route because it has a higher metric.

A RIP metric of 16 (hops) means that the destination is not reachable.

Recently some routers started supporting RIP II (RIP version 2; RFC 1388). RIP II is an enhancement over RIP that includes the subnet mask in its routes and variable length subnets, which enables subnet information to be passed on correctly. Also, authentication on routing update messages can be performed.

Not all RIP routers support RIP II. Make sure that your routers use the same protocol.

Some routers, such as Novell's Multiprotocol Router, can support RIP I and RIP II simultaneously.

The biggest disadvantage of distance-vector protocols such as RIP is the time it takes for the information to spread to all routers. This period is known as the *convergence* time. For a large network, the convergence time can indeed be long; and during this time, data frames have a much greater chance of getting misrouted and lost because of the "count-to-infinity" problem illustrated as follows.

Using the distance-vector algorithm, the distances between Network D and the various routers are as follows (see fig. 5.10):

➤ One hop from Router 3 (directly connected)

➤ Two hops from Router 2 (through Router 3)

➤ Three hops from Router 1 (through Routers 2 and 3)

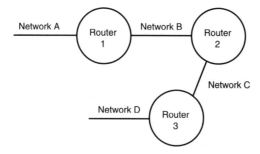

## Figure 5.10:

A simple count-to-infinity problem.

If Router 3 fails or the link between Routers 2 and 3 is down, Router 2 removes Network D's route from its routing table by setting the metric for Network D to 16. However, Router 2 sends a RIP update to Router 3 indicating that it can reach Network D at a lower cost (two hops). Router 3 then adds one hop count to this route and updates its routing table with this new route (reach Network D through Router 2).

Router 2 thinks it can reach Network D through Router 3 (in two hops), and Router 3 thinks it can reach Network D through Router 2 (in three hops). You now have a routing loop! In this case, any data destined for Network D is routed back and forth between Routers 2 and 3 until its time-to-live counter expires.

However, over time as the routers continue to update among themselves, the hop count to Network D continually increases and eventually reaches 16 hops (Infinity; unreachable), and the entry is removed from all routers. But as you can see, it can take a while, especially if you have a large network of routers.

RIP uses a technique called *split horizon* to prevent such routing loops—no routing information is passed back in the direction from which it was received. For example, Router 1 informs Router 2 that it is one hop away from Network A. Router 2 takes that information, adds one to the hop count for Network A, and passes that to Router 3 on Network C, but *not* back to Router 1 because that is the router from which it received the information.

Split horizon helps solve the count-to-infinity problem if you have a linear network. Most networks, however, contain redundant routes for fault-tolerant purposes, which reduces the effectiveness of split horizon. Figure 5.11 shows a network with multiple paths.

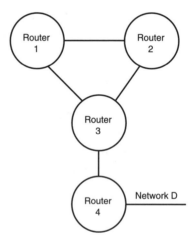

**Figure 5.11:**
A complex count-to-infinity problem that involves multiple paths.

Router 3 informs Routers 1 and 2 that Network D is two hops away from it; thus the routing tables in Routers 1 and 2 list Network D as three hops away. If Router 4 fails or the link between Routers 3 and 4 goes down, Router 3 will know that Network D is no longer reachable and will inform Routers 1 and 2 of the fact. Through split horizon, Routers 1 and 2 cannot tell Router 3 about their routes to Network D right away. However, between Routers 1 and 2 a "valid" path still exists.

Router 1 learns from Router 2 that it is two hops away from Network D. Router 1 adds one hop to that route and passes the information (3 hops to Network D) to Router 3, but not to Router 2 because of split horizon. Router 1 can pass information about Network D to Router 3 because Router 3 no longer advertises a route to Network D. Router 3 now thinks it is four hops away from Network D through Router 1. Router 3 passes that information to Router 2. Router 2 now thinks it is five hops away from Network D through Router 3. Router 2 propagates this to Router 1. Router 1 turns this into six hops, and passes this information to Router 3. Eventually, a hop count of 16 is reached, and split horizon didn't help much!

What can you do? You can use two more tricks: *poisoned reverse* and *triggered updates*, described in the following paragraphs.

With split horizon, routes are not advertised back onto the interface from which they were learned. With *poisoned reverse* enabled, however, such routes *are* advertised back to the same interface from which they are learned, but with a metric of 16. This immediately breaks the routing loop between any two routers. It helps to speed up the convergence time in the count-to-infinity problem, but does not necessarily eliminate it entirely.

Following are two packet captures taken using Novell's LANalyzer for Windows v2.1. This sample IP network has two routers. Router 1 is connected to IP networks 126.0.0.0 (with address 126.1.1.1) and 125.0.0.0 (with IP address 125.1.1.1). Router 2 is connected to IP networks 126.0.0.0 (IP address 126.2.2.2) and 120.0.0.0 (IP address 120.1.1.1). Router 2 has poisoned reverse enabled. Following is the RIP update from Router 126.1.1.1:

```
Station:126.1.1.1 ---->255.255.255.255
Protocol: UDP
    Version: 4
    Header Length (32 bit words): 5
    Precedence: Routine
           Normal Delay, Normal Throughput,
           Normal Reliability
    Total length:  52
```

```
                 Identification:      802
                 Fragmentation allowed, Last fragment
                 Fragment Offset: 0
                 Time to Live: 128 seconds
                 Checksum: 0xB895(Valid)
      udp: ================= User Datagram Protocol
           =================
                 Source Port: ROUTER
                 Destination Port: ROUTER
                 Length = 32
                 Checksum: 0x0000(checksum not used)
      rip: ============== Routing Information Protocol
           ===============
                 Command: Response
                 Version: 1
                 Family ID: IP
                       IP Address: 125.0.0.0
                       Distance: 1
```

The RIP update from Router 126.2.2.2 when poisoned reverse is
used is as follows:

```
      Station:126.2.2.2 ---->255.255.255.255
      ...
      Precedence: Routine
                  Normal Delay, Normal Throughput,
                  Normal Reliability
      Total length: 92
      ...
     udp: =================== User Datagram Protocol
          =================
      Source Port: ROUTER
      Destination Port: ROUTER
      Length = 72
      Checksum: 0x0000(checksum not used)
    rip: =============== Routing Information Protocol
         ==============
      Command: Response
      Version: 1
      Family ID: IP
            IP Address: 120.0.0.0
```

```
        Distance: 1
Family ID: IP
    IP Address: 125.0.0.0
    Distance: Not Reachable
Family ID: IP
    IP Address: 126.0.0.0
    Distance: Not Reachable
```

As you see in the first of the preceding two examples, Router 1 advertises to network 126.0.0.0 a route to network 125.0.0.0 with a hop count (distance) of one as expected. In the second example, Router 2 advertises a route to network 120.0.0.0 with a hop count of one, also as expected. Because it has poisoned reverse enabled, however, Router 2 also advertises network 125.0.0.0 (its local network) and network 126.0.0.0 (learned from Router 1) as not reachable.

A quick comparison between the RIP packets in the preceding examples shows that poisoned reverse generates more update traffic (larger update messages). On a large network, especially on a backbone, this level of traffic can cause traffic problems.

Consider the case of a building backbone connecting a number of different floors. On each floor, a router connects the backbone to a local network. Using split horizon, only the local network information is broadcast onto the backbone. But with poisoned reverse, the router's update message includes all the routes it learned from the backbone (with a metric of 16), as well as its own local network. For a large network, almost all the entries in the routing update message indicate unreachable networks.

In many cases, network administrators choose simply to use split horizon *without* poisoned reverse to conserve bandwidth and accept the slower convergence time.

If your router supports triggered updates coupling it with poisoned reverse can greatly minimize convergence time. *Triggered updates* cause the router to send a RIP update when a route's metric is changed, even if it is not yet time for a regular update message.

Be careful in the use of triggered updates because they can cause much broadcast traffic, similar to a broadcast storm.

The count-to-infinity problem in using RIP can be avoided by designing your network without router loops. If you must have multiple paths for redundancy, consider using a routing protocol other than RIP, such as OSPF as discussed later. Or simply keep in mind how RIP works, fix your downed link as soon as you can, or reset the routers to force a new routing table to be built.

# Configuring Interface Routes

At boot time most hosts run a network configuration file, and each interface is configured. A routing table entry also is created for each interface. The interface is normally configured by the TCP/IP ifconfig command, as shown in the following example:

```
ifconfig lan0 9.67.111.214 netmask 255.255.240.0
```

This command configures the lan0 interface with an IP address of 9.67.111.214 and a netmask of 255.255.240.0. This IP address is on network 9.67.96.0 (obtained by performing a BITWISE AND between 9.67.111.214 and 255.255.240). The following routing table entry is created for the interface:

```
destination        router    flags intrf
    9.67.96.0   9.67.111.214    U     lan0
```

The H flag is not set because this is not a route to a host, and the G flag is not set because this is not a route to a router.

# Assigning Static Routes

For simple networks, or networks whose configuration changes relatively infrequently, creating a static routing table using the TCP/IP route command is often efficient. This command provides a mechanism to manipulate the routing table by adding, modifying, and deleting table entries. For example, you can use the following command to create a default route to a network router whose IP address is 9.67.96.1:

```
route add default 9.67.96.1 1
```

The digit 1 following the IP address is referred to as the "hop count" and represents the distance (in number of routers) to the destination host or network.

# Interior Gateway Routing Protocol (IGRP)

For a long time on the Internet, routers used the *Interior Gateway Routing Protocol* (IGRP) to exchange routing information. Although IGRP is a distance-vector routing protocol, it uses a number of variables to determine the metric, including the following:

➤ Bandwidth of the link

➤ Delay due to the link

➤ Load on the link

➤ Reliability of the link

By considering these variables, IGRP has a much better, and real-time, handle on the link status between routers. IGRP is much more flexible than RIP, which is based solely on hop count. IGRP can better reflect the type of link and choose a more appropriate path than RIP. In figure 5.11, the links between Router 1 and Router 3 and Router 1 and Router 2 are T1 links, whereas the link between Router 2 and Router 3 is a 56K line. RIP doesn't know the difference in line speed between the paths and sends traffic over the slower 56K line rather than the T1 lines simply because it has a lower hop count. IGRP uses the more efficient T1 lines.

The update interval for IGRP is every 90 seconds, as compared to every 30 seconds for RIP. However, like RIP, when an update is sent, the whole routing table is sent also.

IGRP was developed by Cisco Systems, Inc., which is why for a long time when you acquired a link to the Internet, you were required to use a Cisco router. Now IGRP is supported by many other router vendors.

# Open Shortest Path First (OSPF)

*Open Shortest Path First* (OSPF) is a link state routing protocol first introduced in 1989 (RFC 1131/1247/1583). More and more IP sites are converting to OSPF from RIP because of its much lower traffic overhead and because it completely eliminates the count-to-infinity problem.

Using "cost" as the metric, OSPF can support a much larger internet than RIP. Remember in a RIP-based internet, you cannot have more than 15 routers between any two networks, which sometimes results in having to implement more links for large networks.

Similar to RIP II, OSPF supports variable length subnetting, which enables the network administrator to use a different subnet mask for each segment of the network. Variable length subnetting greatly increases the flexibility and number of subnets and hosts possible for a single network address. OSPF also supports authentication on update messages.

Using cost, an OSPF metric can be as large as 65535.

Other than exchanging routing information within an autonomous system, OSPF also can exchange routing information with other routing protocols, such as RIP and *Exterior Gateway Protocol* (EGP). This exchange can be performed using an *autonomous system border router.*

If you are using multivendor routers in a mixed RIP and OSPF environment, make sure that routes are redistributed between routing protocols in a consistent manner. To create routing loops because a vendor does not increment the hop count when going from RIP to OSPF and back to RIP is possible.

To go into the details of OSPF concepts, OSPF areas, and other OSPF protocols (such as the OSPF Hello Protocol) is beyond the scope of this chapter. Refer to RFC 1583 for the latest definition of OSPF Version 2.

# Internet Control Message Protocol (ICMP)

Sometimes even if you have not configured dynamic routing on an IP router, routes can be automatically added to your routing table by the *Internet Control Message Protocol* (ICMP).

ICMP was first introduced in 1980 (RFC 792/1256). Its function is to provide a dynamic means to ensure that your system has an up-to-date routing table. ICMP is part of any TCP/IP implementation and is enabled automatically. No configuration is necessary. ICMP messages provide many functions, including route redirection.

If your workstation forwards a packet to a router, for example, and that router is aware of a shorter path to your destination, the router sends your workstation a "redirection" message informing it of the shorter route.

The newer implementation of ICMP (RFC 1256) contains a *router discovery* feature. Strictly speaking, router discovery is not a routing protocol, but a way of finding neighboring routers. When a router starts up, it sends a router discovery request (multicast address 244.0.0.2; broadcast only if the interface does not support multicast) asking neighboring routers to identify themselves. Only routers directly attached to the network that the new router is on respond.

Router discovery is a rather new implementation for some routers and therefore is not supported by all routers.

# Other Routing Protocols

The protocols discussed earlier are all *interior gateway protocols* (IGPs), and they are by far the most often encountered routing protocols in the field. However, at times you might encounter some exterior routing protocols. *Exterior routing protocols* are used to connect two or more autonomous systems (see fig. 5.12). Two exterior routing protocols—*Exterior Gateway Protocol* (EGP; RFC 827/904) and *Border Gateway Protocol* (BGP; RFC 1105/ 1163/1267)—are briefly discussed in this section so that you can become familiar with them.

Introduced in 1982, EGP is the earliest exterior routing protocol. Routers using EGP are called *exterior routers*. Exterior routers share only reachability information with their neighboring exterior routers. EGP provides no routing information—an EGP router simply advertises *a* route to a network; therefore no load-balancing is possible on an EGP network.

In 1989, BGP was introduced. BGP uses TCP as the transport layer connection to exchange messages. Full path information is exchanged between BGP routers, thus the best route is used between autonomous systems.

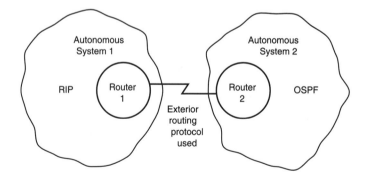

**Figure 5.12:**

Linking two autonomous sytems using an exterior routing protocol.

# Default Routes

In general, to create a separate routing table entry for every remote network in your internetwork is not necessary. If a *default network* (sometimes called *default router* or simply *default route*) entry exists in your routing table, then packets destined for networks not specifically listed in the routing table are forwarded to that router.

A default router entry is simply an entry in the routing table whose destination is network 0.0.0.0. Figure 5.13 shows an example of such an entry for a NetWare server/router. In this setup, any packets for, say, network 120.1.1.15 are forwarded to router at 126.2.2.2 because the local router doesn't know how to handle it, and 126.2.2.2 is listed as the default router.

```
TCP/IP Console  v1.01 (910801)          NetWare 386 Loadable Module

Host: 126.1.1.1              Uptime:   0 Days  1 Hour   32 Minutes 51 Seconds
Novell NetWare v3.11 (250 user)  2/20/91

ipReceives:      1,285 │ ipTransmits:      1,524 │ ipForwards:          0
tcpReceives:         0 │ tcpTransmits:         0 │ tcpConnects:         0
udpReceives:     1,246 │ udpTransmits:     1,505 │

                          ┌─────────────────────┐
                          │    TCP/IP Tables     │
              ┌───────────┴─────────────────────┴───────────┐
              │              Routing Table                   │
              │ Destination        Next Hop      Intf  Cost  Type   │
              │ 0.0.0.0            126.2.2.2       1     3    remote │
              │ 125.0.0.0          125.1.1.1       3     1    direct │
              │ 126.0.0.0          126.1.1.1       1     1    direct │
              │ <End of Table>                                      │
              └─────────────────────────────────────────────┘
```

## Figure 5.13:

A default route entry on a NetWare server/router.

A default route entry is useful when you are not using any routing protocols on your network—for example, if you turned off RIP to save on the bandwidth, but your routers don't support other routing protocols such as OSPF. You do not need to create a static route for each router on your network or subnets on your internet. You can use a default router entry on most routers to "point" to a few central routers that have more complete routing tables.

Some Internet service providers do not use RIP for their connections. Therefore, if you are connected through such a service provider, you might need to use a default router entry to gain access to the Internet.

# Path of an IP Packet

Now that you know how routes are determined between your networks and subnet, look at what happens to a frame when it is sent from a workstation to a host as it crosses bridges and routers. The sample network in figure 5.14 consists of two segments bridged together and a router connecting them to a third segment; the default network masks are used—255.0.0.0 for network 126.0.0.0 and 255.255.0.0 for network 133.7.0.0.

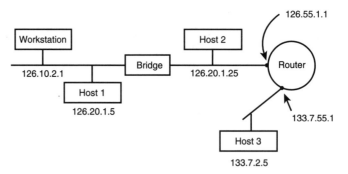

**Figure 5.14:**

A sample network that consists of two bridged segments and one routed segment.

# Local Segment

In figure 5.14, the workstation (126.10.2.1) wants to communicate with Host 1 (126.20.1.5). The TCP/IP software in the workstation determines that the destination is on the same network (126.0.0.0); therefore sending data between Workstation 1 and Host 1 does not need to involve a router.

To compose the frame at the data link layer, the TCP/IP software needs the hardware address, also known as the *Data Link Control* (DLC) address or *Media Access Control* (MAC) address, of Host 1. The TCP/IP software finds the hardware address using the *Address Resolution Protocol* (ARP). TCP/IP inserts the DLC address in the destination address field of the frame and its own DLC address (determined from the NIC installed) in the source address field. The frame is then transmitted onto the wire.

Both Host 1 and the bridge "see" this frame. The bridge, however, based on its learned table of addresses, knows Host 1 is on the same side as the workstation; therefore the bridge ignores the frame.

Host 1 sees its own address in the destination field, takes the frame, and processes it. Host 1 uses the DLC address in the source address field as the destination address in its reply messages. In this manner two devices learn about each other's DLC addresses.

# Bridged Segment

The communication process in a bridged IP network environment is not much different than the local segment scenario discussed previously. Should the frame need to cross the bridge (to reach Host 2), the workstation uses ARP to obtain the DLC address for Host 2. The workstation then uses the DLC address in the destination field, puts its own address in the source field, and transmits the frame onto the wire.

In this case, the bridge notices that the destination address is listed on its other segment. Therefore, the bridge makes a copy of the frame and puts a copy on the other side—without changing anything, not even the DLC addresses.

Host 2 sees the frame and processes it, not knowing it actually came across a bridge. Remember, bridges are transparent to protocols.

# Routed Segment

In a routed environment, the data frame addressing is a little more complicated than in the two cases previously covered. First, the workstation determines that the destination (Host 3) is *not* on its own network; therefore, it needs to use a router. However, which router is used if multiple routers are on the segment? When you install the TCP/IP software on a workstation, you are generally asked to specify a default router. This entry is not used if you are communicating locally. When you need to communicate outside your network, however, all frames are addressed to this default router.

Some workstation software (such as Novell's LAN WorkPlace for DOS v4.1 and higher) enables you to define multiple default routers, which give you some backup paths. Be careful, however, in load-balancing the specification so that no given router is overloaded.

The workstation finds the DLC address of the router by using ARP as in the preceding two cases. The TCP/IP network drive software puts the router's DLC address as the destination, rather than Host 3's address. This key concept is very important—in a bridged environment, the DLC address of the bridge is not involved in data frame addressing. In a routed environment, however, the router's DLC address (and IP address) is involved.

After the router receives the frame, it "unpacks" the frame by stripping off the DLC information. The router looks at the IP information (IP destination address) and checks with its routing table to see where the next stop is. If the destination is on a network directly connected to this router (as in the earlier simple example), the router uses the ARP protocol to determine the DLC address of Host 3 and creates a new *frame* using that information and its own DLC address. Host 3 knows the frame came from a router because the source IP network within the frame is different from its own network. The replies from Host 3 back to the workstation follow the reverse path.

If, however, the first router is not directly connected to the destination network, the router looks in its routing table to find where the next hop is, uses the ARP protocol to determine that router's DLC address, and sends a new frame with the new information. This process continues until the frame reaches a router directly connected to the destination network.

Now you can see why it is important to have the routing tables of *all* your routers up-to-date and consistent with each other. Any old routing information along the path of the frame results in lost data, causing retransmission in the best case and application crashes and incapability to communicate throughout your internet in the worst case.

## Summary

This chapter introduced and defined the various devices used in internetworking, such as bridges and routers. Two simple case studies were used to illustrate how to select the appropriate device for a given environment. The various IP routing protocols, such as RIP and OSPF, were discussed in depth, including their strengths and limitations. The chapter discussed the classic count-to-infinity problem and various options, such as poisoned reverse and split horizon, to minimize this effect. Finally, the IP routing process was illustrated.

# Chapter 6

# IPng

The *IP layer* is the foundation of the TCP/IP protocol suite.
Perhaps the IP layer's most critical function is addressing. The IP
address structure was developed with the expectation that it
should meet current and future requirements. The current
implementation of IP, also known as version 4, which utilizes a
32-bit addressing space, does provide for a large addressing
space.

This is illustrated in the following table:

**Table 6.1   IP Version 4 Addressing Capabilities**

| Address Class | First Octet Range | Number of Networks | Number of Nodes per Network |
|---|---|---|---|
| A | 1–127 | 127 | 16,277,214 |
| B | 128–191 | 16,383 | 65,534 |
| C | 192–223 | 2,097,151 | 254 |

IP version 4's addressing capacity met the internetwork community's requirements when first implemented but has rapidly been exhausted, owing principally to the enormous growth of devices that utilize IP addresses.

The computer environment currently is the largest group of devices that utilize IP addresses and one of the fastest growing areas of technology. Now being purchased in the thousands are personal computers, many of which utilize TCP/IP as a communications protocol and therefore have an IP address. More and more platforms, such as mainframes, utilize TCP/IP and have IP addresses.

The Internet has experienced phenomenal growth over the past several years, and that rate of growth is likely only to increase. As of October 1994, estimations suggested that the Internet consisted of approximately 40,000 networks. Since then, the number of networks in the Internet is rapidly increasing each year. At the same time, the number of users within these networks also is increasing owing to the rapid growth in use of the Internet in both the business and home communities. Another example of the growth in the Internet is quantified by the number of World Wide Web servers.

Systems and network management also has contributed to exhausting IP addresses. Network and device management is critical for organizations that implement local and wide area networks and for client-server environments that require monitoring, control, and fault detection. Using technologies based on Simple Network Management Protocol (SNMP), an IP-based protocol, requires that each device—a network hub, a network interface card in a personal computer, a file server, a router, a LAN switch or other communications equipment—have an IP address.

Although the computer and network market's growth has been explosive, it might not experience the amount of growth now only priming to erupt in the consumer entertainment market. By providing services such as cable television, video on demand, home shopping, and information access, every television could become an Internet device with an IP address. The growth that this market alone can be expected to drive will demand an architecture that provides efficient, easy-to-implement, and easy-to-monitor large scale addressing and routing.

# History of IP Next Generation

IP Next Generation, or version 6, actually is the evolution and compilation of a number of proposals and efforts over the last three years within the standards communities. Numerous proposals have addressed some but not all of the IP version 4 issues.

By the end of 1992, the Internet community had developed three primary proposals for consideration: *TCP and UDP with Bigger Addresses* (TUBA), *Common Architecture for the Internet* (CATNIP), and the *Simple Internet Protocol Plus* (SIPP).

# TUBA—TCP and UDP with Bigger Addresses

By design, TUBA's primary objective is to address the IP address exhaustion issue; specifically, to provide a significantly larger address space by replacing the current IP layer with CLNP. CLNP uses an address format known as Network Service Access Point (NSAP) addresses, which are significantly larger than the IP version 4 32-bit addresses. Furthermore, the hierarchy that can be structured into these address structures would enhance the scalability of the Internet environment and increase the levels of efficiency of routing data through the Internet.

One of TUBA's strongest points is that it doesn't require completely replacing the current transport (TCP and UDP) protocols or application protocols (FTP, TELNET, SMTP, SNMP, HTTP, and so on). TUBA doesn't imply a complete transition to the OSI protocol suite—rather it just replaces the current network layer with CLNP.

Integral to the TUBA proposal is a migration strategy that would allow a gradual transition of Internet devices. The primary devices affected during this migration phase would be host systems that serve as platforms for Internet applications and *Domain Name Server* (DNS) platforms that provide host name to address translation functions. This migration strategy would allow both traditional IP version 4 addresses and NSAP addresses to coexist in the Internet, and this would allow for a smooth transition rather than a large scale conversion effort all at once.

# CATNIP—Common Architecture for the Internet

The concept driving CATNIP is to establish a commonality between several of the most prominent protocol environments you see in today's networks: namely, in the Internet, which is predominately TCP/IP based, OSI, and Novell IPX. The objective is to eliminate the architectural and protocol barriers between these environments and to facilitate growth of the Internet. The goal is to extend the life of the Internet and to increase the performance of it.

The CATNIP concept specifies that any of the current transport layer protocols (TCP, UDP, IPX, SPX, TP4 and CLTP) be able to function on any of the prominent layer three protocols (CLNP, IP version 4, IPX, and CATNIP). It also would permit one device that might use IP as a network layer protocol to interoperate with a device that uses IPX as a network layer protocol.

Like TUBA, CATNIP implements OSI Network Service Access Point (NSAP) format addresses.

# SIPP—Simple Internet Protocol Plus

Perhaps the primary consideration behind the design of the Simple Internet Protocol is to develop a protocol that would provide an easy transition from IP version 4. It is expected that SIPP would function well in high performance network environments, such as FDDI and ATM, as well as in lower performance networks, such as low bandwidth wide area networks (WANs) or wireless networks. The two primary areas addressed are addressing and structure of the IP packet.

The Simple Internet Protocol increases the size of the IP address from 32 to 64 bits, and this larger address space allows for a significantly larger number of addressable devices as well as for a higher degree of hierarchical structure in a network. This would dramatically increase the efficiency of routing data in large networks such as the Internet. Furthermore, the architecture allows the 64-bit address space to be expanded even further in 64-bit increments. Given this, it is projected that SIPP could have a longer viable lifespan than earlier versions of IP.

The structure of the IP packet also has been revised. Functions and fields not functional or deemed unnecessary have been eliminated. Required enhancements have been added to the specifications. A certain capability was added, for example, to enable identifying packets as being part of a "conversation" between two devices that might need special handling as they are transported through an internetwork.

# IP Next Generation Overview

Each of the preceding proposals resolved some of the existing issues with IP version 4 and also introduced new functionality necessary for the future requirements of the IP protocol. None of them, however, addressed all of the relevant issues. IP Next Generation, as it is currently defined, is in fact the result of adopting the salient features of these three prominent proposals.

One of the primary objectives of IP version 6 design is to maintain compatibility with higher level protocols that rely on it, such as SMTP, SNMP, FTP, and HTTP. By design, it is meant to be evolutionary, so that it doesn't require completely redesigning the applications that thousands of users currently utilize.

The evolution of IP version 6 can be categorized into several areas:

➤ Expanded addressing and routing capabilities

➤ Header format simplification and improved support for options

➤ Quality of service capabilities

➤ Security and privacy

➤ IP mobility

The following sections discuss how IP version 6 seeks to address the issues and limitations of the current implementation of IP in each of these areas.

# IP Next Generation Addressing

One of the most noticeable differences between IP versions 4 and 6 comes in the area of addressing. IP version 4 utilizes a 32-bit address space, whereas IP version 6 increases this address space from 32 bits to 128 bits, which allows a much greater number of addressable devices—a total of 340,282,366,920,938,463,463, 374,607,431,768,211,456 addresses. This is 4 billion times 4 billion the number of addresses that are possible with IP version 4.

IP version 6 has three types of addresses, as follow:

➤ **Unicast.** Unicast addresses identify a specific interface on a device. By definition, only one device can be assigned to a specific unicast address.

➤ **Anycast.** Anycast addresses identify a group of interfaces in which a single member of the group receives any packet sent to the multicast address. The device that is "closest"— closest according to the routing metric—receives any packet sent to an anycast address. (The *routing metric* is the unit of measure provided by a routing protocol such as RIP or OSPF, to quantify the end-to-end path between two networkd devices.)

Anycast addresses are identical in format to unicast addresses. The only difference is that more than one device can be assigned to a specific anycast address and the device can be specifically configured to know that it has an anycast address.

➤ **Multicast.** Multicast addresses identify a group of interfaces in which all members of the group receive any packet sent to the multicast address.

The type of IPng address is determined by the leading bits in the address. This variable length field is called the Format Prefix (FP).

IP version 4 addresses are distinguished by class, but this is not so with IPng addresses. The IPng concept resembles *Classless Inter Domain Routing* (CIDR), which is discussed in detail in RFC 1338.

This RFC does not explain IPng addressing. It is a source for a similar mechanism, and the reference is provided for someone who might want more technical information.

The leading bits in the address indicate the specific type of IPng address. The variable-length field that comprises these leading bits is called the *Format Prefix* (FP). The initial allocation of these prefixes is as follows:

### Table 6.2   Address Distribution for IP Version 6

| Allocation | Prefix (binary) | Fraction of Address Space |
|---|---|---|
| Reserved | 0000 0000 | 1/256 |
| Unassigned | 0000 0001 | 1/256 |
| Reserved for NSAP Allocation | 0000 001 | 1/128 |
| Reserved for IPX Allocation | 0000 010 | 1/128 |
| Unassigned | 0000 011 | 1/128 |
| Unassigned | 0000 1 | 1/32 |
| Unassigned | 0001 | 1/16 |
| Unassigned | 001 | 1/8 |
| Provider-Based Unicast Address | 010 | 1/8 |
| Unassigned | 011 | 1/8 |
| **Reserved for Neutral-Interconnect-Based** | | |
| Unicast Addresses | 100 | 1/8 |
| Unassigned | 101 | 1/8 |
| Unassigned | 110 | 1/8 |
| Unassigned | 1110 | 1/16 |
| Unassigned | 1111 0 | 1/32 |

| Allocation | Prefix (binary) | Fraction of Address Space |
|---|---|---|
| Unassigned | 1111 10 | 1/64 |
| Unassigned | 1111 110 | 1/128 |
| Unassigned | 1111 1110 0 | 1/512 |
| Link Local Use Addresses | 1111 1110 10 | 1/1024 |
| Site Local Use Addresses | 1111 1110 11 | 1/1024 |
| Multicast Addresses | 1111 1111 | 1/256 |

*Source: R. Hinden, http://www.playground.sun.com/pub/ipng/html/pingmain.html

Based on this scheme, approximately 15 percent of the address space has been reserved and 85 percent is available for future use.

# Routing

One of the objectives with IPng was to minimize the effect on other protocols and technologies that rely on the IP protocol. One such example is routing.

Routing in IPng is very similar to routing in IP version 4 environments using CIDR, except for the actual addresses used for routing; that is, IPng addresses being 128 bits long rather than 32 bits.

Therefore, current routing protocols, such as RIP, OSPF, IS-IS, and IDRP can be used to route IPng with modification rather than force the development of entirely new protocols. This too will facilitate the transition to IP version 6.

One of the new capabilities of routing in IP version 6 environments is facilitated by the IPng routing option. An IPng source device uses the routing option to list one or more intermediate nodes it must pass through on its way to a specified destination. This functionality allows the source device to dictate the path that its data takes, enabling such things as provider selection. To illustrate this concept, examine the network depicted in figure 6.1.

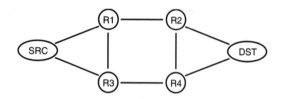

**Figure 6.1:**

Source routing in an IP version 6 environment.

In the network illustrated in figure 6.1, if device SRC (representing a source device) transmits data to device DST (representing a destination device), the routing protocol in use determines its path through the network. A routing protocol may determine the optimal path based on characteristics of the individual connections and devices between the source and destination nodes, such as bandwidth, delay, or hop counts. The path of transmitted data, for example, might be SRC-R1-R2-DST, because the routing metric for this path is the least among the possible paths.

Using the IPng routing option, the device SRC can specify the path of its data through this internetwork. Essentially, this enables the source device, such as a personal computer, to override the router and dictate its path through the network. If the connection between R1 and R2 is subject to high amounts of delay and the data in question is delay sensitive, for example, SRC might want to specify that the path of its data be SRC-R3-R4-DST.

The IPng routing option can also provide source devices with the capability to select which Internet Access Provider (IAP) might handle specific flows of data. If the connection between R1 and R2 is provided by an IAP that might be undesirable for the traffic flow for reasons of cost, bandwidth, delay, or reliability, the source device can direct network traffic onto a favorable path.

# IP Next Generation Packet and Header Formats

As mentioned previously, many of the new capabilities of IP version 6 are made possible by a restructuring of the IP header. In this section, you examine the components of the IP version 6 header and explain the capabilities made possible by these components.

The sizes of the fields shown in figure 6.2 are illustrative only. The actual size of each field and its function are explained in the following:

➤ **Ver.** 4-bit Internet Protocol version number. The purpose of this field is to identify which version of the IP protocol is being used. For example, the number in this field is 4 in the current implementation of IP. This field will be 6 in the headers of IP version 6 packets.

➤ **Prio.** 4-bit Priority value. This allows the source device to mark packets as higher or lower priority relative to other packets from the same source. This will be discussed further in the section titled "IP Version 6 Priority."

➤ **Flow Label.** 24-bit field. The purpose of this is to allow the source device to identify packets transmitted between a source and destination device that are part of a specific conversation or "flow." An example of this might be a multimedia transmission of time and delay sensitive video and audio material. This will be discussed further in the section titled "Flow Labels."

➤ **Payload Length.** 16-bit unsigned integer. This file identifies the length of the payload of the packet in octets. The payload is the remainder of the packet following the IPng header.

➤ **Next Hdr.** 8-bit selector. Identifies the type of header immediately following the IPng header. The values for this field are listed in RFC 1700.

➤ **Hop Limit.** 8-bit unsigned integer. The initial value of this field is specified by the source device. It is decreased by 1 by each node that forwards the packet, such as a router. If the value reaches 0, the packet is discarded by the node that is handling it.

➤ **Source Address.** 128 bits. The address of the sender of the packet.

➤ **Destination Address.** 128 bits. The address of the intended target recipient of the packet.

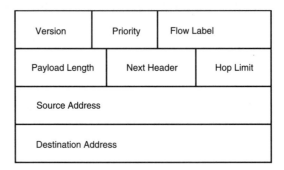

**Figure 6.2:**

The IP version 6 header format.

# IPng Extensions

In IP version 6, optional IP layer information is placed in separate headers between the IP version 6 header and the transport layer headers of TCP or UDP. A single packet can contain zero, one, or several extension headers. Primarily, only the receiving or destination device uses these headers, and intermediary devices such as routers do not examine them, with the single exception being the Hop-by-Hop Options header (discussed later in this chapter). This serves to improve the performance of routers that process packets that contain IP version 6 options. Unlike IP version 4 headers, IPng extension headers have any length in multiples of 8 octets without IP version 4's 40-byte option limitation.

The header formats shown in figures 6.3 through 6.5 illustrate several possibilities.

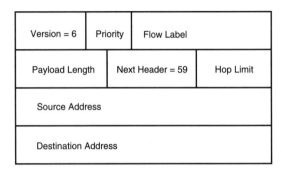

### Figure 6.3:

The IP version 6 header with no options.

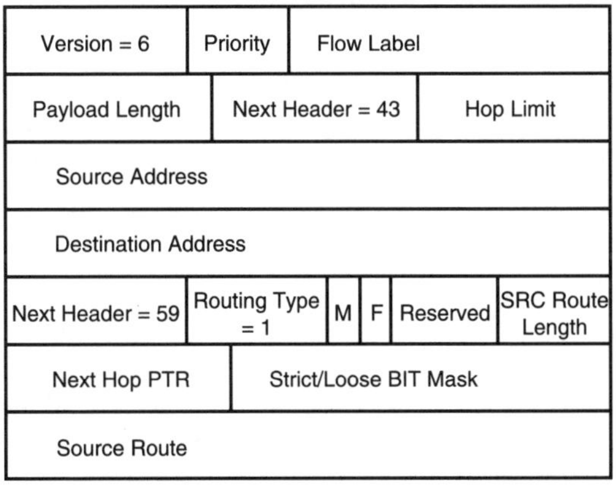

### Figure 6.4:

The IP version 6 header with a single option field.

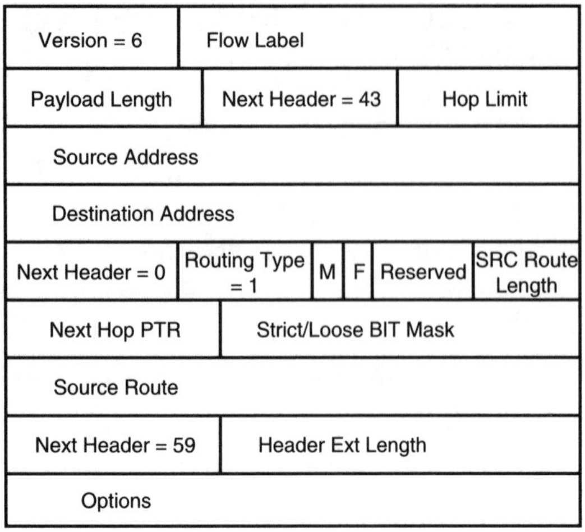

| Version = 6 | Flow Label | |
|---|---|---|
| Payload Length | Next Header = 43 | Hop Limit |
| Source Address | | |
| Destination Address | | |
| Next Header = 0 | Routing Type = 1 | M | F | Reserved | SRC Route Length |
| Next Hop PTR | Strict/Loose BIT Mask | |
| Source Route | | |
| Next Header = 59 | Header Ext Length | |
| Options | | |

**Figure 6.5:**

The IP version 6 header with multiple option fields.

At this time, the following IPng headers have been defined: Routing, Fragmentation, Authentication, Encapsulation, Hop-by-Hop Options, Destination, and No Next Header. The following sections discuss each of these headers and the function each provides to the IP version 6 protocol.

## Routing

The function of the Routing header is to specify one or more intermediate devices to be visited as a packet is forwarded to its destination (see fig. 6.6). This allows a source to specify the "route" to a destination and essentially override the route that might ordinarily have been determined by the routing protocol.

The Routing header is identified by a Next Header value of 43 in the header that precedes it. This is illustrated more clearly in figure 6.5, in which the entire IP version 6 is illustrated.

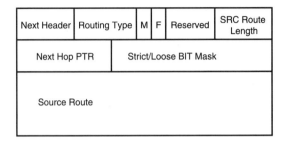

| Next Header | Routing Type | M | F | Reserved | SRC Route Length |
|---|---|---|---|---|---|
| Next Hop PTR | | Strict/Loose BIT Mask | | | |
| Source Route | | | | | |

**Figure 6.6:**
The format of a Routing header.

# Fragmentation

In an IP version 6 environment, the source node uses the Fragmentation header to send packets that are too large to fit in the maximum packet size or MTU of the destination. By function, the Fragmentation header addresses the possibility that the network to which the receiving station is attached, or any intermediate networks, cannot accommodate packets as large as the sending station. A device connected to an FDDI network, for example, could send packets as large as 4,000 bytes, whereas a receiving device connected to an Ethernet network could only receive a packet of 1,518 bytes.

In this case, the source node divides, or fragments, the larger packet into smaller packets that can fit the receiving device's MTU. Each fragmented packet would have a Fragmentation header that identifies it as a large fragmented packet (see fig. 6.8). When the receiving node receives the fragments, it recombines the fragments into a single packet and processes it accordingly.

| Next Header | Reserved | Fragment | Reserved | M |
|---|---|---|---|---|
| Identification | | | | |

**Figure 6.7:**
The format of a Fragmentation header.

IP version 6 fragmentation works much differently than with IP version 4. Whereas with IP version 4, intermediary devices, such as routers, can handle fragmentation, only the source node performs fragmentation with IP version 6. The Fragmentation header is always identified by a Next Header value of 44 in the preceding header.

## Authentication

The Authentication header exists specifically to ensure two significant facts:

➤ The destination node receives data that matches the data the source node sends.

➤ The sender that the source address identifies truly is the sender of the data.

To accomplish this, the sending station calculates a value based on the headers, payload, and user information within the packet. The receiving node then calculates the value based on the same headers, payload, and user information. If these two values match, the receiver considers the packet authentic as defined; if not, it rejects the packet.

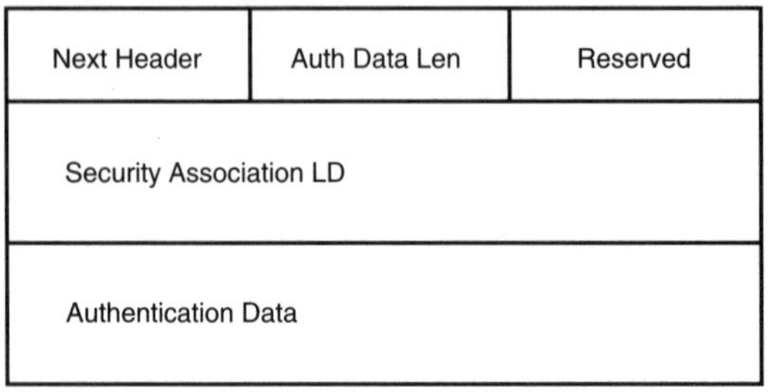

| Next Header | Auth Data Len | Reserved |
|---|---|---|
| Security Association LD | | |
| Authentication Data | | |

**Figure 6.8:**
The format of an Authentication header.

The section "Security" discusses authentication in detail later in this chapter.

# Encapsulation

The Encapsulation header seeks to provide the same security functions as authentication but also provides confidentiality between the sender and receiver. It achieves confidentiality by taking the IP version 6 datagram and encrypting the data, which is known as the Encapsulated Security Payload (ESP). Then a new IP version 6 header is attached to the ESP for transmission through the network. The new header is illustrated in figure 6.9.

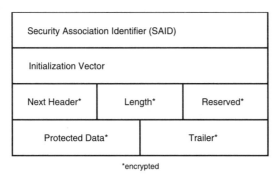

*encrypted

**Figure 6.9:**
The format of an Encapsulation header.

After the destination device receives the packet, it removes the new header, decrypts the ESP, and then processes the original IP version 6 datagram.

Obviously, coordination of these encryption formats between the source and destination nodes is critical for the receiver to be able to decrypt the packet. Equally critical is the confidentiality of these encryption keys. The section "Security" later in this chapter discusses the principle of encapsulation in IP version 6 in detail.

# Hop-by-Hop Options

The Hop-by-Hop Options header (see fig. 6.10) is the one header option that each node or device examines or reviews along the delivery path to the destination. Its function is to identify specific handling that the intermediary nodes between the source and destination nodes require. It is identified by a Next Header value of 0 in the Next Header field of the IP version 6 header.

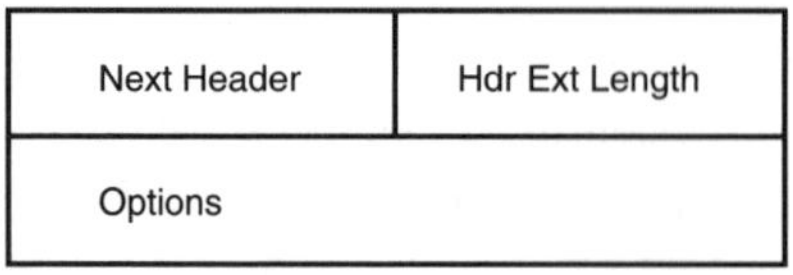

| Next Header | Hdr Ext Length |
|---|---|
| Options | |

**Figure 6.10:**
The format of a Hop-by-Hop Options header.

## Destination Options

The Destination Options header (see fig. 6.11) accommodates information that only the destination device for the packet or packets will handle. It is identified by a Next Header value of 60 in the preceding header.

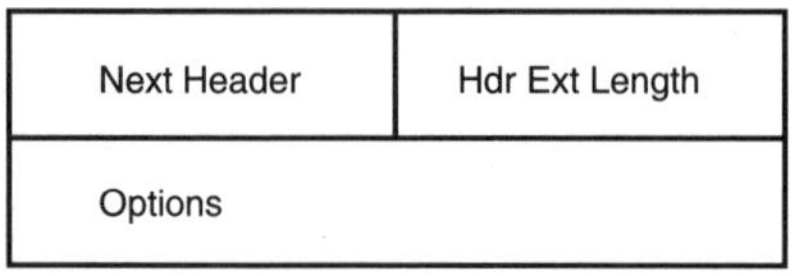

| Next Header | Hdr Ext Length |
|---|---|
| Options | |

**Figure 6.11:**
The format of a Destination Options header.

## No Next Header Option

The value of 59 in the Next Header value of the IP version 6 header or that of any extension header indicates that no options follow.

As mentioned previously, one of the advantages of IP version 6 is the capability to have larger headers than is possible with IP version 4. This advantage will allow new IP version 6 header options to be defined as new requirements are discovered.

# Quality of Service

One of the fastest growing technologies in the internetwork arena is applications that rely on "real-time" data, such as multimedia, multicast, or video applications. These applications have several critical requirements:

➤ A constant level of throughput to ensure adequate bandwidth between the source and destination nodes. If a user tries to view a video presentation using a network, for example, the bandwidth or capacity of the network must be sufficient to deliver the data.

➤ A constant level of delay.

➤ A constant level of *jitter*, where jitter refers to varying amounts of latency in the transmission of packets through a network.

A host can use the flow label and the priority fields in the IPng header to identify packets that might require special handling by IPng routers to ensure throughput, delay, and jitter to meet application requirements.

# Flow Labels

A *flow* is defined as a series of packets sent from a specific source device to a specific destination that requires special handling by any intermediary IPng routers. RFC 1363 defines a flow as "a data structure used by internetwork hosts to request special services of the internetwork, often guarantees about how the internetwork will handle some of the hosts' traffic." The destination can be a single device (using unicast addresses as a destination) or multiple devices (using multicast addresses as a destination). One example of a flow would be the transmission of a multimedia presentation from a server to a group of client personal computers.

The flow label field of the IP version 6 header is 24 bits long. A flow is identified by having a value other than zero in the flow label field of the IP version 6 header. A packet that isn't part of a flow would contain a flow label value of 0, which a control protocol, such as *Resource Reservation Protocol* (RSVP), would then use. RSVP is an example of a protocol designed to reserve a path through an internetwork that meets the application's requirements for bandwidth, delay, and jitter.

A device that doesn't support use of a flow label must do one of the following:

➤ Set the field to zero if it originates the packet, the function of a destination node that doesn't support flow labels, such as a workstation or server.

➤ Pass the field on unchanged when it forwards the packet, the function of a router that might not yet support flow labels.

➤ Disregard the field if receiving the packet, the function of a destination node that doesn't support flow labels, such as a workstation or server.

Any packets transmitted as part of a flow must contain the same IP version 6 header information, including the source address, destination address, and flow label value, as well as information in any extension headers, such as Routing headers or the Hop-by-Hop Options header.

Flow labels and the protocols that would utilize them still are being designed and can be expected to change, owing to the requirements that present themselves.

# IP Version 6 Priority

Often, to meet application requirements in internetworks, you might need to assign certain data higher priority than other traffic from the source. The priority in the IP version 6 header is a 4-bit field, which offers a value range of 0 to 15. The purpose of this field is to allow a source node to identify the priority level for delivering packets. Data that has a priority level of 12, for example, should be delivered before packets that have a priority level of 3.

The traffic to be transmitted is separated into the two following classes:

➤ Traffic in which the source device (a file server, for example) can provide congestion control. Here, in the event of network congestion, the device can "throttle back" until the congestion dissipates entirely. For example, this type of traffic uses TCP as a transport protocol, such as FTP, Telnet, or HTTP. The priority values for this traffic currently range from 0 to 7, with the following categories:

| Priority | Description |
| --- | --- |
| 0 | Uncharacterized traffic |
| 1 | "Filler" traffic (e.g., netnews) |
| 2 | Unattended data transfer (e.g., email) |
| 3 | (Reserved) |
| 4 | Attended bulk transfer (e.g., FTP, HTTP, NFS) |
| 5 | (Reserved) |
| 6 | Interactive traffic (e.g., telnet, X) |
| 7 | Internet control traffic (e.g., routing protocols, SNMP) |

➤ Traffic that cannot be "throttled back" to resolve network congestion: multimedia transmissions that consist of video and audio information, for example. You would use a priority value between 8 and 15 for this type of traffic. A value of 8 identifies real-time traffic that is more acceptable to be discarded in the event of network congestion whereas a value of 15 identifies traffic that is far less acceptable to be discarded.

# Security

IP version 6 contains two mechanisms to address security in networks, both of which are optional extensions to the IP version 6 header. The first is the Authentication header, which guarantees delivery of the packet intact and authenticity of the source address. It does not guarantee confidentiality, however; some other device between the sender and the receiving station could potentially also receive the transmission.

The sending value computes a value based on the headers that don't change during delivery to the destination and the payload of the transmission. When the destination node receives the transmission, it also computes a value based on the headers and payload. If these two values match, then the station addresses and the packet's payload are considered authentic and therefore processed. If these two values do not match, the packet is discarded. The algorithm currently used to compute the value for the authentication header is the *MD5 algorithm.*

Using of the Authentication header impacts the processing performance of IP version 6 devices and the communications latency between them, owing to the need to calculate the authentication value in the source and destination devices and to compare the two computed values in the destination node.

Secondly, IP version 6 provides a feature called Encapsulating Security Payload (ESP). As does using the Authentication header, ESP ensures the integrity of the transmitted data and authenticates the sender and receiver. In addition, ESP ensures the privacy of the transmission. Using an encryption algorithm that only the sender and the receiving device maintain prevents other devices from decrypting and processing the transmission unless they too possess the encryption key.

# IP Mobility

Assuming that a network user maintains a single unchanging specific location would frequently lead to error nowadays. Many network users are highly mobile, and many work at home or even in different parts of an organization. IP mobility is in fact not unique to IP version 6 and currently is addressed with IP version 4—and can easily be modified to work with IP version 6. The definition of IP version 6 provides a significant opportunity to implement functionality to meet the unique needs of the mobile network user.

In the Internet draft document from the IP version 6 Working Group titled "Mobility Support in IP version 6," by Charles Perkins and David Johnson, it clearly states the primary issue to be dealt with by IP mobility.

"We believe that the most important function needed to support mobility is the reliable and timely notification of a mobile node's current location to other nodes that need it. The home agent needs this location information in order to forward intercepted packets from the home network to the mobile node, and correspondent nodes need this information in order to send their own packets directly to the mobile node."

IP mobility requires that mobile computers have at least two addresses defined for them—one permanent and any others temporary or care of address. The mobile user would obtain the care of address from a local router or server and then notify the home agent of its temporary location.

You could send information such as e-mail, for example, to a mobile user at the permanent address. If the mobile user is at that location, they receive it. If not, a home agent receives the transmission and redirects the data to the care of the address.

# Transitioning to IP Version 6

Clearly, the success of IP Next Generation depends highly on the level of complexity and difficulty in transitioning to this new protocol. A complex, high cost migration plan would dramatically hinder its potential of becoming widely deployed. IPng, however, has number of features that greatly facilitate its implementation.

The most significant feature is the provision for a "phased" implementation. IP version 4 devices, such as client workstations, servers, or routers, can be upgraded gradually with minimal effects on each other. This is due, in part, to the fact that devices upgraded to IP version 6 will essentially run both the IP version 6 and the IP version 4 protocols. This will enable communications with devices that have not yet been upgraded.

The addressing structure of IP version 6 will also ease the burden of transition. Devices that have been upgraded can continue to use their IP version 4 addresses. A server, for example, might be upgraded to support IP version 6 but would still support an IP version 4 address to enable communications to clients that are still using IP version 4. Furthermore, IP version 4 addresses can be "embedded" in the larger address space made possible by IP version 6.

By design, the transition to IP version 6 has been architected to be a smooth, gradual migration. For this reason, it is very likely that the deployment and acceptance of IP version 6 will be swift.

## Summary

IP version 6 is designed to be an evolutionary step from IP version 4. It seeks to address known issues with IP version 4 and to introduce functionality to address future requirements of this protocol.

From the start, the issue of migration has been dealt with extensively. As discussed earlier, the addressing techniques designed for IP version 6 allow for the inclusion of IP version 4 addresses to facilitate migration. Hosts that are converted to IP version 6 will be able to maintain their current IP version 4 addresses. By design, IP version 6 hosts will be able to communicate with IP version 4 hosts.

IP version 6 has been designed to work on a variety of networks, ranging from slower technologies such as wireless networks to high speed networks using technologies such as ATM and FDDI.

Perhaps most importantly, IP Next Generation seeks to meet the requirements of the Internet, Next Generation: a large, scaleable, and useable worldwide network.

# Sources of Information on IP Next Generation

S. Bradner, A. Mankin, RFC 1752, "The Recommendation for the IP Next Generation Protocol," January 1995.

V. Fuller, et al, "Supernetting: an Address Assignment and Aggregation Strategy," RFC 1338, June 1992.

S. Deering, "Simple Internet Protocol Plus (SIPP) Specification (128-bit address version)," Internet Draft, July 1994.

R. Hinden, Editor, "IP Version 6 Addressing Architecture," Internet Draft, April 1995.

R. Gilligan, E. Nordmark, "Transition Mechanisms for IP version 6 Hosts and Routers," Internet Draft, March 1995.

# Part III

## Configuring Internet Information Server Publishing Services

# Chapter 7

# Configuring the WWW Publishing Service

Not long ago, the world was perceived as being flat—two dimensional. The written word and knowledge traveled very slowly. Today we live in a technological age of advancements that enable us to view the world in a new way. Since the advent and acceptance of the Internet as a global publishing medium, knowledge is now distributed to millions of people in a matter of seconds. The WWW Publishing Service will be your tool to publish information to the global Internet community. This chapter will guide you through the steps necessary to install and configure the WWW Publishing Service.

## Preparing for the Installation

When preparing to install the WWW Publishing Service, you should have an overall understanding of the possible methods of installation, as well as the common terms used when discussing the operation and configuration of the Internet Information Server. You must also understand the prerequisites necessary to install the Internet Information Server.

# Installation Methods

There are a variety of methods available to install the Internet Information Server. All methods will provide the same results. The installation method you choose will largely depend upon your particular needs.

Configuration of the individual Internet Information Server component services is performed after the initial installation procedure is completed by using the Internet Service Manager. The Internet Service Manager is located in the Microsoft Internet Server folder. The use of the Internet Service Manager is discussed later in this chapter, in the section called "Understanding the Internet Service Manager."

The possible installation methods are as follows:

➤ The first method of installation is to select the installation of the Internet Information Server during the process of NT 4.0 setup. During NT 4.0 setup, a dialog box will appear, asking if you want to install the Internet Information Server.

➤ The second method is to run the Install Internet Information Server Icon located on the desktop. This may not be present on your NT Server installation, depending upon whether your NT 4.0 installation was an upgrade or a fresh installation.

➤ The third method is to add the Internet Information Server by selecting the Services Tab from the Network Icon located in the Control Panel. You then choose the Add button and select Microsoft Internet Information Server 2.0.

➤ The fourth method is to run the Internet Information Server installation setup program from the NT CD-ROM.

➤ The fifth method is to run the Internet Information Server installation program from a network drive. This method may be chosen if you do not have a compact disk drive available on your NT Server. Often, the option to install the Internet Information Server is bypassed during the initial NT 4.0 Server setup procedure. When the decision is made later to install the Internet services contained within the Internet Information Server, the most commonly used method of installation is the installation procedure from the compact disk. This installation procedure will be discussed later in this chapter, in the section called "Installation Procedures."

# Understanding Related Terms

The WWW Publishing Service is the key component of Internet Information Server. Many other components of the NT Server installation process relate to IIS installation. You should have a general understanding of each of the terms and components involved in planning the WWW Publishing Service installation.

The following terms and components will be discussed:

➤ Internet

➤ Intranet

➤ HTML and HTTP

➤ Hyperlinks

➤ Internet Information Server

➤ URL

➤ Browser Requests

➤ ISAPI Filter

➤ ISAPI Application

➤ Dynamic HTML Page

➤ Static HTML Page

➤ CGI Script

# Internet

The term Internet refers to the global network of computers that communicate using the TCP/IP protocol. The Internet is the largest network of computers in the world.

One aspect of the Internet is the World Wide Web. The World Wide Web is the most common perception of the Internet. The World Wide Web displays information in a graphical manner. When information is published on the World Wide Web, it can be interrelated and linked to other sources of information. This global structure of interrelated and linked information is what comprises the World Wide Web.

# Intranets

The term intranet refers to a TCP/IP network that is not directly connected to the Internet. An intranet network is usually considered to be a private network, or private network segment.

Many intranet networks have a secure connection to the Internet through a firewall. Often, computers on an intranet can be allowed access to the Internet through a firewall implementation. A firewall implementation can restrict and prevent access to computers on an intranet from computers on the Internet.

IIS will operate on an intranet in the same manner as if it were connected to the Internet. All features and functionality will be available to the users on your private network.

# HTML and HTTP

HTML and HTTP are abbreviations that have recently made their way into everyday vocabulary. These abbreviations are becoming commonplace in advertising.

The WWW Publishing Service will transmit information written in the HyperText Markup Language, using the HyperText Transport Protocol. The HyperText Markup Language is commonly referred to as HTML, and the HyperText Transport Protocol is referred to as HTTP. Information you publish on the World Wide Web will usually be in the form of HTML pages.

# Hyperlinks

When viewing HTML pages of text and graphics with a Web browser, you will often see highlighted text in a different color, or graphics with a similarly colored border. These are links to other sources of information on the World Wide Web. These links are referred to as hyperlinks.

Hyperlinks are text and graphics, defined within HTML pages, that have Web addresses embedded in them. When you click on a hyperlink, you send a Web Server a request for an HTML page located elsewhere on the Internet.

# Internet Information Server

The Internet Information Server is an NT Server running one or more integrated Internet services. The WWW Publishing Service, the FTP Publishing Service, and the Gopher Publishing Service are the Internet services that comprise the Internet Information Server. An NT Server running any or all of these services is also commonly called an Internet Server.

Using the Internet Information Server, you will be able to publish your information in a variety of ways. Home pages, newsletters, informational documents, catalogs, database information re-trieval, and interactive programs are but a few examples of the potential and power of publishing on the Internet.

The Internet Information Server's operation can be equated to this simple process: It listens for requests for information from other computers, and responds.

The following sections discuss terms related to the Internet Information Server.

# URLs

The Uniform Resource Locator, known as the URL, is the full address used by a Web browser to request information on the World Wide Web. The format of an URL begins with the specific protocol, the domain name, the path to the requested information, and then the name of the file.

**ftp://ftp.yourcompany.com/software/updates/versions.txt**

Protocol

   Domain name

      Path

         Filename

Here are a few sample URLs:

**gopher://gopher.yourcompany.com/marketing/reports/index.html**

**http://www.yourcompany.com/sales/catalog.html**

**https://www.yourcompany.com/sales/orders.html**

The protocol descriptor https:// requests a secure session.

# Browser Requests

Browser requests are URLs sent from a Web browser to the Internet Information Server. When the Internet Information Server receives the URL, it responds accordingly, sending the requested information back to the Web browser.

# ISAPI Filters

An Internet Server Application Programming Interface (ISAPI) Filter, is a software DLL that is loaded with the Internet Information Server, and enhances the functionality or operation of the WWW Publishing Service. ISAPI Filters are loaded by modifying a Key Value in the Registry. See Chapter 18, "ISAPI," for more information.

# ISAPI Applications

An ISAPI Application is a DLL that performs a specific action as a result of a request. For example, you may choose to allow searches for information within your WWW server documents. In this case, you would implement an ISAPI filter that would perform the task of searching through your WWW server documents. The WWW Publishing Service can be enhanced by utilizing customized ISAPI Applications.

Here is an example of an ISAPI URL:

**http://www.yourcompany.com/isapi/search.dll?TEXT=findthis**

# Dynamic HTML Pages

A Dynamic HTML Page does not exist as an HTML page on a drive. It is created as a response to a request, dynamically on-the-fly, by an application or process running in association with the Internet Information Server. A Dynamic HTML page name is not explicitly called out from within an URL.

Dynamic HTML page generation is of great benefit to the Webmaster or Administrator in charge of maintaining the Web site. For example, if a Web site had a catalog of thousands of products, normally each product would need its own HTML page stored on the WWW server. Each HTML page would need to be created and maintained by the Webmaster or Administrator. If the HTML pages were generated as Dynamic HTML pages, the task of Web server administration is greatly reduced.

ISAPI and Internet Database Connector requests have the capability to create Dynamic HTML pages. See Chapter 18, "ISAPI," and Chapter 16, "Database Interfaces," for more information.

## Static HTML Pages

A Static HTML page is a term used to refer to an existing HTML page that is stored on a drive. You can edit static HTML pages. To request a Static page, the URL might look like this:

**http://www.yourcompany.com/sales/catalog.html**

## CGI Scripts

A CGI script performs a specific task, as a result of a request. The functionality of the WWW Publishing Service can be enhanced by utilizing customized CGI scripts. Here is an example of a CGI script URL:

**http://www.yourcompany.com/cgi-bin/counter.pl?homepage**

See Chapter 15, "CGI Basics," for more information.

# Understanding the Internet Service Manager

In the past, the most common complaints related to managing and maintaining a Web server have been the difficulty involved or the lack of a friendly configuration program. The primary program used to configure the WWW Publishing Service is the Internet Service Manager. This program is very well designed, and will be easy for you to use. After you have completed and tested your installation, you can use the Internet Service Manager and other programs to configure advanced features of the WWW Publishing Service.

Within the Internet Service Manager, you will be able to configure advanced features of the WWW Publishing Service, the FTP Publishing Service, and the Gopher Service. Configuration of the

WWW Publishing Service is discussed in this chapter. Advanced configuration issues related to the WWW Publishing Service are discussed in Chapter 8, "Multihoming: Creating Multiple Domains."

Configuration of the FTP Publishing Service and Gopher Service are discussed in Chapter 9, "Configuring the FTP Publishing Services," and Chapter 10, "Configuring the Gopher Publishing Services," respectively.

The following is a list of what you can configure within the Internet Service Manager:

➤ Default settings

➤ Home directories and Virtual directories

➤ Access permissions

➤ Bandwidth usage

➤ Logon security

➤ Multiple domain virtual servers

➤ Encryption requirements

➤ Other Internet Information Servers

➤ Comments and Messages

➤ Logging

## Internet Service Manager Views

When working in the Internet Service Manager, there are three views available. You can select a view to display the available Servers and Services, as needed. The views available from the Internet Service Manager are as follows:

➤ Servers view

➤ Services view

➤ Report view

## Servers View

The Servers view displays Internet Information Server Services running on NT Servers by server name. You can click the plus symbol next to a server name to see which services a server has available. You can double-click a service name to see and configure its property sheets. The Servers view is usually selected when you have multiple computers and you need to configure or know the status of whether a service is running or stopped, and the services installed on a specific computer.

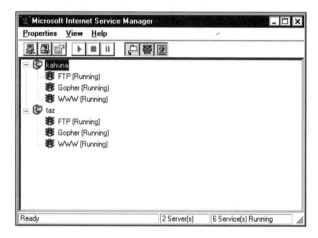

**Figure 7.1:**

Servers view.

## Services View

The Services view enables you to list the Internet Information Services on selected NT Servers, grouped by service name. You can click the plus symbol next to a service name to see which servers are running that service. You can double-click the server name under a service to display and configure its property sheets. The Services view is usually selected when you need to configure or know which computers are running a specific service.

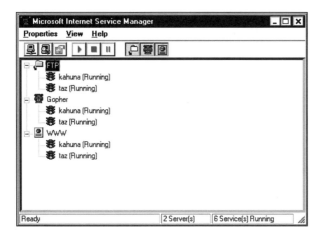

**Figure 7.2:**

Services view.

# Report View

The Report view is the default view and is the most common. The Report view lists Internet Information Servers alphabetically, with each available service shown on a separate line. The list can be sorted alphabetically by clicking the column headings. The Report view is usually selected when you only have one or two servers running Internet Information Server.

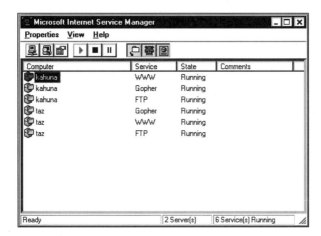

**Figure 7.3:**

Report view.

# Connecting to an Internet Information Server

To connect to an Internet Information Server from the Internet Service Manager, you have two options. You can have the Internet Service Manager find available servers or you can select a specific server to connect to.

## Finding Available Servers

To find and connect to available Internet Information Servers, follow these steps:

1.  From the Properties menu in the Internet Services Manager, select Find All Servers.

2.  From the list of servers displayed, double-click the server that you want to connect to.

## Selecting a Server

To select a specific server to connect to, you will need to know the server name, IP address, or the NETBIOS name of the server. To select a specific server to connect to, follow these steps:

1.  From the Properties menu in the Internet Service Manager, select Connect to Server.

2.  In the Server Name box, type the server name, IP address, or NETBIOS name.

# Starting, Stopping, and Pausing Services

The Internet Service Manager will enable you to start, stop, or pause individual services on a specific server, as necessary. For example, when installing a new ISAPI Filter, you will need to stop the WWW service and restart the service after the ISAPI Filter has been installed. This will enable the WWW service to load the ISAPI Filter. If you pause a specific service, all users connected to the service will be disconnected.

To start, stop, or pause a service, follow these steps:

1. Connect to an Internet Information Server.

2. Select the service you want to start, stop, or pause.

3. From the Properties menu, select Start Service, Stop Service, or Pause Service.

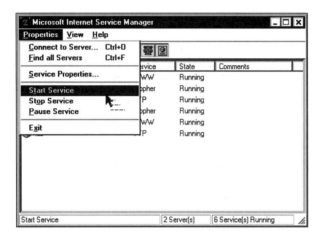

**Figure 7.4:**
Starting, Stopping, and Pausing Services.

# Installing the WWW Publishing Service

The WWW Publishing Service is one of three component services that can be selected during the Internet Information Server installation. The other services are the FTP Publishing Service and the Gopher Publishing Service. The Internet Information Server installation Setup program will enable you to selectively install the individual component services. Therefore, to install the WWW Publishing Service, the general procedure to install the Internet Information Server should be followed.

# Installation Prerequisites

To install the WWW Publishing Service, you must first be logged on as a user who is a member of the Administrators group. You can verify whether you are a member of the Administrators group by looking in the User Manager for Domains, located within the Administrative Tools folder.

In addition, you should confirm the following:

➤ NT Server is installed on an NTFS partition, and your Server is functioning normally. For security reasons, your WWW Publishing Service must be installed on an NTFS partition.

➤ TCP/IP Protocol is loaded and has been properly configured.

➤ Name Resolution has been set up through the use of either DNS, WINS Server, HOSTS file, or an LMHOSTS file.

➤ Security procedures have been reviewed and are in order. Do not allow unauthorized access to your NT Server from the Internet. Ensure that all users defined in the User Manager have unique passwords. See Chapter 13, "Server Security Basics," for detailed security information.

# Installation Procedures

The following procedure will guide you through the WWW Publishing Service installation. During the installation process, you can change some of the installation options. Bare in mind that the default installation configuration is fully operational and may be reconfigured later using the Internet Service Manager.

To perform the WWW Publishing Service installation follow these steps:

1. Insert the NT Server compact disk into an available compact disk drive. If you do not have a compact disk drive on your NT Server, the installation can be performed from a network drive.

2. Run either the Explorer or File Manager, or open a Command Prompt window.

3. Locate and change the INETSRV directory within the appropriate directory for your hardware platform. For example, change to I386\INETSRV for Intel platform. If your NT Server was loaded from a network drive, you can copy the entire contents of the appropriate INETSRV directory tree to an available network drive.

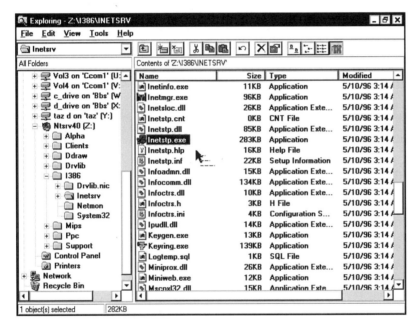

**Figure 7.5:**

Explorer.

4. In the Explorer or File Manager, locate and run the file named INETSTP.EXE by double-clicking on the filename. If you are working in a Command Prompt window, enter **INETSTP** to start the installation program.

5. At the Microsoft Internet Information Server 2.0 Setup Welcome dialog box, choose OK.

**Figure 7.6:**

Welcome dialog box.

6. You will see a list of available options in the Add/Remove, Reinstall, Remove All options dialog box. Choose Add/Remove.

**Figure 7.7:**

Add/Remove, Reinstall, Remove All options dialog box.

7.  In the Location dialog box you will see the location of the
    installation files. Choose OK.

**Figure 7.8:**
Location of Installation Files dialog box.

8.  A list of installation options is now visible in the Installation
    Options and Directory Location dialog box. For a complete
    installation of the WWW Publishing Service, you must verify
    that the following boxes, located on the Installation Options
    and Directory Location dialog box, are checked:

    ➤ Internet Service Manager: The Internet Information
      Server Configuration Manager

    ➤ World Wide Web Service: The WWW Publishing
      Service

    ➤ Help & Sample Files: Online Help and Sample
      HyperText Markup Language files

There are other installation options on the list. If you do not want
to install a particular installation option, clear the check box next
to it.

If you plan to provide access to databases through the Internet
Information Server, you will need to check the box next to ODBC
Drivers and Administration. This will install the Open Database
Connectivity drivers, commonly referred to as ODBC, and the
ODBC Control Panel Applet. This option is required for logging
on to ODBC database files and for enabling ODBC access for the
WWW Publishing Services Internet Database Connector. If you

currently have an application running that uses ODBC, you might encounter an error message telling you that one or more ODBC components are in use. Before proceeding, close all applications and services that are currently using ODBC components.

If you have chosen to include ODBC Drivers and Administration, you will see the Install Drivers dialog box. After you have made your ODBC selections, choose OK.

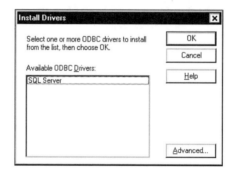

**Figure 7.9:**

Install Drivers dialog box.

See Chapter 16, "Database Interfaces," for more information.

9.  The installation directory path can now be chosen. You can accept the default path or specify a new directory path. If this is your first time installing the Internet Information Server, you will be able to change the installation directory path. If you have previously installed Internet Information Server, and want to reinstall into a different directory path, you must first remove the "INetStp" Key from the Registry. The following is the Registry path to the Key:

    \HKEY_LOCAL_MACHINE\SOFTWARE\Microsoft\INetStp

    If this key is present in the Registry from a previous installation, the Change Directory button will be dimmed, and you will be unable to change the directory path. If you get to this point and decide that the key must be removed, you will need to restart the installation setup program after you delete the key.

To accept the default installation directory path, choose OK.

To specify a new directory path, click the Change Directory button and type the new directory path. Choose OK.

The installation program will begin a partial file copy process.

10. The directory you specify in the Publishing Directories dialog box will become your World Wide Web Server home directory. This is where the default Home Page will be located for your domain. You can choose to accept the default directory path for the WWW Publishing Service, or you can change the directory path to another location.

**Figure 7.10:**
Publishing Directories dialog box.

If you already have HTTP files ready to publish that exist else-where on the same drive as Internet Information Server, you can enter the full path to their location. If you accept the default directory path, you can move your HTTP files to the default location.

If your HTTP files are located on an accessible NTFS network drive, you should accept the default directory for the moment. After setup has completed, you can use the Internet Service Manager to change your default home directory to the path for the network directory containing your HTTP files. The following is an example of a network path:

**\\ServerName\ShareName\WebFileDir**

You will also need to verify that the security permissions on the network drive are correct. See Chapter 13, "Server Security Basics," for more information.

The Installation Setup program will prompt you to create the WWW Publishing Service directory. Click Yes.

11.   The Create Internet Account dialog box appears.

This is the user account name assigned for all anonymous access to the Internet Information Server. Select the option to enter a password and confirm the password for this user account name. See Chapter 13, "Server Security Basics," for more information.

12.   Choose OK. The Installation Setup program will copy all of the remaining Internet Information Server files to your drive. When the Installation Setup completion dialog box appears, click OK.

You may use the Installation program later, to add or remove individual components. The Installation program can also be used to reload or remove all Internet Information Server-related components.

# Testing the Installation

To test the WWW Publishing Service you will need access to a Web browser. Ideally, you should test from another computer on your intranet, or from the Internet. You can test the basic functionality of the WWW Publishing Service from your NT Server; however, this might not confirm the proper operation of other related components. To test the WWW Publishing Service, do the following:

1. Start your favorite Web Browser.

2. Enter the URL for your Web Server into the Location field of your Web Browser. The URL you enter will begin with "http://", and will be followed by the name of your Web Server, and end in a slash "/". It should appear similar to the following example: "http://hostname.domain.com/".

   If you performed a default installation and everything is functioning properly, you will see a sample home page displayed in your Web browser. The HTML file being displayed was loaded with the Help & Sample Files option, and is called "default.htm".

3. Close your Web Browser.

# Configuring WWW Publishing Services

Configuration of the WWW Publishing Service is primarily performed using the Internet Service Manager. There are many other programs that you can use, related to advanced configuration and management.

The following sections describe configuration and will provide you with an understanding of related configuration programs.

# Viewing and Configuring Property Sheets

In the Internet Service Manager, property sheets are used to view and configure the individual Internet Information Server Services. Each Internet Information Server Service has its own set of property sheets.

The WWW Publishing Service has four main property sheets for viewing and configuration. There are many configuration options within each property sheet. The property sheets are listed as follows:

➤ Service

➤ Directories

➤ Logging

➤ Advanced

To view or configure the property sheets of a selected server, follow these steps:

1. Select a server.

2. Double-click a service to view or configure.

3. Choose the property sheet to view or configure by clicking the tab at the top of the property sheet display page.

4. View or configure options as necessary.

5. Click OK to return to the main Internet Service Manager window.

Detailed information about advanced property sheet configuration options can be found in related chapters on security, multihoming, and logging. See Chapter 13, "Server Security Basics," and Chapter 8, "Multihoming: Creating Multiple Domains."

## Service Property Sheet

The Service Property Sheet is used to control access rights to the WWW Publishing Service. The account name used for anonymous client requests must be specified. The default user name, in the format **IUSR_computername**, is used for anonymous logons. The default user name is set up during the Internet Information Server installation. All anonymous logons to the service will use this user name. If you decide to allow anonymous logons, you should still verify that the security permissions for this user name are correct.

You have the option to specify another user name. You can specify an existing user name, or create a new user account. In either case, you must configure its security permissions relevant to your requirements. It is recommended that the default account name be used. Use the default account name relevant to your security requirements unless you have a specific need to implement another one.

The password you select is used internally by the NT Server. The password is not presented by another computer during the logon process. See Chapter 13, "Server Security Basics," for more information.

In the Comment option field, you can enter a comment or note, which will be visible in the Internet Service Manager, Report View window. This comment is sometimes used as a reference for the service. For example, for reference purposes, you could enter the IP address or the physical location of the server.

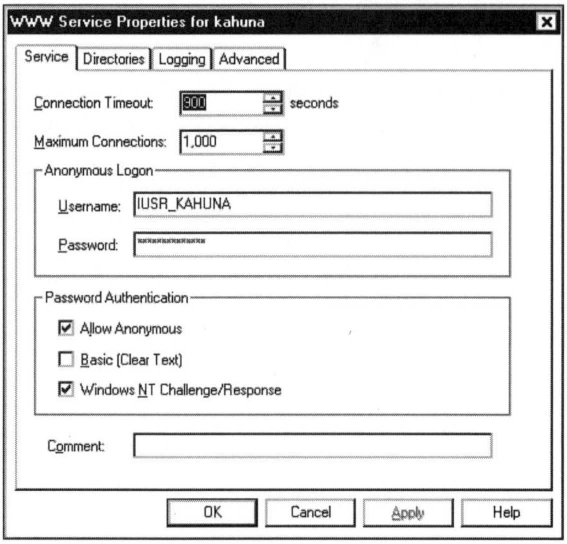

**Figure 7.11:**
Service Property Sheet.

## Directories Property Sheet

Within the Directories Property Sheet, you can configure directory paths available to users, set access permissions, configure virtual servers, and define virtual directories.

You can also define the Default Document, and decide whether or not to enable Directory Browsing. Default Document and Directory Browsing options are discussed later in this chapter.

The following sections will discuss the Directories Property Sheet options related to a single domain WWW Publishing Service.

The WWW Publishing Service can also be configured for multiple domains on a single Internet Information Server. See Chapter 8, "Multihoming: Creating Multiple Domains," for more information.

**Figure 7.12:**
Directories Property Sheet.

## Directory Paths

During the Internet Information Server installation procedure, a default home directory for the WWW Publishing Service was created. The default directory name is \Wwwroot. This is also known as the default Home Directory for your Web server, and the root of your Web server directory tree. You can change this directory path as needed.

You can place your Home Page or Default document into the Home Directory. You can create other directories within this directory. By default, files you place within the Home Directory tree of the WWW Publishing Service will be available to Web browsers.

You can also add other directories outside of the home directory tree structure as needed. These directories will appear to a Web browser as subdirectories of the home directory. These directories are called virtual directories, and can be elsewhere on your NT Server or on an available network drive.

In addition to being able to configure virtual directories, you can assign Alias names to physical directories. You might want to assign an Alias to a physical directory, for reasons of security, or to simplify the physical directory name. For example, if the physical directory name was long, you could assign a shorter, simplified Alias to the directory name.

The following is an example of a long directory name and its Alias:

**Directory name: F:\SouthwesternSalesGroupMarketingReports**

**Alias: /SWReports**

If you assign virtual directories to network drives, be sure that you specify a username and password to connect to them from your NT Server. Ensure that your security procedures are correct. See Chapter 13, "Server Security Basics," for more information.

## Default Document

The WWW Publishing Service has the capability to respond to browser requests that do not specify a filename. If you enable the default document option, specify a default document name and place a default document in each directory; the WWW Publishing Service will return the default document to the Web Browser when it receives an URL request that does not specify a filename. For example, if your default document is named "index.html", and you place an HTML page of this name into your home directory, this HTML page will become your Home Page.

The following is an example of an URL used to access the default document, which in this case is the home page of the Web site:

**http://www.yourcompany.com/**

In another related example, if you place an HTML page named "index.html" into another directory within your WWW service tree structure and an URL that does not specify a specific filename is used to access the directory, the WWW Publishing Service will return the default document named "index.html" to the Web browser.

The following is an example of an URL used to retrieve the default document from another directory and place it within the WWW Service directory tree structure:

**http://www.yourcompany.com/catalog/**

If an HTML page with the same name as the document name configured within the default document option for the WWW Publishing Service exists in the home directory, it is known as the Home Page. The Home Page is typically an HTML page used to greet Web browsers, and usually contains hypertext links to other pages within your Web server.

The default document option is a global setting used by the WWW Publishing Service for the entire directory structure.

## Directory Browsing

Directory browsing and the Default Document option are inter-related. If the WWW Publishing Service receives a browser request without a specific filename and the Default Document is not present in the directory, a hypertext directory listing of the directory is sent to the Web browser.

Most often, directory browsing is not enabled. If it is enabled, Web browsers will be able to see all of the files and navigate through directories within your WWW Publishing Service tree structure. For example, if you have files or directories within your Web server tree structure which are there for administrative purposes only, you usually would not want to make them available to Web browsers. This option is a global WWW Publishing Service setting, and affects all of the directories within the Web server.

# Logging Property Sheet

The Internet Information Server can log the activity of the WWW Publishing Service. Enabling logging is recommended. Logs can provide important information, and can be used for security and statistical review. The logs can tell you how your server is being used.

The IIS log file will contain the IP address of the Web browser, date and time of access, service name, hostname of service, service IP address, service status codes and bytes sent, and the name of the file accessed. For detailed information on how to read IIS log files, see Chapter 11, "Monitoring Server Activity and Performance."

The following is an example of an IIS log file:

206.27.214.226, -, 7/13/96, 10:52:51, W3SVC, KAHUNA, 206.173.231.39, 1011, 291, 4809, 200, 0, GET, /jobs.html, -,

206.27.214.226, -, 7/13/96, 10:52:53, W3SVC, KAHUNA, 206.173.231.39, 80, 231, 5623, 200, 0, GET, /images/ jobsites_header.gif, -,

206.27.214.226, -, 7/13/96, 10:52:53, W3SVC, KAHUNA, 206.173.231.39, 0, 219, 1397, 200, 0, GET, /images/ltb.gif, -,

206.103.73.9, -, 7/13/96, 10:56:29, W3SVC, KAHUNA, 206.173.231.39, 11, 224, 111, 404, 2, GET, /cmed.html, -,

206.171.21.21, -, 7/13/96, 11:15:31, W3SVC, KAHUNA, 206.173.231.34, 0, 169, 476, 403, 5, GET, /webdesign.html, -,

206.173.231.39, -, 7/13/96, 11:21:05, W3SVC, KAHUNA, 206.173.231.39, 120, 185, 29, 304, 0, GET, /index.html, -,

206.173.231.39, -, 7/13/96, 11:21:07, W3SVC, KAHUNA, 206.173.231.39, 70, 293, 29, 304, 0, GET, /images/ coolsites_bb.gif, -,

You can choose to have the log data written to files or to an SQL/ ODBC database. If you have multiple Internet Information Servers or Services on your network, you can log all of their activity to a single file or database on a specific network computer.

If you would like to have individual log files for specific services, you can choose Log to File. Individual log files can simplify the task of viewing the statistics for a specific service. If you choose Log to File, you must also specify how often to create new logs and where to log files. Check the box for the frequency of how often you want the Internet Information Server to create new log files and specify the Log file directory location.

If you want to log the World Wide Web Service activity to a SQL/ ODBC data source, you must specify the ODBC Data Source Name (DSN), table, user name, and password to the database. Logging to a SQL/ODBC database will enable you to review the statistics for all of your IIS services from a single file. For detailed information on ODBC logging, see Chapter 11, "Monitoring Server Activity and Performance."

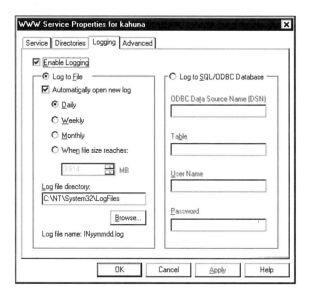

**Figure 7.13:**
Logging Property Sheet.

## Advanced Property Sheet

The Advanced Property Sheet can be used to configure access restrictions to the WWW Publishing Service, and limit the total outbound bandwidth of the Internet Information Server Services. You might want to restrict access to your Web server for security reasons, or limit outbound bandwidth from your IIS server to satisfy network bandwidth limitations.

**Figure 7.14:**

Advanced Property Sheet.

## Restricting IP Access

The WWW Publishing Service can be configured to have the Internet Information Server grant or deny access from specified IP addresses. You can use this option to restrict access to your server from a specific computer or a group of computers. For example, if the content of the Web server was intended for your research and development engineers only, you could restrict access to the Internet Information Server from only the designated IP addresses associated to the engineers' computers.

By default, access to your WWW Publishing Service is granted to all IP addresses. You can choose to specify the IP addresses of computers you want to deny access to.

You can also choose to change the option to deny access to all IP addresses. If you choose this option, you can specify the IP addresses of computers you want to grant exclusive access for.

## Limiting Network Bandwidth

You can limit the outbound network bandwidth used by all of the Internet Information Server Services on your NT Server. This option will control the maximum outbound network bandwidth for your Internet Information Server. If you have limited bandwidth, or are running other Internet services on the NT Server, you might want to enable and set this option to meet your needs. See Chapter 11, "Monitoring Server Activity and Performance," for more information.

If you choose to limit the outbound bandwidth used by the Internet Information Server Services, you must have an understanding of the possible implications:

> When the actual bandwidth usage remains below the level you set, the read, write, and transfer functions will remain enabled.

> If the actual bandwidth usage approximates the limit you have set, reads will be temporarily blocked.

> If the actual bandwidth exceeds the limit you set, reads will be rejected, and file transfers will be temporarily blocked.

The Internet Information Server will return to normal operation when the bandwidth usage equals or falls below the maximum limit.

# Other Configuration Programs and Utilities

The Internet Service Manager is the primary configuration program used to configure the WWW Publishing Service. You can use other programs and utilities, included with NT Server 4.0, to enhance functionality, perform advanced configuration, and monitor the Internet Information Server Services. This section references other configuration programs and utilities, and explains how they are related to the WWW Publishing Service.

This section references the following:

➤ HTML Administrator

➤ Control Panel Configuration Options

➤ Explorer

➤ User Manager for Domains

➤ Registry Editor

➤ Performance Monitor

➤ Event Viewer

## HTML Administrator

The WWW Publishing Service can be remotely administered across the Internet with your Web browser by accessing the HTML. The HTML Administrator program is loaded during the Internet Information Server installation. The HTML Administrator program has the same configuration options as Internet Service Manager.

To be able to securely log on to the remote Internet Information Server, you should use a Web browser that is capable of Windows NT Challenge/Response authentication. The Microsoft Internet Explorer has this capability.

If your Web browser is not capable of a secure logon, you can log on using basic clear text. Be aware that in order to use the HTML

Administrator, you will need to log on to the remote Internet Information Server as a user with Administrators Rights. For this reason, a logon using basic clear text across the Internet is not recommended, because this could compromise the security of your password. To use HTML Administrator, follow these steps:

1.  Run your Web Browser.

2.  In the Location field, Enter the URL in the following format:
    **http://www.yourcompany.com/htmla/htmla.htm**

3.  Log on as a user who is a member of the Administrator Group.

4.  View or configure options as needed.

# Control Panel Configuration Options

In the Control Panel, you will find Applets related to basic and advanced configuration options of the Internet Information Server. You can configure options related to the Internet Information Server and its Services in the following Applets:

➤ Network Applet

➤ Services Applet

➤ ODBC Applet

Each of these is discussed in the following sections.

## Network Applet

The Network applet, located in the Control Panel, can be used to configure your TCP/IP protocol settings and other network services and protocols. The TCP/IP protocol advanced configuration property sheet can be used to add additional IP addresses, up to a total of five, for use with multiple domain names within your Web server. When more than five IP address need to be added to the TCP/IP protocol configuration, you must use the Registry Editor to manually add additional IP addresses.

## Services Applet

The Services applet can be used to start, stop, and pause the individual Internet Information Server Services, as well as control startup options.

After you highlight a service name, you can use the Startup button to enable or disable the individual Internet Information Server Services from loading during the NT Server boot process.

You can also configure the Log On As option for the WWW Publishing Service. The Log On As option contains the user name used internally by the Internet Information Server to log on to the service. The default setting for the Log On As option is set during the Internet Information Server installation. You would normally only need to change this setting for security reasons. For example, if you change the account user name in the Service property sheet for an Internet service from the Internet Service Manager, you must also change the Log On As name for the service to the same name.

## ODBC Applet

The ODBC applet, found within the Control Panel, is used to configure ODBC connectivity options. The ODBC applet will be present if you chose to install ODBC during the IIS installation procedure or if it was installed as a necessary feature of other software.

Within the ODBC applet, you can add, remove, and configure User Data Source Drivers and System Data Source Drivers. Configuration and selection of ODBC Data Source Drivers is dependent upon your specific needs and installed software related to the IIS.

# Setting Permissions with the Explorer

By default, security permissions placed upon files and directories within the individual IIS services directory tree structure are adequate for most installations. You might have a need to modify the security permission for files or directories within your IIS tree structure for security reasons.

If you find it necessary to change security permissions on files or directories within the WWW server directory tree structure, you can use the Explorer. For example, if you have a file or directory that contains sensitive or secure data, and you want to restrict access to a specific user or group of users, you can use the Explorer to set or change the security permissions. See Chapter 13, "Server Security Basics," for more information on WWW security issues.

To use the Explorer to set or change directory and file permissions on Windows NTFS drives, follow these steps:

1. Click the right mouse button on a file or directory name.

2. Click Properties.

3. Click the Security tab.

4. Click the Permissions button.

5. Set the Permissions as needed.

See Chapter 12, "Site Administration Utilities," for more information on permissions.

## User Manager for Domains

The User Manager for Domains is used to manage security policies, user accounts, and groups for your NT Server. The User Manager for Domains is located in the Administrative Tools folder.

You can use the User Manager for Domains to modify and implement security procedures relevant to the operation of your Internet Information Server.

See Chapter 12, "Site Administration Utilities," for more information on using the User Manager for Domains.

## Registry Editor

The Registry Editor can be used to edit Registry Keys and Values related to the Internet Information Server.

One of the most common uses for the Registry Editor, related to the Internet Information Server, is for adding IP addresses for use with multiple domains. If you are running a multiple domain Web server and need more than five IP addresses or five domain names linked to your NT Server, you must use the Registry Editor to manually add the additional IP addresses to the registry. See Chapter 8, "Multihoming: Creating Multiple Domains," for information on creating multiple domains.

You might also find it necessary to use the Registry Editor for other tasks, such as loading ISAPI Filters. The procedure for loading ISAPI Filters, in most instances, requires that you manually edit or add a registry key or value in the registry. See Chapter 18, "ISAPI," for more information.

## Performance Monitor

The Performance Monitor is a powerful and useful tool that provides a graphical interface which can be used to view real-time statistics and evaluate the overall operation of the Internet Information Server Services. It can also be used to evaluate and diagnose problems related to the individual Internet Information Server component services, such as the WWW Publishing Service.

With the Performance Monitor, you can view statistics in real time. For example, you can use the Performance Monitor to show how many connections are active on all IIS services or an individual Internet service. See Chapter 11, "Monitoring Server Activity and Performance," for more information.

## HTTP Performance Counters

The Internet Information Server installation loads Windows NT Performance Monitor counters for the WWW Publishing Service, as well as the FTP Publishing Service and the Gopher Publishing Service.

The Object name used in the Performance Monitor for the WWW Publishing Service is HTTP service. The following is a list of Counters used to monitor the HTTP service object:

➤ Bytes Received/sec: The rate that data bytes are received by the HTTP Server.

➤ Bytes Sent/sec: The rate that data bytes are sent by the HTTP Server.

➤ Bytes Total/sec: The sum of Bytes Sent/sec and Bytes Received/sec. This is the total rate of bytes transferred by the HTTP Server.

➤ CGI Requests: Custom gateway executables (.exe) that the administrator can install to add forms processing or other dynamic data sources.

➤ Connection Attempts: The number of connection attempts that have been made to the HTTP Server.

➤ Connections/sec: The number of HTTP requests being handled per second.

➤ Current Anonymous Users: The number of anonymous users currently connected to the HTTP Server.

➤ Current CGI Requests: The current number of CGI requests that are simultaneously being processed by the HTTP Server. This includes WAIS index queries.

➤ Current Connections: The current number of connections to the HTTP Server.

➤ Current ISAPI Extension Requests. The current number of Extension requests that are simultaneously being processed by the HTTP Server.

➤ Current NonAnonymous Users: The number of nonanonymous users currently connected to the HTTP Server.

➤ Files Received: The total number of files received by the HTTP Server.

➤ Files Sent: The total number of files sent by the HTTP Server.

➤ Files Total: The sum of Files Sent and Files Received. This is the total number of files transferred by the HTTP Server.

➤ Get Requests: The number of HTTP requests using the GET method. Get requests are generally used for basic file retrievals or image maps, though they can be used with forms.

➤ Head Requests: The number of HTTP requests using the Head method. Head requests generally indicate a client is querying the state of a document they already have to see if it needs to be refreshed.

➤ ISAPI Extension Requests: Custom gateway Dynamic Link Libraries (.dll) that the administrator can install to add forms processing or other dynamic data sources.

➤ Logon Attempts: The number of logon attempts that have been made by the HTTP Server.

➤ Maximum Anonymous Users: The maximum number of anonymous users simultaneously connected to the HTTP Server.

➤ Maximum CGI Requests: The maximum number of CGI requests that have been simultaneously processed by the HTTP Server. This includes WAIS index queries.

➤ Maximum Connections: The maximum number of simultaneous connections to the HTTP Server.

➤ Maximun ISAPI Extension Requests: The maximum number of extension requests that have been simultaneously processed by the HTTP Server.

➤ Maximum NonAnonymous Users: The maximum number of nonanonymous users simultaneously connected to the HTTP Server.

➤ Not Found Errors: The number of requests that couldn't be satisfied by the server because the requested document could not be found. These are generally reported as an HTTP 404 error code to the client.

➤ Other Request Methods: The number of HTTP requests that are not GET, POST, or HEAD methods. These might include PUT, DELETE, LINK, or other methods supported by gateway applications.

➤ Post Requests: The number of HTTP requests using the POST method. Post requests are generally used for forms or gateway requests.

➤ Total Anonymous Users: The total number of anonymous users that have ever connected to the HTTP Server.

➤ Total NonAnonymous Users: The total number of nonanonymous users that have ever connected to the HTTP Server.

## IIS Global Performance Counters

The Object name for the Internet Information Server is Internet Information Services Global.

The following is a list of Counters used to monitor the Internet Information Services Global object:

➤ Cache Flushes: The number of times a portion of the memory cache has been expired due to file or directory changes in an Internet Information Services directory tree.

➤ Cache Hits: The total number of times a file open, directory listing, or service-specific objects request was found in the cache.

➤ Cache Hits %: The ratio of cache hits to all cache requests.

➤ Cache Misses: The total number of times a file open, directory listing, or service-specific objects request was not found in the cache.

➤ Cache Size: The configured maximum size of the shared HTTP, FTP, and Gopher memory cache.

➤ Cache Used: The total number of bytes currently containing cached data in the shared memory cache. This includes directory listings, file handle tracking, and service-specific objects.

➤ Cached File Handles: The number of open file handles cached by all of the Internet Information Services.

➤ Current Blocked Async I/O Requests: The number of current async I/O requests blocked by bandwidth throttler.

➤ Directory Listings: The number of cached directory listings cached by all of the Internet Information Services.

➤ Measured Async I/O Bandwidth usage: The measured bandwidth of async I/O averaged over a minute.

➤ Objects: The number of objects cached by all of the Internet Information Services. The objects include file handle tracking objects, directory listing objects, and service-specific objects.

➤ Total Allowed Async I/O Requests: The total number of async I/O requests allowed by bandwidth throttler.

➤ Total Blocked Async I/O Requests: The total number of async I/O requests blocked by bandwidth throttler.

➤ Total Rejected Async I/O Requests: The total number of async I/O requests rejected by bandwidth throttler.

See Chapter 11, "Monitoring Server Activity and Performance," for more information.

## Event Viewer

The Event Viewer in the Administrative Tools folder is a tool that you can use to monitor system, security, and application events in your system. You can use the Event Viewer to view and manage system, security, and application event logs. The Event Viewer can notify administrators of critical events, such as a stopped or failed service, and unauthorized access attempts by displaying pop-up messages, or by adding event information to log files. The information enables you to better understand the sequence and types of events that lead up to a particular state or situation.

See Chapter 12, "Site Administration Utilities," for more information.

# Summary

In this chapter, you learned about the installation issues for the WWW Publishing Service. Many of the installation concepts needed to understand the Internet Information Server configuration, such as installation methods and related terms, were discussed prior to showing you the installation procedure. The Internet Service Manager was discussed in detail and other configuration tools were noted.

The installation and configuration procedures discussed in this chapter should suffice for the majority of installation situations. The next chapter discusses advanced configuration issues, multihoming, and multiple domains.

# Chapter 8

# Multihoming: Creating Multiple Domains

Single domain Web sites are reasonably simple to set up and maintain. Often, the task of planning and implementing a multiple domain Web server is considered to be a formidable procedure. The Internet Information Server is designed to support multiple domains, and will allow you to configure multiple domain options with ease.

Web content files, stored on single domain Web servers, are often found within the server root directory tree structure. When you configure the Internet Information Server to use a network directory, or a directory outside of the server root directory tree structure, you create what is called a virtual directory.

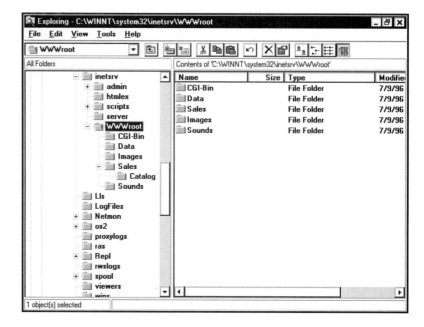

**Figure 8.1:**

Server root directory tree structure.

A single domain Internet Information Server is usually configured to respond to requests from one assigned IP address. When you configure IIS to support multiple domains, it will respond to the requests from more than one IP address. IP address configurations are also discussed in Chapter 2, "Configuring Windows NT Server."

When IIS is configured to respond to requests from multiple IP addresses, it will be perceived as multiple servers. In a nutshell, you can configure a single Internet Information Server to appear as many servers. These additional servers are known as virtual servers.

The World Wide Web Publishing Service of IIS can be configured to support multiple domains. Each domain within the Web server can have its own Home Directory. Multihoming is a term used to describe a Web server that is configured to support multiple domains.

This chapter will discuss the following:

➤ Home Directories

➤ Managing Directories

➤ Content Directories

➤ Directory Browsing and Default Document

➤ Virtual Directories

➤ Virtual Servers

# Home Directories

All of the individual IIS services are configured with default content directories. These directories are also known as the Home Directories. Every IIS service must have a Home Directory assigned. The Home Directory is the location where the tree structure of the service originates. Without a Home Directory assigned, the service will not function properly.

The Home Directory for each IIS service is also known as the root directory for the service. By default, the Home Directory and all of the content subdirectories that you create within will be available to users. Subdirectories within the Home Directory can be used to organize content and make administration easier.

The following is an example of a WWW server Home Directory tree structure:

**C:\inetsrv\wwwroot**

   **\images**

   **\sales**

   **\sales\catalog**

   **\sales\promotions**

The Home Directory is the location used to store the default document for a specific Internet service. Other content files can also be located in the Home Directory. In the above example, the wwwroot directory is the Home Directory. The other subdirectories are used for organizational structuring.

The physical directory name of the Home Directory is not known to the user using a Web browser. The Home Directory appears to the Web browser as the root of the directory structure. The IIS server allows access only to the Home Directory, subdirectories within the Home Directory, and virtual directories that you configure in the Directories Property Sheet.

A browser request, sent to the WWW Publishing Service ending in only a "/", directs the Web server to look in the specified Home Directory for the default document. The following examples all refer to Home Directories.

**http://www.yourcompany.com**

**http://www.yourcompany.com/**

**http://www.yourcompany.com/home.html**

A browser request, sent to the FTP Publishing Service ending in only a "/", directs the FTP server to look for a subdirectory under the specified Home Directory that matches the name of the user logging on. By default, during an anonymous FTP logon, the FTP server looks for a directory called "anonymous." If the "anonymous" subdirectory does not exist, the user will be sent to the Home Directory. The use of an "anonymous" directory for anonymous logons is optional.

The following example refers to a Home Directory:

**ftp://ftp.yourcompany.com/**

During an anonymous FTP logon, if a filename is included on the URL, and the file exists, the file will be sent to the Web browser without error. The following is an example:

**ftp://ftp.yourcompany.com/GetThisFile.txt**

If during a non-anonymous FTP logon, for example, a user named BOB attempts an authorized FTP logon, and a subdirectory named "bob" exists, the "bob" subdirectory will be BOB's Home Directory. In this case, BOB's FTP session will begin in the "bob" subdirectory. This can be BOB's private FTP directory as well. In this example, to restrict access to allow only BOB access to the directory, you will need to set the security permissions for the directory. See Chapter 14, "Security Utilities and Testing," for more information.

# Managing Directories

In the Directories Property Sheet of the Internet Service Manager, you can change the Home Directory path, as well as create additional directories or delete existing directories. You can create and delete directories as needed to satisfy organizational needs and changing content.

Follow these steps to change your Home Directory:

1. In the Internet Service Manager, select a Server.

2. Choose the Service for which you want to change the Home Directory.

3. Click the Directories tab.

4. Select Home Directory from the Directory list.

5. Click Edit Properties.

6. In the Directory box, type the full directory path, or select a directory by using the Browse button.

7. In the Access box, choose the type of access.

8. Click OK.

9. Click Apply.

10. Click OK to return to the main window.

**Figure 8.2:**

Directories Property Sheet.

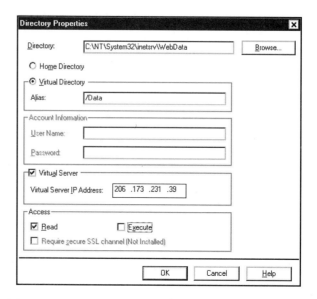

**Figure 8.3:**

Directory Properties dialog box.

Follow these steps to create a Home Directory:

1. In the Internet Service Manager, select a Server.
2. Choose the Service for which you want to add a directory.
3. Click the Directories tab.
4. Click Add.
5. In the Directory box, type the full directory path, or select a directory by using the Browse button.
6. Select the Home Directory option.
7. In the Access box, choose the type of access.
8. Click OK.
9. Click Apply.
10. Click OK to return to the main window.

Follow these steps to delete a Home Directory:

1. In the Internet Service Manager, select a Server.
2. Choose the Service from which you want to delete a directory.
3. Click the Directories tab.
4. In the Directory list, select the directory you want to delete.
5. Click Remove.
6. Click Apply.
7. Click OK to return to the main window.

# Content Directories

In general, you can refer to all of the directories available to your IIS services as Content Directories. Content Directories can be subdirectories within or outside of the Home Directory tree structure, or on other network drives. Content Directories are directories used to store HTML pages, other files, and images for the Internet Services.

All of the subdirectories that you create within your Home Directory tree are available to users by default. You do not need to add these subdirectories to the Directories Property Sheet, Directory List.

If you have files elsewhere; outside of the Home Directory tree structure, or on other network drives, and you want to make the directories available to IIS services, you will need to create virtual directories. Virtual directories are discussed later in this chapter.

# Directory Browsing and Default Document

The Directory Browsing and Default Document options in the Directories Property Sheet are interrelated. Each option affects the other, and controls the manner in which the IIS services operate.

The Directory Browsing option controls an IIS service's capability to allow Web Browsers to see file lists.

The Default Document option controls an IIS service's capability to display a default document.

The WWW Publishing Service has the capability to respond to browser requests that do not specify a designated filename. If you enable this option and place a default document in each directory, the WWW Publishing Service will return the default document to the Web browser. If a default document does not exist in a specified directory, the Service will return an error, unless directory browsing is enabled.

If you choose to do so, default documents can be placed into all of the WWW Publishing Service directories. The Default Document option, located in the Directory Properties Sheet, is a global setting used by the WWW Publishing Service. Use this option if you plan to include default documents in all content directories.

The Directory Browsing option, located in the Directory Properties Sheet, is a global setting that acts upon all WWW directories.

When Directory Browsing and Default Document options are both enabled, if the WWW Publishing Service receives a browser request without a specific filename, and a default document is not present in the directory, a hypertext directory listing of the directory is sent to the Web browser. Directory browsing enables a Web browser to see a complete listing of the requested directory contents. Enable this option if you want users to be able to navigate through your World Wide Web directories. This will allow users to see all of the files available, and is usually not enabled on the WWW service.

When browsing WWW Publishing Service directories, virtual directories will not be visible from the Home Directory. By convention, the WWW service operates in this manner.

The Virtual Directory alias needs to be specified by the Web browser in order to list files contained within the Virtual Directory. Directory annotations can be used to list Virtual Directories in the FTP Publishing Service. Explicit links can be created in descriptive tag files for the Gopher Publishing Service so that users have access to Virtual Directories. Tag files, in the Gopher Service, enable you to augment the Gopher display list with descriptive information, and provide links to other computers.

Directory browsing from the WWW Publishing Service is similar to browsing in the FTP Publishing Service. Both listings will provide file and directory information for navigation.

# Virtual Directories

Web content files, stored on single domain Web servers, are often found within the server Home Directory tree structure. When you configure IIS to use a network directory (or a directory outside of the server root directory tree structure) you create what is called a

Virtual Directory. Each IIS Publishing Service can have one Home Directory, in addition to many other publishing content directories.

Virtual Directories assigned to network drives must exist within the same domain as the Internet Information Server, or they will not be accessible. You must also have access permission to the network drives from the Internet Information Server. Access permissions for network drives can be configured by using the User Manager for Domains and the Explorer. See Chapter 14, "Security Utilities and Testing," for more information.

## Aliases

When configuring Virtual Directories in the Directory Properties Sheet, you must assign the Virtual Directory an alias. You can choose to use the same name as the directory name or choose an alternate name. The alias is the subdirectory name that will be used by Web browsers to access information in the Virtual Directory. If alias names for Virtual Directories are not specified, an alias name is generated automatically by the Internet Service Manager. The alias name will be the same name as the Virtual Directory name. The alias name that you choose will only be visible to Web browsers if the name is known by the user. When you choose an alias name in the Internet Service Managers Directory Properties dialog box, the name must begin with a slash, "/". For example, the IIS installation program creates a default "/Data" Virtual Directory (see fig. 8.3).

## Home Directories

The root of a Virtual Directory can be referred to as a Home Directory of the Virtual Directory. Subdirectories can be created within the Virtual Directory root, and will be available to Web browsers. The virtual home directory is the root of the Virtual Directory tree, and each Virtual Directory tree is addressed as if it were a subdirectory of the primary non-virtual home directory. In this manner, Virtual Directories are linked to the Home Directory.

The following is an example of a WWW service tree structure:

> **C:\inetsrv\wwwroot**
>> **\images**
>>
>> **\sales**
>>
>> **\sales\catalog**
>>
>> **\sales\promotions**

The following is an example of a virtual directory tree structure:

> **D:\d-sales   (virtual directory root)**
>> **\d-sales\catalog**
>>
>> **\d-sales\promotions**

When listed, the directory structure will appear as follows:

> **C:\inetsrv\wwwroot**
>> **\images**
>>
>> **\sales**
>>
>> **\sales\catalog**
>>
>> **\sales\promotions**
>>
>> **\d-sales**
>>> **\d-sales\catalog**
>>>
>>> **\d-sales\promotions**

# Creating Virtual Directories

The Directories Property dialog box is used to create virtual directories. To create a virtual directory, follow these steps:

1. In the Internet Service Manager, select a server.

2. Choose the Service for which you want to create the virtual directory.

3.  Click the Directories tab.

4.  Click Add.

5.  In the Directory box, type the full network directory path, local directory path, or select a directory by using the Browse button.

6.  Select the Virtual Directory option.

7.  Type the name of the virtual directory in the Alias box.

8.  Choose the type of access in the Access box.

9.  Click OK.

10. Click Apply.

11. Click OK to return to the main window.

## Examples of Virtual Directory Structure

Understanding the possibilities of Virtual Directory Structure will assist you in developing your IIS content directory layout. The following examples are provided to acquaint you with the potential configuration variations of virtual directories.

The following are example directory paths and associated URLs of a sample WWW Publishing Service directory structure. The sample directory structure consists of a home directory, virtual directories on local drives, and virtual directories on network drives.

1.  **C:\inetsrv\wwwroot:** Home Directory, Local drive, No Alias name assigned. From a Web browser, the URL used to access the above Home Directory would appear in the following format:

    **http://www.yourcompany.com/**

    If this Home Directory contains the subdirectory C:\inetsrv\CGI-Bin, "CGI-Bin", the URL used to access the subdirectory would appear in the following format:

    **http://www.yourcompany.com/CGI-Bin/**

2. **C:\inetsrv\Scripts:** Virtual Directory, Local drive, Alias name "Scripts".

   From a Web browser, the URL used to access the Virtual Directory would appear in the following format:

   **http://www.yourcompany.com/Scripts/**

3. **C:\inetsrv\DataFiles:** Virtual Directory, Local drive, Alias name "DataFiles".

   From a Web browser, the URL used to access the Virtual Directory would appear in the following format:

   **http://www.yourcompany.com/DataFiles/**

4. **D:\sales\MarketingData:** Virtual Directory, Local drive, Alias name "SalesM".

   From a Web browser, the URL used to access the Virtual Directory would appear in the following format:

   **http://www.yourcompany.com/SalesM/**

5. **\\ServerName\ShareName\webstuff\MarketingData:** Virtual Directory, Network Drive, Alias name "SalesData".

   From a Web browser, the URL used to access the Virtual Directory would appear in the following format:

   **http://www.yourcompany.com/SalesData/**

   If this Virtual Directory contains the subdirectory \\ServerName\ShareName\webstuff\MarketingData\1996Data, "1996Data", the URL used to access the subdirectory would appear in the following format:

   **http://www.yourcompany.com/SalesData/1996Data/**

   The creation of virtual directories is not limited to a single domain Internet Information Server. When you create a virtual directory on a multiple domain Internet Information Server, you must specify the IP address of the domain name for which the directory is assigned. This procedure will be discussed later in this chapter, in the section "Virtual Servers."

# Account Information

The Account Information option will become visible only if you have selected a network directory share using a Universal Naming Convention (UNC) path. If you have selected a network directory share by using a UNC path, you must enter a username that has permission to access the network directory and enter a valid password for the username (refer to fig. 8.3).

A Universal Naming Convention (UNC) path is a path used to access a network directory share on another computer within your domain. The following is an example of a UNC:

**\\ServerName\Sharename\directoryName**

# Access Checkboxes

There are three checkboxes within the Access option: Read, Execute, and Require secure SSL channel (refer to fig. 8.3).

➤ Read: The default option used for content directories.

➤ Execute: This option can be selected for directories containing programs, scripts, and ISAPI applications. If you select the Execute option, ensure that the Read option is not selected. If the Read option is also selected, Web browsers will be able to see the executable files in the directory.

➤ Require secure SSL channel: This option is necessary if you require encrypted access to a directory. For more information on Secure Sockets Layer (SSL), see Chapter 13, "Server Security Basics."

# Virtual Servers

By default, IIS is configured to answer requests addressed to a single domain name. If for example, your domain name is **www.yourcompany.com**, all of the IIS Publishing Services will answer requests for this domain name.

The following are example URLs used to connect to IIS services on a single domain name computer:

**http://www.yourcompany.com/**

**ftp://www.yourcompany.com/**

**gopher://www.yourcompany.com/**

# Assigning IP Addresses

Each domain name is assigned to a single IP address. Likewise, each IP address is assigned to a single domain name. You can add IP addresses to the TCP/IP configuration of your NT Server. To create virtual servers within IIS, you will need to add more IP addresses to the TCP/IP protocol configuration and resolve the additional IP addresses to domain names. You will need to configure DNS, WINS, LMHOSTS, or a HOSTS file to resolve the IP addresses to domain names.

Multiple IP addresses can be assigned to a single network adapter card, or to multiple network cards. Use the Network Applet in the Control Panel to bind the additional IP addresses to your network adapter card. See Chapter 4, "Introduction to TCP/IP," for more information. To add more than five IP addresses to a network card, you will need to change Registry Key Values. See Chapter 12, "Site Administration Utilities," for more information.

Usually, a single computer has a single domain name and a single IP address. This is the common perception of a computer on the Internet. When you add IP addresses to the TCP/IP configuration of your NT Server and the IP addresses are resolved to domain names, your Internet Information Server will be able to answer requests for these additional domain names. This will enable you to host multiple domains on a single IIS server.

# Multiple Domain Names

The WWW Publishing Service can be configured to answer requests for more than one single domain name. When it is configured in this manner, the additional WWW Publishing Services are known as virtual servers within the Internet Information Server. This makes the single Web server appear as if it were many Web servers.

The main benefit derived from the use of Virtual Servers is that you do not need a different computer for each domain name. For example, you may have different departments within your company that need a presence on the World Wide Web. If you obtain a unique domain name for each department, you will be able to configure Virtual Servers for all of the domain names on one Internet Information Server computer. To do this, you must obtain IP addresses for the primary server and for each additional Virtual Server that you want to create.

## Virtual Server Directories

You must create a unique Home Directory for each Virtual Server that you create. Each Virtual Server must have a home directory specified for proper operation of the IIS service. You must specify an IP address when you create a home directory or a Virtual Server. If you do not specify an IP address for the home directory, the virtual directory will be linked to the default primary server domain name. In the Directories Property Sheet, select the Virtual Server box and enter an IP address associated to the domain name for which you want the home directory assigned. The IP address links the directory to a domain name. Home Directories can be on local or network drives within your domain, depending upon your requirements.

You can also create other virtual directories, and assign them to a specific Virtual Server by assigning an IP address associated to a specific domain name.

## Creating a Virtual Server

To create a Virtual Server, follow these steps:

1. In the Internet Service Manager, select a server.

2. Select the World Wide Web Service.

3. Click the Directories tab.

4. Click the Add button.

5. In the Directory box, type the full directory path, or select a directory by clicking the Browse button.

6. Select the Virtual Directory option.

7. In the Alias box, type the name of the virtual directory.

8. Type the IP address for the virtual server.

9. In the Access box, choose the type of access.

10. Click OK.

11. Click Apply.

12. Click OK to return to the main window.

# Virtual Server Directories

When you implement virtual servers within the WWW Publishing Service, IP addresses must be specified for virtual directories. If you do not specify an IP address for a directory, the directory will be visible to all virtual servers. If you need to share a virtual directory with all of the configured virtual servers, you can leave the IP address blank.

The default directories created during IIS installation do not specify IP addresses for the service's home directory. You may need to specify IP addresses for the default directories when you add virtual servers.

# Summary

In this chapter, you learned about the advanced configuration issues related to multiple domains. Many of the concepts needed to understand the configuration of virtual servers were discussed.

The configuration procedures discussed in this chapter should suffice for the majority of installation situations. The next two chapters discuss configuration of the FTP and Gopher Services.

# Chapter 9

# Configuring the FTP Publishing Service

The FTP Publishing Service—one of three component services within the Internet Information Server is based upon the File Transfer Protocol, known as FTP. FTP is one of the earliest protocols to be implemented on TCP/IP networks and is still widely accepted today. FTP enables file transfers between computers. FTP is especially useful in transferring files between computers of different operating systems, which may have no other means of compatibility. Implementing the capabilities of FTP on the Internet Information Server requires some fundamental knowledge and creative tweeking abilities. This chapter will prepare you to create a successful FTP site with discussion of the following:

➤ Understanding the FTP Publishing Service

➤ Installation

➤ Configuration

➤ Related Tools

# Understanding the FTP Publishing Service

The first FTP client programs used were character-based. Users were required to enter commands manually at a command prompt to be able to logon, list, and copy files. Character-based FTP programs are still widely used today. Windows NT includes a character-based FTP program that can be run from the command prompt as shown in the following figure.

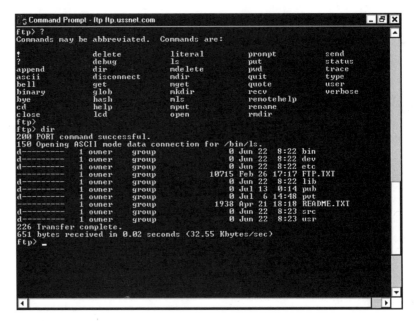

**Figure 9.1:**

FTP command prompt.

Today there are a variety of graphical user interface FTP client programs available, such as WS_FTP and Cute FTP. These FTP clients have simplified the tasks of logging on, listing, and copying files.

The Internet Explorer, as well as other Web browsers, can be used to anonymously log on to the FTP service, browse directories, transfer files from the FTP service, and log off.

The FTP service displays directory listings to Web browsers as dynamically generated hypertext links. These hypertext links are displayed in the Web browser as directory listings. The directory listings of hypertext links enable the user to navigate through directories with the simple point and click of a mouse. In the same manner, a click on a filename within the directory listing requests the file from the FTP service and starts the file transfer process.

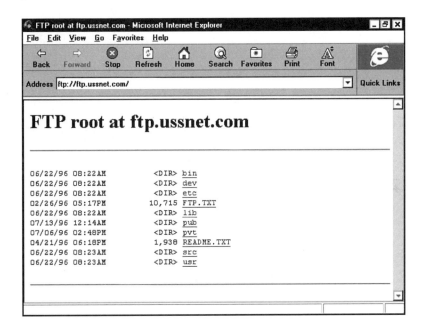

**Figure 9.2:**
Internet Explorer FTP directory listing.

In addition to enabling anonymous logons, the FTP service can be configured to allow secure user logons. When a user performs a secure logon, access can be granted to allow the user to transfer files, either to or from the FTP service. Secure, non-anonymous

FTP logons are usually accomplished by using an FTP client. Most Web browsers only allow anonymous FTP logons.

The WWW service has replaced much of the functionality and need for FTP. The WWW service enables users to request and transfer files from the Internet Information Server. However, of the three IIS component services, only the FTP Publishing Service can be used to transfer files from a remote computer to the Internet Information Server. For example, if the FTP service is used to distribute shareware files, authors could send the latest versions of their shareware to the FTP service to create a dynamic repository for new software.

The content and format of the files made available through the FTP service are without restriction. For example, text, multimedia, executable, and compressed files can be made available for transfer.

# Installing the FTP Publishing Service

The FTP Publishing Service is one of three component services that may be selected during the Internet Information Server installation. The IIS installation setup program will enable you to selectively install the FTP Publishing Service. To install the FTP Publishing Service, refer to the general procedure for installing the Internet Information Server, previously outlined in Chapter 7, "Configuring the WWW Publishing Service" and substitute the FTP options for the WWW options.

# Configuring the FTP Publishing Service

The FTP Publishing Service is configured through property sheets accessed from within the Internet Service Manager. The FTP service has five main property sheets for viewing and configuration. There are many configuration options within each property sheet.

Configuration issues, related to the following, will be discussed:

➤   Service Property Sheet

➤   Messages Property Sheet

➤   Directories Property Sheet

➤   Logging Property Sheet

➤   Advanced Property Sheet

➤   Creating Annotation Files

➤   Directory Structuring

# Configuring the Service Property Sheet

The Service property sheet located in the Internet Service Manager enables the administrator to control access to the service, set the connection timeout, set maximum connections, and enter connection messages.

**Figure 9.3:**

Service Property Sheet.

The following sections discuss the Service Property Sheet configuration options for the FTP Publishing Service.

## Connection Timeout

The Connection Timeout option sets the length of time (in seconds) for a connection before the server disconnects an inactive user. This is often referred to as the inactivity timeout. As a guideline, it is recommended that you should not set this number lower than 100 seconds. The default connection timeout value is 900 seconds (15 minutes). The maximum connection timeout value you can set is 32,767 seconds. This value ensures that all connections are closed if the FTP protocol fails to close a connection.

## Maximum Connections

The Maximum Connections option limits the number of simultaneous user connections to the FTP server. If bandwidth is limited, and you have many users transferring files from the FTP server, you can lower the setting value to help conserve bandwidth usage.

## Allow Anonymous Connections

By default, anonymous connections are allowed on the FTP Publishing Service. If you disable anonymous connections, only authorized secure logons will be allowed.

If you choose to allow anonymous connections, the account name and password used for anonymous client requests must be specified. The default account username, in the format **IUSR_computername**, is used internally by the Internet Information Server for anonymous logon security. Anonymous logon users are linked to this account username. The default account username is set up during the Internet Information Server installation. All anonymous logons to the service will use this account username. To clarify this issue, when an anonymous user logs on to the FTP server, the IIS server uses the account username for security restriction information.

The password you select for the account username in the Service Property Sheet is used internally by the NT Server. This password is not known or set during the anonymous user logon process by the remote computer.

Anonymous FTP users usually log on using their e-mail addresses as passwords. Web browsers, such as the Internet Explorer, are by default, configured to present the e-mail address of the user as the password during an anonymous FTP logon.

If you decide to allow anonymous FTP logons, you should still verify that the security permissions for this account username are correct. You have the option to keep the default username, specify another existing username, or create a new user account. In any case, you must configure its security permissions relevant to your requirements. Use the User Manager for Domains to configure or verify security permissions, or refer to Chapter 13, "Server Security Basics," for more information.

## Allow Only Anonymous Connections

In addition to anonymous FTP logons, FTP clients are also permitted to log on with a valid Windows NT account username and password.

Select the Allow Only Anonymous Connections check box, located in the Service Property Sheet, to prevent valid Windows NT users from accessing the FTP service through username account logons. When this check box is enabled, only anonymous connections are allowed. For security reasons, this option is usually enabled, to prevent unauthorized access and protect user passwords. See Chapter 14, "Security Utilities and Testing," for more information.

## Comment Option

The Comment option, located in the Service Property Sheet, is most often used to enter the text description of the service. The Comment option is commonly used for reference purposes. This comment will appear in the Internet Service Manager, Report

View window. On networks with many IIS services, some system administrators enter the IP address of the service for reference.

## Configuring the Messages Property Sheet

The Messages Property Sheet, located in the Service Property Sheet, is used to customize the Welcome, Exit, and Maximum Connections messages. By default, these entries are empty. Typically, these message options are used and should be configured to meet your needs. These messages are usually used to personalize the FTP server.

➤ The Welcome Message is displayed to the user during the logon process. This is commonly used to tell users something about the FTP server's content.

➤ The Exit Message is displayed to a user when disconnecting from the FTP server.

➤ The Maximum Connections Message is displayed to a user when the maximum number of connected users has been exceeded.

**Figure 9.4:**

Messages Property Sheet.

# Configuring the Directories Property Sheet

Within the Directories Property Sheet of the FTP Publishing Service, you can configure directory paths available to users, set access permissions, define a Home directory, define virtual directories, and select a Directory Listing Style.

**Figure 9.5:**

FTP Directories Property Sheet.

The following sections discuss the Directories Property Sheet configuration options of the FTP Publishing Service.

# Home Directory

During the IIS installation, a default Home directory for the FTP Publishing Service is created. The default directory name is **\Ftproot**. By default, this directory is actually a subdirectory within the existing IIS directory tree, and is not created in the root of the drive. The actual directory path will appear similar to the following example:

**C:\WINNT\System32\InetSrv\Ftproot**

You can change the location of the FTP Home directory as long as the directory you assign is located on an NTFS drive within your domain.

The FTP server will not operate properly without an assigned Home directory. Assigning a Home directory is a requirement for the proper operation of the FTP server. If you do not assign a Home directory, all users will be denied access during FTP logon.

When configuring or changing the FTP Home directory, there is another important option to choose. You must select the type of access permission for the directory. By default, the Home directory is assigned Read access permission only. If you want to allow users to upload files to the Home directory, you must also select the Write option. It is generally not recommended to enable the Write option for the Home directory. Only enable the Write option for the Home directory if you have a specific need.

If you want to allow users to be able to upload files to the FTP server, it is recommended that you create other directories to accept transfers, and configure them with the Write permission.

The Home directory is percieved as being the root directory of the FTP server tree structure. You can create other directories within the Home directory. By default, other directories and their contents will be available to anonymous logon users.

The following is an example of an FTP server Home directory tree structure:

**C:\WINNT\System32\InetSrv\Ftproot**

> **\public**
>
> **\info**
>
> **\software**

In the preceding example, the FTP server will not allow FTP clients to gain access to the \InetSrv directory. By default, the FTP server will allow FTP clients to gain access to the \public, \info, and \software directories within the \Ftproot Home directory.

You can place your FTP files into the Home directory and other subdirectories that you create within the Home directory. Directories created within the Home directory can be created to organize your FTP contents. By default, the files you place within the Home directory tree of the FTP server will be available to anonymous users.

During an anonymous logon, when accessing the IIS server with a domain name-only URL such as `ftp:\\www.yourcompany.com\`, the FTP service operates in a slightly different manner than the WWW service. The WWW service will look for the default document or list the directory contents of the Home directory. The FTP service will first look for the presence of an "\anonymous" directory within the FTP Home directory. If it exists, the anonymous user will be given the "\anonymous" directory contents, in the form of a hypertext listing. If the "\anonymous" directory does not exist, the user will then be given the contents of the actual FTP Home directory, in the form of a hypertext listing.

The following is an example of an FTP Home directory tree structure, with an \anonymous directory:

**C:\WINNT\System32\InetSrv\Ftproot**

        **\public**

        **\info**

        **\software**

        **\anonymous**

During the FTP logon process, the FTP service will always look for a directory that matches the username. If a matching directory name does not exist, the user will be directed to the FTP Home directory.

The creation and use of an "\anonymous" directory within the FTP Home directory is optional. For example, you may want to use an "\anonymous" directory to direct anonymous users to specific content when the FTP service is configured to also allow non-anonymous logons to the FTP server.

The following is a sample domain URL, used to access the WWW service:

**http://www.yourcompany.com/**

The following is a sample domain URL, used to access the FTP service, on the same Internet Information Server:

**ftp://www.yourcompany.com/**

## Create or Change the FTP Home Directory

You can change the Home Directory path, if needed. The Home Directory can be located on a local NTFS drive or on an available NTFS network drive within your domain.

To create or change the FTP Home Directory, follow these steps:

1. In the Internet Service Manager, select a Server.
2. Choose the FTP Service for which you want to change the Home Directory.
3. Click the Directories tab.
4. In the Directory list, select the Home Directory.
5. Click Edit Properties.
6. In the Directory properties box, type the full directory path, or select a directory by using the Browse button.
7. In the Access box, choose the type of access needed.
8. Click OK.
9. Click Apply.
10. Click OK to return to the main window.

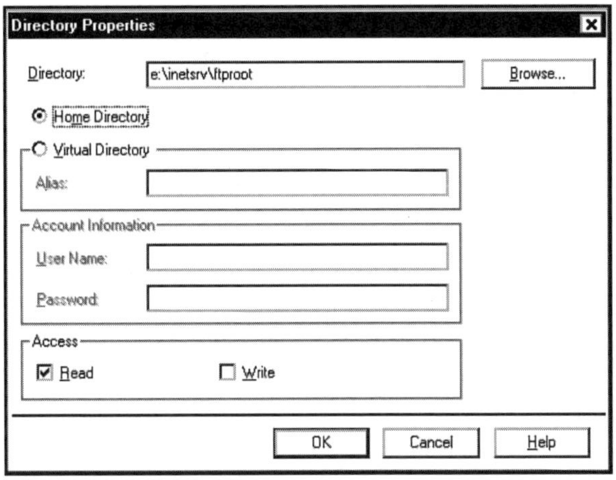

**Figure 9.6:**
Directory Properties Dialog Box.

You can create other directories within the Home Directory. By default, these directories will be both available and visible to FTP clients. You can create other directories within the Home Directory by using the Explorer.

The following are examples of other directories created within the default Home directory.

**C:\WINNT\System32\InetSrv\Ftproot\public**

**C:\WINNT\System32\InetSrv\Ftproot\info**

**C:\WINNT\System32\InetSrv\Ftproot\software**

# Virtual Directories

You can also add other directories outside of the Home directory tree structure. These directories will appear to a user as sub-directories of the Home directory. These directories are called virtual directories, and can be located anywhere on your NT Server or on an available NTFS network drive. For security reasons, you should use NTFS drives to store your FTP files.

Virtual directories are effectively implemented when you want to access directory contents existing on another NT server within your domain or network.

When you configure virtual FTP directories, you must assign the virtual directory an alias name. An alias name is a name linked to the actual physical directory. Users can access the physical directory only if they know the alias name. You may want to assign an alias name to a physical directory for security reasons or to simplify the physical directory name.

If you assign virtual directories to network drives, you must specify a username and password. The username must have sufficient security permission to access the network directory. Ensure that your security procedures are correct. Refer to Chapter 13, "Server Security Basics," for more information.

When you use virtual FTP directories, the virtual directories will not be visible to the user browsing the FTP Home directory. This is a technical limitation of the FTP protocol as implemented within the FTP publishing service. Users can browse a virtual directory if they know the alias of the virtual directory.

If a user is accessing the FTP service with a Web browser, hypertext links can be embedded within the HTML page to direct the user to the virtual directory name. Typically, a index.text file is incorporated as a guide to the site contents and will direct the user to the hidden virtual directories.

## Read and Write Permissions

By default, the Read permission is enabled for all directories within the FTP server. You can use the Read and Write options in various combinations.

Read: The Read option allows an FTP client to see a directory listing and transfer files from that directory.

Write: The Write option allows an FTP client to transfer files to a directory. Enabling the Write permission on a specific directory will allow users to transfer files to your FTP server.

If you disable the Read option and enable the Write option on a specific directory, users will be able to transfer files to that directory, but will not be able to see a directory listing or transfer files from the directory. If the Read and Write options are both enabled for a specific directory, users will be able to transfer files to and from the directory, and see a directory listing. For example, if you need a directory to accept file transfers from users, and do not want the files transferred to be visible to other users, enable the Write option only.

## Directory Listing Styles

The Directory Listing Style option enables you to choose how the directory listing will appear to an FTP client. There are two styles to choose from—UNIX and MS-DOS. It is usually recommended that this option be set to the UNIX format directory listing style. This will ensure maximum compatibility for Web browsers that require a UNIX format directory listing. The following figures show directory listings in both UNIX and MS-DOS format.

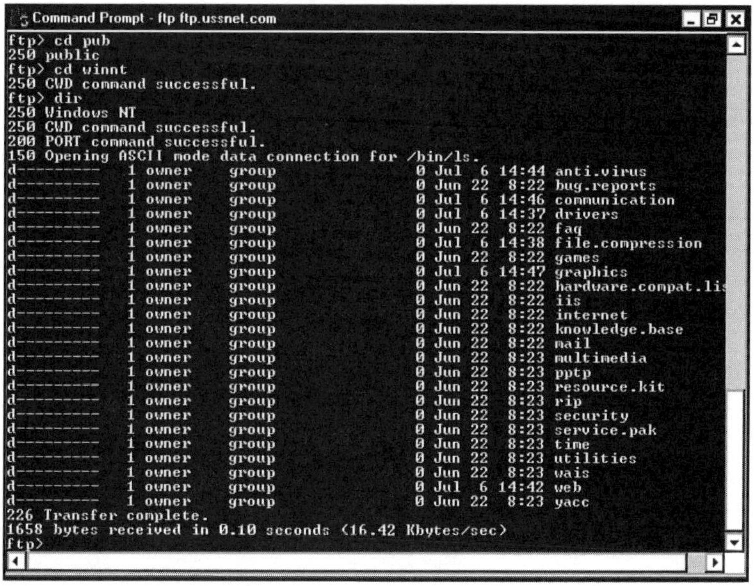

**Figure 9.7:**
UNIX Style Directory Listing.

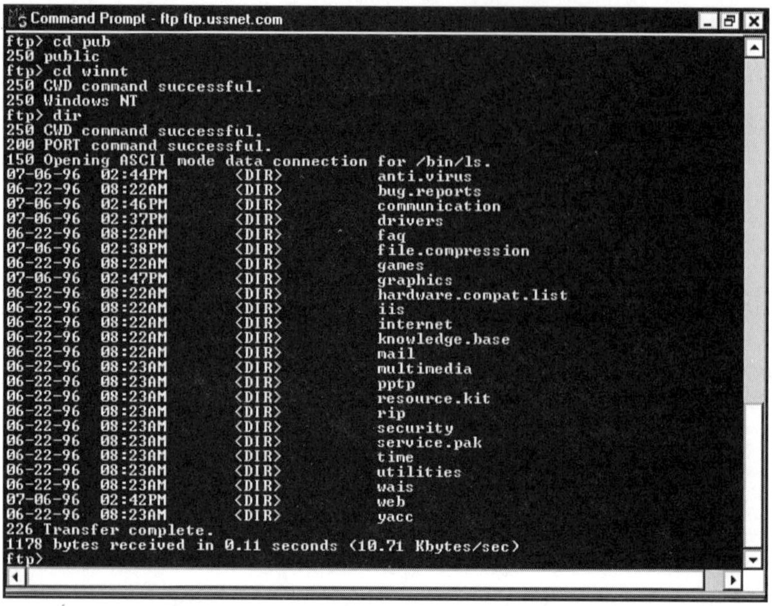

```
Command Prompt - ftp ftp.ussnet.com
ftp> cd pub
250 public
ftp> cd winnt
250 CWD command successful.
250 Windows NT
ftp> dir
250 CWD command successful.
200 PORT command successful.
150 Opening ASCII mode data connection for /bin/ls.
07-06-96  02:44PM       <DIR>          anti.virus
06-22-96  08:22AM       <DIR>          bug.reports
07-06-96  02:46PM       <DIR>          communication
07-06-96  02:37PM       <DIR>          drivers
06-22-96  08:22AM       <DIR>          faq
07-06-96  02:38PM       <DIR>          file.compression
06-22-96  08:22AM       <DIR>          games
07-06-96  02:47PM       <DIR>          graphics
06-22-96  08:22AM       <DIR>          hardware.compat.list
06-22-96  08:22AM       <DIR>          iis
06-22-96  08:22AM       <DIR>          internet
06-22-96  08:22AM       <DIR>          knowledge.base
06-22-96  08:22AM       <DIR>          mail
06-22-96  08:23AM       <DIR>          multimedia
06-22-96  08:23AM       <DIR>          pptp
06-22-96  08:23AM       <DIR>          resource.kit
06-22-96  08:23AM       <DIR>          rip
06-22-96  08:23AM       <DIR>          security
06-22-96  08:23AM       <DIR>          service.pak
06-22-96  08:23AM       <DIR>          time
06-22-96  08:23AM       <DIR>          utilities
06-22-96  08:23AM       <DIR>          wais
07-06-96  02:42PM       <DIR>          web
06-22-96  08:23AM       <DIR>          yacc
226 Transfer complete.
1178 bytes received in 0.11 seconds (10.71 Kbytes/sec)
ftp>
```

**Figure 9.8:**

MS-DOS Style Directory Listing.

## Logging Property Sheet

The Internet Information Server can log the activity of the FTP Publishing Service. Enabling logging is recommended. Logs can provide important information and can be used for security and statistical review. Fundamentally, logs can tell you how your server is being used.

You can choose to have the log data written to a file or to an ODBC database. If you have multiple Internet Information Servers or Services on your network, you can log all of their activity to a single file or database on a specific network computer.

If you want to log the FTP service activity to files, you can specify how often to create new logs and where to log files.

If you want to log the FTP service activity to an ODBC data source, you must specify the ODBC Data Source Name, table, username, and password to the database. The advantage of logging to an ODBC data source is that the activity from all three IIS services can be logged to one file and set up as parsed HTML information to be viewed on a Web page.

See Chapter 16, "Database Interfaces," and Chapter 17, "Introduction to Database Connectivity with Microsoft SQL Server and Oracle CGI Scripting," for more information.

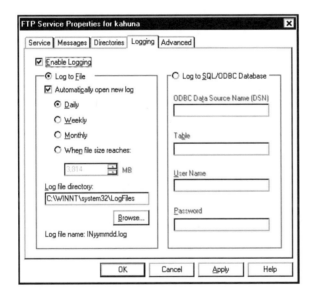

**Figure 9.9:**
Logging Property Sheet.

# Advanced Property Sheet

The Advanced Property Sheet enables the administrator to configure access restrictions to the FTP Publishing Service and limit the total outbound bandwidth of the Internet Information Server services.

**Figure 9.10:**
Advanced Property Sheet.

## Restricting IP Access

The FTP Publishing Service can be configured to have the Internet Information Server grant or deny access from specified IP addresses. You can use this option to restrict access to your server from a specific computer, or a group of computers.

By default, access to your FTP Publishing Service is granted to all IP addresses. You can choose to specify the IP addresses of computers you want to deny access to.

You can choose to change the option to deny access to all IP addresses. If you choose this option, you can specify the IP addresses of computers you want to grant access to. There should not be a need to restrict IP addresses in a public anonymous access FTP environment.

One example of proper implementation of IP address restriction would be if the research and development department of your company had an FTP server, and you wanted to restrict access to only the engineers within the department, you could specify the IP addresses of the engineers.

## Limiting Network Bandwidth

If you are running multiple Internet services and have insufficient bandwidth to meet all the needs of your IIS services, you can limit the outbound network bandwidth used by all of the Internet Information Server services on your NT Server. This option will control the maximum outbound network bandwidth for your Internet Information Server. If you have limited bandwidth, or are running other Internet services on the NT Server, you may want to enable and set this option to meet your needs. See Chapter 11, "Monitoring Server Activity and Performance," for more information.

If you choose to limit the outbound bandwidth used by the Internet Information Server Services, you must have an understanding of the possible implications.

When the actual bandwidth usage remains below the level you set, the read, write, and transfer functions will remain enabled. If the actual bandwidth usage approximates the limit you have set, reads will be temporarily blocked. If the actual bandwidth exceeds the limit you set, reads will be rejected and file transfers will be temporarily blocked. The Internet Information Server will return to normal operation when the bandwidth usage equals or falls below the maximum limit.

# Creating Annotation Files

In the FTP Publishing Service, annotation files are sometimes used to summarize the directory description for a specific directory. Each directory within the FTP server can contain an annotation file. Directory descriptions are used to inform FTP users of the contents of a directory on the FTP server. The contents of the annotation file will appear automatically to a Web browser when the user views a directory listing.

The name used by the FTP server for annotation files is
**~ftpsvc~.ckm**. The name annotation file should remain hidden.
When the file is hidden, the annotation file will not be listed in
the directory listing. To change the attribute of an annotation file
to hidden, use the Explorer.

To be able to use the annotation file feature of the FTP service,
you will need to add a key to the Registry. By default, this registry
key is not defined in the Registry. If you want to enable directory
annotation, you must add an entry to the registry subtree by
using the Registry Editor. Refer to Chapter 12, "Site Administration Utilities," for detailed information on using the Registry
Editor.

To create annotation files, follow these steps:

1.  Create a file called ~ftpsvc~.ckm, and place the file into the
    directory you want to annotate.

2.  In the Explorer, select the file, click the right mouse button,
    and check hidden within the Attributes option section of the
    Properties dialog box.

3.  Use the Registry Editor to enable annotated directories by
    adding the value of "1" to the HKEY_LOCAL_MACHINE
    subtree key called "AnnotateDirectories":.

The following is the full path to the registry key:

**HKEY_LOCAL_MACHINE\SYSTEM\CurrentControlSet\Services\
MSFTPSVC\Parameters\AnnotateDirectories**

Registry subtree key: AnnotateDirectories

Add the value: REG_DWORD

Range: 0 or 1

Default = "0" (off)

set to "1" (on)

The preceding value, "0" or "1", defines the behavior of directory annotation. When this value is 1, directory annotation is enabled. When the value is 0, directory annotation is disabled.

If directory annotation is enabled on your FTP service, some Web browsers may display error messages when browsing FTP directories. These errors can be eliminated by limiting each annotation file to one line or by disabling directory annotation.

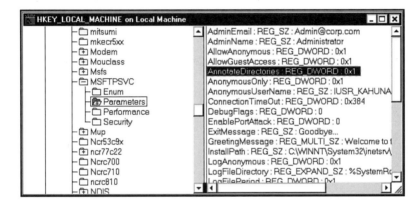

**Figure 9.11:**
Registry Editor.

# Monitoring FTP Session Connections

The Internet Service Manager can be used to monitor connections to the FTP service. Within the FTP Service Property Sheet of the Internet Service Manager, you will see a list of users connected to the FTP service. You will have the ability to disconnect an individual user or disconnect all users. This is valuable if you detect an unauthorized user in a secure nonanonymous FTP environment.

To monitor users currently connected to your FTP site, follow these steps:

1. In the Internet Service Manager, select an FTP server.

2. Double-click the FTP service to display its property sheets.

3.  Click the Service tab.

4.  Click Current Sessions.

5.  If you want to disconnect a specific user, select the user and then click Disconnect. To disconnect all user connections, click Disconnect All.

6.  Click Close.

7.  Click OK to return to the main menu.

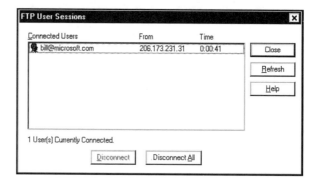

**Figure 9.12:**

FTP Service Properties Sheet, FTP User Sessions.

## Performance Monitor

The Performance Monitor is a very powerful and useful tool that provides a graphical interface that can be used to view real-time statistics and evaluate the overall operation of the Internet Information Server Services. It can also be used to evaluate and diagnose problems related to the individual Internet Information Server component services, such as the FTP Publishing Service.

With the Performance Monitor, you can view statistics in real-time. For example, you can use the Performance Monitor to show how many connections are active on all IIS services, or an individual Internet service. See Chapter 11, "Monitoring Server Activity and Performance," for more information.

# FTP Server Performance Counters

The Object name used in the Performance Monitor for the FTP
Publishing Service is FTP Server. The following is a list of
Counters used to monitor the FTP Server object:

➤ **Bytes Received/sec**: Indicates the rate that data bytes are
received by the FTP Server.

➤ **Bytes Sent/sec**: Indicates the rate that data bytes are sent by
the FTP Server.

➤ **Bytes Total/sec**: Indicates the sum of Bytes Sent/sec and
Bytes Received/sec. This is the total rate of bytes transferred
by the FTP Server.

➤ **Connection Attempts**: Indicates the number of connection
attempts that have been made to the FTP Server.

➤ **Current Anonymous Users**: Indicates the number of
anonymous users currently connected to the FTP Server.

➤ **Current Connections**: Indicates the current number of
connections to the FTP Server.

➤ **Current NonAnonymous Users**: Indicates the number of
nonanonymous users currently connected to the FTP
Server.

➤ **Files Received**: Indicates the total number of files received
by the FTP Server.

➤ **Files Sent**: Indicates the total number of files sent by the
FTP Server.

➤ **Files Total**: Indicates the sum of files sent and received. This
is the total number of files transferred by the FTP server.

➤ **Logon Attempts**: Indicates the number of logon attempts
that have been made by the FTP server.

➤ **Maximum Anonymous Users**: Indicates the maximum
number of anonymous users simultaneously connected to
the FTP Server.

➤ **Maximum Connections**: Indicates the maximum number of simultaneous connections to the FTP Server.

➤ **Maximum NonAnonymous Users**: Indicates the maximum number of nonanonymous users simultaneously connected to the FTP Server.

➤ **Total Anonymous Users**: Indicates the total number of anonymous users that have ever connected to the FTP Server.

➤ **Total NonAnonymous Users**: Indicates the total number of nonanonymous users that have ever connected to the FTP Server.

## IIS Global Performance Counters

The Object name for the Internet Information Server is Internet Information Services Global. The following is a list of Counters used to monitor the Internet Information Services Global object:

➤ **Cache Flushes**: Indicates the number of times a portion of the memory cache has been expired due to file or directory changes in an Internet Information Services directory tree.

➤ **Cache Hits**: Indicates the total number of times a file open, directory listing, or service-specific objects request was found in the cache.

➤ **Cache Hits %**: Indicates the ratio of cache hits to all cache requests.

➤ **Cache Misses**: Indicates the total number of times a file open, directory listing, or service-specific objects request was not found in the cache.

➤ **Cache Size**: Indicates the configured maximum size of the shared HTTP, FTP, and Gopher memory cache.

➤ **Cache Used**: Indicates the total number of bytes currently containing cached data in the shared memory cache. This includes directory listings, file handle tracking, and service-specific objects.

➤ **Cached File Handles**: Indicates the number of open file handles cached by all of the Internet Information Services.

➤ **Current Blocked Async I/O Requests**: Indicates the current async I/O requests blocked by bandwidth throttler.

➤ **Directory Listings**: Indicates the number of cached directory listings cached by all of the Internet Information Services.

➤ **Measured Async I/O Bandwidth usage**: Indicates the measured bandwidth of async I/O averaged over a minute.

➤ **Objects**: Indicates the number of objects cached by all of the Internet Information Services. These include file handle tracking objects, directory listing objects, and service-specific objects.

➤ **Total Allowed Async I/O Requests**: Indicates the total async I/O requests allowed by bandwidth throttler.

➤ **Total Blocked Async I/O Requests**: Indicates the total async I/O requests blocked by bandwidth throttler.

➤ **Total Rejected Async I/O Requests**: Indicates the total async I/O requests rejected by bandwidth throttler.

See Chapter 11, "Monitoring Server Activity and Performance," for more information.

# Summary

In this chapter you learned about the configuration issues for the FTP Publishing Service. Many advanced configuration concepts required to understand the FTP Publishing Service were discussed.

The configuration procedures discussed in this chapter should suffice for the majority of installation situations. The next chapter discusses configuration of the Gopher Publishing Service.

# Chapter 10

# Configuring the Gopher Publishing Service

The Gopher Publishing Service (GPS), third of the three major service options available for installation in your IIS system, is available for implementation when you want to make collections of files available for searching, browsing, and transfer by remote Gopher clients, such as Archie and VERONICA. The GPS is selected and activated by the IIS installation setup program previously outlined in Chapter 7, "Configuring the WWW Publishing Service."

This chapter will discuss the following:

➤ Understanding the Gopher service

➤ Installing GPS and configuring property sheets

➤ WAIS activation and tag files

➤ Performance monitoring

# Understanding the Gopher Publishing Service

Rather than scanning endlessly through directory listings at innumerable FTP server sites or by indirectly accessing information through Web search engines, many people use Gopher clients to find information on the Internet. Gopher is a reliable, user-friendly, client/server system with distinct advantages over the Web and FTP for finding files on remote systems. Unlike FTP servers, Gopher servers are searchable by keyword. Gopher servers process specified search requests—Boolean-style queries—executed from client workstations and return results in menu-style lists. This makes finding and identifying relevant material for selection efficient and accurate. Gopher performance does not depend upon or vary according to client system platform, graphical capability, or browser make and model—all of which have become major concerns with the upheaval of Web popularity.

The Microsoft Internet Information Server Gopher Publishing Service connects your server system to the international Gopher searching community. It supports all Gopher features, including "Gopher plus" selector strings, which return additional information to the client such as administrator name, modification date, and MIME type.

The Gopher Publishing Service is not limited to searches by Gopher clients alone. Gopher sites can be accessed by Web browsers with a Gopher URL or by a hot link on a Web page. From the viewpoint of access by Web browsers, the GPS resembles and behaves much like the FTP service, and can be used effectively to maintain and publish certain file collections in a more organized manner than those in the FTP directories. As an example, you might amass a large collection of MIDI files in a directory on your FTP service, and find at some point that you need to sort the collection into multiple directories reflecting different types of musical content or different musical artists. In this situation, the GPS is available as an alternative way of organizing and publishing your MIDI file collection. The installation and configuration procedures for the two services are similar, and if you've succeeded with those for the FTP service, you will find those for the Gopher Publishing Service to be simple and straightforward.

# Installing and Configuring the GPS

The Gopher Publishing Service is selected and activated by the Internet Information Server installation setup program previously outlined in Chapter 7, "Configuring the WWW Publishing Service." The installation process creates a Home Directory for the GPS with the default name Inetsrv\Gophroot.

As in the FTP service, collections of files to be published can be sorted into any number of subdirectories under the Home Directory. The names you give these subdirectories, usually using the Explorer, are arbitrary, but you will want them to reflect characteristic subject matter relevant to the file content of each. Directories and files in both FTP and Gopher should be named so as to include as much specific subject-related information as possible. Alphanumeric-only and arcane directory or filenames are rarely user-friendly in FTP or Gopher environments, particularly when the file content is something other than simple readable text.

With the directory tree for your Gopherspace in place and content files moved to the appropriate directories, the next step is to run the IIS Internet Service Manager and complete the four GPS property sheets: Service, Directories, Logging, and Advanced.

Gopherspace is the environment containing Gopher files and directories, similar to a Web site environment on the WWW.

# Service Property Sheet

The Service property sheet, located in the Internet Service Manager, is used to configure the following:

➤ Connection timeouts

➤ Maximum connections

➤ Service administrator

➤ Anonymous connections

➤ Comments

The configuration options of the Service property sheet of the Gopher Publishing Service will be discussed in detail in the following sections.

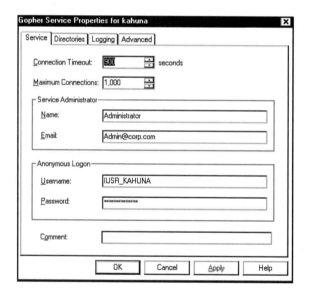

**Figure 10.1:**

The Service property sheet of the Gopher Publishing Service.

## Connection Timeout

The Connection Timeout option sets the length of time (in seconds) for a connection before the server disconnects an inactive user. This is also often referred to as the inactivity timeout. As a guideline, it is recommended that you should not set this number lower than 100 seconds. The default is 900 seconds (15 minutes) for the connection timeout value. The maximum you can set is 32,767 seconds. This value ensures that all connections are closed if the protocol fails to close a connection.

## Maximum Connections

The Maximum Connections option is used to limit the number of simultaneous user connections to the Gopher Publishing Service. If you have limited bandwidth and you have many users transferring files from the Gopher server, you can change the default setting by lowering its value to help control bandwidth usage.

## Service Administrator

The Service Administrator option controls who has administrative access to the Gopher Publishing Service. You must choose a user name and password.

To set user name and password security, do the following:

1.  In Internet Service Manager, double-click the IIS GPS to display its property sheets and then click the Service tab.

2.  In the Anonymous Logon box, type the username and password that you want the service to use when accessing resources on behalf of a client.

    By default *IUSR_computername* is used for anonymous logons. You can also use any valid Windows NT account set up in the Windows NT User Manager.

3.  Click OK.

## Allow Anonymous Connections

By default, only anonymous connections are allowed on the
Gopher Publishing Service. The account name used for anonymous client requests and password must be specified. The
default account user name, in the format IUSR_computername,
is used internally by the Internet Information Server for anonymous logon security. The default account user name is established during the Internet Information Server installation.
All anonymous logons to the service are linked to and use
IUSR_computername as the account user name. To clarify
this issue, when an anonymous user logs on to the GPS server,
the IIS server acknowledges the security restriction information
of the account username.

The password you select for the account user name in the Service
Property Sheet is used internally by the NT Server. This password
is not known or presented by another computer during the
anonymous logon process.

Most often, anonymous GPS users log on using their e-mail
addresses as passwords. Web browsers, such as the Internet
Explorer, are by default configured to present the e-mail address
of the user as the password during an anonymous logon.

When you decide to allow anonymous GPS log ons, you should
still verify that the security permissions for the account user
name are correct. You have the option to keep the default user
name, specify another existing user name, or create a new user
account. With any of these account user names, you must configure its security permissions relevant to your security requirements. Use the User Manager for Domains to configure or verify
security permissions, or refer to Chapter 13, "Server Security
Basics," for more information.

## Comment Option

The Comment option is primarily used for reference purposes
with a simple text description of the service. This comment
will appear in the Report View window of the Internet Service

Manager. For example, on networks with many IIS services, some
system administrators will enter the IP address of the service here
for reference.

# Directories Property Sheet

Within the Directories property sheet, you can configure the
Gopher Home Directory and create virtual directories.

**Figure 10.2:**

The Directories property sheet of the Gopher Publishing Service.

The configuration options of the Directories property sheet of the
Gopher Publishing Service will be discussed in detail in the
following sections.

# Home Directory

During Internet Information Server's installation, a default Home
Directory for the Gopher Publishing Service is created. The
default directory name is \Gophroot. By default, this directory is

actually a subdirectory within the existing IIS directory tree, and is not created in the root of the drive. The actual directory path will appear similar to the following example:

**C:\WINNT\System32\InetSrv\gophroot**

You can change the location of the GPS Home Directory as long as the directory you assign is located on an NTFS drive within your domain.

Assigning a Home Directory is a requirement for the proper operation of the server. The Gopher server will not operate properly without a Home Directory assigned. If you do not assign a Home Directory, all users will be denied access.

When configuring or changing the GPS Home Directory, there is another important option to choose. You must select the type of access permission for the directory. By default, the Home Directory is given Read access permission only. If you want to allow users to be able to transfer files to the Home Directory, you must also select the Write option. It is generally not recommended to enable the Write option for the Home Directory. Only enable the Write option for the Home Directory if you have a specific need.

The Home Directory is perceived as being the root directory of the GPS tree structure. You can create other directories within the Home Directory. By default, other directories and their contents will be available to Gopher client queries.

The following is an example of a GPS Home Directory tree structure:

**C:\WINNT\System32\InetSrv\gophroot**

> **\rockmidi**

> **\jazzmidi**

> **\popmidi**

In the preceding example, the GPS will not allow Gopher clients to gain access to the \InetSrv directory; however, Gopher clients will be able to gain access to the \rockmidi, \jazzmidi, and \popmidi directories within the \Gophroot Home Directory.

You can place your content files into the Home Directory and other subdirectories that you create within the Home Directory. Directories created within the Home Directory can be created to organize your content file collection. By default, the files you place within the Home Directory tree of the GPS will be available to anonymous users.

## Create or Change the GPS Home Directory

The Directory Properties dialog box enables you to change the Home Directory path, if needed. The Home Directory can be located on a local NTFS drive or on an available NTFS network drive within your domain.

To create or change the GPS Home Directory, follow these steps:

1. In the Internet Service Manager, select a Server.

2. Choose the GPS Service for which you want to change the Home Directory.

3. Click the Directories tab.

4. In the Directory list, select the Home directory.

5. Click Edit Properties.

6. In the Directory properties box, type the full directory path, or select a directory by using the Browse button.

7. In the Access box, choose the type of access needed.

8. Click OK.

9. Click Apply.

10. Click OK to return to the main window.

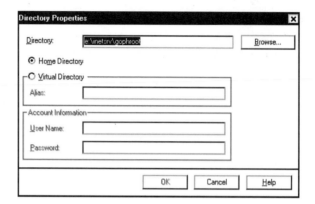

**Figure 10.3:**
The Directory Properties dialog box of GPS.

You can create other directories within the Home Directory. By default, these directories will be both available and visible to Gopher clients. You can create other directories within the Home Directory by using the Explorer.

The following are examples of other directories created within the default Home Directory.

**C:\WINNT\System32\InetSrv\Gophroot\rockmidi**

**C:\WINNT\System32\InetSrv\Gophroot\jazzmidi**

**C:\WINNT\System32\InetSrv\Gophroot\popmidi**

## Virtual Directories

You can also add other directories outside of the Home Directory tree structure. These directories will appear to a user as sub-directories of the Home Directory. These directories are called virtual directories, and can be located elsewhere on your NT Server or on an available NTFS network drive.

For security reasons, you should use NTFS drives to store your Gopher files.

When you configure virtual Gopher directories, you must assign an alias name to the virtual directory. An alias name is a name linked to the actual physical directory. Users can access the physical directory only if they know the alias name. You might want to assign an alias name to a physical directory for security reasons or to simplify the physical directory name.

If you assign virtual directories to network drives, you must specify a user name and password. The user name must have sufficient security permission to access the network directory. Ensure that your security procedures are correct. See Chapter 13, "Server Security Basics," for more information.

# Logging Property Sheet

The Logging Property Sheet allows you to enable, disable, and choose the characteristics of logging.

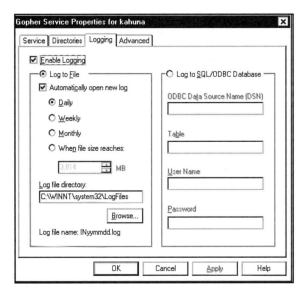

**Figure 10.4:**
The Logging Property Sheet of the Gopher Publishing Service.

The configuration options of the Logging Property Sheet of the Gopher Publishing Service will be discussed in detail in the following sections.

## Logging Property Sheet

The Internet Information Server can log the activity of the Gopher Publishing Service. Enabling logging is recommended. Logs provide important server information, and can be used for security and statistical review. In the end, logs can tell you how your server is being used.

You can choose to have the log data written to a file or to an ODBC database. If you have multiple Internet Information Servers or Services on your network, you can log all of their activity to a single file or database on a specific network computer.

If you want to log Gopher server activity to files, you can specify how often to create new logs and where to log files.

If you want to log the Gopher server activity to an ODBC data source, you must specify the ODBC Data Source Name, table, user name, and password to the database. See Chapter 16, "Database Interfaces," for more information.

# Advanced Property Sheet

The configuration options of the Advanced Property Sheet of the Gopher Publishing Service will be discussed in detail in the following sections.

## Restricting IP Access

The Gopher Publishing Service can be configured to have the Internet Information Server grant or deny access from specified IP addresses. You can use this option to restrict access to your server from a specific computer or from a group of computers.

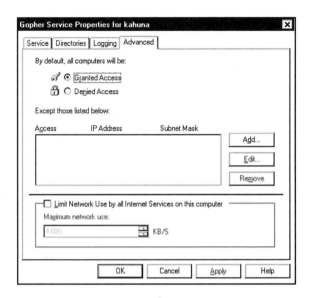

**Figure 10.5:**
The Advanced Property Sheet of the Gopher Publishing Service.

By default, access to the GPS is granted to all IP addresses. You can choose to specify the IP addresses of computers you want to deny access to.

If you want to grant access to only a select number of IP addresses, change this option to deny access to all IP addresses and then specify the IP addresses of computers you want to grant access to.

## Limiting Network Bandwidth

You can limit the outbound network bandwidth used by all of the Internet Information Server Services on your NT Server. This option will control the maximum outbound network bandwidth for your Internet Information Server. If you have limited bandwidth or are running other Internet services on the NT Server, you might want to enable and set this option to conserve bandwidth. See Chapter 11, "Monitoring Server Activity and Performance," for more information.

If you choose to limit the outbound bandwidth used by the Internet Information Server Services, you should be aware of the possible implications:

1. When the actual bandwidth usage remains below the level you set, the read, write, and transfer functions will remain enabled.

2. If the actual bandwidth usage approximates the limit you have set, reads will be temporarily blocked.

3. If the actual bandwidth exceeds the limit you set, reads will be rejected and file transfers will be temporarily blocked.

4. The Internet Information Server will return to normal operation when the bandwidth usage equals or falls below the maximum limit.

## Setting Up WAIS Index Queries

Enabling Wide Area Information Searches (WAIS) on the Gopher Publishing Service makes your Gopherspace searchable by remote Gopher clients.

To enable Wide Area Information Search (WAIS) index searching, you must change the following entry in the Windows NT Registry from 0 (disabled) to 1 (enabled):

**HKEY_LOCAL_MACHINE\SYSTEM**

**\CurrentControlSet**

**\Services**

**\GopherSVC**

**\CheckForWAISDB**

## Tag Files

Tag files are used to add searchable information to listings for content files. This enables you to supplement the standard Gopher display returned to clients with additional information and to provide links to other computers.

All information about a file that is sent to a client comes from tag files. This information includes the name of the file displayed for the client. Typical tag files contain the following:

Display names

Host names

Port numbers

Tag files are hidden files. Use Explorer to set the hidden attribute for tag files.

If you are running Gopher plus, you can add more information to each tag file, such as the server administrator's name and e-mail name, the file's date of creation, and the date of last modification.

## Creating Tag Files

Tags for your Gopher site are created with the command line utility called GDSSET and then stored on the server. To see the complete syntax of the gdsset command, type **gdsset** at the command line with no parameters.

By default, GDSSET is located in the \winnt\system32 directory, and is in your search path. The GDSSET program automatically hides the tag files you create.

To create a tag file, enter the following syntax on the command line:

```
gdsset -c -gn -f "description of file" -a"administrator's
name" -e e-mail filename
```

The following are explanations of command line switches:

➤ **-c:** Use this flag to edit or create a new file.

➤ **-gn:** The value for n can be any single-digit code from 0 to 9. If you omit this flag, the code for the file type will default to 9, binary.

➤ **-a:** "administrator's name"—The value between the quotation marks is the administrator's name. If you omit this flag, the value defaults to the service administrator's name in the Service dialog box of the Microsoft Internet Service Manager.

➤ **-e**: e-mail—This value is the administrator's e-mail address. If you omit this flag, the value defaults to the service administrator's e-mail name in the Service dialog box of the Microsoft Internet Service Manager.

➤ **filename**: This value is the name of the tag file you are creating or editing.

The following is an example of syntax used to create a batch command that tags a series of files that have the same type—a series of text files, for example:

```
for %1 in (*.txt) do <echo %i&& gdsset -c -gn -f %i %I
```

To create a link from your local Gopher site to a directory on another computer, run the gdsset command with the following syntax:

```
gdsset -c -gn -f "file description" -a "administrator's
➥name" -e e-mail -h hostname filename
```

The following are explanations of command line switches:

➤ **-c:** Edits or creates a new file.

➤ **-gn:** The value for n can be any single-digit code from 0 to 9. If you omit this flag, the code for the file type will default to 9, binary. For a list of type codes, see the following section, "Interpreting Item Types."

➤ **-f: "file description"**—This value is a descriptive phrase or string of keywords reflecting the subject matter of the file.

➤ **-a: "administrator's name"**—This is the value between the quotation marks in the administrator's name. If you omit this flag, the value defaults to the service administrator's name in the Service property sheet of the Internet Service Manager.

➤ **-e: e-mail**—This value is the administrator's e-mail address. If you omit this flag, the value defaults to the service administrator's e-mail address in the Service property sheet of the Internet Service Manager.

➤ **-h: hostname filename**—This value specifies the name of the computer to link to, followed by the name of the file for which you want to create a tag file.

Gdsset automatically hides the tag files you create. The following command displays information stored in a tag file:

```
gdsset -r filename
```

To create a batch command to tag a series of files that have the same type, such as a series of text files, use the following syntax:

```
for %i in (*.txt) do <echo %i && gdsset -c -g0 -f %i %I
```

## Naming Tag Files on FAT File Systems

On drives formatted using the FAT file system, the tag filename is appended with **.gtg** and is the same as the file it describes. For example, if the content filename is **Catalog.txt**, then the tag filename would be **Catalog.txt.gtg**. Tag files stored on FAT volumes can be edited using most ASCII-based text editors, such as Notepad. The file may need to be unhidden to edit it.

## Naming Tag Files on NTFS File Systems

On drives formatted using NTFS, the tag filename is appended with **:gtg** and is the same as the file it describes. NTFS tag files are stored in an alternate data stream. For example, if the content filename is **Catalog.txt,** then the tag filename would be **Catalog.txt:gtg**. A colon marks the tag file extension rather than the period used on FAT file systems. Tag files stored on NTFS volumes cannot be edited by most text editors because the file is stored in an alternate data stream.

If your server is configured for NTFS, you must move the tag file manually when you move the corresponding data files. To move the tag file, first make it visible (because tag files are hidden files), then move the file and make it hidden again. You can use File Manager to make files hidden or visible. If disk space is critical, make sure that you include the hidden tag files when you calculate how much space your files will take up.

# Interpreting Item Types

The following table shows all possible Gopher item type codes and what they mean. The first character is the type code.

| Type Code | Definition |
|-----------|------------|
| 0 | A file, usually a flat text file. |
| 1 | Gopher directory. |
| 2 | CSO phone-book server. |
| 3 | An error. |
| 4 | Macintosh file in Binhex format. |
| 5 | MS-DOS binary archive. |
| 6 | UNIX Uuencoded file. |
| 7 | Index-search server. |
| 8 | Telnet session. |
| 9 | Binary file. |
| c | Calendar or calendar of events. |
| g | Graphic interchange file (GIF) graphic. |
| h | HTML World Wide Web hypertext page. |
| I | Inline text that is not an item. |
| I | Another kind of image file. |
| m | BSD format mbox file. |
| P | PDF document. |
| T | TN3270 mainframe session. |
| : | Bitmap image (use Gopher plus information for type of image). |

# Performance Monitor

The Performance Monitor can be used to view real-time statistics, and evaluate the overall operation of the Internet Information Server Services. It can also be used to evaluate and diagnose problems related to the individual Internet Information Server component services.

The Internet Information Server installation loads Windows NT Performance Monitor counters for the Gopher Publishing Service, as well as the FTP Publishing Service, and the World Wide Web Publishing Service.

# Gopher Service Performance Counters

The Object name used in the Performance Monitor for the Gopher Publishing Service is Gopher Service. The following is a list of counters used to monitor the Gopher Service object:

➤ Aborted Connections: Indicates the total number of connections made to the Gopher Server that were aborted due to error or exceeding request limits.

➤ Bytes Received/sec: Indicates the rate that data bytes are received by the Gopher Server.

➤ Bytes Sent/sec: Indicates the rate that data bytes are sent by the Gopher Server.

➤ Bytes Total/sec: Indicates the sum of Bytes Sent/sec and Bytes Received/sec. This is the total rate of bytes transferred by the Gopher Server.

➤ Connection Attempts: Indicates the number of connection attempts that have been made to the Gopher Server.

➤ Connections in Error: Indicates the number of connections that had errors when processed by the Gopher Server.

➤ Current Anonymous Users: Indicates the number of anonymous users currently connected to the Gopher Server.

➤ Current Connections: Indicates the current number of connections to the Gopher Server.

➤ Current NonAnonymous Users: Indicates the number of non-anonymous users currently connected to the Gopher Server.

➤ Directory Listings Sent: Indicates the total number of directory listings sent by the Gopher Server.

➤ Files Sent: Indicates the total number of files sent by the Gopher Server.

➤ Gopher Plus Requests: Indicates the number of Gopher Plus requests received by Gopher Server.

➤ Logon Attempts: Indicates the number of logon attempts that have been made by the Gopher Server.

➤ Maximum Anonymous Users: Indicates the maximum number of anonymous users simultaneously connected to the Gopher Server.

➤ Maximum Connections: Indicates the maximum number of simultaneous connections to the Gopher Server.

➤ Maximum NonAnonymous Users: Indicates the maximum number of non-anonymous users simultaneously connected to the Gopher Server.

➤ Searches Sent: Indicates the total number of searches performed by the Gopher Server.

➤ Total Anonymous Users: Indicates the total number of anonymous users that have ever connected to the Gopher Server.

➤ Total NonAnonymous Users: Indicates the total number of non-anonymous users that have ever connected to the Gopher Server.

## IIS Global Performance Counters

The Object name for the Internet Information Server is Internet Information Services Global. The following is a list of Counters used to monitor the Internet Information Services Global object:

➤ Cache Flushes: Indicates the number of times a portion of the memory cache has been expired due to file or directory changes in an Internet Information Services directory tree.

➤ Cache Hits: Indicates the total number of times a file open, directory listing, or service-specific objects request was found in the cache.

➤ Cache Hits: %: Indicates the ratio of cache hits to all cache requests.

➤ Cache Misses: Indicates the total number of times a file open, directory listing, or service-specific objects request was not found in the cache.

➤ Cache Size: Indicates the configured maximum size of the shared HTTP, FTP, and Gopher memory cache.

➤ Cache Used: Indicates the total number of bytes currently containing cached data in the shared memory cache. This includes directory listings, file handle tracking, and service-specific objects.

➤ Cached File Handles: Indicates the number of open file handles cached by all of the Internet Information Services.

➤ Current Blocked Async I/O Requests: Indicates the current async I/O requests blocked by the bandwidth throttler.

➤ Directory Listings: Indicates the number directory listings cached by all of the Internet Information Services.

➤ Measured Async I/O Bandwidth Usage: Indicates the measured bandwidth of async I/O averaged over a minute.

➤ Objects: Indicates the number of objects cached by all of the Internet Information Services. The objects include file handle tracking objects, directory listing objects, and service-specific objects.

➤ Total Allowed Async I/O Requests: Indicates the total async I/O requests allowed by the bandwidth throttler.

➤ Total Blocked Async I/O Requests: Indicates the total async I/O requests blocked by the bandwidth throttler.

➤ Total Rejected Async I/O Requests: Indicates the total async I/O requests rejected by the bandwidth throttler.

See Chapter 11, "Monitoring Server Activity and Performance," for more information.

## Summary

In this chapter, you learned about the configuration issues and concepts necessary for executing a smooth-running Gopher Publishing Service. The configuration procedures discussed in this chapter should suffice for the majority of installation situations. The next chapter discusses monitoring server activity and performance.

# Part IV

## Managing Internet Information Server

# Chapter 11

# Monitoring Server Activity and Performance

Monitoring the activity and performance of your server is one of your most important jobs. By monitoring the activity on your server, you can learn which documents are being accessed the most and can get an idea of who is visiting your site. Fortunately, performance monitoring your server is easy because IIS can keep a log of all server activity. You can also use Windows NT's included server administration tools to monitor IIS. In this chapter, you will learn how to effectively monitor server activity and performance and how to apply the information you gather to improve the performance of your server.

# Configuring Logging

Part of the process of setting up Internet Information Server involves enabling logging so you can see who has been accessing the server and how often they have been accessing the information stored on it. To configure logging, follow these steps:

1. With the Internet Service Manager open, double-click the service you want to enable logging for (see fig. 11.1).

**Figure 11.1:**

The Microsoft Internet Service Manager window.

2. Click on the Logging tab to display the Logging property sheet (see fig. 11.2).

3. The Enable Logging check box must be selected to start logging. If you ever want to disable logging, you must uncheck it.

You have two options for logging. You can either log to a file or log to an SQL/ODBC Database. Logging to a file is usually better because it enables you to use popular log analyzing features to automatically give you data about your site's activity. However, if it is necessary, it is also just as easy to log in to any ODBC-compliant file. You can use the 32-bit ODBC administrator, located in the the ODBC program group, to configure ODBC data sources (see fig. 11.3).

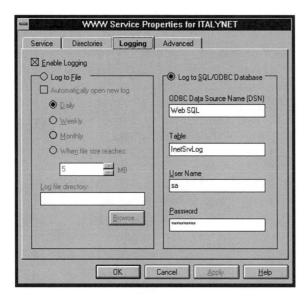

**Figure 11.2:**

Logging panel for the WWW Service.

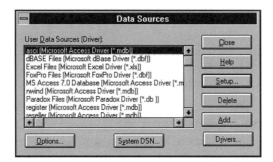

**Figure 11.3:**

The ODBC Data Sources Administrator.

## Logging to Files

To log to a file you must check the Log to File radio button. If your site will be receiving enough traffic that you don't think you will be able to keep track of it all in one large log file, you will want to select the option to Automatically open a new log. Depending on the amount of traffic your site receives, you can have it open a new log daily, weekly, or monthly. Or, for even more control, you can have IIS open a new log file when it reaches a size that you specify. The next thing you must do is choose a directory for log files. At the bottom of the Logging panel is the name IIS will use for the log file. If you are using the same directory for the logging of multiple services, they will log to the same file.

## Logging to SQL/ODBC Databases

If you want to log to an SQL/ODBC database, you should select that option. All you need to do is enter the Data Source Name (DSN), the table, and the user name and password used when logging in to the database. One of the primary benefits of doing this is that you can use any ODBC-compliant application (such as FoxPro or Access) to view the log data. Furthermore, if you need to be able to view the logs on the Web, all you need to do is hook up the database using the Internet Database Connector.

Logging to a database increases the load on the HTTP server. For sites with heavy traffic, it is probably a better idea to log to a file for better performance.

## Reading Log Files

In general, it is not very difficult to decipher the log files generated by IIS. The log files tell you all you need to know, including the IP address of the client, their user name (if one was supplied), the date and time of their connection, the service they were using (such as W3SVC for the Web service), the name of the computer they connected to, and the IP address of the server. You can also get an idea of the activity on the server by looking at the processing time and the bytes sent and received. Additionally, the logs also tell you what operation was being performed (such as accessing a file or entering a password) and what the operation was being performed on.

# Log Analysis Utilities

However, reading straight log files can be time-consuming, especially if they are very large. There are a number of log analyzing tools available. For most purposes, small CGI applets with names such as **"'http- "'http-analyze"'analyze"'http-analyze"** (available at **http://www.netstore.de/Supply/http-analyze/**) can analyze the logs well and give you a good idea of such things as what locations are accessing your site the most, which files are the most popular, how many hits per day a site is receiving, and what times of the day the server is accessed the most. However, some people will opt for more commercial utilities, such as WebTrends (available at **http://www.webtrends.com**), which can create a report from your log file providing the kind of information advertisers would look for, such as demographics, what areas of your site are the most popular, and so forth. These log analyzing utilities are worth a look because they make the job of monitoring server activity much easier.

# Converting Log Files

In order to use the log files Internet Information Server generates, you must convert them to other log formats. To do this, you can use the Convlog.exe program, available in the \Inetserv\Admin directory. Open a command prompt and type **convlog** to see syntax and examples on how to use the Microsoft Internet Log Converter. ConvlogIt will convert to either European MS Windows NT Academic Centre (EMWAC) format or the Common Log File format, both of which are readable by most log analyzers. You need to use convlog because IIS has a new log file format that isn't supported by other utilities yet. However, most utilities for analyzing log files will be updated to support the IIS log file format.

# Monitoring Server Performance with Performance Monitor

The best way to monitor performance is to use NT's included Performance Monitor, available in the Administrative Tools program group. Among other things, it is very helpful in trouble-shooting performance problems. Performance Monitor is especially useful because Internet Information Server comes with a number of counters you can use.

NT's Performance Monitor is best to use for the following reasons:

➤ Flexibility and extensibility.

➤ Provides a number of counters to use.

➤ Monitors the performance of both the computer and the server software at the same time.

## Using Performance Monitor

Performance Monitor enables you to measure the performance of your server. It uses groups of objects to monitor different aspects of your computer, such as its CPU and processes. Each object is associated with counters that let you monitor different aspects of the object. An object represents a different part of the computer, such as the CPU or RAM or server software. Each counter in-cluded with an object helps keep a tally of the number of times a specific event occurred.

Performance Monitor provides a number of options for viewing this information. Its capabilities include charting, alerting, and reporting the current activity on the server, as follows:

➤ The Alert View provides information about events that go over or go under user-defined limits. You can monitor as many conditions as you want at a time. This view is best if you want to focus on specific events occurring that you want to keep track of.

➤ The Chart View enables you to display information graphically, which is good for immediately spotting problems (see fig. 11.6). The Chart View is best if you want a graphical representation of the activity on the site, especially because it is usually quicker to detect a problem this way.

➤ The Log View enables you to send information to a disk file, but this isn't really necessary because IIS provides its own logging (see fig. 11.4). This view is best only if you don't want to use IIS's built-in logging.

➤ The Report View displays a simple text-based report of events you want to display (see fig. 11.5). The Report View is best if you want to have just a no-frills report of what is happening with the server.

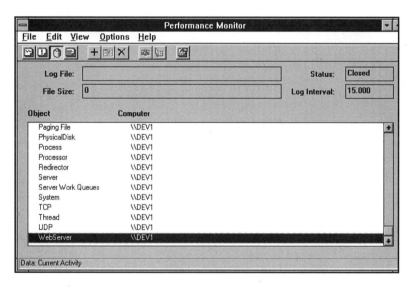

**Figure 11.4:**

Performance Monitor's Log View.

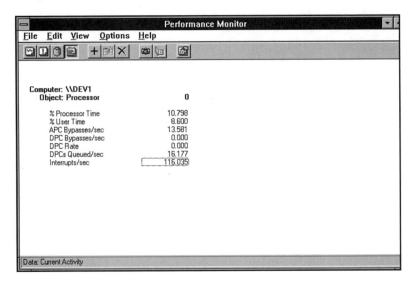

**Figure 11.5:**

Performance Monitor's Report View.

Performance Monitor's toolbar is the same for all four views. The buttons are also used in the same way (that is, the Delete button is used in all views to delete an element).

➤ The plus sign button enables you to add items to be monitored.

➤ The next button, a pencil erase, enables you to edit the values for the parameters you have already entered.

➤ The X button is used to remove elements.

➤ The camera button, referred to as the Update Now button, is used to let Windows NT know that you want to start monitoring immediately. This can also be done by selecting Options, Update Now from the Options menu.

➤ If you want to change the method used to update the display, select either Periodic or Manual Updating from the Options menu. If you select Periodic Updating, you will need to enter a value for the frequency of the updates.

➤ If you want to bookmark the current place where activity is being monitored, you can click on the button with the opened book on it. If a specific event occurs that you want to be able to get back to quickly without having to remember when it occurred, it is best to use a bookmark.

➤ The last button, which looks like a piece of paper, enables you to look at the options for the monitor.

To start monitoring performance, launch Performance Monitor. Go to the View menu and select Add to Chart. This will bring up the Add to Chart dialog box (see fig. 11.6).

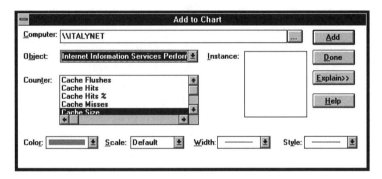

### Figure 11.6:
Performance Monitor's Add to Chart dialog box.

The name of the computer you want to monitor appears in the Computer field. Select the object that contains the counters you want to add. For the Object pop-up menu, you should select the Object that contains the counters you want to add. An Object is meant to represent a group of counters. The IIS object represents all the counters you can use to monitor IIS.

Before you start monitoring the performance of IIS, you should start monitoring the performance of the computer itself. You can use Performance Monitor to see how much load is being placed on the available resources, which include the microprocessor, memory, hard disk, and networking hardware. You should see what the load is on these resources. If you have your server hooked up and people are connecting to it, it is usually a bad sign if the processor, disk drives, and so forth are already close to being overloaded. Read "Improving Performance" later in this chapter to find information on improving performance.

## Monitoring Current Activity

To monitor the current activity of the site, you must first launch Performance Monitor. You can use any combination of the Chart, Alert, Log, and Report views to monitor performance.

1. With Performance Monitor open, choose a new settings file from the File menu.

2. From the Edit menu, choose Edit, the Add To Menu item. This will bring up a dialog box where you can select the objects and counters you want to use. To select multiple counters, just press and hold down the Shift key and drag to select items that are grouped together. Press and hold the Ctrl key to select items that aren't grouped together. Click the Add button to add counters and the Done button when you are finished (refer to fig. 11.5).

3. You can switch from Chart, Alert, Log, and Report views from the View menu. One technique is to create multiple windows and view the different views at once. You can either save individual views or more than one window by saving the Workspace from the File menu.

## Setting Alerts in Performance Monitor

One of the good things about Performance Monitor is that you can enable alerts to automatically inform you if a counter reaches a certain value that you want to be notified about. For example, you might want to be alerted if the number of hits to the server reaches 100,000. This frees you up from having to continually monitor performance all the time. You can do all this from the Alert View (see fig. 11.7).

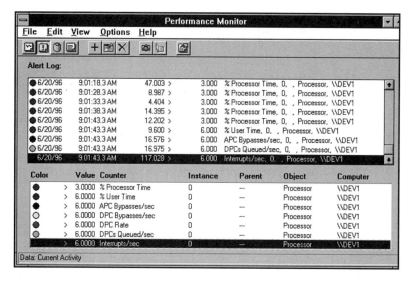

**Figure 11.7:**

Performance Monitor's Alert View.

This is how to add a counter to the Alert View:

1. First, choose Alert from the View menu.

2. Choose New Alert Settings from the File menu.

3. Choose Add to Alert from the Edit menu.

The Add to Alert dialog box appears (see fig. 11.8).

4. Choose the objects and counters you want to use and then click the Add button.

5. In the Alert If box, select either Over or Under and add a value. For example, if you wanted to be alerted every time a counter went over 6, for example, you would select Over and enter 6 in the field.

Now, whenever a counter reaches a point you specified you will be alerted.

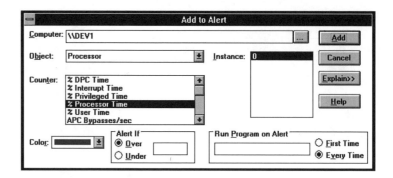

**Figure 11.8:**
The Add to Alert Dialog Box.

# Using IIS Counters to Interpret Traffic to the Site

IIS includes Objects for Internet Information Server, FTP server, Gopher server, and HTTP server. Highlight a counter you want to include and add it by clicking on Add. Once you have found a counter you want to add, click Add while it is highlighted and it will be automatically added. After you have added the counters you want to use, click on Done. Now you will see a representation of the activity for each of the counters you selected, all of which are color-coded (see fig. 11.9).

Following are explanations of every counter included with Internet Information Server. For the counters that represent the total number of something, it is important to note that it is only the total number since the service was started. If you had stopped the server and then started again, the Total counters will only show the latest numbers.

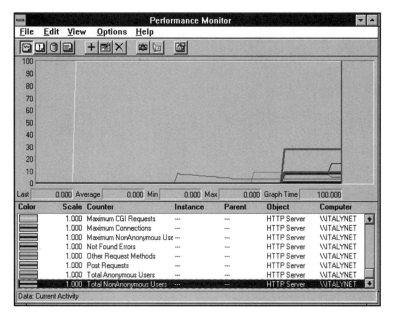

**Figure 11.9:**
Performance Monitor with the included IIS counters.

# The Internet Information Server Object

The IIS Object contains counters that enable you to monitor the performance of Internet Information Server. These counters are for monitoring all-purpose aspects of IIS, as shown in the following list:

➤ **Cache Hits:** Indicates how many times a request for a file directory listing or object was found in the cache. This is important because it gives you an idea of how often the same files that are already being stored in the cache are being requested.

➤ **Cache Misses:** Indicates how many times a request for something was not found in the cache.

➤ **Cache Hits %:** Indicates the number of cache hits related to the entire number of cache requests. If this is a low number, it means that a number of the files being requested are not currently in the cache, which could be one reason for a particularly slow server.

➤ **Cache Size:** Indicates the configured size is for the memory cache, which is shared by the HTTP, FTP, and Gopher servers.

➤ **Cache Used:** Indicates how many bytes of the cache are currently being used.

➤ **Cached File Handles:** Indicates the total number of file handles cached by Internet Information Server.

➤ **Current Blocked Async I/O Requests:** Indicates how many asynchronous I/O requests are currently being blocked by bandwidth throttling. If this number is a high value it is a good indication that you need a connection capable of handling more throughput. Bandwidth throttling is something you can control so that you can ensure that performance of the server is good. However, if a lot of requests are being blocked, then you really should look into getting more bandwidth for the server.

Bandwidth throttling is the name for the process in which requests for additional bandwidth are denied when a specified amount of bandwidth is being used.

➤ **Directory Listings:** Indicates how many directory listings are cached.

➤ **Measured Async I/O Bandwidth Usage:** Indicates the average indication of bandwidth in bytes over one minute of I/O.

➤ **Objects:** Indicates the total number of objects being cached by IIS. This includes file handle tracking, directory listing, and service-specific objects.

➤ **Total Allowed Async I/O Requests:** Indicates the total number of requests allowed.

➤ **Total Blocked Async I/O Requests:** Indicates the total number of blocked requests. Again, if this is a high number it is a good indication that you need to move to a faster connection.

# The FTP Server Object

You will see each of these counters when you select the FTP Server Object in the Performance Monitor.

➤ **Bytes Received/sec:** Indicates the rate that the FTP server receives data in bytes.

➤ **Bytes Sent/sec:** Indicates the rate that the FTP server sends data. This is particularly important if your FTP server is one of your major services.

➤ **Bytes Total/sec:** Indicates the rate that the FTP server transfers data.

➤ **Connection Attempts:** The total number of times connections have been attempted to the FTP server. This number is one good indication of how much your FTP server is being used.

➤ **Current Anonymous Users:** Indicates the current number of connected users using the Anonymous login account. If you have opted to disable the Anonymous login, this counter isn't necessary.

➤ **Current Connections:** Indicates the current number of connections to your FTP server.

➤ **Current Non-anonymous Users:** Indicates the current number of users connected using specific accounts other than the Anonymous account.

➤ **Files Received:** Indicates the total number of files received by the FTP server.

➤ **Files Sent:** Indicates the total number of files requested and sent by the FTP server. This is also a good way to see how much the FTP server is being used.

➤ **Logon Attempts:** Indicates the total number of attempts made to log on to the FTP server.

➤ **Maximum Anonymous Users:** Indicates the highest number of concurrent connections by anonymous users. If you have already set a maximum, this counter will reflect that. For example, if you have set a limit of 100 anonymous users, this counter won't go over 100.

➤ **Maximum Connections:** Indicates the highest number of concurrent connections by all users at one time. Depending on the amount of bandwidth available this could be a very large number or a very small number.

➤ **Maximum Non-anonymous Connections:** Indicates the largest number of concurrent non-anonymous users.

➤ **Total Anonymous Users:** Indicates the total number of anonymous users who have connected to the FTP server.

➤ **Total Non-anonymous Users:** Indicates the total number of non-anonymous users who have connected to the FTP server.

## The Gopher Server Object

You will see these counters when you select the Gopher Server Object in the Performance Monitor.

➤ **Aborted Connections:** Indicates the total number of terminated connections. You should pay close attention to this counter because these connections are usually aborted because of an error or too many requests being made to the Gopher server.

➤ **Bytes Received/sec:** Indicates the rate at which data is received.

➤ **Bytes Sent/sec:** Indicates the rate at which data is sent.

➤ **Bytes Total/sec:** Indicates the rate at which data is being sent and received.

➤ **Connection Attempts:** Indicates the total number of attempted connections to the Gopher server.

➤ **Connections in Error:** Indicates the total number of connections that produced errors when the Gopher server processed them. If this number is a high value, it is a good indication that something is wrong with the Gopher server.

➤ **Current Anonymous Users:** Indicates the current number of people connected to the Gopher server anonymously.

➤ **Current Connections:** Indicates the number of connections by both anonymous and non-anonymous users.

➤ **Current Non-anonymous Users:** Indicates the current number of users who are using accounts other than the anonymous accounts.

➤ **Directory Listings Sent:** Because the Gopher server's activity consists largely of sending directory listings, this counter provides a good indication of the usage of the Gopher service.

➤ **Files Sent:** The Gopher server's activity also consists of sending files. This counter, in conjunction with Directory Listings Sent, provides a good indication of the activity.

➤ **Gopher Plus Requests:** Indicates the number of requests for Gopher Plus-related services. Because most people don't use Gopher Plus, this number will probably be fairly small. Gopher Plus is an enhanced version of Gopher, but it never got time to catch on because most people were already switching to the Web.

➤ **Logon Attempts:** Indicates the total number of attempts to log on recorded by the Gopher server.

➤ **Maximum Anonymous Users:** Indicates the maximum amount of anonymous users connected at one time.

➤ **Maximum Connections:** Indicates the maximum amount of all users allowed to connected at one time. If your Gopher server is popular, this will be an especially good indication of how much the Gopher server can handle.

➤ **Maximum Non-anonymous Users:** Indicates the largest amount of non-anonymous users ever connected at one time.

➤ **Searches Sent:** Indicates the number of searches that the Gopher server performed.

➤ **Total Anonymous Users:** Indicates the total number of anonymous users, another good indication of the popularity of your Gopher service.

➤ **Total Non-anonymous Users:** Indicates the total number of non-anonymous users to the Gopher server in the given time span.

## The HTTP Server Object

You will see these options when you select the HTTP Server Object in Performance Monitor.

➤ **Bytes Received/sec:** Indicates the rate at which the HTTP server receives data.

➤ **Bytes Sent/sec:** Indicates the rate at which data is sent by the HTTP server.

➤ **Bytes Total/sec:** Indicates the rate at which the HTTP server sends and receives data.

➤ **CGI Requests:** Indicates the number of times a CGI script has been requested to be executed. Because CGI executable files take more processor time than simple HTML files, a large number of CGI requests can seriously affect the performance of the server. CGI scripts affect performance because they require the CPU to execute the application. It is OK if the site isn't busy, but if you are running a busy site with CGI, you will want to have a Pentium or Pentium Pro for a server.

➤ **Connection Attempts:** Indicates the number of times a connection has been attempted to the HTTP server.

➤ **Connections/sec:** Indicates how many connections per second the server is receiving. This is one of the essential counters in telling how busy the server is.

➤ **Current Anonymous Users:** Indicates the current total of anonymous logons to the HTTP server.

➤ **Current Non-anonymous Users:** There normally won't be any non-anonymous users unless you have implemented some form of authentication in which you require an account to access your site.

➤ **Current CGI Requests:** Indicates the sum of current CGI requests to the HTTP server.

➤ **Current Connections:** Indicates the current number of anonymous and non-anonymous users. This number shouldn't be different from the current number of anonymous users alone unless you have some method of authentication set up, in which case you would want to keep track of non-anonymous users.

➤ **Current ISAPI Extensions Requests:** Indicates the current number of ISAPI extension requests that the HTTP server is processing. Like CGI requests, this number can also affect the performance of the server. These are custom DLLs, which can be installed to add services such as form processing.

➤ **Files Received:** Indicates the total number of files the HTTP server has received. This should be a small number because the server shouldn't be receiving too many files, unless you have implemented extra services, such as cookies, where the server would be requesting data from the computer connecting to it.

➤ **Files Sent:** Indicates the total number of files sent from the HTTP server. This is a good indication of the traffic on your site.

➤ **Files Total:** Indicates the total number of files sent and received.

➤ **Get Requests:** This keeps tracks of GET requests sent to the server. This is especially good to monitor If you use imagemaps and forms.

➤ **Head Requests:** Indicates the total number of "HEAD" requests received by the server. This is usually an indication that a client is trying to see what the state of a document is (such as its last modification date) to see if it needs to be refreshed.

➤ **ISAPI Extension Requests:** Indicates the total number of requests for ISAPI Extensions received by the HTTP server.

➤ **Logon Attempts:** This counter doesn't usually matter unless you need to keep track of logons (such as in the case of an intranet or a site that requires a logon by a non-anonymous user account).

➤ **Maximum Anonymous Users:** Indicates the largest number of anonymous users ever connected at one time. This number won't be that big because the HTTP server doesn't usually leave a user connected for that long. If this number is large, it might indicate a problem with both performance and the HTTP server itself.

➤ **Maximum Connections:** Indicates the largest number of connections allowed to the HTTP server at one time. Again, if this number is particularly large, it indicates that there is either a problem or that the site is very busy.

➤ **Not Found Errors:** Indicates the number of times the server responds with a Not Found Error after someone requests a document. If this number is high, you should check to make sure that all the links on your own system are working. You should then try to check to see if some other site is linking to a non-existent file on your server.

➤ **Other Request Methods:** Indicates the number of requests for other methods, such as PUT, DELETE, and LINK. These are usually rare though, and this number should be small.

➤ **Post Requests:** Indicates the total number of POST requests, usually used by forms.

➤ **Total Anonymous Users:** Indicates the total number of anonymous users. For most sites this is a good indication of the total number of hits.

➤ **Total Non-anonymous Users:** This is a good counter if you have areas that require authentication. It can give you a good idea of how much these areas are being used.

# Improving Performance

After you have started monitoring the activity and performance, you will discover that your server might not be performing as well as it should be. One of the most important jobs of an administrator is tuning and improving the performance of the server and the computer it is running on.

# CPU Performance Tuning

The first thing you should do is try to tune the CPU. It is difficult to tune the CPU to its maximum performance, but you can use Performance Monitor to see if the CPU is being maxed out, and then take steps to fix this problem. In most cases you could simply run some applications on another machine, but for the best performance, you should try to avoid using the server machine for anything other than running IIS. Usually, the best thing to do to improve CPU performance is to install a faster processor. For example, if you are currently running NT with a 486/66 and 12 MB of RAM, you will be able to improve performance dramatically by switching the CPU with a Pentium or Pentium Pro. Adding some more RAM can't hurt either.

You can use Performance Monitor to see how the CPU is doing. You should pay close attention to the % Total Processor Time counter. This is the total percentage of time the CPU is spending doing work necessary to your server. If this number is close to 100 percent, it is a good indication that the CPU is limiting the server. Unless you switch to a faster processor, NT will be forced to slow down to handle the server (see fig. 11.10).

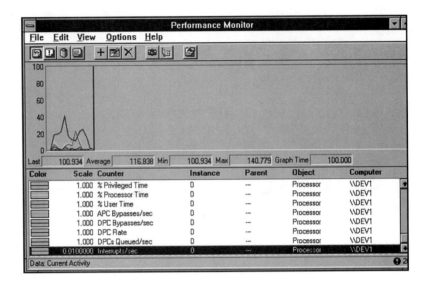

**Figure 11.10:**

Performance Monitor monitoring the CPU.

# Memory Performance Tuning

It is also good to keep an eye on memory, using the Memory Object. By using the Pool Nonpaged Bytes counter, which can be accessed in the Memory Object, you can get a good idea of the number of bytes in nonpaged memory. Nonpaged memory is memory that cannot be moved to virtual memory. Essentially, it is the total amount of RAM that must remain in physical memory. Performance will suffer if this number gets within 4 megabytes of the total amount of memory. For example, if you have a machine with 24 megs of RAM, the amount of nonpaged memory should not get within 20 megs. If it does, NT will begin to swap memory frequently, dramatically slowing down the computer (see fig. 11.11). In a worst-case scenario, NT will swap memory constantly and the server will come crashing to a halt until you fix the page file.

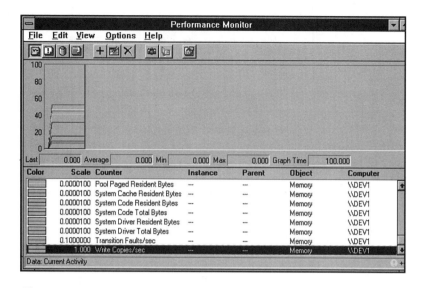

**Figure 11.11:**

Performance Monitor monitoring memory.

You can also use the Commit Available Bytes, Committed Bytes, and Commit Limit counters together to get an idea of the state of the virtual memory management subsystem. The Commit Available Bytes counter indicates the amount of available virtual memory. Unfortunately, it doesn't indicate the total amount of memory available reliably. To do that, you use the Committed Bytes counter to indicate the total amount of virtual memory that must be available. The Commit Limit is the total amount of space that can be committed, and is roughly equal to the amount of physical memory plus the size of the page file. You should watch this to see if the Committed Bytes counter gets close to the same amount as the Commit Limit. When these numbers converge, virtual memory is running out, and you must manually increase the size of the page file. Doing this helps to avoid performance problems. Now that you know how to add alerts, you can add alerts whenever the Committed Bytes size gets to a point close to the Commit Limit. You then can have it alert you when it does, letting you know when you need to expand the page file (see fig. 11.12). All of these counters can be accessed in the Memory Object.

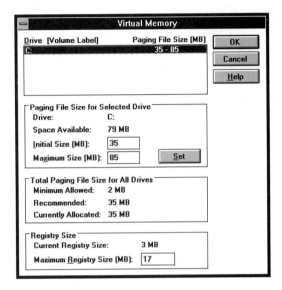

**Figure 11.12:**
Changing the size of the page file in the Virtual Memory settings.

# Network Performance Tuning

After you have identified and overcome system bottlenecks, you need to move on to improving network performance. The performance of the network is probably the most important thing, especially if all the machine is being used for is Internet Information Server. The chances are good that there could be networking problems that are hampering performance more than anything else. Again, it is best to use Protocol Analyzers. You should use the Internet Information Server counters, as well as the counters for other parts of the computer, to analyze performance. For example, the Bytes Total/sec. represents the total transfer of data in bytes. By looking at the IIS counters, you can usually spot potential problems. If the Bytes Total/sec. number is very low, it means that it isn't transferring data at a reliable rate.

You can also look at the Redirector object. The Redirector is a software component that determines when data transfers should be handled by local resources and when they should be handled over the network. This is one of the best places to look for potential network bottlenecks (see fig. 11.13).

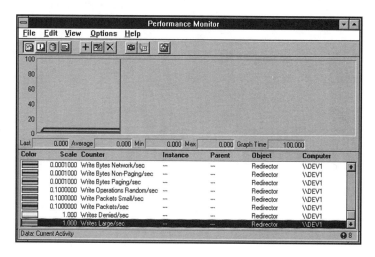

**Figure 11.13:**
Performance Monitor with Redirector object.

# Using Counters for Performance Tuning

The first counter to look at is the Redirect Current Commands counter. This tells how many commands are queued. If this number ever gets higher than one per network card and stays there, then that usually indicates that there is a bottleneck in the Redirector component itself. More likely there is a problem in the network hardware. If the network itself is slow, or you're getting slow response to a server, then it is likely that the Redirector is becoming a bottleneck. If this is the case, you need to go into the Registry and increase the Maximum Number of Commands in the HKEY_LOCAL_MACHINE/SYSTEM/Current ControlSet/ Services/LanmanWorkstations/Parameters sections. The default is 50. It can be raised to as high as 255, and should be if the Current Commands Counter is at least 5 (see fig 11.14). However, a better solution would be to try to determine why the commands are being queued. Usually it is because the network is bogged down, or the server performance is slow. If that is the case, you need to check these out. You can run diagnostic tests and try to access data from another computer on the network to see how well it is performing. If performance is inadequate, you need to check the connection and network adapter card.

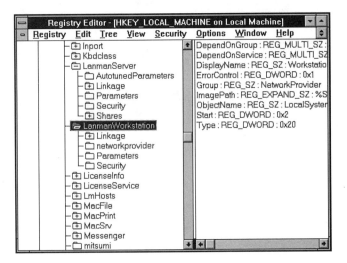

**Figure 11.14:**
Increasing MaximumNumberofCommands in RegEdit.

# Limiting Network Use for Performance Tuning

Internet Information Server also provides a way to improve performance by limiting network use. To do this, click on any service in the Internet Service Manager. Click on the Advanced tab to go to the Advanced panel. Select Limit Network Use by all Internet Services on this computer (see fig. 11.15). You can try different settings. Adjusting these settings gives you control over a technique called bandwidth throttling. A good place to start is 4,096 KB/sec. Bandwidth throttling is the term used to describe the process of limiting the amount of data that can be transferred per second. By limiting the amount of network resources available, requests will be refused until the traffic subsides. This might irritate some users, but it is better than having the entire server get bogged down. You should check the Blocked Requests counter. If that number is high, it is an indication that your server is getting overloaded too often and needs more bandwidth.

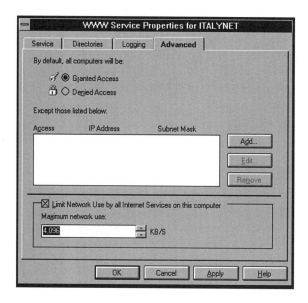

**Figure 11.15:**

Advanced Panel of Internet Service Manager.

# Summary

Now you should be able to effectively monitor the activity and performance of your site. You should make a habit of setting up alerts and keeping an eye on the server. It might seem like it takes too much time, but preventative maintenance is always better than having to make emergency repairs. One of your most important duties will be keeping track of how the server is performing, and constantly tuning it to perform as close to its full potential as possible.

# Chapter 12

# Site Administration Utilities

After you have installed Internet Information Server, you can use the Internet Service Manager and various components of Windows NT to further configure and administrate your site.

## Administration Using Internet Service Manager

You can use Internet Service Manager to further configure your server. It makes it easy to monitor all the Internet services running on any Windows NT Server on the network. Internet Service Manager provides a Report view, a Server view, and a Services view. You can quickly switch among these views by selecting them from the View menu (see fig. 12.1).

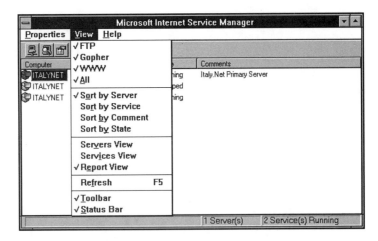

**Figure 12.1:**
Selecting views in Internet Service Manager.

# Report View

The Report View is the view you see by default when you open up
Internet Service Manager (see fig. 12.2).

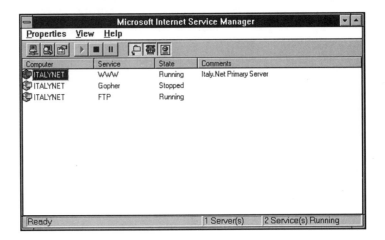

**Figure 12.2:**
Report View of Internet Service Manager.

This view lists the computers and which Internet services they are running. In figure 12.2, there is one computer with three services. The state column indicates that the WWW service is running, the Gopher service is stopped, and the FTP service is running. You can easily use the Internet Service Manager to control these servers. The button bar at the top provides access to the commands you will need to use, which are also available from the menu bar. The first button of the toolbar enables you to connect to the selected Internet server. The second button automatically finds all servers on the network (see fig. 12.3). These servers are any other computers that are hooked up to the network. The third button displays property sheets to configure the service that is selected (which can also be done by double-clicking the service). The fourth button starts the selected service (only available only if the selected service is either stopped or paused). The fifth button stops the selected service and the sixth button pauses the selected service. The seventh button displays the FTP service in the main window, the eighth button displays the Gopher service in the main window, and the ninth button displays the WWW service in the main window. At the bottom of the window you can get a quick summary of the current status of the servers (for example, 1 Server, 2 Services Running).

**Figure 12.3:**

Finding all servers connected to the network.

# Servers and Services View

The Servers View simply displays the services running on the network referenced by computer name. This is mainly useful if you have multiple computers running IIS on the network. Clicking the Plus symbol next to a computer name will show which services it is running. The Services View organizes the list by Service, and shows which computers on the network are running each service.

# Property Sheets

When you double-click on a service, it displays the property sheets for that service. You can use these property sheets to configure Internet Information Server's more advanced features.

## Service Property Sheet

The Service Property Sheet (see fig. 12.4) is used to specify who has access to the server. You can choose which account will be used for anonymous requests to log on. To allow anonymous logons you should fill in a username and password, and select Allow Anonymous. The Password Authentication section is used for security purposes, which are covered more in-depth in Chapter 14, "Security Utilities and Testing." You will want to allow anonymous logons for most public sites simply because that is the standard practice for most Web sites on the Internet.

## Directories Property Sheet

The Directories Property Sheet (see fig. 12.5) lists the directories on networked computers available to users. The Alias column lets you select an Alias to use for the Internet address. For example, if the site's URL was **http://www.foobar.com**, you could set the alias for the C:\Admin directory to be /admin, which would be accessed over HTTP by **http://www.foobar.com/ admin**. The address column lists the IP address that the directory can be accessed from.

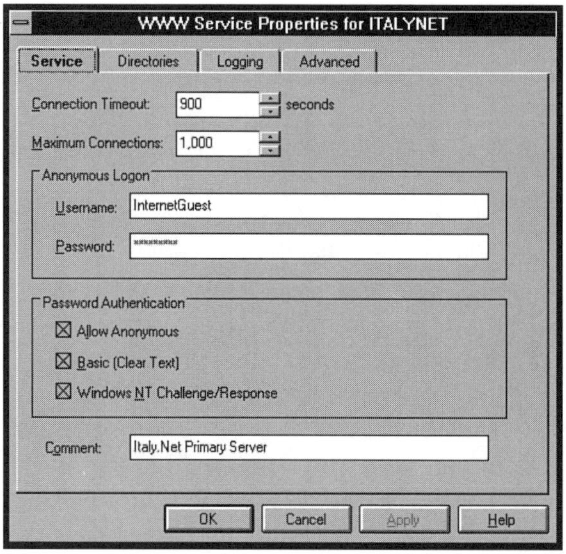

**Figure 12.4:**

The Services Property Sheet.

**Figure 12.5:**

The Directories Property Sheet.

You can use the Enable Default Document setting to specify which file will be used if a user doesn't specify the specific file that they want when they access your Web site. For example, if C:\www\foobar has the URL of **http://www.foobar.com**, when someone enters that URL, they will need to have a default file. The Internet Information Server standard states that the name of this file be Default.htm. However, it is more common that most index files are usually called index.htm or index.html. Assuming you choose Default.htm, that means that whenever someone requests **http://www.foobar.com**, IIS will look for the file Default.htm in the C:\www\foobar directory and serve it automatically. If IIS doesn't find a Default.htm file, it will instead serve an HTML Directory Listing of the contents of C:\www\foobar. If you want information to be served in this way, you can also choose to Enable Directory Browsing, which will let people browse the site using the Directory Listings, much like they would browse a Gopher site.

Default files are usually good to use because they make sure that only the files that people make links to are accessible. Directory indexes are only good if you want people to be able to see every file on your server (which you usually won't).

To change the properties of a directory, highlight the directory you want to edit and click Edit Properties. By default, Internet Information Server provides directories called \Wwwroot, \Gophroot, and \Ftproot as home directories for the three different servers. You can make any directory a home directory by selecting Home Directory in its Directory Properties. Otherwise, you can select Virtual Directory. A virtual directory appears as a subdirectory of the home directory. This is useful if you want to have many different directories appear under one home directory. All you need to do is specify the path (and drive if it is on another drive or a network drive) and the Alias for it. For example, if you make the alias **foo** it will appear as **http://www.foobar.com/foo**. If you choose to use a network drive as a virtual directory, you need to provide a username and password to log in to the drive. If you want to make a drive a virtual server, you need to select that option and specify an IP address for it. For access, you can allow people to read and/or execute files. You will need to set it to execute files if you want to run things like CGI. You can also provide secure transfers by requiring a secure SSL channel. For more information on this, refer to Chapter 8, "Multihoming: Creating Multiple Domains." A home directory is used for a specific IP address. A Virtual Directory is a directory that points to somewhere else on the computer.

## Logging Properties Sheet

The Logging Properties Sheet allows you to enable logging either to a file or to an SQL/ODBC database (see fig. 12.6). This property sheet is covered more in-depth in Chapter 11, "Monitoring Server Activity and Performance."

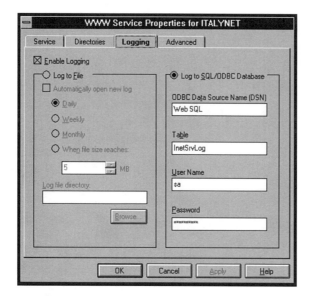

**Figure 12.6:**

The Logging Properties Sheet.

## Advanced Properties Sheet

The Advanced Properties Sheet (see fig. 12.7), is used to configure advanced options,. This allows you to specify whether all computers will be granted or denied access. For control, you can add specific computers to the list by clicking the Add button. You can choose whether a specific computer's access will be Granted or Denied. For an open system, you can make the default ensuring that all computers are granted access. You should only deny access if the server is private or should be accessible only to specific computers. All you need to do is specify the IP address for the computer you want to grant or deny access to. In a low-security environment you would want to automatically grant access to all computers. Usually it is better to handle security issues on a case by case basis. The only reason to do otherwise is if you only want a few computers to be able to access something.

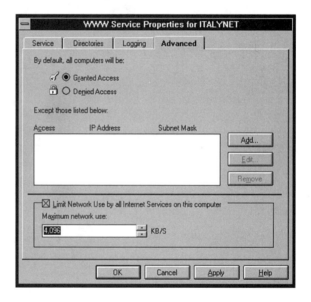

**Figure 12.7:**
The Advanced Properties Sheet.

The "Limit Network Use by all Internet Services on this computer" option gives you control over a technique called *bandwidth throttling,* which lets you specify exactly how much bandwidth is allowed for the Internet services. This is something you should do if you have limited bandwidth and want to ensure the performance of the computer.

# Administration Using Windows NT

One of the best things about Internet Information Server is its integration with Windows NT. As you saw in Chapter 11, "Monitoring Server Activity and Performance," Internet Information Server lets you use Performance Monitor to oversee monitor performance and activity. The following text will explain how to use other features of NT to help in administrating Internet Information Server.

This section covers:

➤ The Network Control Panel

➤ TCP-IP and Networking Bindings

➤ The Services Control Panel

➤ The Server Control Panel

➤ The User Manager for Domains

# Network Control Panel

The Network Control Panel (see fig. 12.8) is useful for adding Network Software, changing the name of the computer, and changing the domain name. To launch it, double-click Control Panels, located in the Main program group, and then double-click on the Network Control Panel.

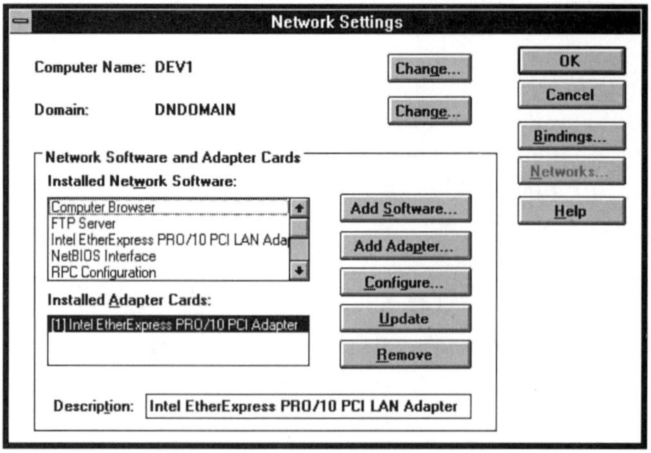

**Figure 12.8:**

The Network Control Panel.

You can use this control panel to configure the TCP/IP settings. To do this, double-click the TCP/IP Protocol in the Installed Network Software listing. This brings up the TCP/IP Configuration dialog box. From the TCP/IP Configuration dialog box you can also configure the DNS settings. The TCP/IP and DNS settings are vital to ensuring that your server works properly on the Internet.

## Changing Computer Names

One thing that you might have to do is change the name of the computer. To change the name of the computer, click the Change button next to the computer name. Rename the computer using the dialog box that appears. You must make sure that you don't give the computer the same name as another computer on the network. You might need to change the computer name if it is necessary for identifying it, or if someone else wants the computer to have a specific name on the network.

# Changing Domain Names

Changing the Domain name is a little more tricky. To do this you have to re-enter the domain name on each server and workstation that is part of the domain.

You should make sure that the domains are already set up correctly because you can't move a server from one domain to another without reinstalling Windows NT on that machine. Furthermore, you can't make two domains one merged domain without reinstalling NT on all of them. Also, it is usually not a good idea to mess around with domain names unless you are willing to put a lot of work into it. The benefit of merging domains is simply that it enables you to manage things a little more easily, especially when using a tool like User Manager for Domains.

# Installing Network Software

You normally shouldn't have to install any new network software, but it may be necessary if you add new hardware, such as an adapter card, to your server. Here is how to add new network software:

1. With the Network Settings control panel open, click the Add Software button. A dialog box appears with a list of available components.

2. A dialog box will appear with a list of available components. Select the component you want to install and click the Continue button. If the component isn't available, but you have a disk, click the Other button. Follow the instructions to either insert a disk or enter the path name for where the component can be found on a disk.

Be aware that you might be asked for Windows NT Installation disks. You should have them ready at all times.

After you have made the changes, you will be required to restart the computer.

## Network Bindings

Another thing you can do with the Network control panel is show the Bindings for the various installed components (see fig. 12.9). The network is made up of many different layers that consist of software that do things for the other pieces of software ahead of it and behind it in the layer. The normal configuration is such that all network components are bound to make sure they are being used. However, you can choose to disconnect (or unbind) something like a network adapter card if it isn't being used. This will free up some memory and might also help to troubleshoot problems.

Network Bindings show the services and software connected to the different hardware items of your server.

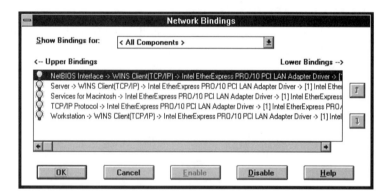

**Figure 12.9:**
The Network Bindings dialog box.

# Services Control Panel

The Services control panel is used to start, stop, and pause the WWW, Gopher, and FTP Publishing services (see fig. 12.10). This can also be done directly from the Internet Service Manager. One of the things you can do is select a service and click the Startup button. This enables the service to start up automatically. If you don't want the service to start up automatically, then you can set it to manual. If you want to, you can also override the account set up in the Internet Service Manager, but this usually isn't a good idea. The Services applet is useful because it not only gives you a quick way to see the status of your Internet services, it displays the status of the services, which might help in finding a problem.

It is useful to be able to start, pause, and stop the services quickly and easily in case you need to test a piece of software or reboot. Using these controls is safer than just shutting the computer down with the services still running.

In this case, the word applet refers to a small NT application that serves a specific purpose. The concept of applets has been made more popular with the Internet, as people design specific applets to do various tasks, programmed in languages like Java, or to run on the client computer as an NT app.

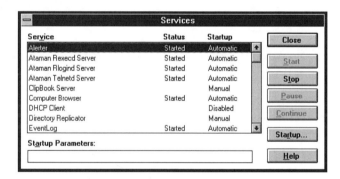

**Figure 12.10:**
The Services control panel.

# The Server Control Panel

The Server control panel provides a quick glance at the current connections to your computer and the resources being used (see fig. 12.11). This control panel is useful if you want to keep track of who is using your computer, and how they are using it. For example, you might be able to use this control panel to see that a lot of people are connecting to access a specific document, which could serve as an indication that you might want to move that file to another server to help offset the load being caused by all the users connecting.

➤ The Sessions item indicates the number of people are who are currently connected to your computer.

➤ The Open Files item tells how many shared resources are currently open.

➤ The File Locks and Open Named Pipes indicate how many file locks and named pipes are currently on the computers.

You can further administer the site by choosing the buttons at the bottom of the Server control panel.

➤ The Users button enables you to see a list of all the users who are currently connected. If it is necessary, you can quickly disconnect one or more users. For example, if you were about to take the server down, you might want to disconnect any connected users first. You will be able to see the time they have been connected, how many resources they have open, and if they are a Guest or not.

➤ The Shares buttons enables you to see a list of the shared resources, and the users connected to them. Again, you can disconnect users here as well.

➤ The In Use buttons provides a list of the resources currently in use, and enables you to close them.

➤ The Replication button enables you to easily manage directory replication and specify a path to user logon scripts.

➤ The Alerts button provides a list of users and computers that are alerted when an administrative alert occurs.

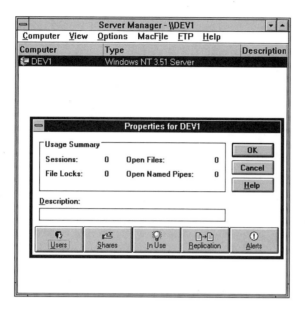

**Figure 12.11:**
The Server control panel.

# User Manager for Domains

The User Manager for Domains grants complete control over users to your server. Depending on your setup and, especially if you are running an intranet or a private server, the User Manager for Domains is a very good tool for creating and maintaining users for your system.

# Starting User Manager for Domains

To start User Manager for Domains, open up the Administrative Tools program group and double-click on User Manager for Domains. To use User Manager for Domains, you must be a member of the Administrators group, the Domain Admins group, or the Account Operators group. The User Manager for Domains window will appear as shown in figure 12.12.

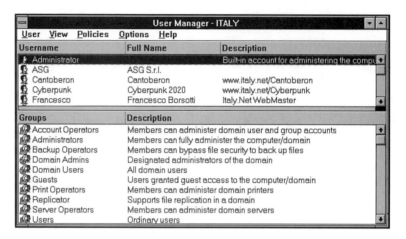

**Figure 12.12:**

The User Manager for Domains window.

When User Manager for Domains starts, it displays the domain that you are logged into in the title bar. The top half of the Window lists the user accounts, and the bottom half lists the groups.

 Users are the different people who have access to your computer. Each user must belong to one or more groups, which gives you control over who has access to what on your server.

To move to a different Domain, choose Select Domain from the User menu.

# Managing User Accounts

One of the most useful things you can do is manage user accounts. A user account contains all the information Windows NT needs to know about users, such as their usernames and passwords, their permissions, and what groups they belong to. Windows NT has built-in accounts for the Administrator and for Guest users. Adding user accounts is easy.

## Creating User Accounts

1. To create a new user account, choose New User from the User menu.

2. Type the username the user will use to logon. This name
   must be unique, and no longer than 20 characters. You can
   enter the user's full name as well in the Full Name entry
   field, but it isn't necessary. You can also enter a description
   of the user if you wish.

3. You need to enter a password, and then confirm it. You do
   this as the administrator.

## Configuring Options for Passwords

The New User dialog box provides some additional options as
well. If you choose that the users must change passwords at next
logon, this forces them to change their passwords. You can also
make it so the users *can't* change their passwords, by selecting the
Password Never Expires option. This is usually a good idea if you
have an account that more than one person uses. You should do
this for the accounts that your services use to log on. You can also
quickly disable accounts by selecting the Disable Account option.

## Configuring User Groups

After you have entered all the necessary information, you can
click the Groups button to choose which groups users will belong
to. You can use the Profile button to choose a home directory for
a user, particularly useful if your are giving users space on your
ftp and Web servers. If you want to, you can choose the Hours
button to limit the times people can connect. For example, you
might make it so some users can't connect during peak hours.
After you choose all of this, you can click the Add button to add
them. Later on you can modify accounts by double-clicking on
the account name you want to modify from the User Manager for
Domains window.

Home directories are important because they determine where a user's
files are stored, especially when giving them ftp access.

# Duplicating User Accounts

If you need to make a lot of accounts with the same kind of information, permissions, and so on, you can duplicate existing accounts to save some time.

1. First, highlight a user account you want to duplicate from the User Manager for Domains window, and then choose Copy from the User menu.

2. This will bring up the Copy of dialog box, where you can configure the account. For the most part, all you will usually have to change is the username, Full Name, and password. If necessary, you might also have to change a description or profile.

3. Click the Add button to add the account. After you add it, the Copy of dialog box will go back to its original state, allowing you to add another account or close it.

# Managing User Groups

User Manager for Domains also makes it easy to manage groups.

To create a new group, just follow these steps:.

1. First, select the user accounts that you want to use as members of the groups you are going to create using the User Manager for Domains.

2. Choose New Global Group from the User menu. The New Global Group dialog box appears. If you had any users selected, they will appear in the Members list.

3. Type the name of the group in the Group Name field. The group name should be unique and no longer than 20 characters. Then type a description of the group in the Description field.

4. To add a member, select their name from the Not Members list and click the Add button.

5.  To remove a member, select their name from the Members list and click the Remove button.

6.  Once you are satisfied with the group's membership, click the OK button.

## Duplicating User Groups

You can save yourself some time if you are creating multiple groups that you want to have the same members by copying an existing group.

1.  First, select a global group you want to copy and then choose Copy from the User menu.

2.  Enter a group name and define it. You also can add or remove members. When you are satisfied, click the OK button.

## Managing Global User Groups

To manage a global group, double-click on the Group name in the User Manager for Domains window. This brings up the Global Group Properties dialog box (see figure 12.13). You can then add or remove members, change the Group name, and change the Group description.

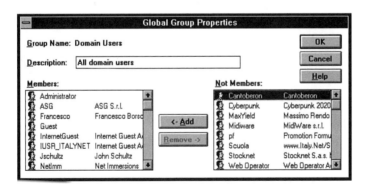

**Figure 12.13:**

Global Group Properties window.

## Viewing User Group Properties

You can also view the properties of groups by double-clicking them. Doing this brings up the Local Group Properties window (see fig. 12.14).

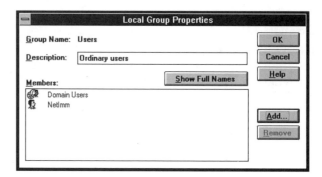

**Figure 12.14:**

The Local Group Properties window.

## Changing Security Policies

Another feature of User Manager for Domains is that it enables you to change many of the security policies. These include the Account policy, which defines properties for passwords. The User Rights policy enables you to control the rights given to users and groups. The Audit policy defines which security events should be logged. Finally, the Trust Relationships policy enables you to specify the domains that the current domains trust. These policies are covered more in-depth in Chapter 14, "Security Utilities and Testing."

# Event Viewer

Events are considered to be anything that occurs on the machine that would be considered significant. Essentially, anything that happens on the computer (even the invisible events that you aren't aware of) are considered to be events. If you are experiencing any problems, the Event Viewer is one of the best places to look to see what could be causing it.

The Event Viewer can be used to monitor most of the important events that occur on your system. Important events are different for each administrator, because each administrator will want to keep track of different events. Windows NT records many different events. The system log is for events that are made by Windows NT components. This is where you will find problems such as a driver failing to load. Application events are logged in the application. Finally, the security log registers security events.

## Starting Event Viewer

To launch the Event Viewer, double-click on the Event Viewer, located in the Administrative Tools program group. The Event Viewer window opens (see fig. 12.15).

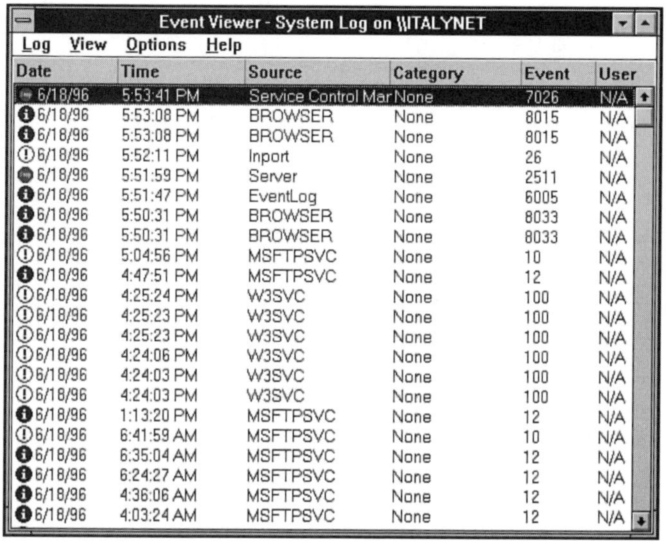
Event Viewer - System Log on \\ITALYNET
Log View Options Help
Date Time Source Category Event User
6/18/96 5:53:41 PM Service Control Mar None 7026 N/A
6/18/96 5:53:08 PM BROWSER None 8015 N/A
6/18/96 5:53:08 PM BROWSER None 8015 N/A
6/18/96 5:52:11 PM Inport None 26 N/A
6/18/96 5:51:59 PM Server None 2511 N/A
6/18/96 5:51:47 PM EventLog None 6005 N/A
6/18/96 5:50:31 PM BROWSER None 8033 N/A
6/18/96 5:50:31 PM BROWSER None 8033 N/A
6/18/96 5:04:56 PM MSFTPSVC None 10 N/A
6/18/96 4:47:51 PM MSFTPSVC None 12 N/A
6/18/96 4:25:24 PM W3SVC None 100 N/A
6/18/96 4:25:23 PM W3SVC None 100 N/A
6/18/96 4:25:23 PM W3SVC None 100 N/A
6/18/96 4:24:06 PM W3SVC None 100 N/A
6/18/96 4:24:03 PM W3SVC None 100 N/A
6/18/96 4:24:03 PM W3SVC None 100 N/A
6/18/96 1:13:20 PM MSFTPSVC None 12 N/A
6/18/96 6:41:59 AM MSFTPSVC None 10 N/A
6/18/96 6:35:04 AM MSFTPSVC None 12 N/A
6/18/96 6:24:27 AM MSFTPSVC None 12 N/A
6/18/96 4:36:06 AM MSFTPSVC None 12 N/A
6/18/96 4:03:24 AM MSFTPSVC None 12 N/A

**Figure 12.15:**
The main Event Viewer window.

## Displaying Event Information

Each line of the display shows the necessary information about an event. The lines tell the date and time the event occurred, what the source of the event was, and the computer on which it oc-curred. This information is best used if you want to get an idea of who did something to your server, which is especially good for letting people know not to do something, or for tracking down people trying to damage your server.

The source is the name of the software that the event occurred on. For example, if an event was logged by the Web service, it would report the source as W3SVC. The category is the type of event that the event falls into. For example, it might be a Logon, Object access, or something else. The event number indicates exactly what the event is, which is usually most useful when reporting a problem to tech support. The User is the name of the user who was logged on and using the computer when the event occurred. The Computer is the name of the computer on which the event occurred.

Next to each event is a small icon. These icons indicate the status of the event.

➤ The stop icon indicates an error, usually a serious problem.

➤ The exclamation icon is a warning, which usually indicates that something might be wrong and should be checked out before a real error does occur.

➤ The i icon is for information. Some programs may log an event here when it completes a task.

➤ The lock icon indicates that an audit occurred successfully. An example of this is when someone logs on successfully.

➤ The key icon indicates a failed audit. This means that a user attempted to log on unsuccessfully. If you see a lot of these, especially from one user, it could be that they are trying to access something they shouldn't, and it should be checked out.

To find out more details about a specific event, double-click on it. This will bring up the Event Detail window (see fig. 12.16).

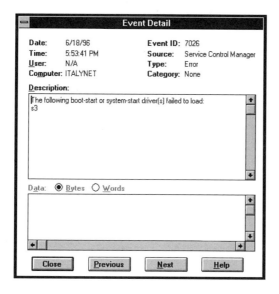

**Figure 12.16:**
The Event Detail window.

# Finding Events

By default, Event Viewer shows all events that occur. To find events faster, you can filter them by doing the following:

1.  Select Filter Events from the View menu. The Filter dialog box appears.

    You can either simply view from the first event through the last event or specify the exact times you want to view. This is helpful, especially if you already know what time a problem might have occurred.

2.  Next, you can choose which events should be shown. For example, if you only want to view errors, you should deselect Information, Warning, Success Audit, and Failure Audit.

3.  You can narrow it down even further by looking for a specific user, a specific computer, or a specific event ID. For example, you can find all instances of events with the ID 2511.

4.  After you have selected the information you want to be displayed, click the OK button to view the filtered event log.

5.  You can go back to the default setting by clicking on the Clear button in the Filter dialog box.

6.  To go back to viewing all events, select All Events from the View menu.

## Summary

In addition to familiarizing yourself with Internet Server Manager, User Manager for Domains, and Event Viewer, you will soon discover that administering Internet Information Server and administering the computer will seem to become one and the same. One of the biggest advantages to using Internet Information Server is that it integrates these two seemingly separate functions.

# Part V

# Internet Information Server Security

# Chapter 13

# Server Security Basics

The Internet is a vast public network connecting millions of hosts. Anyone with a computer can get connected to the Internet and partake in the endless sharing of information. Unfortunately, the public nature of the Internet has also spawned a new class of hackers and cyberthiefs. These malevolent individuals attempt to disrupt the cooperative culture of the Internet by participating in illegal activities—such as theft and the illegal penetration of computer systems. Last year, the Pentagon alone received 250,000 attempted break-ins to its network. Your best line of defense to thwart attackers is to actively prepare for security breaches. Don't wait for a security breach to occur before you take action!

This chapter first explores the Web Security Model that defines categories of security pertaining to the Web. Secondly, the chapter takes you through server security on Windows NT Server and Internet Information Server. In addition, the chapter includes information on protecting data between the Web server and the Web browser by using secure channel protocols, and also includes tools that protect your Web server itself (shockingly, some of these tools even enable you to capture lost passwords!). And finally, the chapter takes you to the realm of forbidden knowledge, studying common security attacks used by Internet hackers.

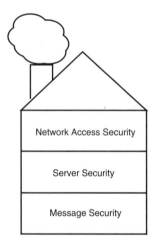

**Figure 13.1:**
A house with three security levels.

# The Web Security Model

The Web Security Model approaches the study of Web security in three levels. A picture is worth a thousand words; therefore, refer to figure 13.1.

You can place security controls only on what is yours. Based on this notion, the diagram depicts a house with three floors—anything that occurs within your house is your responsibility and duty to protect. As soon as someone exits your residence, you are no longer liable for their actions. Each floor represents a higher level of security. Most of your guests are normally entertained in the guest room or living room on the ground level. The second floor might contain your children's bedrooms, and on the top floor is your master bedroom. Each level requires a higher level of access—on the top level, you might only let in your best friends or relatives. And the stairway plays an important role in allowing travel to each floor or access point.

Now compare the analogy of the home to the Web Security Model. When a user sends an e-mail message (ground floor) across the Internet, it travels through the internal network and reaches the mail server (second level). Only messages destined for the Internet exit your network via the router.

A router is an intelligent hardware device that picks the best route for your data to travel.

All messages not destined for the Internet are determined to be local and go no further than your mail server.

Technically, an e-mail message is considered local if the destination IP network address is the same as the source IP network address. So, if the source address of the e-mail packet is 164.55.12.10 and the destination address is 164.55.12.2, the e-mail is local because the network IP address (164.55.0.0) is the same. Likewise, remote e-mail would have a different IP network address in the source and destination portion of the packet (suppose the source address is 164.55.12.2 and the destination address is 157.57.12.3—the network addresses are 164.55.0.0 and 157.57.12.3, respectively). E-mail messages are likely to traverse countless numbers of networks with each network being a possible access point for an intruder.

Without any form of message security, local or Internet e-mails can be read, altered, or even deleted by an unauthorized party. For a more comprehensive understanding of Web security, let's take a detailed approach toward examining each security level.

# Message Security

Referring to the analogy of the home in figure 13.1, imagine if Phil and Alvie (your guests) bring over a case of white wine to celebrate your renewed friendship. A close examination of this scenario will help you to better understand the four tenets of message security—Authentication, Confidentiality, Data Integrity, and Dialogue Verification.

Phil and Alvie walk into your house and you happily acknowledge their presence. (Authentication. You make eye contact with Phil and Alvie. You recognize them as good friends that you have known for years.)

While in the guest room, Phil hands you the case of wine. (Confidentiality. This event is occurring in the privacy of your own home.)

You graciously take the case of wine and thank Phil. (Data Integrity. The act of Phil handing you the case of wine and you receiving it intact ensures integrity.)

Phil engages you in a stimulating conversation about Japanese sushi. Alvie checks her watch and notices that it's time to eat. She comments that your conversation with Phil is making her hungry. (Dialogue Verification. Alvie records the time of the conversation in her memory and verifies that the conversation took place by her participation. Alvie can later recall the conversation with reference to the time when the event took place.)

Let's extend this metaphor and step through a scenario on the Internet where all four types of message security take place.

➤ Authentication: Peter and Joe are CEOs and would like to exchange a confidential e-mail on the Internet, but they both would like assurances of each other's identity. After speaking to their system administrators and having their identities verified (by company id), they are both issued a security token and a secret password. The CEOs then utilize the security token and their password to gain access to the e-mail system.

➤ Confidentiality: To ensure that only Peter and Joe read the e-mail message, Peter (the sender) encrypts the e-mail message using the Data Encryption System (DES)—a government-developed encryption algorithm. A secret key computed by the DES software is then sent to Joe via a private courier. Upon receipt of the e-mail and the secret key, Joe deciphers the message using the secret key and produces plaintext which can then be read.

➤ Data Integrity: Because data packets can be distorted or dropped during their travels on the Internet, a mechanism must exist to verify the contents of the transmission. The e-mail software program that our CEOs are using automatically computes a checksum (via an algorithm of some type) for each e-mail sent. Once the e-mail reaches Joe, a checksum is computed by the e-mail software and compared to the original checksum (which is embedded within the contents of the file). If there is a mismatch then the e-mail is considered distorted and a request for retransmission of the e-mail is initiated.

➤ Dialogue Verification: To verify that the electronic conversation between the CEOs took place, the e-mail server records in a log the time and date of all messages sent and received. If either CEO repudiates the occurrence of the event, the log would serve as proof that the event did take place.

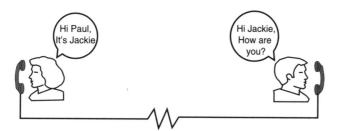

**Figure 13.2:**
Authentication—Verifying that senders of messages are really who they say they are.

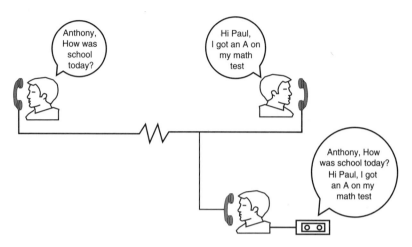

## Figure 13.3:

Confidentiality—Ensuring that the message will not be read by anyone else other than the intended receiver.

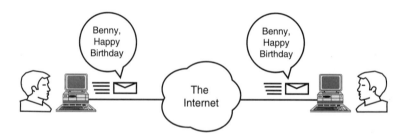

## Figure 13.4:

Data Integrity—The message reaching its destination without modification.

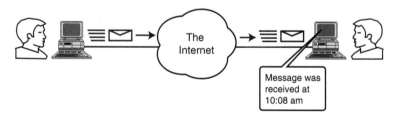

## Figure 13.5:

Dialogue Verification—Proving that the conversation took place either through a time stamp or an audit log.

Table 13.1 refers to the four basic message methods that you may encounter on the Internet. The left column lists each message security component. The right column lists some technical implementations for each message security component. Following the table is a detailed explanation of each implementation.

**Table 13.1   Message Security Methods**

| Method | Where It Is Used |
|---|---|
| Authentication | Basic authentication, public key technology, digital certificates, security tokens |
| Confidentiality | Encryption, secure channel protocols |
| Data Integrity | Packet checksums, transport Control Protocol, application level retransmissions |
| Dialogue Verification | Time stamps, audit logs |

# Authentication

On the Internet, authentication by visual verification is all but impossible. Until video conferencing takes off and becomes the preferred method of communicating on the Internet, we have to rely on alternate methods of verifying the identity of senders and receivers. As we know, the content of e-mail varies in importance. An e-mail you send to grandma congratulating her on her birthday can be intercepted and read by an unauthorized individual. The consequence of the previous example is harmless and no damage is done to either party; however, if an e-mail containing confidential company finacial records is intercepted and read by a competitor, the damage could be very substantial. Authentication implementations such as Basic Authentication, Public Key Cryptography, Digital Certificates, and Security Tokens are widely used on the Internet and are explained in the following sections.

# Basic Authentication

The user specifies his login name and a secret password. This is the simplest and weakest form of authentication because the user name and password are sent in encoded form known as base64. It is important to understand the difference between message encoding and message encryption. In message encoding, any person with the encoding algorithm can decode the message and read its contents. Base64 is the encoding method use in MIME— the Internet standard for sending files of different formats. Additionally, if the user enters a dictionary password, it can be easily retrieved by employing a brute force attack. For more information on brute force attacks, refer to the section "Common Security Attacks" later in the chapter.

IIS allows for the use of Basic Authentication. By selecting this option, user names and passwords would be sent in encoded cleartext and can be easily captured and decoded. By default, for security reasons this box is unchecked.

The advantage of Basic Authentication is that it is widely supported among WWW servers (including IIS) and clients. The disadvantage is that the user name and password are sent in cleartext and can be easily captured.

## Public Key Cryptography

If you have rented a safe deposit box in a bank, then you are already familiar with the concept of public and private keys. Each safe deposit box contains two key holes: one key belongs to the bank (public key), while the other key (private key) is given to the safe deposit box owner. The bank's key can be handled by any authorized employee of the bank while the other key is held privately by the owner of the safe deposit box. The key pair is unique to each safe deposit box. The bank is allowed to make duplicates of its key, but not the key of the customer. The lock is designed so that both keys must be used in order to unlock the box (the keys are complementary). If the box is unlocked, then we know the identity of the key holder has been verified. (In reality, the bank would request a signature or a bank document before you are allowed into the safe deposit box area. This is known as a two factor authentication.) Once the box is open, the customer can view, take, or place items into the box. After the box is closed and returned to its proper location, the bank key is returned to the key rack (to be accessed later by any authorized bank personnel). Meanwhile, the other key is carried away to be kept secretly by the customer.

Public Key Cryptography functions in much the same manner as our safe deposit box analogy. Each individual holds two complementary keys (also known as a key pair)—a public and a private key. Each key can unlock the ciphertext (or code) made with the other key. The public key is openly distributed, whereas the private or secret key is never revealed. To encrypt a message, the sender would use the public key of the recipient. The recipient would then decrypt the message by using his secret key. Because the two keys are complementary, one key unlocks the other key. Authentication is accomplished when the sender  digitally signs the message. A digital signature is created when the message is encrypted with the sender's private key. To authenticate the identity of the sender, one can obtain the public key of the sender and attempt to decrypt the message. If the message is decrypted sucessfully, then we can postulate that:

1.  The two keys are complementary (the keys are from the same person).

2.  The secret key is possessed only by the sender.

3.  Therefore, we can conclude that the sender's identity is indeed authentic.

In IIS, public and private keys are generated with the *keygen* program located in c:\inetsrv\server. Refer to implementing SSL on IIS later in this chapter for more information.

The advantages of public key cryptography are that it provides both authentication and encryption, but does not require a secure channel for the transmission of keys and messages. The disadvantage of this method of authentication is that security is compromised if the secret key is lost or stolen. Also, the identity of the key holder cannot be verified by the other party unless a digital certificate exists.

## Digital Certificates

How do you confirm that the person holding the keys is in fact the legitimate holder? This is a real dilemma because if an unauthorized person obtains the keys of someone, that intruder can masquerade as another person and perform malicious acts. Because the key information is sent via an unsecured channel (the Internet), any data (encrypted or plaintext) can be plucked and retransmitted. This technique is known as *replay*. Refer to the "Common Security Attacks" section for more information.

To solve this problem, key certificates are used to verify the authenticity of the sender and receiver. A key certificate can be issued to an individual or to a server. A key certificate for an individual holds the key information of the user, the key owner's id (user name), and a time stamp of when the key pair was created. Similarly, key certificates issued to WWW servers contain key and server-specific information. Key certificates are processed and issued by a Certificate Authority (CA). A CA is a third party key-escrow service whose job is to validate the identity of a WWW client or WWW server. A certificate is issued by the Certificate Authority only after the user's keys (public and secret), identification information (such as a passport), and other documentation are obtained. The following example presents a self-signed digital certificate from Netscape:

Certificate:

```
Data:
      Version: 0 (0x0)
      Serial Number: 1 (0x1)
      Signature Algorithm: MD5 digest with RSA Encryption
      Issuer: C=US, OU=Test CA, O=Netscape Communications
►Corp.
      Validity:
           Not Before: Wed Nov 23 14:30:35 1994
           Not After: Fri Nov 22 14:30:35 1996
      Subject: C=US, OU=Test CA, O=Netscape Communications
►Corp.
         Subject Public Key Info:
             Public Key Algorithm: RSA Encryption
```

```
                Public Key:
                    Modulus:
                        00:b4:6c:8a:ec:ba:18:7b:72:a1:3c:cb:
➥e9:81:15:
                        2d:df:9b:b2:82:5b:13:50:02:2a:fe:7c:
➥51:07:e6:
                        14:c3:60:ad:15:56:de:f0:a7:32:c1:a0:
➥34:95:a3:
                        6a:4e:bf:21:48:4a:4a:21:7d:6b:37:12:
➥59:8a:b8:
                        c9:65:ff:a7:45:a0:16:b7:e1:b8:cb:52:
➥0e:16:bd:
                        e0:16:dd:dd:a7:36:67:3e:09:b9:db:33:
➥bd:74:fc:
                        de:58:94:cf:28:b3:96:d5:8e:33:61:1f:
➥cb:40:3f:
                        2a:29:2d:0b:68:87:15:68:fd:09:00:e0:
➥77:4e:d2:
                        40:1a:3e:5f:9c:d3:cc:16:63
                    Exponent: 3 (0x3)
            Signature Algorithm: MD5 digest with RSA Encryption
            Signature:
                55:79:c0:97:88:44:77:48:8a:48:7e:16:6a:d7:e5:3e:e2:f7:
                17:d0:d4:80:d8:92:95:e8:7c:12:9f:be:78:4b:a6:cb:e5:25:
                c9:db:d4:e0:d3:e7:c2:7b:56:03:f9:2a:7a:d5:09:53:48:86:
                37:b1:be:0b:21:1a:f5:0c:6c:96:2b:bf:70:8a:6e:c4:fd:ea:
                0f:90:35:7f:66:05:eb:f2:05:c2:20:3d:72:fa:52:ab:88:41:
                7b:3e:d8:10:23:59:e5:82:f9:71:86:66:12:ca:c5:f7:46:47:
                84:ad:56:66:a4:50:1c:ff:ac:12:a4:69:65:4a:d4:11:b7:a4:
                b1:4e
```

Here is the raw X.509 certificate, uuencoded:

```
begin 664 netscape-test-ca.der
M,((!^S"""60"'0$P#P#08)*H9(AO<-'0$$!0'P1S$+,'D&'U4$$!A,
➥"55,Q$#'.
M!@-5!'L3!U1E<W0Q!T$C'D!@-5!'H3'4YE='-C87!E($$-O;6UU;
➥FEC871I
M;VYS($-O<G'N,!X7#3DT#3$R,S(R,S(V,3(R,35H7#3DV,3$R,3$R
➥C(R,T'S-5HP1S$+
M,'D&'U4$$!A,"55,Q$#'.!@-5!'L3!U1E<W0Q!0$-O;6UU;FEC871I
➥4YE='-C87!E($$-O<G'.-'C'
```

```
M87!E($-0;6UU;FEC871I;VYS($-0<G'N,(&=,'T&"2J&2
➡(;W#0$!'04"X&+
M'#"!AP*!!@0"T;(KLNAA[<J$\R^F!%2W?F[*"6Q-0'BK^?%$'
➡YA3#8*T55M[P
MIS+!H#25HVI.0R%(2DHA?6LW$EEF**N,EE_Z=%H!:WX;C+4@X6O>
➡'6W=VG-F<^
M";G;,[UT_-Y8E,\HLY;5CCC-A'\M'/RHI+0MHHAAQ5H_0D'X'=.TD':/
➡E^<T\P6
M8P(!'S'-!@DJADBJ]PT!'00%".!@0!5><"7B$1W2
➡(I(?A9JU^4^X0<7T-2'
MV)*5Z'P2G[YX2Z;+Y27)V]3@T^?'"">U8#^^2IZU0E32(8WL;X+(1KU#&R6*[]P
MBF[$_>H/H/D#[5_9@7K\@7"(#[UR^E*K]*B[/M@@(UGe@0eQAF82RL7W1D>
➡$K59F
0I%'<_ZP2I&EE2M01MZ2Q3CUR
'
end
```

Verisign Inc. is a Certificate Authority endorsed by industry leaders such as Microsoft and Netscape to issue digital certificates. Verisign was founded in 1995 as a subsidiary of RSA data security. RSA stands for the initials of its founders—Ron Rivest, Adi Shamir, and Leonard Adleman. Rivest, Shamir, and Adleman were responsible for inventing the first public key cryptosystem known as RSA encryption. To obtain more information on obtaining certificates from Verisign, point to **http://www.verisign.com**.

In Internet Information Server 1.0, Microsoft is only supporting digital certificates on the server. When generating key data using Keygen, keep in mind that Verisign requires the submission of a **Distinguished Name**. Because servers across an organization may have the same name, a **Distinguished Name** is created to differentiate each certificate owner. A **Distinguished Name** contains the following fields of information that helps make each certificate owner unique:

**Fields in a Distinguished Name**

Country=US

State/Province=NEW YORK

Locality=NYC

Organization=EXAMPLE

Organizational Unit=MARKETING

Common Name=www.mycompany.com

Because duplicate key values violate the principles of authentication and confidentiality, the algorithm that generates the keys must provide a high degree of randomness.

The advantage of using digital certificates is that a key holder's identity can be verified by a certificate authority. The disadvantage of using this method of authentication is that the sender and receiver must rely on the ability of the certificate authority to verify the key holder's identity and maintain the safety of the keys. Another drawback is that there is an annual maintenance fee charged for each certificate.

# Security Tokens

Authentication of user identity can be proven by using a variety of methods. One method of verifying authentication is with the use of security tokens. Access to a system is granted to those who possess the card and a secret password (this is similar to the operation of an ATM cash card and PIN number). A security token resembles the size of a bank ATM card with an LCD display and a keypad. To use the token, one must enter the secret password on the keypad. The authentication device (in this case, a personal computer) sends a challenge (displayed on the screen as a series of characters). The user keys in the challenge on the token's keypad. A response is then generated on the LCD. The user then types the string of characters displayed on the security token into the PC. Based on the software algorithm on the authentication device, the response is generated internally and compared to the characters inputted by the user. If the strings match, then the identity of the user has been confirmed and access to the system is granted.

Many security tokens rely on two-form factor security. This states that a user must have something that he knows (a PIN) and something that he has (the token).

Security tokens provide strong two-factor authentication (something that you have and something that you know). The only disadvantage to this method of authentication is that users must carry a token at all times to use the system. If users forget the PIN, the token has to be reinitialized by the system administrator. If they become lost, replacements can be expensive. Effective usage of security tokens depends entirely upon the responsibility of the token carrier.

# Confidentiality

Our right to privacy is as American as apple pie. Whether it's sending a piece of mail through the postal system or talking on the phone, we expect our communication to be private and unavailable to unauthorized parties. In the case of the postal system or the phone company, there exists a governing body to ensure that privacy is enforced. On the Internet there exists no such entity; therefore, message confidentiality must be enforced by the communicating parties. There are several techniques available to us to ensure message confidentiality.

# Encryption

*Encryption* is the process by which the original message (plaintext) is scrambled to produce a new message that is unreadable (ciphertext). In *single* (or symmetric) *key encryption*, one key is used by both the originator and the recipient to unlock the message. *Public* (or asymmetric) *key encryption* requires two keys for each individual, a public key and a private key (see "Public Key Cryptography"). Single key encryption is most appropriately used in encoding files for individuals because the transmission of the key requires a secure channel. (If a secure channel already existed, we would have no need for keys!) *Data Encryption Standard* (DES) is a single key encryption scheme widely supported by the U.S. government and the security industry. DES uses single key encryption and key sizes of 56 bits. DES requires a secure channel for the transmission of the key and therefore, is unsuitable for use over the Internet. DES should be used for simple file encryption. Conversely, public key cryptography does not require a secure channel for key transmission and is more appropriate for Internet use.

There is much discussion around the strength of the 56-bit key used in DES. To increase the cryptographic strength of DES, many proponents of the standard have recommended doubling the size of the DES secret key to 112 bits.

# Data Integrity

The volume of Internet traffic is predicted to double every year. The reliability of data transfers across the Internet could decrease if we tax the network to its limits. During peak periods of the day, the user will experience slower performance due to the frequent retransmission of packets. Because network equipment has a finite amount of storage and processing capability, packets can be discarded due to network congestion. In addition, intentional or unintentional modifications of a packet should be a concern. Because packets must travel in the open on the public information highway, a hacker can intentionally disrupt service by capturing network packets and then reinjecting the packets back onto the network. Unintentional disruptions such as the failing of network hardware or cabling can result in packets being discarded or altered.

Data Integrity ensures that the information is received by the intended party and that the message has not been modified intentionally or unintentionally. Fortunately, there are mechanisms that can detect when a packet does not reach its destination or when a packet has been altered. Mechanisms that verify data integrity are transparent to the user and are present in the Internet in the form of hardware logic, network protocols, and checksum algorithms.

There are protocols within the OSI model that ensure the successful delivery and verfication of data.

The Open Systems Interconnection (OSI) model was developed by the International Standards Organization (ISO) and serves as a framework for network communication.

A reliable transport layer protocol such as TCP (Transmission Control Protocol) performs data verification by confirming that a packet has been received without modification. Before the sender can transmit the next packet in the sequence, an acknowledgment must be received. If a network error occurs and the data packet is distorted or lost, the sender will not receive an acknowledgment and the packet is retransmitted. UDP (User Datagram Protocol) is an unreliable transport protocol that does not require acknowledgments and consequently relies on higher layer programs (such as e-mail servers) to perform retransmission.

The commercialization of the Internet backbone has improved the overall data integrity on the Internet. Commercial providers have introduced faster routers and bigger network pipes into the backbone, which result in lower packet loss.

## Dialogue Verification

E-mail systems create time stamps of incoming and outgoing messages. Network operating systems keep track of who logs on and when they do it. Phone calls made from your home phone are time stamped and recorded in the phone company's mainframe computers. Dialogue verification is not only important in network security, but also serves as the basis for billing and accounting.

Internet commerce is swiftly becoming a reality. The capability to confirm that a transaction took place between two parties is a vital requirement. By attaching a time stamp and adding an entry in the audit logs, neither party can repudiate the existence of the transaction.

# Securing Your Message with Pretty Good Privacy (PGP)

Millions of e-mail messages travel in cyberspace every day. Yet a large number of these e-mails are sent in clear text. If Benny sends Arthur an e-mail, an unsuspected third person can snoop at the e-mail and even modify the original message and resend the message masquerading as Benny. When Arthur receives the message, he would not know that the message has been modified and would assume it came from the rightful owner. If Benny and Arthur had practiced message security, their e-mail would never have been compromised. Fortunately, a freely available program called Pretty Good Privacy is available on the Internet to protect your information from snoops and fakes.

PGP is a popular software application created by Philip Zimmerman that provides authentication and confidentiality for sending electronic mail and files over the Internet. The intention of the author was to develop an easy-to-use cryptography system for the masses and, based on its use on the Internet, it looks like Mr. Zimmerman has succeeded.

PGP is available as freeware on the following platforms: Unix, MS-DOS, and the Macintosh. PGP combines public key cryptography with single key cryptography to provide fast encryption of the plaintext file. As of this writing, the current version of PGP is 2.6.2.

Phil Zimmerman, the author of Pretty Good Privacy (PGP), was charged in 1995 by the U.S. government for violating federal cryptography export restrictions. For three years Phil Zimmerman was the target of a criminal investigation by the U.S. Customs Service that assumed that laws were broken when PGP spread outside the U.S. That investigation was closed without indictment in January 1996. Earlier this year, the Justice Department dropped its case against Mr. Zimmerman after overwhelming support from the Internet community.

Most businesses frown on using PGP because the PGP system involves using a "Web of Trust" rather than a Certificate Authority to authenticate the identity of key owners. The Web of Trust states that if User A trusts User B, and User B trusts User C, then User A trusts User C. The system falls apart if someone masquerades as User B. Nonetheless, PGP has become the de facto standard for thousands of users to transmit information safely on the Internet.

Pretty Good Privacy is a public key encryption scheme and can be generally described by the following steps:

1.  The sender decides to send a confidential e-mail across the Internet using PGP software. Recall that the sender and the recipient each hold two keys—a public key and a secret key.

2.  A temporary key is created for this session by the PGP software, and the plaintext message is encrypted using this temporary key. This step is hidden to the user and is executed in the background.

3.  The temporary key is enciphered with the recipient's public key.

4.  The ciphertext and the cipher session key are sent to the recipient.

5.  The recipient uses his secret key to decode the encipher session key.

6.  Using single key cryptography, the plaintext session key can now be used to encrypt the ciphertext.

7.  The ciphertext is converted to plaintext and is now readable by the recipient.

You can learn more about PGP and download the distribution files at **http://web.mit.edu/network/pgp.html**.

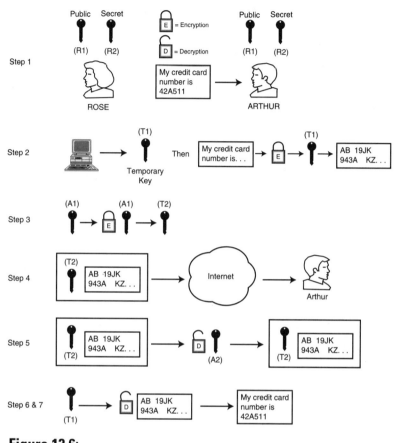

**Figure 13.6:**

PGP.

# Server Security

The Web server in many ways serves as the electronic ambassador for your company. The information contained on the server might include news releases, stock prices, or sales information. If the information is modified, the damage can be substantial.

Therefore, Web server data must be protected at all times. Windows NT and IIS provide much-needed security at the operating system and application level to thwart intruders. Your Web server can be secured by implementing C2 security, NT File System (NTFS) security, strong passwords, security protocols, application security, and limited physical access.

Windows NT Server is one of the first graphical-based network operating systems to be certified for government C2 security. Originally, the U.S. National Security Agency (NSA) created the C2 security class to secure U.S. government installations. But any business requiring the need to secure sensitive information can benefit from C2 certification.

NTFS implements strong security by restricting access to resources to only the owner and users authorized by the owner. Each user is uniquely identified with a security identifier known as the SID. The SID prevents a user from masquerading as another user by simply duplicating the user name—because each user created is assigned a unique SID regardless of the name. Furthermore, all entities or objects that have a name (such as a file or a directory) are secured with an Access Control List (ACL). The ACL contains entries that describe access and auditing permissions for the object.

Strong passwords protect access to the Web server so intruders cannot easily guess the password. Your security policy should dictate the avoidance of dictionary passwords on servers. Instead, use passwords that provide a healthy mix of letters—uppercase and lowercase—and numbers.

There are various server security protocols available to secure the conversation between the Web server and the client. Security protocols such as Secure Sockets Layer and Secure HTTP perform authentication in addition to data verification.

Application security introduces an extra layer of protection on top of whatever security the operating system has already implemented. In addition to Internet Information Server's high integration with NT's security, IIS provides additional access control with directory and IP restrictions.

Finally, limiting physical access can protect your Web server from unauthorized persons. Because data is the most important resource of many companies, data centers are often guarded and entrance is permitted only with an authorized identification card. Protecting your server does not have to be an expensive ordeal because simply placing your server under lock and key can be a simple solution to protecting your server resources. The components of server security are disussed in more detail in the following sections.

# Network Access Security

Once your network is connected to the Internet, your internal network is no longer private. In essense, your corporate network has become an extension of the Internet and anyone with an Internet connection can readily access resources on your site. Devices such as routers and firewalls can be configured to filter incoming as well as outgoing traffic. When these devices are correctly configured and strategically placed, they become your best protection in guarding your site against unwanted intrusion.

## Internet Routers

The Internet is a conglomeration of diverse networks connected to each other via network devices known as routers. Internally, a *router* is a hardware device connecting the company's local network segments to the outside world. In addition to providing connectivity between networks, routers can also find optimal routes, translate protocols, and connect dissimilar media (between Ethernet and Token Ring, for example). Today's routers from major vendors such as Cisco and Wellfleet are capable of processing gigabits of data per second.

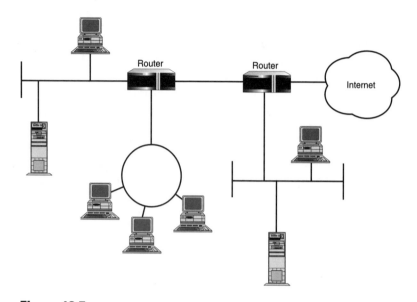

**Figure 13.7:**

A router connecting local segments and connecting to the Internet.

Understandably, the router is your network's first line of defense. But you should not envision the router as an almighty fortress that is able to stop all intruder attacks. Packet-screening devices, such as routers, primarily concentrate on the network and transport layers (no facilities are available to screen application-level programs). The configuration and administration of a router require high levels of knowledge in protocols such as OSPF (Open Shortest Path First), IGRP (Interior Gateway Routing Protocol), and TCP/IP (Tranmission Control Protocol/Internet Protocol). Excessive use of the router as a packet-filtering device consumes a great deal of the router's processing power and thus reduces its capability to route packets quickly. Also, a router's auditing and logging features lack administrative functionality that is crucial in tracking security violators.

## Router Configurations for Packet Filtering

Remember that the core function of a router is to direct traffic to its proper destination and provide physical connectivity. As a secondary service, routers also provide packet filtering. A router can examine the guts of a packet and determine if the packet should be forwarded or dropped. In a router configuration, an access list can be defined to restrict both incoming and outgoing traffic. A simple access list might state "Let's restrict all outgoing traffic that is not destined for network 148.87.0.0." An extended access list might say "Let's restrict all outgoing traffic from 148.57.98.27 not destined for 148.57.0.0 and allow all other traffic out except TCP packets with port 23."

A sample Cisco router configuration:

```
hostname sandbox
enable secret 5 $1$ST4X$oOfjeDxDgBh20sXaJ6Oyup0
enable password shovel
line vty 0 4
password pail
snmp-server community
xremote tftp host 123.123.123.246
!
ip routing
decnet routing 1.1
decnet node-type area
ipx routing
xns routing
appletalk routing
apollo routing
clns routing
router iso-igrp pubsgroup
net 78.8885.0013.0000.0C01.0D1D.00
vines routing
bridge 1 protocol dec
no mop enabled
access-list 1 permit 16.32.0.3
access-list 1 deny 16.0.0.0  0.255.255.255
access-list 102 permit tcp 0.0.0.0 255.255.255.255
➦128.88.0.0 0.0.255.255 gt 1023
access-liot 102 permit tcp 0.0.0.0 255.255.255.255
➦128.88.1.2 0.0.0.0 eq 25
!
interface BRI0
```

```
no ip address
!
interface Ethernet0
ip address 16.0.0.10
ip access-group 1 in
ipx network 10
xns network 2
clns router iso-igrp pubsgroup
vines metric
bridge-group 1
no mop enabled
lat enabled
!
interface Serial0
ip address 128.88.0.42
ip access-group 102 in
clns router iso-igrp pubsgroup
vines metric
bridge-group 1
no mop enabled
no lat enabled
!
router igrp 15
network 131.108.0.0
!
```

endTraffic can be filtered on a TCP/IP network based on the following:

➤ IP addresses

    Individual IP addresses (158.57.98.27)

    Entire networks (158.57.0.0)

➤ Protocols

    IP

    UDP

    TCP

➤ Ports

    TCP—Telnet (port 23), FTP (port 21), SMTP (port 25)

    UDP—e.g., tftp (port 69), time (port 37)

## Configuring Router ACLs

Extending upon the sample Cisco router configuration in the preceding section, the following examples are simple ACL configurations. ACL 1 states that the router should permit only traffic with an IP address 16.32.0.3 while denying everything else:

```
access-list 1 permit 16.32.0.3
access-list 1 deny 16.0.0.0  0.0.255.255
```

The next example shows an extended access list that permits any incoming TCP connections with destination ports greater than 1023:

```
access-list 102 permit tcp 0.0.0.0 255.255.255.255
➥128.88.0.0 0.0.255.255 gt 1023
```

The next example permits incoming TCP connections to the SMTP (simple mail transport protocol) port of host 128.88.1.2:

```
access-list 102 permit tcp 0.0.0.0 255.255.255.255
➥128.88.1.2 0.0.0.0 eq 25
```

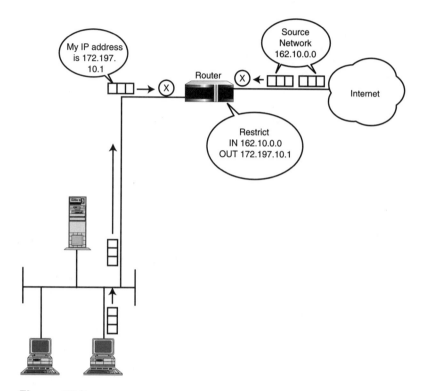

**Figure 13.8:**

Router restricts IP addresses and networks (in and out).

## Firewalls

A *firewall* is simply a mechanism that permits and restricts incoming and outgoing network traffic. A firewall is the network's primary defense in deterring intruders. Because all traffic is funneled through this device, the firewall is often known as the "choke point."

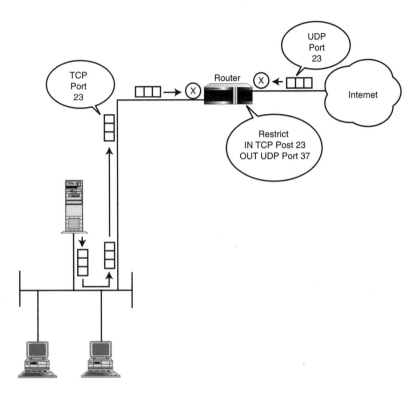

**Figure 13.9:**
Router restricts ports (in and out).

The firewall is a software package loaded onto a host that has network connections to both the corporate network and the Internet. The computer where the firewall software resides is called a *bastion host.* A bastion host with two network interface cards (NICs) connecting to two different networks is known as a *dual-homed host.* Because the firewall serves as a dedicated security device, it includes sophisticated rules-based administration and auditing features that are needed in monitoring your network. A rule defined in a firewall might state that only traffic coming from host *pizza* destined to host *pepperoni* can pass if the following criteria are met:

1. Traffic can pass only after 4:00 p.m.

2. Only FTP Get, Telnet, and HTTP services are allowed.

3. Security tokens are required to authenticate the users.

4. Only users from the finance group are allowed.

 **NOTE** Many sites on the Internet have been compromised due to misconfiguration of the firewall software. Configuration and setup should be left to security professionals with extensive experience in setting up firewalls.

## Firewall Placement

A firewall is best placed behind your router connecting to the Internet. All network traffic must first hit the router, which performs the first level of packet filtering. The packets then enter the firewall through one network interface, go through a filtering process, and exit to the second interface that connects to the internal network. The Gauntlet from Trusted Information System, Firewall-1 from CheckPoint Software Technologies, and Eagle from Raptor Systems Inc. are some of the more popularly used firewalls. Of the three, Eagle is the only product that runs on Windows NT, whereas the other two products support only Unix.

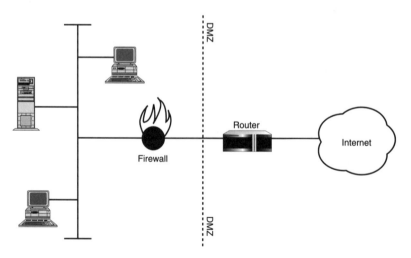

**Figure 13.10:**
The location of the firewall, router, local segments, DMZ, and connection to the Internet.

A Demilitarized Zone (DMZ) is the region between the router and firewall.

## Adding Additional Bastion Hosts and DMZs

To improve on the previous design you can introduce a second bastion host and a second DMZ. Introducing a second bastion host creates two domains where the first domain guards against outside intrusion while the second domain guards against internal attacks. Therefore, it is recommended that you place hosts with less sensitive data on the second DMZ and hosts with the most sensitive material behind the second bastion host. For example, file and print servers can be positioned on the second DMZ while a SQL Server containing payroll information can be located behind the second bastion host. Because firewall configuration can get very complex and mistakes can lead to a security breach, you might want to use a different staff to configure each firewall. Before implementing this setup, it might be to your benefit to determine the estimated cost of the project. Keep in mind that cost includes hardware, software, and personnel.

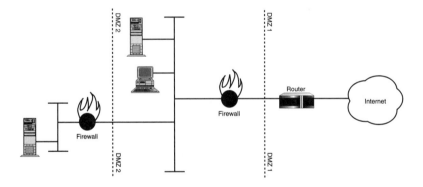

### Figure 13.11:
Dual DMZ and bastion hosts.

## Web Server Placement

Deciding on the physical location of the Web server is an important security decision. If a public Web server is placed within the internal network, the firewall must be configured to pass through all Web clients. If not, once inside, an intruder can hack away at your private network since they have already penetrated your strongest defenses.

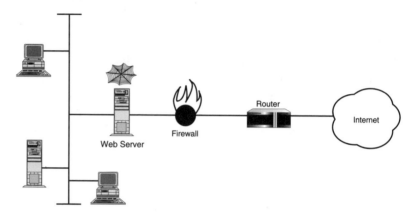

**Figure 13.12:**
Where not to put your Web server.

Instead, place your Web server in the DMZ, because if an intruder bypasses the security on the Web server, they will still have to contend with breaching the firewall.

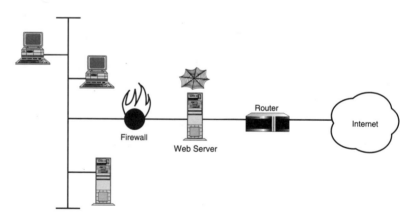

**Figure 13.13:**
Where to place your Web server.

The firewall is your primary defense in stopping unwanted intruders from the Internet. Because improper configuration of a firewall is as dangerous as having no firewall, you should ensure that the implementation is done by a qualified person. As the need in your company arises, additional security can be implemented with a secondary bastion host. But be forewarned that installing a second host requires increased administration and financial resources. When it is time to pick a firewall, I recommend getting the June 17,1996 copy of LAN TIMES Special Internet Issue. This issue rates the seven leading firewalls and includes a thorough comparison of each product.

# Defining a Corporate Security Plan

Whether you like it or not, part of your job as Webmaster or network administrator is to protect corporate data. Today, almost all companies recognize this and have initiated implementing a security policy. As the outbreak of computer viruses and security attacks make front page headlines, business managers will want to know how their corporate data is being protected. Implementing network security is complex and a formal set of procedures is vital in ensuring that your implementation satisfies the needs of the organization.

Setting a corporate policy of any kind requires the full support of upper management. Similarly, the creation of a corporate security policy requires substantial political and financial commitment. The implementation of a security policy impacts business units and the input of line managers is important to understanding the need of the corporation. Before approaching management to start a security initiative, it is important that you develop a well thought-out plan. The following operations order provides you with a template in devising your Corporate Security Plan.

## Implementing a Security Plan in Four Steps

The template for implementing a security plan includes establishing and defining four components: Situation, Mission

Statement, Implementation, and Staffing. By addressing the issues and questions presented in each section, you should be able to produce a formal security plan from the results.

## Security Situations

This section presents an overview of the current security environment and provides evidence of why a security plan is needed.

1. Describe your current situation.

2. What steps prompted you to create this report?

3. Have there been recent security attacks?

4. Was a computer-savvy disgruntled employee recently let go?

5. What security systems do you have in place? Identify any obvious security holes.

6. Define, in dollar amounts, current and future possible losses due to security breaches.

7. Define the budget for this project.

## Security Mission Statement

The Mission Statement should be a short paragraph stating corporate policy regarding computer security.

To define your security policy fundamentals, determine the following:

➤ Data Access—Determining who can access what data.

➤ Data Integrity—Ensuring that the data is not modified between sender and receiver.

➤ Confidentiality—Guaranteeing that messages cannot be found by snoopers.

➤ Accountability—Holding employees responsible for the enforcement of security procedures.

➤ Security Violators—Determining what to do with violators.

A sample mission statement:

To provide a high a degree of data reliability and protection for all users of the corporate information system by enforcing account-ability for all systems employees; to report violators to the proper authorities; and to seek prosecution for violators.

# Security Implementation

This section is the core of your security plan and should be the largest section of the plan. Take time to read this section over thoroughly because weak security is an invitation for intruders to break into your network. The implementation of network security requires skilled individuals. If you lack such individuals, you may want to contract a security professional to help with the implementation. It may also be prudent to keep the implement-ation team small in order to control the access of detailed infor-mation. The following steps outline the process of implementing security:

1. Decide if you have the expertise or resources to initiate the security plan. Consult security vendors if necessary.

2. Form a security team.

3. Gather Information about your site.

4. Speak with line managers about their security concerns.

5. Define your current network infrastructure. Include recent network diagrams that show connectivity to internal and external networks.

6. From your network diagrams, identify all access points and rank each according to the level of threat.

7. Identify Network Operating Systems in your organization and any security flaws.

8. Select security products for evaluation.

9. Define testing criteria and performance expectation.

10. Initiate proof of concept testing.

11. Deploy security product in incremental fashion, if possible.

12. Develop procedures to monitor security events.

13. Determine what you will do if you detect a break-in. Will you capture as much information as possible and contact the authorities?

14. Decide how often and when monitoring will take place.

15. Consider hiring an outside security firm to perform a control penetration of your site.

16. Create network policy documentation to educate management and users.

## Staffing for Security

List all individuals involved in the security project. It is to your advantage to keep this group as small as possible.

1. State their roles and tasks.

2. Determine their availability.

Example of a security implementation team:

**Project Manager**: Oversees the planning and execution of the security plan. This person may be a network manager or the head of the security department.

**Network Engineer**: Familiar with the internal network infrastructure and can provide insight into possible security holes. This person is responsible for assisting the Security Expert with the implementation.

**Network Administrator**: Carries out the implementation at the user level and provides security training to users.

**Security Expert**: Has previous experience in implementing firewalls and router security. If you do not have the expertise in-house you may want to subcontract this position.

# Securing Transactions on the Internet

Doing business on the World Wide Web is still in its infancy. With 30 million potential customers, merchants big and small have flocked to the Web in hopes of cashing in on this new market. Unfortunately, the biggest show stopper is the absence of a standardized payment system on the Internet. Currently a variety of encryption/authentication methods (i.e. Secure Socket Layer protocol) and third party payment systems (such as Cybercash) enable electronic transactions; however, for Internet commerce to prosper, the standardization of a single system that encompasses encryption and payment procedures must be available.

The attributes of a payment system must include:

➤ Authentication of the cardholder's identity

➤ Authentication of the merchant's identity

➤ Confidentiality and data integrity of payment information

➤ Standard procedures dictating the processing of the payment information

# SET

Bowing to market reality, the two credit card giants, MasterCard and Visa, have cooperated to develop the basis of a standard payment system for the Internet called Secure Electronic Transaction (SET). Industry players such as Netscape, Microsoft, IBM, and GTE have pledged support for SET. Given the strength of the endorsers, it is only a matter of time before SET becomes a reality. As of this writing, SET is in the form of an Internet draft and may be ratified by the time you are reading this book.

According to the SET specifications, seven business requirements are addressed:

➤ Payment and order information must be transmitted confidentially.

➤ Data integrity for all interactions.

➤ Authentication that the cardholder is a valid user of a branded bankcard account.

➤ Authentication that the merchant can accept the cardholder's branded bankcard with its financial institution.

➤ Provide the very best in security and systems techniques to guard the transaction of all parties involved.

➤ Creation of a system-independent protocol.

➤ Interoperability across different software and network providers.

Here is how SET works:

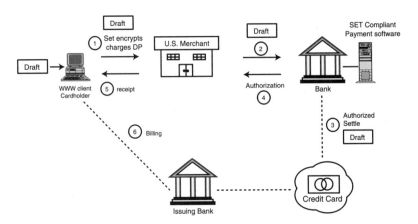

**Figure 13.14:**

SET Implementation.

# CyberCash

CyberCash is an independent Internet payment service that provides secure transactions for consumers and merchants. The CyberCash system can be described in the following six steps:

1. A consumer selects an item to purchase. The merchant's server returns with product description, order ID, and payment information.

2. The consumer launches a CyberCash Wallet by clicking on to the "Pay" button. The buyer then selects a credit card from their "wallet" and clicks OK. The payment and order information is sent encrypted to the merchant.

3. The merchant sends the payment information encrypted with his private key along with a digital signature to the CyberCash server. The consumer's credit card information is never revealed to the merchant.

4. The Cybercash server receives the transaction and sends it to the merchant's bank over private lines.

5. The merchant's bank then sends the authorization request to the cardholder's bank via the card association (i.e. MasterCard, Visa) or directly to American Express or Discover.

6. An approval or denial code is then sent back to the merchant from CyberCash. The approval or denial information is eventually passed by to the consumer.

It usually takes between 15-20 seconds for the entire transaction to be completed.

# VeriFone

VeriFone designs, manufactures, markets, and supports Transaction Automation solutions, including Internet payment services. VeriFone played a major role in expanding the opportunities for Transaction Automation in the payment processing market by offering the first low-cost terminals for electronic credit card authorization. You can find more information for VeriFone at **http://www.verifone.com**.

## Open Market

Open Market, Inc. develops high-performance software products for conducting commerce on the Internet. Open Market provides a complete Internet payment service for merchants to securely run their business on the World Wide Web. Open Market can be reached at **http://www.openmarket.com**.

## Server Security Basics

"As the Webmaster of the American Teddy Bear Co., you have been assigned the task—should you choose to accept—to guard the Web Server from unauthorized access. You have two days to complete the mission. This tape will self-destruct in thirty seconds...."

## C2 Security

Luckily, your job is not as impossible as it may seem. If you are running Windows NT, you may already know that NT provides a robust and stable platform to run your Web server. But did you know that Windows NT contains superb security features such as government-certified C2 security, user account security, auditing, and file system security?

Unlike Unix, Windows NT was developed with security in mind. One of the design goals was to obtain government C2 level certification, which provides "discretionary [need to know] protection and, through the inclusion of audit capabilities, accountability of subjects and the actions they initiate." Basically, C2 security means resource owners have the ability to protect access to data and the system has the capability to track how and when data is accessed.

# NTFS Security

The file system is one of the most important components of an operating system. A robust file system should enable data to be stored and retrieved in a fast and reliable manner. Even as the amount of data stored on a server increases, the file system must be able to maintain a consistent level of performance. A file system residing on a desktop is inherently less critical than that of a file server. Support for large disks, security, auditing, data protection, and recoverability are some features that should be on your shopping list when choosing a file system for your server.

Windows NT Server supports FAT (File Allocation Table), NTFS (NT File System), and HPFS (High Performance File System) file systems. Of the three, NTFS is your best choice. Tables 13.3–13.5 help to illustrate this choice.

### Table 13.3    File Allocation Table

| Advantages | Disadvantages |
| --- | --- |
| Works fast on small disks | No security, auditing, and data protection |
| Widely supported | No bad block remapping |
| Standard format for floppy disks | Single FAT volume can hold up to only 65,518 files |
| | Performance decreases as amount of storage grows |
| | Restricted to 8 by 3 file names |

### Table 13.4    NTFS

| Advantages | Disadvantages |
| --- | --- |
| Has NTFS security, auditing, and data protection capabilities (disk striping, disk mirroring, for example) | Performance decreases for small disk |
| Can perform bad block remapping | Large overhead |

*continues*

**Table 13.4    Continued**

| Advantages | Disadvantages |
| --- | --- |
| Disk compression | |
| Recoverable file system | |
| File names can be up to 256 characters | |
| Linear performance even as the amount of storage grows | |
| Support for very large disk (up to 32 tetrabytes) | |
| POSIX support | |

To remain secure, NTFS restricts access from other operating systems. Recently, a public domain program called NTFSDOS.EXE (from Numega Technologies) has surfaced that bypasses NT security and lets DOS and Windows open and copy files on NTFS. If NTFSDOS.EXE is placed on a floppy and booted from a server, your files are no longer secure. Microsoft has responded by stating that programs such as NTFSDOS.EXE only confirm the importance of having tough physical security for your servers.

**Table 13.5    HPFS**

| Advantages | Disadvantages |
| --- | --- |
| Support for file names up to 255 characters | Rapidly losing market share |
| HPFS volumes can access up to 2 GB-based systems | Inherits design restrictions from OS/2 |
| Can perform bad block remapping | Not as robust and expandable as NTFS |

## User Account Security

WWW clients accessing the Internet Information Server do not get authenticated by NT's normal logon services and must rely on a special account (IUSR_computername) created for Internet users. If my computer name is PAULT, then the Internet user (IUSR) account would be named IUSR PAULT. Thus, you must protect all aspects of this special account.

# Ensuring a Secure Environment

A combination of Windows NT and IIS security enables the Webmaster to exert a finer degree of control over who can access the Web server. To ensure that excessive rights are not granted and misconfiguration does not occur, several account security settings should be reviewed. To ensure a secure environment for IIS, log on as an administrator and review the following:

➤ Account Policy

➤ User rights for IUSR_computername

➤ Administrator accounts

# Windows NT Account Policy Capabilities

In Windows NT, it is possible for network administrators to restrict access based on system-wide settings known as account policies. The settings in the Account Policy screen should be reviewed carefully for excessive rights.

Windows NT Account Policy enables you to:

➤ Change password restrictions

➤ Perform account lock-outs

➤ Force remote users to be disconnected when their log on hours expire

➤ Select whether users must log on in order to change password

# Viewing and Implementing Account Policy Settings

To view your Account Policy settings:

1. Double-click on the User Manager for Domains icon.

2. Select Policies, Account. The Account Policy screen appears.

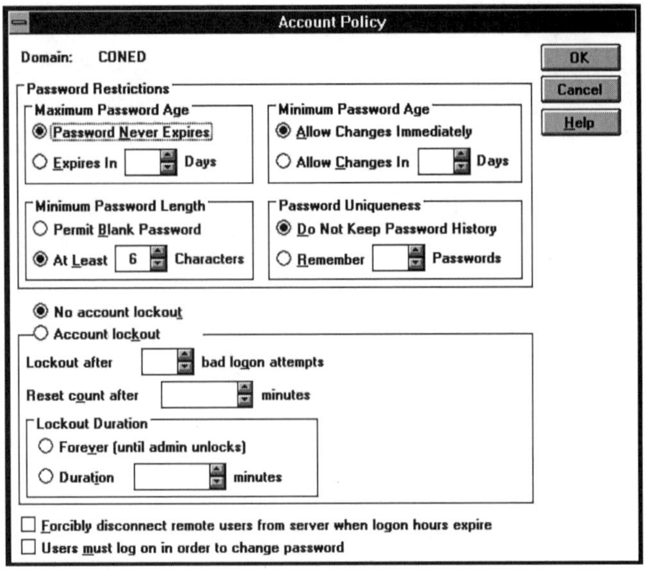

**Figure 13.15:**

Viewing Account Policy settings.

To tailor your Account Policy settings for IIS here are recommended settings:

**Maximum Password Age**: 30 days

**Miminim Password Age**: Allow Changes Immediately

**Minimum Password Length**: At Least 8 Characters

**Password Uniqueness**: Remember 3 Password

**Account lockout**: selected

**Lockout after**: 5 bad logon attempts

**Reset count after**: 30 minutes

**Lockout Duration**: 30 minutes

The Account Policy settings are global and affect all users!

# Reviewing IUSR_computername Account

The IUSR_computername account is created by default when you install IIS. All IIS clients use this account to log on. To prevent access to other internal server data, the IUSR_computername account enables users to only logon locally.

To review the IUSR_computername account:

1. Double-click on User Manager for Domains.

2. Double-click on the IUSR_computername account.

3. User Cannot Change Password and Password Never Expires should be checked.

4. Click on Groups. Delete any unnecessary group memberships for the account.

5. Click on Hours. Does the account have 7 by 24 access?

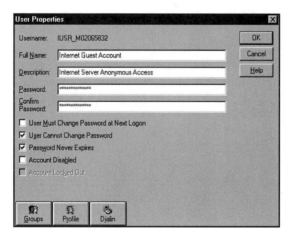

**Figure 13.16:**

IUSR_computername dialog box.

# Reviewing the User Rights Policy

User Rights Policies dictate what actions can be performed by users. Actions such as Force shutdown from a remote system should only be performed by Administrators or Server Operators.

To simplify administration, user rights should be assigned to groups instead of users. The "Logon locally" right is of special importance to IIS. To maintain a secured environment, IIS clients should be restricted to log on only to the local IIS server.

To review the User Rights Policy:

1. Select Policy and User Rights from the User Manager for Domains.

2. Select Log on Locally from the drop-down list box.

3. Check that IUSR_computername is in the Grant To box.

Administrator accounts can perform all system tasks without restrictions. Therefore, you should grant administrator access to only a selected few.

## Auditing

Auditing is the process of tracking access to system resources. Windows NT provides auditing information in three logs: Application, System, and Security. The information generated in the logs are useful for billing, security, system maintenance, and troubleshooting. Windows NT allows for the successful and failed audits of system events and file access. If a WWW client attempts to access unauthorized files, an entry would be created in the Security log. The log would state the time the user logged on and the files that user was trying to access. Repeated failed audits from the same user should be viewed as a potential security attack and appropriate steps should be taken (What does your security policy say about dealing with offenders?). It is the responsibility of the Webmaster or network administrator to periodically view the entries in the Security log to look for unauthorized access.

## Implementing Auditing

The auditing process is as follows:

1. Log on as an administrator.

2. Run User Manager for Domains.

3. Click Policies and then Audit.

4. To start auditing, click Audit These Events.

5. Select the check box for events you would like to audit.

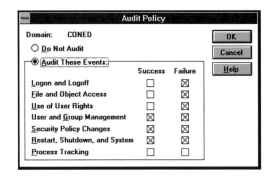

**Figure 13.17:**
Audit Policy screen.

## Recommended Events for Auditing

In the IIS environment, Web clients typically perform two actions—logging in and out, and file access. At the minimum, you should audit these two events. You can do so by highlighting the success and failure box for "Logon and Logoff" and "File and Object Access." It is recommended that the following events be audited on IIS:

➤ **Logon and Logoff**—records when user logs on and logs off. Important for tracking unauthorized access to your IIS system

➤ **File and Object Access**—records any access to files and directories. Lets you know when an IIS user attempts to access restricted files, directories, and objects (any entity that contains a name is an object, such as a printer).

➤ **User and Group Management**—modifies user account information. Ensure that the permissions of the IUSR_computername account and the groups assigned to this account are not modified.

➤ **Security Policy Changes**—records changes to audit, user rights, and trust policies. Auditing this entry would notify you of user right changes to the IUSR computername account. (Remember that this account should be allowed to only log on locally.)

## Auditing Directories/Files

You can track access to specific files and directories on Windows NT. There are six events that can be audited: Read, Write, Execute, Delete, Change Permissions, and Take Ownership. One directory that you may want to audit for write permission is the C:\WINNT\SYSTEM32 directory. This directory contains executables, DLLs, and system-related files. In IIS, you may want to turn on Write, Change Permissions, and Take ownership for the following directories: <home>, /scripts, and /cgi-bin (this directory is not created by default, but is a popular name for Common Gateway Interface scripts). To audit a file or directory, do the following:

1. Log on as an administrator.

2. Start File Manager.

3. Highlight a file or directory you want to audit.

4. Select Security, Auditing.

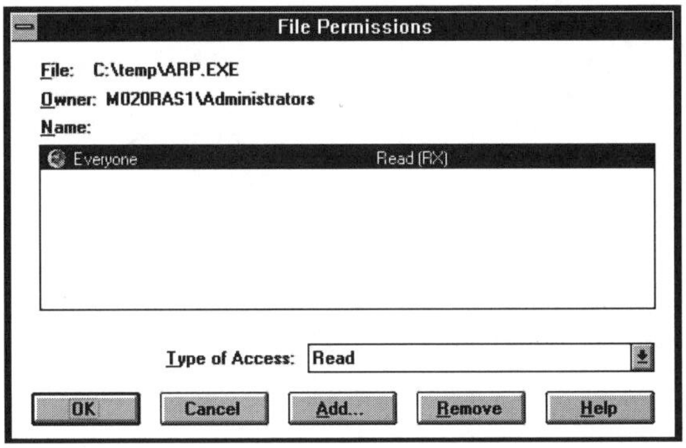

**Figure 13.18:**

File audit screen.

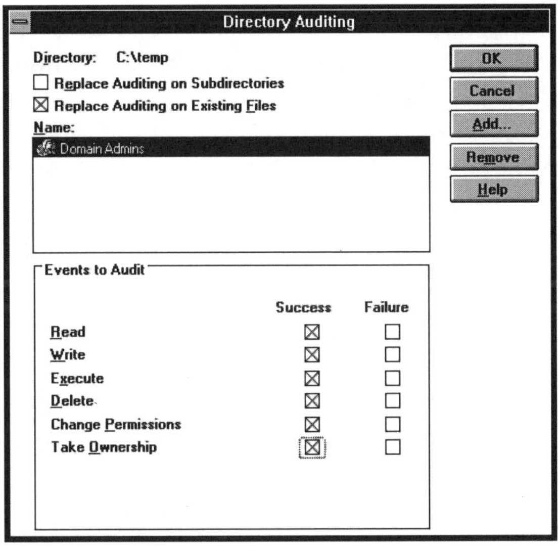

**Figure 13.19:**

Directory audit screen.

# IIS Security

IIS is tightly integrated with NT security and provides a high level of security with the following outlined features.

➤ Anonymous Access with IUSR_computername

➤ IP Address Restrictions

➤ Directory Permissions on IIS

➤ Secure Channel Protocols

## Anonymous Access with IUSR_computername

As you may know, anonymous access is available with a special user account (IUSR_computername). An anonymous user is defined as any user who has not been granted a username with permissions to use the system. The IUSR_computername account gives administrators a finer degree of control by funneling Internet users into a special account. As a result, monitoring security of Internet users has become much simpler.

The IUSR_computername account is set up, by default, to log on locally only. This safeguard prevents any untrusted user from gaining access to any other server on the network. In addition, the IUSR_computername account is assigned to be part of the Guest group and Everyone group. To provide maximum protection, review your settings (refer to the Recommended Events for Auditing section) to make sure these two groups can log on locally only.

## IP Address Restrictions

If you have a router or a firewall on your network, access restrictions for IP addresses might already exist. You can further control and limit access to IIS by defining your own set of trusted IP addresses. For instance, you are setting up an internal Web server, and you only want to grant access to selected users. This can be easily accomplished by clicking the Granted Access button and adding the respective IP addresses of the users. IP restrictions or access can be defined for a single computer or an entire network by specifying the subnet mask.

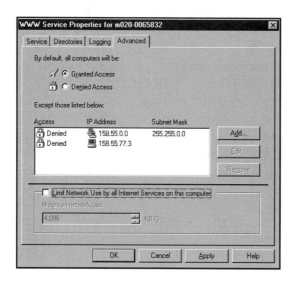

**Figure 13.20:**
Configuring advance settings for the WWW service.

## Directory Permissions on IIS

By using File Manager, you can easily set directory and file permissions on IIS. Refer to table 13.6 to set up directory restrictions

**Table 13.6    Directory Restriction Settings**

| Type of content | Access |
| --- | --- |
| HTML files, graphic files (Gifs, JPEGs) | Read-Only |
| Scripting programs (Perl and Visual Basic) | Read and Execute |
| CGI and ISAPI applications | Read and Write |
| SQL SERVER and other kinds of databases | Read and Write |

If there is contention between IIS security and NTFS security, the system will default to the more secure setting.

# Secure Channel Protocols

Secure channel protocols such as S-HTTP, SSL, and PCT enable information to traverse the Internet in a secure manner. Credit card and payment information can now be sent with assurances that the data will not be altered or viewed by unintended parties. Though these protocols do a fine job securing your transaction, no facilities exist that authenticate the identities of cardholders, merchants, and issuers. None of the three secure channel protocols being discussed here have been ratified by any standards body (such as the IETF or W3C group on security).

 The Secure Electronic Transaction (SET) protocol, developed jointly by MasterCard and Visa, addresses deficiencies in secure channel protocols. Look for SET to become a major specification in Internet commerce (refer to the discussion of SET in the section "Securing Transactions on the Internet").

## Secure HTTP

S-HTTP is a secure end-to-end transaction protocol proposed by Enterprise Integration Technologies in order to provide authentication, privacy, and data integrity. S-HTTP is HTTP with security enhancements and, thus, functions on the application layer of the OSI model. S-HTTP does not provide any protection with protocols other than HTTP. To access an S-HTTP site, you must specify **shttp://** in your URL instead of the usual **http://**. S-HTTP utilizes public key encryption from RSA Data Security (**http://www.rsa.com**) as its core security mechanism.

 Microsoft's Internet Information Server does not support S-HTTP.

# Secure Sockets Layer

SSL is a secure communications protocol developed by Netscape Corporation that features privacy, authentication, and data compression. IIS and Microsoft Explorer 2.0 for Windows 95 support SSL.

Netscape designed SSL to provide message security from the network layer to the application layer of the OSI model. Unlike S-HHTP, SSL can provide security regardless of what application layer program (http, Telnet, ftp, smtp, and so on) is used. Both the client and the server must support SSL. In order for the server to use SSL, you must specify an **https://**. For non-SSL applications, you may continue to use the familiar **http://**. The Internet Assigned Numbers Authority has specifically assigned port number 443 for the use of SSL.

The Internet Assigned Numbers Authority (IANA) is a central authority responsible for the assignment of IP addresses and other Internet-related numbering (such as port numbers). This duty has been given to the InterNIC (www.rs.internic.net). In January of 1993 the InterNIC was established as a collaborative project between AT&T, General Atomics and Network Solutions, Inc. and supported by three five-year cooperative agreements with the National Science Foundation. AT&T was assigned the InterNIC Directory and Database Services project. NSI was assigned the Registration Services project and General Atomics was given Information Services project.

The details of an SSL dialogue is as follows:

1.  A "Hello" message is sent by the SSL client to the SSL server.

2.  The SSL server responds by sending a certificate that includes the public key of the server. Currently only server-side certificates are supported in IIS.

3.  Using RC4 (a symmetric key encryption from RSA), a session key is generated. This key is encrypted using the server's public key.

4. The SSL server receives the session key and decrypts it using its secret key.

5. A secure channel has been created. All subsequent session information (URLs, all HTTP requests and responses, content data, and so on) is sent in encrypted form.

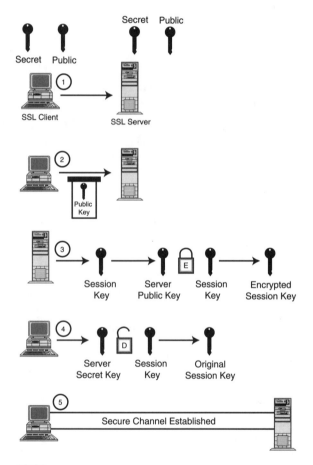

**Figure 13.21:**

SSL dialogue.

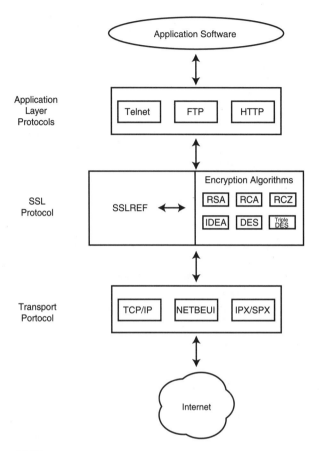

**Figure 13.22:**

SSL stack.

The steps for implementing SSL on IIS are as follows:

1. Generate a key pair file and a request file.

2. Request a certificate from a Certification Authority.

3. Install the certificate on your server.

4. Activate PCT/SSL security on a WWW service directory.

### Step 1. Generating a key pair file and a request file

SSL uses symmetric key technology. Your first step is to generate a key pair (keypair.key) that contains a private and a public key for the server. In addition, a request file (request.req) containing the server's Distinguished Name (DN) needs to be created and sent to VeriSign. In IIS 2.0, there are two methods to creating a key pair and a request file. The first method is with the graphical utility called Key Manager. The second method is with the command-line utility called Keygen. Because VeriSign requests information from the command-line utility, the examples presented are to be used with Keygen.

```
c:\winnt40\system32\inetsrv\server>keygen MyPassword1
keypair.key request.req "C=US, S=NEWJERSEY, L=OLDBRIDGE,
O=EXAMPLE, OU=ACCOUNTING, CN=www.mycompany.com"
PCT/SSL Key generation utility, Version 1.0
Copyright (c) 1995 Microsoft Corporation
Generating key pair of length 1024 bits...
Completed.
```

Send the generated request file, Request.req, to your Certificate Authority for signing.

 **NOTE**    If you prefer to use Key Manager instead of Keygen, you would need to replicate the Keygen command-line syntax because this is required by VeriSign.

### Step 2. Requesting a certificate from a Certification Authority

Next, you need to request a certificate from VeriSign. SSL cannot be enabled on IIS until a digital certificate is installed. Send an e-mail to VeriSign with the Keygen command-line syntax and the key request file. You can use Notepad to copy the contents of the key request file into the clipboard and then paste it into your e-mail.

```
From: webmaster@mycompany.com
To: microsoft-request-id@verisign.com
Subject: Certificate Request

C:\inetsrv\server>keygen <be sure to remove your pass-
word> keypair.key request.req "C=US, S=NEWJERSEY,
L=OLDBRIDGE, O=EXAMPLE, OU=ACCOUNTING,
CN=www.mycompany.com"

----BEGIN NEW CERTIFICATE REQUEST----
GkD1iN3sEPfSTGxNJXY58XH3JoZ4nrF7mIfvpghNi1taYimvhbBPNqYe4y
➥LPAgMB
MIIB0DCCAXoCAQAwDQYJKoZIhvcNAQECBQAwczELMAkGA1UEBhMCVVMxID
➥AeBgNVB
AoTF1JTQSBEYXRhIFNlY3VyaXR5LCBJbmMuMRwwGgYDVQQLExNQZXJz
b25hIENlcnRpZmljYXRlMSQwIgYDVQQDExtPcGVuIE1hcmtldCBUZXN0IFN
➥lcnZlci
AxMTAwHhcNOTUwNzE5MjAyNzMwWhcNOTYwNTE0MjAyOTEwWjBzMQswCQY
➥DVQQGEwJVUzEgM
B4GA1UEChMXUlNBIERhdGEgU2VjdXJpdHksIEluYy4xHDAaBgNVBAs
TE1BlcnNvbmEgQ2VydGlmaWNhdGUxJDAiBgNVBAMTG09wZW4gTWFya2a2
➥V0IFRlc
3QgU2VydmVyIDExMDBcMA0GCSqGSIb3DQEBAQUAA0sAMEgCQQDU7lrgR6
vkVNX40BAq1poGdSmpfhv+iP8m+bF66HNDUlFz8ZrVOu3WQapgLPV90
kIskNKXX3a+8NY8khckgyHN2LLcnRpZmljYXRlMSQwIgYDVQ
QDExtPcGVuIE1hcmtldCBUZXN0
------END NEW CERTIFICATE REQUEST----
```

## Step 3. Installing the certificate on your server

Once you received your signed certificate from VeriSign, you
must install the certificate into IIS. Use a text editor such as
Notepad to copy the following text to a file (i.e., cert.txt).

```
From: certificate@verisign.com
To:   webmaster@mycompany.com
Subject: Certificate Response
```

*continues*

```
----BEGIN NEW CERTIFICATE REQUEST----
MIIBnDCCAQUCAQAwXjELMAkGA1UEBhMCVVMxCzAJBgNVBAgTAk5ZMQww
➡CgYDVQQH
EwNOWUMxDjAMBgNVBAoTBWNvbmVkMQswCQYDVQQLEwJpcjEXMBUGA1UEAx
➡QOdHNv
cEBjb25lZC5jb20wgZ8wDQYJKoZIhvcNAQEBBQADgY0AMIGJAoGBAIKM
➡dhj43UxU
SVprLPfpi1wTmcdfmRVKahhSzsnmzkGr+0W17ZgYjVdo0JxzTCB6P2gni9
➡zpbJvd
wfUC9Mt1gsJTCoUQoDBnVtmBXuLeETfk7DwiKYFvLO/
eKt0PMv+PRMiMY2mH29B4
/
qNa7FaanSJvlkw7msD6BVxSqnTqXg55AgMBAAEwDQYJKoZIhvcNAQEBQ
➡ADgYEA
MH1y/
gH9UE5nh6190eet4yydgexW8pGd0rKNweXx4eylhOD+aYW7PwQ0F70c/
z5j
9tDJBvbTEc6Py8yN8FCOxCAyAjnJXW7Bh/RxJWhlrpBuL1gtE8rht/
UTdu/oHfSl
2+89AKYIgATep1VnZ0plGyCdjlfA2MCwpfDPI0WTKVo=
----END NEW CERTIFICATE REQUEST----
```

Next, use Setkey to install the certificate into IIS:

```
setkey MyPassword keypair.key cert.txt
```

If you are using Key Manager, click on **Key** and then **Install Key Certificate.**

## Step 4. Activating PCT/SSL security on a WWW service directory

1. Run Internet Service Manager to activate PCT/SSL security.

2. Double-click on the WWW Service for the IIS computer.

3. Click on the Directory tab.

4. Double-click on the directory where you want to install SSL.

5. Click on the Require secure SSL channel check box.

# Private Communication Technology Protocol (PCT)

Microsoft Corporation devised the PCT protocol to correct inadequacies and introduce enhancements to the SSL protocol. The goal of Microsoft is not to replace SSL, but to strive for the convergence of the two protocols. The PCT protocol resembles the SSL protocol, for the most part. Most of the changes revolve around the details in the "handshaking phase" of the SSL protocol. For more detailed information, refer to the Internet Draft on PCT: **http://pct.microsoft.com/pct/pct.htm**.

# Security Utilities for Windows NT

Windows NT contains many robust security features such as C2 security, NTFS, and file auditing. But even with that arsenal of tools, the lack of proper configuration can render the system defenseless. The tools described here help reveal gaping security holes in your system by analyzing your current security configuration. Used appropriately, the following tools will strengthen the walls that protect your NT server.

# Security Log

Windows NT provides auditing and logging for security events such as failed logons, file and directory access, and system shutdowns. To view successful and failed security audits, run event viewer and select Log and Security. A key symbol denotes a successful audit; a lock symbol denotes a failed audit. A failed audit denotes an unauthorized attempt by a user to access restricted resource. Some failed audits are the result of unintentional access while others signify deliberate attempts to hack into your systems. Look for a trend in the security log to determine if someone is staging an attack on your server. Because attacks can occur at any time, the security log should be viewed periodically to ensure there are no violations.

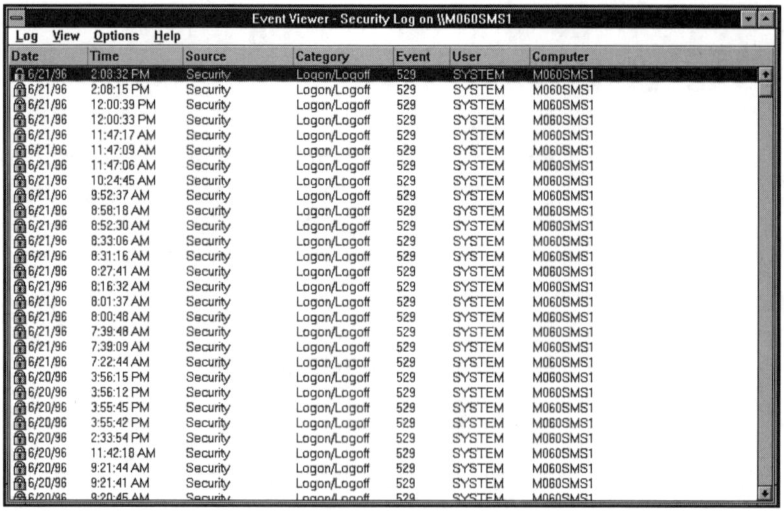
Event Viewer - Security Log on \\M060SMS1

Log View Options Help

| Date | Time | Source | Category | Event | User | Computer |
|---|---|---|---|---|---|---|
| 6/21/96 | 2:08:32 PM | Security | Logon/Logoff | 529 | SYSTEM | M060SMS1 |
| 6/21/96 | 2:08:15 PM | Security | Logon/Logoff | 529 | SYSTEM | M060SMS1 |
| 6/21/96 | 12:00:39 PM | Security | Logon/Logoff | 529 | SYSTEM | M060SMS1 |
| 6/21/96 | 12:00:33 PM | Security | Logon/Logoff | 529 | SYSTEM | M060SMS1 |
| 6/21/96 | 11:47:17 AM | Security | Logon/Logoff | 529 | SYSTEM | M060SMS1 |
| 6/21/96 | 11:47:09 AM | Security | Logon/Logoff | 529 | SYSTEM | M060SMS1 |
| 6/21/96 | 11:47:06 AM | Security | Logon/Logoff | 529 | SYSTEM | M060SMS1 |
| 6/21/96 | 10:24:45 AM | Security | Logon/Logoff | 529 | SYSTEM | M060SMS1 |
| 6/21/96 | 9:52:37 AM | Security | Logon/Logoff | 529 | SYSTEM | M060SMS1 |
| 6/21/96 | 8:58:18 AM | Security | Logon/Logoff | 529 | SYSTEM | M060SMS1 |
| 6/21/96 | 8:52:30 AM | Security | Logon/Logoff | 529 | SYSTEM | M060SMS1 |
| 6/21/96 | 8:33:06 AM | Security | Logon/Logoff | 529 | SYSTEM | M060SMS1 |
| 6/21/96 | 8:31:16 AM | Security | Logon/Logoff | 529 | SYSTEM | M060SMS1 |
| 6/21/96 | 8:27:41 AM | Security | Logon/Logoff | 529 | SYSTEM | M060SMS1 |
| 6/21/96 | 8:16:32 AM | Security | Logon/Logoff | 529 | SYSTEM | M060SMS1 |
| 6/21/96 | 8:01:37 AM | Security | Logon/Logoff | 529 | SYSTEM | M060SMS1 |
| 6/21/96 | 8:00:48 AM | Security | Logon/Logoff | 529 | SYSTEM | M060SMS1 |
| 6/21/96 | 7:39:48 AM | Security | Logon/Logoff | 529 | SYSTEM | M060SMS1 |
| 6/21/96 | 7:39:09 AM | Security | Logon/Logoff | 529 | SYSTEM | M060SMS1 |
| 6/21/96 | 7:22:44 AM | Security | Logon/Logoff | 529 | SYSTEM | M060SMS1 |
| 6/20/96 | 3:56:15 PM | Security | Logon/Logoff | 529 | SYSTEM | M060SMS1 |
| 6/20/96 | 3:56:12 PM | Security | Logon/Logoff | 529 | SYSTEM | M060SMS1 |
| 6/20/96 | 3:55:45 PM | Security | Logon/Logoff | 529 | SYSTEM | M060SMS1 |
| 6/20/96 | 3:55:42 PM | Security | Logon/Logoff | 529 | SYSTEM | M060SMS1 |
| 6/20/96 | 2:33:54 PM | Security | Logon/Logoff | 529 | SYSTEM | M060SMS1 |
| 6/20/96 | 11:42:18 AM | Security | Logon/Logoff | 529 | SYSTEM | M060SMS1 |
| 6/20/96 | 9:21:44 AM | Security | Logon/Logoff | 529 | SYSTEM | M060SMS1 |
| 6/20/96 | 9:21:41 AM | Security | Logon/Logoff | 529 | SYSTEM | M060SMS1 |
| 6/20/96 | 9:20:45 AM | Security | Logon/Logoff | 529 | SYSTEM | M060SMS1 |

**Figure 13.23:**
Security log.

# The Kane Security Analyst (KSA)

The Kane Security Analyst was developed by Intrusion Detection Inc., a New York-based company specializing in network security software. The KSA provides assessment of your overall NT security environment and reports security deficiencies in six areas: password strength, access control, user account restrictions, system monitoring, data integrity, and data confidentiality. An evaluation copy is available for download from **http://www.intrusion.com**.

The KSA can analyze the following security attributes:

- Password cracking test
- C2 security
- Trust relationship
- Scripted passwords
- Audit policy compliance

Excessive rights

Registry security settings

Login violations

Domain security

Security logs

User and group permissions across domains

Password strength

Event logs

Nonsecure partitions

UPS status

Security report cards

Guest ID configuration

NT services

Domains that can't be administered

Down level authentication

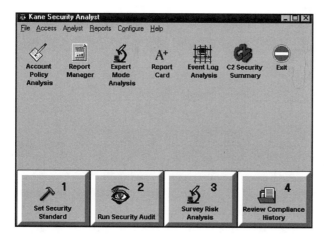

**Figure 13.24:**

KSA.

## Somarsoft DumpAcl V2.7

DumpAcl gathers permissions (or Access Control Lists) from the file system, registry, shares, and printers; and outputs them in an easy-to-read format. This tool can generate a single report that you can use to scan for security holes. DumpAcl can be run from any NT workstation and server. An evaluation copy can be obtained from **http://www.somarsoft.com**.

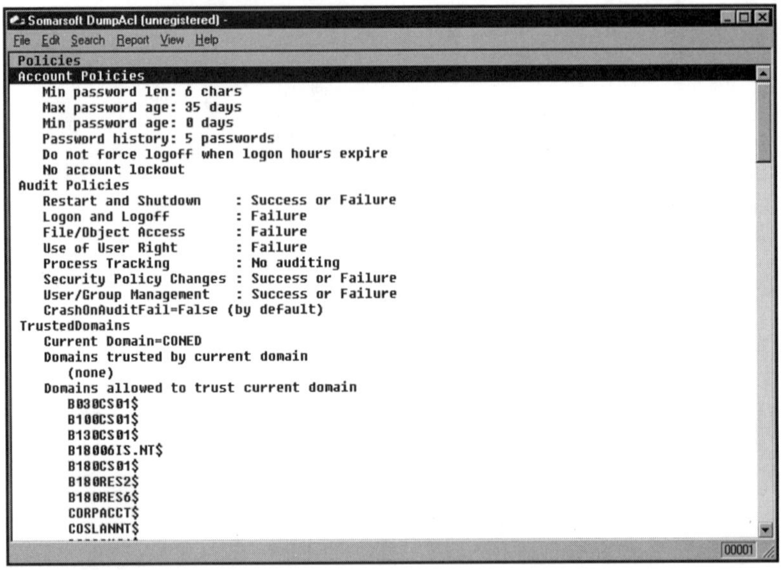

**Figure 13.25:**

DumpACL from Somarsoft, Inc.

## Recovering Lost Passwords

If you are unfortunate enough to lose your administrator's password, third-party programs are available to help you recover lost passwords or create a new superuser. These tools require that you have some access to the server—either physical access or access to the registry. These tools are a reminder that strong physical security is still a necessity for securing your Windows NT server.

To avoid having to use a password recovery program, it is good practice to create an emergency repair disk by running "rdisk.exe -s"(the -s updates the sam and security databases). The disk should then be labeled with the administrator's password and stored in a secure compartment.

## ScanNT v 1.1

ScanNT from MWC, Inc. uses the local system account to attempt a brute force attack to recover passwords. The current version can execute 10,000 passwords per minute on a 100 Mhz Pentium with 24 MB RAM. A demo version can be downloaded from **http://www/omna.com/yes/AndyBaron/pk.htm**.

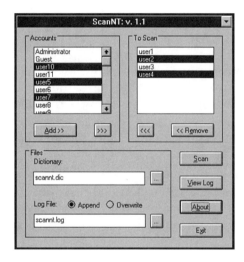

**Figure 13.26:**
ScanNT.

## Password NT

Password NT is a shareware program, also from MWC, Inc., that leverages on NT services that were started under an administrator's account. Because the service can already perform administrative functions, Password NT "asks" the service to change the password to something else. This program assumes you can access the local drive, since it needs to replace the original service executable file with a modified copy. Password NT creates a superuser named Andy and puts it in all global and local groups on the PDC. Password NT can be downloaded from **http://www.omna.com/yes/AndyBaron/recovery.htm**

### MCW Password Recovery Service

If neither ScanNT nor Password NT is able to recover your administrator's password, you can try MCW's guaranteed recovery service with turn around time as little as four hours. If you select the premium emergency service, MCW will dedicate four Pentium 200 machines and their entire security staff to help you retrieve your forgotten password.

## Picking the Right Security Tool

If you need a general tool that can provide the "big picture" of your overall security setup, then your choice is Kane Security Analyst (KSA). This program provides a thorough analysis of the six functional security areas (password strength, access control, user account restrictions, system monitoring, data integrity, and data confidentiality). The interface is well designed and KSA provides the ability to generate complex reports. SomerACL is a good product if you need to analyze NT permissions. If you forgot your NT passwords, try ScanNT and Password NT from MWC Inc. Finally, MWC provides guaranteed password recovery service for those who need immediate access to their NT system.

## Common Security Attacks

By installing a Web server, you are sending an open invitation to the entire world to come visit your network. Most Net surfers are satisfied with perusing the contents of your Web pages; however, others are a bit more adventurous and perform directory listings and file transfers. Finally, there is a third group of Internet individuals who try to gain entry to systems with malicious or criminal intent. It may behoove you to stay up-to-date on the most recent security attacks by visiting **http://www.cert.com**. Some of the more popular tricks of the trade are discussed in the following sections.

The CERT (Computer Emergency Response Team) Coordination Center was formed in 1988 to serve as a focal point for the computer security concerns of Internet users.

# Sniffing

Sniffing is the passive motion of listening on a wire and capturing data as it passes the listening station. Because there is no insertion of data, sniffing is extremely difficult to detect. Sniffing can be initiated by a dedicated network analyzer or a network station. A station can capture network packet information by obtaining a software analyzer and a network card that can be set to promiscuous mode. *Promiscuous mode* enables the network card to listen to *all* conversation on the wire—not just traffic destined for its node address.

It is conceivable to protect your network from sniffing by housing all network cabling in an impenetrable casing and guarding all access points in a forceful manner. Obviously, this approach is neither cost-effective nor very practical. A more common practice is to encrypt all confidential data before it is sent onto the wire. If you are using Systems Management Server, Microsoft has bundled a software analyzer, called the Network Monitor, which can capture packets and decode them for most popular protocols.

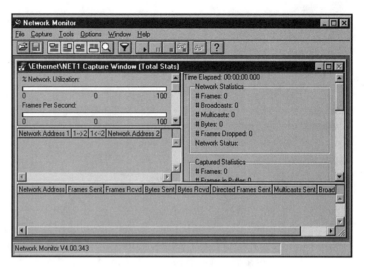

**Figure 13.27:**
Network Monitor from Microsoft's Systems Management Server.

# Replay

Once data is sniffed or captured, the information can be altered and resent back onto the network. Once the information is stored in the intruder's disk or buffer, the captured data can be altered and resent countless times. This technique is known as replay. Spoofing, explained next, is a technique that employs replay.

# Spoofing

Spoofing is simply the act of tricking another computer into believing that you are using the legitimate computer in the conversation when in fact you are not. The objective of a spoof is often to fool the target computer into sending sensitive data or to disrupt service by the transmission of false data. The spoof programs a network analyzer to sniff for events such as logon and file transfers by searching for a specific pattern in the network traffic. Once the pattern is detected, the impersonator hijacks the data and stores it in a file. The capture information can now be viewed or modified and injected back onto the network.

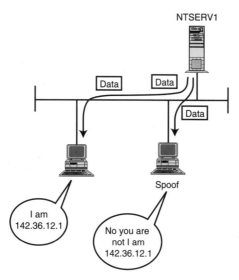

**Figure 13.28:**
Spoofing in action.

One of the more common ways to spoof is to imitate the IP address of another host. On most clients, the IP address is user configurable; this can lead to internal spoofing from your own users. One solution is to set up a Dynamic Host Configuration Protocol (DHCP) server, which dynamically issues IP addresses without user intervention. Nevertheless, most attacks come from untrusted networks, and it is just as simple for an intruder to hijack the packets originating from a designated IP address, modify the contents, and replay it back onto the network.

Windows NT notifies all computers with identical IP addresses. So if you get this message, either a machine has been misconfigured or an intruder has entered your network and is trying to masquerade as someone else.

With a laptop and a software analyzer, anyone can become a spoofer. There are literally thousands of possible access points on your network to plug an analyzer into. Coaxial cables are more vulnerable to being spoofed since *vampire taps* can be placed on the wire without interrupting service. Paradoxically, one of the best ways to protect your network is to use an analyzer to actively monitor the wire for surges in network traffic or repeated attacks at a host.

 A vampire tap is a device that creates an entry point on a coaxial cable so other devices can be connected to the cable. It has sharp metallic teeth that can penetrate the outer shielding to reach the inner copper conductor.

# Brute Force Attacks

Back in the late 1980s, a program called Mikey Hack employed brute force to acquire long distance phone codes by repeatedly dialing an access number with increasing PIN values. Once a call was completed, Mikey Hack would record the PIN into a file. The phone hacker would run the Mikey Hack program overnight, and the next morning he would check if any valid PINs were recorded. Since then, the phone companies have gotten smarter and have started monitoring excessive calls from a single caller.

The concept of brute force exploits the idea that encryption and other security mechanisms require a finite number of attempts before entry is successful. This technique leverages on the massive processing power of today's computers. If the computing power of one machine is not enough, multiple machines can be connected in parallel to compute portions of the equation simultaneously.

The brute force method is easy to detect since the objective is to penetrate the system, not to hide the attacker's identity. With the help of a network analyzer, the offender's packet information can be easily captured and traced.

When brute force is applied to an encryption algorithm, the goal is to find the secret or private key so the ciphertext can be decoded. The trick to protecting your ciphertext is to use a large key size (greater than 40 bits) so it becomes computationally impossible or economically infeasible to find the key in a reasonable amount of time.

# Cracking Keys with Hardware

The brute force method can be used to extract keys of small length. A 16-bit key would take only seconds to decode with today's personal computers. Refer to table 13.7 to see how long it would take to break various key sizes if an algorithm were programmed into a hardware chip and four thousand of these chips were executed in parallel.

**Table 13.7 Time It Takes to Break Certain Keys Using Hardware[1]**

| Key Length (bits) | 1995 | 2000 | 2005 |
|---|---|---|---|
| 40 | 68 seconds | 8.6 seconds | 1.07 seconds |
| 56 | 7.4 weeks | 6.5 days | 19 hours |
| 64 | 36.7 years | 4.6 years | 6.9 months |
| 128 years | 6.7e17 millennia | 8.4e16 millennia | 1.1e16 millennia |

[1] SSLP Reference Project, fig. 2, University of Bristol, Department of Computer Science, Jeremy Bradley.

# Cracking Keys with Software

In August 1995, 100 people volunteered their time to attempt to break a 40 bit key. In only 30 hours , the key and the secret message was decoded by searching only half the keyspace. The time in the table is valid if searching the entire key space.

**Table 13.8 Time Needed to Break Certain Key Sizes Using Software[2]**

| Key Length (bits) | 1995 | 2000 | 2005 |
|---|---|---|---|
| 40 | 1.3 days | 3.8 hours | 28.6 minutes |
| 56 | 228.5 years | 28.6 years | 3.6 years |
| 64 | 58.5 millennia | 7.3 millennia | 914.0 years |
| 128 | 1.1e21 millennia | 1.3e20 millennia | 1.7e19 millennia |

[2] SSLP Reference Project, fig. 4, University of Bristol, Department of Computer Science, Jeremy Bradley.

Cryptography is considered by the U.S. government to be a weapon and is regulated by the International Traffic in Arms Regulations (ITAR, 22 CFR 120-130) of the U.S. State Department, Office of Defense Trade Controls. Government regulations allow only weak cryptography (40 bit key size or less) to be exported. Web browsers exported outside of the U.S. can only generate key sizes of 40 bits or less when used with encryption schemes such as SSL. Therefore, extreme caution should be exercised when transmitting sensitive information overseas.

## The Middle Man

In this scenario, the snooper positions himself between the sender and receiver and unobtrusively captures the conversation. On the Internet, where millions of computers are connected, your network packets traverse many computers before the destination is reached. A snooper can be situated at any of these hops and hijack information without detection. The primary defense against the Middle Man is to use encryption.

## Windows NT Security Issues

The only true security that exists is a server that is not turned on. Fortunately, Windows NT has C2 security, NTFS, and auditing capabilities that are critical for hosting a secure Web server platform. Many of the security holes found in Unix are based on remote logon daemons (rlogin, NFS, NIS, and others), which do not exist in the standard distribution of Windows NT (although there may be third party packages available). Despite the robust security features in NT,  you should still be aware of other security concerns. Your biggest threat may be the introduction of an HTTP server (such as IIS) into your network because alternate methods of data access are readily available (with CGI scripts). Following is a list of security issues specific to Windows NT server.

> **.CMD/.BAT IIS Bug**: Intruders can bypass NT and IIS security by sending commands on the URL to be run on the server. The latest service pack for IIS fixes this problem.

**Default Administrator and Guest Account**: Hackers can use the Administrator account to retrieve the system password with brute force. The guest account by default is set with minimal security. An attacker can use this account to gain access to your server.

**Running Other NT Services with IIS**: Run only services required by IIS. Non-essential services can function as an escape hatch for intruders.

**CGI Scripts**: CGI scripts are notorious for creating hidden security holes. Bad programming is often the culprit.

**Access Restrictions with Server Message Blocks (SMB)**: Windows NT servers uses SMB to communicate with its clients. For example, file and print services relied on SMB to function. To prevent Internet users from performing direct communication with your server, routers have to be configured to filter out incoming SMB traffic.

# .CMD/.BAT Bug in Internet Information Server

The Web server software is complex and consists of thousands of lines of code. As Web server software becomes more feature-rich, the number of lines of code grows proportionally, and the chance that a bug might appear also increases. The basic design of a Web Server is built with security in mind; yet an undiscovered bug can create security holes undetected by the programmer. It is prudent on your part to be up-to-date on software patches and bug fixes from the vendor. If you are still running IIS 1.0, upgrade to the latest IIS service pack now! The ".CMD/.BAT" bug enables users to send a complex string of commands that can be executed on the server. Malicious users can use this information to wreak havoc on your IIS server by issuing system commands on the URL. In addition, the service pack also fixes basic authentication problems between IIS and WWW clients.

For current news on bug fixes and patches visit the IIS site at **http://www.microsoft.com/infoserv**.

# Administrator and Guest Accounts

In general, a limit should be defined for all failed logon attempts because this provides defenses against brute force attacks.

However, because the Administrator account is not affected by this setting (at least one account must have access to the machine), an attacker can use brute force to obtain the password. Therefore, it is recommended that the Administrator account be renamed to something obscure so it cannot be easily determined.

The guest account default setting provides no password and introduces an "open door policy" to intruders. Hackers can use this account to gain access to network shares and cause grave harm to your server. The guest account should be disabled on the IIS server. (IUSR_computername account is automatically added to the local guest group. The local guest group should not be deleted.)

# Running Other Services

The execution of other NT-based services such as the server service on the IIS server can result in compromises in security. If the attacker is able to penetrate security on IIS, and if NT's server service is running, the attacker can use this as an escape hatch to other servers. Other than to disconnect your Web server from the rest of the network, it is prudent to limit services that are only vital to the operation of IIS.

# CGI Scripts

Of all security holes, CGI scripts pose the greatest danger. CGI scripts can be tricked into executing system commands, subsequently bypassing all network security. Also, CGI scripts are often created by novice programmers. Bad programming practices, such as not performing adequate checks on user input, can result in the creation of security back doors to your Web server. Some common checks for user input should include huge or small values, special characters, or large quantity of inputs.

IIS can be configured to accept the execution of CGI scripts from any directory. However, it is recommended that you keep all CGI scripts in the default \Scripts directory because it leads to easier auditing and administration.

# Access Restrictions with Server Message Blocks (SMB)

SMB is an application layer protocol developed by Microsoft. It is the language that defines how NT clients and servers should communicate file, print, and other services. Without SMB, a user can do very little on an NT network. Based on that notion, you can restrict users from having the ability to perform file transfers or administrative functions over the Internet. This is accomplished by disabling UDP ports 137-139 on the Internet router.

On a Cisco router, you can disable incoming UDP traffic for ports 137 to 139 by applying an access list such as

```
access-list 102 deny udp any 202.98.0.0 0.0.255.255 range
137 139
```

and then assigning the access-list to a router interface:

```
interface Ethernet0
ip address 202.98.10.3
ip access-group 102 in
```

# Summary

The Internet has created a new class of hackers and cyber-criminals intent on creating havoc on the data highway. This chapter explores ways to protect the message that you are sending by using authentication and encryption. Network devices such as firewalls and routers help repel the "bugs" of the Internet.

When it's time for your company to implement a major security project, you may want to spend some time to form your battle plan with the help of the security plan template in this chapter. Finally, protecting your Web server can be as simple as lock and key. Other methods include using products such as Kane Security Analyst and SomerACL to keep track of NT's file permissions and user rights. Securing your environment should no longer be a passive task. Take the time to get up to speed on the latest security threats by visiting the Web sites mentioned in the chapter. As is often reminded to every basic trainee in the Army, "Stay Awake, and you will Stay Alive."

# Chapter 14

# Security Utilities and Testing

As soon as you open up your system to the Internet, you open it up to a whole new world of security risks. As any Windows NT administrator can tell you, securing a machine that is simply hooked up to a LAN is difficult enough. Yet on the Internet, you have to secure your site against millions of possible attacks. You must make sure your server is secure; you can use both NT and Internet Information Server to secure your site. If you do not secure your server, a lot of damage can be done both to the services running on it and the machine itself. This damage can range from the server shutting down, to someone destroying all the data and the computer itself.

## Securing a Site Using NT

With Windows NT, you can secure your site by setting up user accounts and securing the NT File system.

Although it isn't always feasible, one of the best ways to ensure the security of your system is to set up user accounts. By doing this, you can make sure that only the people that you want to connect are able to connect. If you require a user account for connection, it will be easy to see who is causing certain problems. You can use the Event Viewer to observe every action that has occurred on the machine, and who is responsible for it (see fig. 14.1).

This is a good way to track user activity, and more importantly, user abuses of the system. For example, you could keep track of how many times someone tries to access files that are clearly off-limits. If users persit in attempting to access off-limit files, you can give them a warning, and then go back to see if they keep on doing it. If they continue after a warning, you can give them one more warning and then revoke their access.

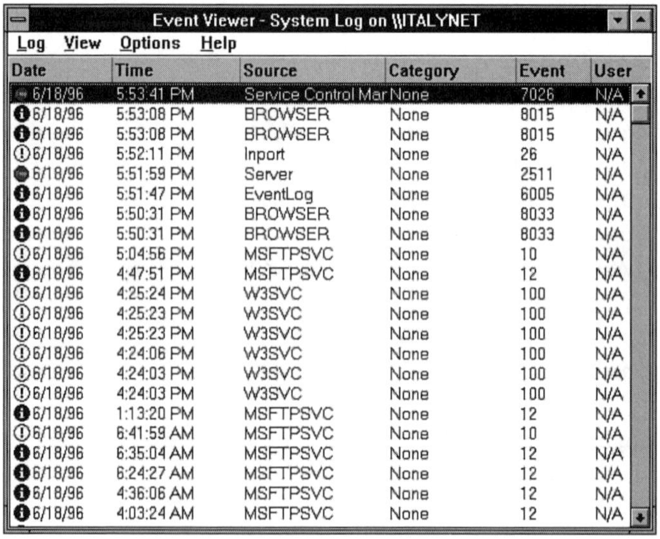

| Event Viewer - System Log on \\ITALYNET | | | | | |
|---|---|---|---|---|---|
| **Log** **View** **Options** **Help** | | | | | |
| **Date** | **Time** | **Source** | **Category** | **Event** | **User** |
| 6/18/96 | 5:53:41 PM | Service Control Mar | None | 7026 | N/A |
| 6/18/96 | 5:53:08 PM | BROWSER | None | 8015 | N/A |
| 6/18/96 | 5:53:08 PM | BROWSER | None | 8015 | N/A |
| 6/18/96 | 5:52:11 PM | Inport | None | 26 | N/A |
| 6/18/96 | 5:51:59 PM | Server | None | 2511 | N/A |
| 6/18/96 | 5:51:47 PM | EventLog | None | 6005 | N/A |
| 6/18/96 | 5:50:31 PM | BROWSER | None | 8033 | N/A |
| 6/18/96 | 5:50:31 PM | BROWSER | None | 8033 | N/A |
| 6/18/96 | 5:04:56 PM | MSFTPSVC | None | 10 | N/A |
| 6/18/96 | 4:47:51 PM | MSFTPSVC | None | 12 | N/A |
| 6/18/96 | 4:25:24 PM | W3SVC | None | 100 | N/A |
| 6/18/96 | 4:25:23 PM | W3SVC | None | 100 | N/A |
| 6/18/96 | 4:25:23 PM | W3SVC | None | 100 | N/A |
| 6/18/96 | 4:24:06 PM | W3SVC | None | 100 | N/A |
| 6/18/96 | 4:24:03 PM | W3SVC | None | 100 | N/A |
| 6/18/96 | 4:24:03 PM | W3SVC | None | 100 | N/A |
| 6/18/96 | 1:13:20 PM | MSFTPSVC | None | 12 | N/A |
| 6/18/96 | 6:41:59 AM | MSFTPSVC | None | 10 | N/A |
| 6/18/96 | 6:35:04 AM | MSFTPSVC | None | 12 | N/A |
| 6/18/96 | 6:24:27 AM | MSFTPSVC | None | 12 | N/A |
| 6/18/96 | 4:36:06 AM | MSFTPSVC | None | 12 | N/A |
| 6/18/96 | 4:03:24 AM | MSFTPSVC | None | 12 | N/A |

**Figure 14.1:**

Viewing events with Event Viewer.

If you want to permit anonymous accounts, you can enable anonymous users to log on using the Service Property Sheet for a server (see fig. 14.2).

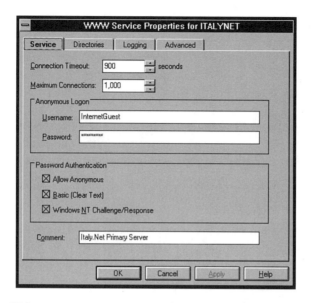

**Figure 14.2:**

Allowing anonymous logons with the Service Property Sheet.

Anonymous logons are made possible by the IUSR_computername account created during Internet Information Server setup. The default is that all of the client requests use this account. This is usually the best way to allow anonymous logons because the account doesn't have any network rights.

The IUSR_computername account name is confusing, but IUSR is simply short for Internet User. Essentially, the account is what every Internet User uses to access the server.

IIS also adds the IUSR_computername account to the Guest group. You should make sure that the Guest group has only the same permissions that you want anyone with access to your servers to have.

Although it may seem like requiring user accounts is the best way to provide security, it might be better to just allow anonymous access. If you allow only anonymous access, it makes it very difficult to log on. If you provide accounts, it is very possible that an account could fall into the wrong hands.

If you do provide user accounts, you should try to ensure that the passwords are unique and difficult to guess. For the best protection, passwords should contain at least one non-letter character somewhere in the middle (for example **ssap!drow**). This makes it harder for people to guess the password.

One other thing you should be aware of is that there is a risk in only requiring Basic authentication in the Service Property Sheet (see fig. 14.2) in that the password is sent encrypted only with Uuencode. The password could be intercepted and then decrypted easily by uudecoding it.

To make sure that passwords aren't so easy to get at, you should also choose Windows NT Challenge/Response from the password section. Doing this enables you to encrypt usernames and passwords. This will provide for a much more secure server. If you select both basic authentication and Windows NT authentication, the only way to connect to your server is with a valid username and password. Selecting both options is best if you want complete control over who can and cannot log onto your server.

## Managing Security Policies with User Manager for Domains

The User Manager for Domains facilitates managing the security policies on your computer. User Manager for Domains enables you to manage the Account policy, which controls the policies regarding passwords. You can manage the User Rights policy, which lets you have control over what users can and cannot do. You can also manage the Audit policy, which gives you control over how Windows NT logs security events. Finally, you can manage the Trust Relationships policy, which lets you specify which domains are trusted and which can trust your domain.

To manage the Account Policy, follow these steps:

1. Choose Account from the Policy menu of the User Manager for Domains.

2. The Account Policy dialog box appears, containing the following categories:

> ➤ The Maximum Password Age—The longest period of time a password can be used before it must be changed.

> ➤ The Minimum Password Age—The shortest amount of time a password can be used before it must be changed.

> ➤ The Minimum Password Length—The shortest length a password can be. To ensure good security, the password should be at least seven characters long.

> ➤ The Password Uniqueness—Very important. It lets you determines how many new passwords a user must create before being able to change to one of their previously used passwords. This requirement is important. The higher the uniqueness value, the more secure your system will be.

3. You can also choose to have the system disconnect a user if their logon hours expire. The logon hours are defined in the User Account.

4. When you are finished, click the OK button.

The next most important thing you can do is implement the User Rights policy. Every right you give to a user enables them to do something different, such as accessing files, or ftping into the server. Rights apply to the entire system, so they are different than just the permissions you give them. The following are some examples of rights you can give users:

➤ The right to access a computer from the network.

➤ The right to back up files and directories. This works over other file and directory permissions.

➤ The right to change the system time. This is a right you shouldn't give to most users.

➤ Forcing shutdown from a remote system is a right you should avoid granting users. It should be given only to administrators.

➤ Logging on locally is good mainly for administrators.

➤ Managing auditing and security logs enables a user to specify what events to audit, and enables them to view the security log. Again, this shouldn't just be given away.

➤ Shutting down the system is another right that should be reserved mainly for administrators.

➤ Taking ownership of files or other objects is another right that can be given to some users, but definitely not to all users.

The best way to manage rights is to simply add a user to a group with those sets of rights you want to give them.

To manage the User Rights policy, follow these steps:

1. Select User Rights from the Policy menu.

2. The Rights pop-up menu provides a list of the available rights. Choose the one you want to grant.

3. After you have granted a right, select the group you want to give the right to from the Grant To box.

4. Choose the Add or Remove option to add or remove a group you don't want to have that right.

5. When you are finished, click the OK button.

You usually grant user rights when you just need to change something quickly for one user. For more sweeping changes, you might want to change the rights for an entire group.

Auditing enables you to track what users are doing. The Audit policy enables you to decide what security logging Windows NT will do. Security logging and auditing is useful because it allows for the tracking of specific rights pertaining to the security of the server. The following text describes the kinds of events that can be audited:

➤ Logon and Logoff

➤ File and Object Access

➤ Use of User Rights

➤ User and Group Management

➤ Security Policy Changes

➤ Restart, Shutdown, and System

➤ Process tracking

To manage these policies, just select Audit from the Policy menu and select which Successes and Failures for which events you want to audit. You would want to audit specific events if you want to track how successful someone was at using the rights that they either do or do not have. A failure can either indicate a small problem with setup, or a potential security threat. It is best to keep track of these to help make your server better for users, and more secure.

# NTFS File Security

The best method of securing your server is to ensure the files are on an NTFS partition. The Windows NT File System provides very good control over the security of your files, and who can access them. You can specify exactly which groups and users can access which files and directories. Before you do anything else, you should make sure that the IUSR Anonymous account is granted access only to the files you want anonymous users to have access to. For more information, refer back to the section on the IUSR Anonymous accounts.

The IUSR account is used almost all the time when you have allowed anonymous users to connect to your server. For example, everytime someone uses a Web browser to get a document, they are getting it by using the IUSR account.

You can also use the User Profile Editor, located in the Administrative Tools program group, to specify what users and groups can do (see fig. 14.3). The User Profile Editor lets you control user access to different folders and files on the NTFS disk, which is an extension of NTFS file security.

### Figure 14.3:
The User Profile Editor window.

 Be careful when giving access to the Everyone group, because that includes the Anonymous account and the Guest group.

For documents, you should grant only Read access. This is because you want people to be able to read the documents, but not change them. For programs like CGI, you should grant read and execute access. CGI programs need to be readable and executable to function properly. For public databases, you should grant read access and write access if you want users to be able to add to the database, or just read access if you want them to be able only to view the database.

Also, you should make sure that only the services that need to be
running are running. You can check this using the gg, located in
the Control Panel (see fig. 14.4). The fewer services you have
running, the less likely it is that you are running something
someone can use to damage your system. If you have some extra
services running, an experienced cracker could use them to their
advantage to communicate with the system and damage it. There
is no easy way to tell which services in particular could be used
this way. It is best to turn off all unnecessary services that aren't
being used for the Internet server. Even harmless services can be
used to damage the system, and it is always best to try to cut off
all potential security holes.

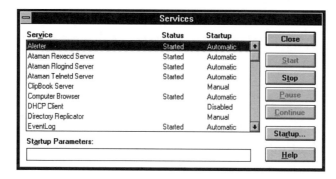

### Figure 14.4:

The Services applet.

You should also check to unbind any unnecessary services, such
as the Server service, from your Internet Adapter cards. You can
do this using the Network applet in the Control Panel (see fig.
14.5). The Server service does not need to be bound to the
Internet Adapter because Internet Information Server already
handles all the communications between the Internet services
and the adapter.

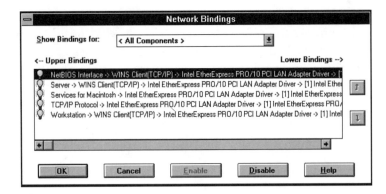

**Figure 14.5:**
The Bindings window of the Network applet.

# Securing Your Site Using IIS Security

Internet Information Server uses a very good method of security by integrating Windows NT's authentication features with the NTFS security. IIS also adds IP address security and control over directory access.

Essentially, Internet Information Server goes through a number of steps to see whether it will accept a request or not from either a local or external user.

1. When IIS receives a request, it first checks to see whether the IP address it is coming from is permitted or not. If the address is permitted, IIS continues the process; if not, it denies access. IIS checks your configuration in the Advanced Property Sheet (see fig. 14.6).

2. IIS then checks to see whether the user is permitted by checking the information in User Manager for Domains. If the user is permitted, IIS continues the process; if not, it denies access.

3. IIS then checks the Internet Server permissions to see whether access is allowed. If it isn't, access is denied; if access is allowed, IIS moves on to the next process.

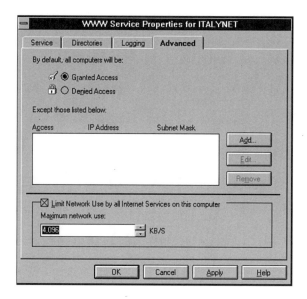

**Figure 14.6:**

The Advanced Property Sheet determines whether an IP Address is permitted.

4.  IIS then checks NTFS permissions to see whether access is allowed.

Internet Information Server also uses IP address security to further protect the server.

For each directory you have set up, you can use the WWW service to allow certain access. If you grant read access, then users can view the files. If you grant execute access, users can execute CGI scripts and ISAPI applications. These would all be implemented when setting up a standard external Web server for the Internet.

You must set execute permissions in both Internet Service Manager (see fig. 14.7) and the File Manager that the applications and scripts are stored in.

**Figure 14.7:**

The Directories Property Sheet.

You can also set IIS to require a Secure Sockets Layer (SSL) channel, which enables users to send information such as form data in a secure, encrypted format.

Secure Sockets Layer (SSL) is a special protocol meant to act as a buffer between the client and the server to ensure that everything transmitted is encrypted and secure. A client must be using an SSL-enabled browser, such as Netscape Navigator 2.0 or higher or Internet Explorer 3 or higher.

You can also configure the WWW service to make it secure data by using the Internet Service Manager. Normally, you should allow anonymous access, but you can further secure the WWW service by requiring a password and Windows NT Challenge/ Response encryption for the passwords. This is also good if you have specific areas you want to restrict access to.

You can control access by IP address using the Advanced Property Sheet of Internet Information Server (see fig. 14.8). You can selectively grant and deny access to individual IP addresses. This is good if you are having a problem with a specific user.

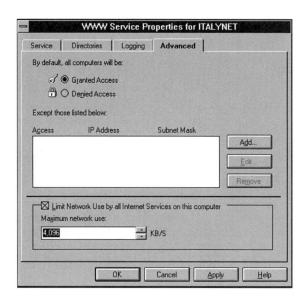

**Figure 14.8:**
The Advanced Property Sheet.

You should also disable directory browsing from the Directories Property Sheet. This is usually good because it will ensure that users can't see everything that is on a site.

# Providing Security using Secure Socket Layers

Using SSL, you can enable encryption to make your site very secure for clients with SSL capable browsers. SSL is a protocol that acts between HTTP and TCP/IP to authenticate and encrypt data (refer to preceding note on SSL).

To enable SSL, you need to follow these steps:.

1. Switch to the directory where you installed IIS.

2. Run keygen.exeKeygen.exe to create the two files you need. Keygen will generate a key file containing the key pair; and the second file is a certificate request file. Type **keygen** to see examples of how to use it.

3. After it has generated the files, e-mail to a certificate authority and ask them to sign it. To ensure that it works, just send the entire output, including what you typed into the command line (although you need to remember to remove the password you entered).

4. The certificate authority e-mails you back with the requested signed certificate. Just copy the text of the message to a text file and save it.

5. Use the SetKey program to install the certificate using the following syntax:

   ```
   setkey YourPassword keypair.key certificate.txt.
   ```

   If you want the certificate to only apply to one IP address, enter it after the name of the certificate.txt file.

6. Finally, open up the Directory Properties and select Require secure SSL channel.

If you are using Windows NT 4.0, you can use the included Key Manager (see fig. 14.9) to use SSL. A benefit of running NT 4.0 is that the Key Manager automates the entire process (including e-mailing the certificate) so you don't have to do it all by hand.

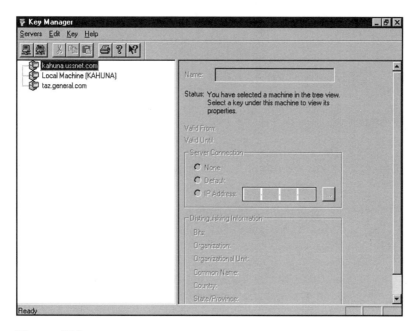

**Figure 14.9:**

The Key Manager of Windows NT 4.

To implement an SSL transaction from Key Manager, perform the following steps:

1. Open up the Key Manager and select Create New Key from the Key menu.

2. The Create New Key and Certificate dialog box appears. For the Key Name, give a name to the key you want to create. Specify the password that will be used to encrypt the key. Enter the length of the key pair in bits. The default is 1024, but you can also select a key that is 512 or 768 bits long. For Organization, enter an ISO-registered name, if possible. For Organizational Unit, enter which department you are in, if applicable. For Common name, enter the domain of your server (www.foobar.com, for example). Enter the ISO Country designation for your country (US, for example).

Enter the full name of the state or province you are in. Enter the name of the city you are in. Finally, type in the name of the Request file that will be created.

3.   Click the OK button.

4.   You will be prompted to retype your password and click. Do it and click OK.

5.   The key appears in the Key Manager window under the computer name. You then need to go through the same process outlined above to acquire a certificate.

6.   Once you get your certificate, select Install Key Certificate from the Key menu and follow the instructions Key Manager gives you.

 You need to pay a certificate authority. You should probably contact VeriSign at **http://www.verisign.com** to get a VeriSign certificate.

# NT Security Issues

The biggest risks to your server will be on the HTTP server. CGI scripts can be especially dangerous, so you should use them with caution.

You should disable the guest account because someone could easily use it to bring down your server by making many logon attempts at one time. You should also make sure that the Everyone group does not have write access to things it shouldn't have. You should also make sure that the permissions are set properly. The most common attacks are against computers that have easy-to-crack user accounts, or have write access from the Everyone Group, or have the Guest account enabled.

# Testing Your Server's Security

Testing security is simple. All you need to do is pretend you are someone who is trying to break into your computer. You should go over the steps you have taken, and then see if they are working or not. If you find a hole, then go through the steps again to improve security.

Unfortunately, even most administrators don't know all the holes that can be found in their system. However, if you take all of the precautions detailed in this section, you can feel safe from most attacks. As of now, there are a number of utilities that test UNIX security automatically, but none exist yet for NT. In essence this is a good sign, because NT was built from the ground up to be an essentially secure platform. As long as you don't provide external users with system administrator level rights, and you make sure that the server is only used for Internet Information Server, your system will be safe.

# Summary

Server security is a very important issue, and you will need to pay particular attention to it to make sure that your server is safe. If you were to take all the precautions listed in this chapter, your system would be unbreakable. However, it is very common for administrators to try to cut corners by leaving some holes un-checked. However remote the possibility, someone could use even the smallest hole to damage your system. The best advice you can take is to focus on preventing security attacks so you can avoid spending time trying to clean up after them.

# Part VI

# Advanced Internet Information Server Tasks

# Chapter 15

# CGI Basics

The *Common Gateway Interface* (CGI) is the interface between a *HyperText Transfer Protocol* (HTTP) server (the program that serves pages for a Web site) and the other resources of the server's host computer.

CGI is not really a language or a protocol in the strictest sense of those terms. It's really just a set of commonly named variables and agreed-upon conventions for passing information from the server to the client and back again. When viewed in this admittedly simplistic light, CGI becomes much less intimidating.

Microsoft's Internet Information Server (IIS) fully supports CGI. IIS's WWW service interprets the CGI requests from the Web client and executes the appropriate responses. Microsoft supports a variety of programming tools such as C, Visual Basic, Perl, and NT batch files for building CGI programs.

Microsoft has introduced a programming interface for IIS known as Internet Server Application Programming Interface (ISAPI). ISAPI programs tend to be much faster and conserve more resources because the ISAPI program is a Dynamic Link Library (DLL) that is loaded once and stays in memory. In contrast, each CGI request spawns a separate process and requires additional memory and processing. See Chapter 18, "ISAPI," for more information on ISAPI.

This chapter covers the following topics:

➤ The environment of CGI

➤ Selecting a programming language

➤ Structure of a CGI program

➤ Using basic authorization

➤ A form-processing example that sends e-mail

➤ Non-parsed header CGI

## The Environment of CGI

CGI is closely tied to both HTTP, the protocol that links Web servers to clients (see the following Note), and the *HyperText Markup Language* (HTML), which is used to write Web pages. It is therefore important that you already have a working knowledge of HTML, and at least a basic understanding of how HTTP works, in order to fully understand CGI.

In this model, the browser is one of a class called clients. Not all HTTP clients are browsers. Spiders, robots, and even proxy servers are HTTP clients at least some of the time.

CGI programs run on the server's host machine. A CGI program gets its input from the server via environment variables and data streams. *Environment variables* are special memory areas set aside by an operating system for passing small amounts of static data between programs. *Data streams* are sequentially organized data that are commonly used for console and file I/O. The *standard input* stream (commonly abbreviated as *stdin*) is used by the server to pass streamed data to CGI programs.

Because CGI programs run in the server's environment, you can test your CGI programs on a Windows NT 3.51 Server running Internet Information Server. With Windows NT 4.0, IIS 2.0 will be included with both the workstation and the server version. Therefore, you no longer need to purchase the server version to run your CGI programs.

You can write CGI programs in any language, although some languages are more suitable than others for any given application. CGI programs are commonly written in C, Perl, and Visual Basic.

# Selecting a Programming Language

There are three major criteria you must consider when deciding what language you will use to write your CGI programs, as follows:

1.  The language must be supported by the operating system on which the server is running.

2.  The language must have sufficient facilities to perform the task that you need from it.

3.  You (the programmer) must be comfortable enough with the language to code in it proficiently.

The first criterion is usually a major factor. According to Georgia Tech's latest GVU Survey, 64.6 percent of Web servers are running some flavor of Unix, where C is universally available, and Perl is also commonplace. In addition, Perl is available on Windows NT running IIS. If you are running a Unix/NT environment, using Perl can help you expedite the porting of Perl scripts between the two platforms. The second and third criteria are more subjective. There are few languages today that don't have the power to perform the necessary tasks—although some are more capable than others. Attempts to quantify the suitability of any given language for any given application, however, usually leads to a discussion that more closely resembles a religious debate than a reasoned, objective analysis of facts and figures.

The examples in this chapter are written in Perl. Perl is available on Windows NT and on many other platforms as well. It is powerful enough to handle most CGI-related tasks efficiently, and there is a large following of Perl users on the Internet who can assist in answering questions.

The version of Perl used for the examples in this chapter is version 4.0.1.8 patch level 36. Perl version 5 is available for Windows NT from Hip Communications Inc. and is backward compatible with Perl version 4. For those who are using MKS toolkit 5.1 for NT, you can download a beta version of MKS's port of Perl5 from `http://www.mks.com/solution/tk/beta/index.htm`.

# Installing Perl5 for Windows NT

Microsoft has commissioned Hip Communications Inc. to provide the port of Perl5 for the Windows NT environment (both workstation and server). The current version as of this writing is 5.108. Perl5 can be downloaded from **http://www.perl.hip.com**.

Not all Unix functions have been ported to the NT version because some Unix functions do not have NT equivalents. Read the Win32 Perl FAQ to learn more about the details.

To install Perl5 on Windows NT, perform the following:

1. Download the 108-i86.zip file.

2. Use WinZip to unzip 108-i86.zip. (Pkzip/Pkunzip does not work because it does not recognize long filenames). WinZip can be downloaded from **http://www.shareware.com**.

3. Add c:\perl5\ntt to your path. This is the directory where the Perl interpreter (PERL.EXE) is located.

4. Associate the .pl extension (or another extension of your choosing) with PERL.EXE by modifying the NT registry.

   a. Run Regedt32.exe and open: HKEY_LOCAL_MACHINE\SYSTEM\CurrentControlSet\ Services\W3SVC\Parameters\ScriptMap.

   b. From the Edit menu, choose Add Value. The Data type is REG_SZ.

   c. Type the .pl extension used for your Perl scripts.

   d. In the String editor, type the full path to the interpreter (i.e. C:\PERL5\NTT\PERL.EXE).

   e. Restart the WWW service.

By default, a /Scripts directory alias is defined with Read and Execute access. It is recommended that you place your Perl scripts here. In addition, you may also want to create a /cgi-bin directory alias for all your CGI programs.

# Structure of a CGI Program

A CGI program can be broken down into three basic tasks that it may or may not perform, depending on the specific application. These tasks are as follows:

➤ Retrieving and decoding input from the server

➤ Formatting the necessary MIME-style headers for HTTP

➤ Creating, formatting, and delivering the correct output to the server

What follows is a discussion of the specific requirements and protocols associated with each of these different segments of a CGI program. Small code fragments are included with the descriptions to illustrate the techniques involved.

# Input from the Server

Most of the data for a CGI program will come from data typed into forms on the user's browser. This data is encoded in a *query string*, in a format that looks like this:

```
name=value&name=value&name=value . . .
```

These *name/value* pairs can be delivered by one of two methods: the GET and POST. Both methods encode the query string in the same manner; they differ only in their delivery method.

The GET uses part of the URL to send variable data from the client to the server. The data is then forwarded to the CGI program in an environment variable called QUERY_STRING. Listing 15.1 is a code fragment in Perl that retrieves the QUERY_STRING environment variable.

The Uniform Resource Locator (URL) is the common format of addressing objects on the World Wide Web. It is described in RFC 1630.

### Listing 15.1   Retrieving the QUERY_STRING Variable

```
# put the QUERY_STRING into a variable
$qs = $ENV{'QUERY_STRING'};

# split it up into an array by the '&' character
@qs = split(/&/,$qs);
```

Because the query string is delivered as part of an URL, the use of certain characters are restricted. Therefore, the query string must be encoded to avoid using these characters. Space characters are replaced with plus (+) characters, and other restricted characters are replaced with their hexadecimal value, preceded by the percent (%) character. A typical QUERY_STRING might look like this:

```
Name=William+E.+Weinman&Email=wew@bearnet.com
```

Any code that retrieves the QUERY_STRING variable will have to decode these characters before it can use them. Listing 15.2 is a Perl code fragment that decodes a query string.

### Listing 15.2    Decoding the QUERY_STRING Variable

```
foreach $i (0 .. $#qs)
  {
  # convert the plus chars to spaces
  $qs[$i] =~ s/\+/ /g;

  # convert the hex characters
  $qs  =~ s/%(..)/pack("c",hex($1))/ge;

  # split each one into name and value
  ($name, $value) = split(/=/,$qs[$i],2);

  # create an associative array
  $qs{$name} = $value;
  }

print "\nVariables:\n\n";

foreach $name (sort keys(%qs))
  { print "$name=", $qs{$name}, "\n" }
```

The POST method delivers data in the same format, but by a different method. Instead of using an environment variable, the POST method delivers the query string via the *standard input* stream.

The major advantage of the POST method over the GET method is that it's not limited by the size of the environment space on the host machine. With the GET method, you can only send as much data as there is space available for environment variables. Because the POST method uses a data stream, there is no such limitation on the amount of data you can send.

Listing 15.3 is a code fragment that retrieves and decodes a POST method query string.

### Listing 15.3  Retrieving and Decoding POST Data

```
$ct = $ENV{"CONTENT_TYPE"};
$cl = $ENV{"CONTENT_LENGTH"};

# check the content-type for validity
if($ct ne "application/x-www-form-urlencoded")
  {
  printf "I don't understand content-type: %s\n", $ct;
  exit 1;
  }

# put the data into a variable
read(STDIN, $qs, $cl);

# split it up into an array by the '&' character
@qs = split(/&/,$qs);

foreach $i (0 .. $#qs)
  {
  # convert the plus chars to spaces
  $qs[$i] =~ s/\+/ /g;

  # convert the hex tokens to characters
  $qs[$i] =~ s/%(..)/pack("c",hex($1))/ge;

  # split into name and value
  ($name, $value) = split(/=/,$qs[$i],2);

  # create the associative element
  $qs{$name} = $value;
  }

print "Variables:\n\n";

foreach $name (sort keys(%qs))
  { printf "$name=%s\n", $qs{$name} }
```

The POST method identifies its data with the special MIME content type, application/x-www-form-urlencoded. According to MIME protocol, the length of the data is also specified with a MIME content-length. This MIME encoding is delivered via the environment variables, CONTENT_TYPE and CONTENT_LENGTH, respectively.

You cannot rely on receiving any end-of-file indication from the standard input stream. It will not always be terminated. Therefore, you must read only the number of bytes specified by the value of the CONTENT_LENGTH variable.

Once your program has retrieved the input from the server, it can begin formatting the output to send back to the client through the server.

## Formatting MIME Headers

Before a CGI program can send data to a client, it must send a *response header* (sometimes called a MIME header because it follows many of the same rules) that identifies the type of data it is sending with a Multipurpose Internet Mail Extanion (MIME) content type. The simplest form of response header contains only the content type, like this:

```
Content-type: text/html
```

MIME is the specification commonly used for Internet mail. It is defined in RFC 1521. Sometimes the MIME content type is simply called the "MIME-type."

The response header must be followed by two newline characters. The following is code fragment that sends a simple response header:

```
print "Content-type: text/html\n\n";
```

Technically, newlines in the response header are supposed to be carriage-return/linefeed pairs, (0D Hex, 0A Hex), but common practice is to use a linefeed (0A Hex) by itself, which is in fact universally supported.

The content type is used by the browser to decide how to render the output that it receives from your program. There are several different content types in common use—table 15.1 contains a brief list.

**Table 15.1    Some Common MIME Content Types**

| Content Type | Usage |
| --- | --- |
| text/html | HTML documents |
| text/plain | Plain text documents |
| image/gif | GIF-formatted images |
| image/jpeg | JPEG-formatted images |
| image/png | PNG[1]-formatted images |
| video/mpeg | MPEG-formatted video |
| video/quicktime | QuickTime-formatted video |

1. PNG is a new graphics format designed to displace GIF. It has many of the same properties as GIF, with a larger possible palette and, more importantly, a non-proprietary compression algorithm. PNG stands for either "Portable Network Graphics" or "PNG's Not GIF."

Mime content types are coordinated by the Internet Assigned Numbers Authority (`http://www.isi.edu/iana/`). Many MIME content types, besides those listed previously, are in common use. For a more complete list, see `ftp://ftp.isi.edu/in-notes/iana/assignments/media-types`.

In most cases, the server will send more components to the response before sending it to the client. The exception to this rule is discussed later, under "Non-Parsed Header CGI."

# Delivering the Output

Output from a CGI program is sent to the standard output stream. In most languages, this is the default behavior for the print command. Listing 15.4 is a Perl code fragment that sends a small HTML fragment to the client.

**Listing 15.4    Sending Output to the Client**

```
print "<html><head><title>Form Response</title></head>\n";
print "<body><h1>Form Response</h1>\n";
print "<p>The name you entered in your form was $name.\n";
print "<p>The address you entered was $address.\n";
print "<hr>\n</body></html>\n";
```

The format of your output must be the format specified in the content type of the response header. In this case, that content type was "text/html", so the output must be in proper HTML format. On the other hand, if the content type were image/gif, the output would have to be a valid GIF formatted image.

# A Brief Discussion of the Standard CGI Variables

Input from the server includes a number of standard CGI environment variables. These variables represent all the information commonly available about the server and client with which your program will be interacting. This section contains a brief description of each of those variables.

You will find that there are other variables available to your CGI program, besides those listed here. What variables your program gets depends on many factors, including the server you're using, the operating system you're using, and often the whims of your system administrator.

Here is a useful CGI program that will list all of the environment variables available on a server:

*continues*

---

**showvars.cgi - Show All Environment Variables**

```
print "content-type: text/plain\n\n";

foreach $v (sort keys(%ENV))
  { print "$v: $ENV{$v}\n"; }
```

---

The standard CGI environment variables fall into three general categories—information about the user, the server, and the specific request that initiated the CGI program. First, let's look at the user information.

# About the User

Some of the standard CGI variables contain information about the user and their environment. The most useful of these are HTTP_USER_AGENT, HTTP_ACCEPT, REMOTE_HOST, and REMOTE_ADDR, discussed in the next sections.

## HTTP_USER_AGENT

The HTTP_USER_AGENT variable contains the name and version of the user's browser in the format "*name/version library/version.*" It also contains information about any proxy gateway (see Note) that the user may be going through. Typically, you won't need information about the proxy gateway, except to know that whenever there is one, the proxy is likely caching data and the connection might or might not represent an individual user.

A *proxy gateway* is a computer that gets between the requests from a group of users and the responses from systems outside their realm. In the case of the World Wide Web, proxies are becoming more popular and are adding quite a bit of complexity to the standards process. In particular, there is a great deal of discussion about how to properly negotiate with proxies to keep their caches up-to-date and make sure their users have access to timely information, while preserving the attendant reduction in traffic they provide for the Net.

Generally, it's not a good idea to count on the format of the
HTTP_USER_AGENT string without having a lot of information in
advance about what each of the different browsers sends there.
As you can see from the next examples, the format varies greatly.
Listing 15.5 is a log of some HTTP_USER_AGENT strings from my Web
site (http://www.bearnet.com/cgibook/).

### Listing 15.5   HTTP_USER_AGENT Strings

```
PRODIGY-WB/1.4b
Mozilla/1.1N (Macintosh; I; 68K)
Microsoft Internet Explorer/4.40.308 (Windows 95)
TCPConnectII/2.3 InterCon-Web-Library/1.2 (Macintosh; 68K)
Mozilla/2.0b3 (X11; I; IRIX 5.3 IP22)
Lynx/2.3.7 BETA  libwww/2.14
NCSA_Mosaic/2.7b1 (X11;SunOS 5.4 i86pc)  libwww/2.12 modified
NCSA Mosaic/2.0 (Windows x86)
Mozilla/1.22 (compatible; MSIE 2.0B; Windows 95)
Microsoft Internet Explorer/0.1 (Win32)
Enhanced_Mosaic/2.10.17S Win16 FTP Software/Spyglass/17S
EINet WinWeb 1.1
IWENG/1.2.000  via proxy gateway  CERN-HTTPD/3.0 libwww/2.17
IBM WebExplorer DLL /v1.03
Mozilla/2.0 (Win95; I)
NetCruiser/V2.1
```

It's worth noting, in this context, that the preceding list is not
representative of the ratios of different browsers that have visited
my site. This log's source had 484 entries, of which 413 were
Netscape (Mozilla) browsers.

The Netscape browser calls itself Mozilla. The official word is that the
word "Netscape" is pronounced "Mozilla." (Consider the fact that the
company is run by a 22-year-old wiz-kid on leave from college.)

The reason for "Mozilla" probably stems from the fact that Netscape was
built on the Mosaic browser, then the college that owns Mosaic forced
Netscape to change its name. The name Mozilla seems to be a play on
words with the name Mosaic. Word-play is popular on the Net.

Listing 15.6 is a listing of some `HTTP_USER_AGENT` strings with proxies.

---

### Listing 15.6   HTTP_USER_AGENT Strings with Proxies

```
Mozilla/2.0b2a (Windows; I; 16bit) via proxy gateway CERN-
➡HTTPD/3.0 libwww/2.1
NCSA Mosaic for the X Window System/2.4-2 libwww/2.12 modified
➡via proxy gateway
IBM WebExplorer DLL /v1.03 via proxy gateway CERN-HTTPD/
➡3.0pre5 libwww/2.16pre
Mozilla/1.1N (X11; I; HP-UX A.09.05 9000/712) via proxy
➡gateway CERN-HTTPD/3.0
```

---

Although the `HTTP_USER_AGENT` string is designed to let you know what brand and version of browser are connecting to your site, it is becoming more difficult to use it for that. The latest version of the *Microsoft Internet Explorer* (MSIE) identifies itself with Netscape's *User-Agent* string. Unlike previous versions of MSIE, there is no indication that it is not the Netscape Navigator. Unfortunately, because MSIE does not support all of the Netscape extensions, it is creating real problems by masquerading as Mozilla. Please see `http://www.bearnet.com/msie-ii.html` for more information.

## HTTP_ACCEPT

The `HTTP_ACCEPT` string provides the MIME content types that the browser can accept. The format of the `HTTP_ACCEPT` string is *type/subtype, type/subtype, [. . .].* As you can see from the examples here, some browsers also add other information that can be used in future versions of HTTP.

In the following examples from my log file, I've put the name of the browser on one line and the `HTTP_ACCEPT` string on the next, so you can tell which browser is generating which string.

```
from Mozilla/2.0b1J --
image/gif, image/x-xbitmap, image/jpeg, image/pjpeg, */*
```

```
from Mozilla/1.22 (Windows; I; 16bit) --
*/*, image/gif, image/x-xbitmap, image/jpeg

from NCSA Mosaic/2.0.0 Final Beta (Windows x86) --
video/mpeg, image/jpeg, image/gif, audio/basic, text/
➥plain, text/html, audio/x-aiff, audio/basic, */*

from Lynx/2.3.7 BETA libwww/2.14 --
*/*, application/x-wais-source, application/html, text/
➥plain, text/html, www/mime, application/x-ksh,
➥application/x-sh, application/x-csh, application/x-sh

from NCSA Mosaic/2.0.0b4 (Windows x86) --
application/pdf, application/winhelp, application/
➥freelance, application/msword, audio/x-midi, application/
➥x-rtf, video/msvideo, video/quicktime, video/mpeg, image/
➥jpeg, image/gif, application/postscript, audio/wav, text/
➥plain, text/html, audio/x-aiff, audio/basic, */*


from NetCruiser/V2.00 --
text/plain, text/html, image/gif, image/jpeg

from NCSA Mosaic(tm) Version 2.0.0a8 for Windows --
audio/x-midi, application/x-rtf, video/msvideo, video/
➥quicktime, video/mpeg, image/jpeg, image/gif, application/
➥postscript, audio/wav, text/plain, text/html, audio/
➥x-aiff, audio/basic, */*

from SPRY_Mosaic/v8.17 (Windows 16-bit) --
application/x-gocserve, audio/basic, audio/x-midi,
➥application/x-rtf, video/msvideo, video/quicktime,
➥video/mpeg, image/targa, image/x-win-bmp, image/jpeg,
➥image/gif, application/postscript, audio/wav, text/
➥plain, text/html; level=3, audio/x-aiff, audio/basic,
➥image/jpeg, image/x-gif24, image/png, image/x-png,
➥image/x-xbitmap, image/gif, application/x-ms-executable,
➥application/x-sprymosaic-hotlist, application/x-
➥airmosaic-patch, application/binary, application/http,
➥www/mime
```

*continues*

```
from Lynx/2.3 BETA libwww/2.14 --
➥application/pdf, application/x-dvi, application/post
➥script, video/*, video/mpeg, image/*, audio/*, */*,
➥application/x-wais-source, text/plain, text/html, www/
➥mime

from NCSA Mosaic/2.0.0 Final Beta (Windows x86) --
➥video/x-msvideo, video format-quick movie format, video/
➥mpeg, text/x-sgml, image/tiff, image/jpeg, image/gif,
➥image/bmp, application/zip, application/x-zip,
➥application/x-tar, application/x-rtf, application/x-hdf,
➥application/x-gzip, application/x-compress, application/
➥postscript, application/pdf, application/octet-stream,
➥application/msword, audio/x-wav, audio/x-midi, audio/x-
➥aiff, audio/wav, audio/basic, text/plain, text/html,
➥audio/x-aiff, audio/basic, */*

from IBM WebExplorer /v1.01 --
➥*/*; q=0.300, application/octet-stream; q=0.100, text/
➥plain, text/html, image/bmp, image/jpeg, image/tiff,
➥image/x-xbitmap, image/gif, application/zip, application
➥/inf, audio/x-wav, audio/x-aiff, audio/basic, video/
➥avs-video, video/x-msvideo, video/quicktime, video/mpeg,
➥image/x-bitmap, image/bmp, image/tiff, image/jpeg,
➥image/gif, application/editor
```

The IBM WebExplorer appears to break the rules more than the other browsers by using semicolons, equal signs, and so on. This is what the MIME folks call *multilevel encoding*. It's not supported by the current HTTP specification, but it might be in the future and doesn't seem to provide any real problems. If you plan to decode the HTTP_ACCEPT variable, you just need to be aware that some browsers will do this.

## REMOTE_HOST and REMOTE_ADDR

The REMOTE_HOST, and REMOTE_ADDR variables provide information about the IP address of the user. REMOTE_ADDR will contain the IP address in dotted-decimal notation. The REMOTE_HOST variable will contain the text-equivalent hostname of the address.

*Dotted-decimal* notation is a common format for expressing the 32-bit IP address used by the Internet Protocol to locate a specific machine on the Internet.

You will find that the REMOTE_ADDR field is always filled in, but the REMOTE_HOST field might not be. Because translating the dotted-decimal address to a hostname (sometimes called *reverse hostname resolution*) takes both time and network bandwidth (it must send requests to a DNS server), many servers turn off this feature for performance and security reasons. If your server has reverse hostname resolution disabled, the REMOTE_HOST variable will be either blank (as it should be) or filled in with the value of REMOTE_ADDR (as it most often is).

# About the Server

The following group of variables provide information about the server and the software that runs it:

➤ The SERVER_SOFTWARE variable contains the name and version of the server software in the format *name/version*.

➤ The SERVER_NAME variable contains the server's hostname, DNS alias, or IP address for use in building self-referencing URLs. Note that this is not always the primary name of the server. The server I use, for example, is a *virtual server* set up by a provider service to look like a private server to the outside world. It should rightfully return the *virtual* name, www.bearnet.com, and it does.

➤ Finally, the GATEWAY_INTERFACE variable contains the revision of the CGI specification that this server uses in the format, *CGI/revision*.

Here's an example of how these variables are set on an Internet Information Server:

```
SERVER_SOFTWARE = Microsoft-IIS-W/2.0
SERVER_NAME = www.bearnet.com
GATEWAY_INTERFACE = CGI/1.1
```

# Request-Specific Variables

The following variables are request-specific in that they change based on the specific request being submitted. In addition to these, the user-specific variables discussed previously are request-specific as well:

➤ QUERY_STRING is probably the most important of these variables. This is the most common method of passing information to a CGI program.

Commonly, a request is made to a CGI program by including a "?" followed by extra information on the URL. For example, if the URL http://www.bearnet.com/cgi/test.cgi?quick.brown.fox is submitted, all the characters after the "?" will be put in the QUERY_STRING variable. The value of the variable will be "quick.brown.fox".

➤ SCRIPT_NAME is set to the filename of the CGI program. This may be useful if you are generating your scripts on-the-fly.

➤ SERVER_PROTOCOL contains the name and revision number of the protocol that this request came in from. It is in the format *protocol/revision*. This will almost certainly be "HTTP/1.0" for now.

➤ The SERVER_PORT variable is the number of the port on which the request came in. It might be significant if your program is servicing requests coming in on different ports, perhaps for different domains or services.

This field will usually be "80", the standard port for HTTP requests.

➤ PATH_INFO and PATH_TRANSLATED represent another way of passing information to a CGI program. You can pass another file path to the program by simply appending it to the URL, like this: "http://www.bearnet.com/cgi-bin/ a/b/c".

Then, PATH_INFO will contain the extra path (/a/b/c) and PATH_TRANSLATED will contain the PATH_INFO appended to the document root path of the server (C:\WINNT\SYSTEM32\INETSRV\CGI-BIN on my server), like this:

```
PATH_INFO = /a/b/c
PATH_TRANSLATED =  C:\WINNT\SYSTEM32\INETSRV\CGI-
BIN\a\b\c
```

➤ CONTENT_TYPE is filled in for queries that have attached information, such as POST requests. It is the MIME content type of the data in the form type/subtype. CONTENT_LENGTH is the number of bytes of data.

A typical set of values would be the following:

```
CONTENT_TYPE = application/x-www-form-urlencoded
CONTENT_LENGTH = 17
```

➤ AUTH_TYPE is used for user authentication. It contains the authentication method used to validate the user. User authentication is discussed further later in this chapter.

➤ REQUEST_METHOD is the method used for the request. It tells you where and how to look for whatever data is passed. Usually it will be either POST or GET.

That covers all the standard CGI variables. In addition to these variables, and whatever other environment variables your server provides to CGI programs, there might also be strings that a browser sends to your server, available with "HTTP_" prepended to the name (the HTTP_ACCEPT string is one of these). Browser-specific variables vary greatly and tend to change from version to version.

# Using Basic Authorization

For some applications, it's important to know authoritatively who is on the other end of the connection. If the service or information you are offering on your Web site is intended for a select group of people, or if you are charging for access to your service, or for any number of other reasons, you might need to implement some method of user authentication.

This section teaches how to use the Basic Authentication Scheme provided in the HTTP/1.0 specification. There are other methods of authentication available such as SHTTP (Secure HyperText Transfer Protocol) and SSL (Secure Sockets Layer). Of the two, the industry seems to be favoring SSL. The two leading Web browsers, Microsoft Internet Explorer and Netscape Navigator, both support SSL as their authentication protocol. The GSS-API, which uses a secret key negotiated on-the-fly between the server and client; HTTP-NG, which provides performance improvements as well as authentication; and a digest authentication scheme from the HTTP working group of the IETF are also under development.

There are still many hurdles ahead, however, before any standard, secure method of user authentication can be widely implemented on the Internet. Not the least of these is that many countries, including the United States, classify encryption technology as munitions, thereby creating legal challenges—on top of the technical challenges—that must be overcome before a new standard can be deployed.

As of the time of this writing, the HTTP Basic Authentication Scheme is the only means of user authentication that is widely supported.

## Is Basic Authorization Secure?

The Basic Authorization Scheme, as described in the HTTP/1.0 specification, uses a BASE64 transfer-encoding scheme borrowed from the MIME specification. BASE64 is not an encryption scheme—it is simply an encoding method designed to ensure the integrity of the authorization data as it travels through the Net from the client to the server. Even if it were designed to be difficult to decode, you wouldn't have to decode it to use it for nefarious purposes—all a miscreant would actually need to break in would be the *encrypted* password, as transferred by the browser.

In IIS, you can turn on Basic Authentication by clicking on the check box in the Internet Service Manager Service property page. By default this box is unchecked.

By selecting Basic Authentication, IIS will send the Windows NT user name and password onto the network in clear text.

The current draft of the HTTP/1.0 specification has this to say about the security value of Basic Authentication:

> The basic authentication scheme is a non-secure method of filtering unauthorized access to resources on an HTTP server. It is based on the assumption that the connection between the client and the server can be regarded as a trusted carrier. As this is not generally true on an open network, the basic authentication scheme should be used accordingly.
>
> —From *http Working Group Internet-Draft*, October 14, 1995, Berners-Lee, Fielding, and Neilsen, Sec. 11.1.

Thus, Basic Authorization is not designed to be secure—all the information a potential intruder needs is available in the response from the browser. A complete solution to the problems of security and user authentication might be forthcoming in time, but for now, all you have to work with is Basic Authorization.

If you are interested in such things, you can find a complete description of BASE64 transfer-encoding in RFC 1521, the document that defines MIME.

# How Basic Authentication Works

The Basic Authentication scheme is a realm-specific method that can assign differing levels of access to different users in various realms of its data structure. Usually these realms are based upon directory trees.

The system works on a simple challenge-response scheme. When the browser requests a file from a restricted realm, the server initiates the authorization transaction with a challenge consisting of the authorization scheme ("basic" in this case), and an identifier representing the realm of the restriction. At this point, the browser will usually prompt the user for a user-ID and password, then respond to the challenge with a response string back to the server. The *response string* contains the credentials of the user for access within that particular realm on that server.

The server then checks the credentials of the user against those in its database to determine their authenticity and authority. Based on the results of the search, the server will respond by either providing the requested data (if it is satisfied that the user is allowed to have it), or an indication that the user is forbidden access.

## The Challenge and the Response

When the server gets a request for a document in a secure area, it begins the authorization transaction by sending a "challenge" back to the client. This challenge includes the 401 (Unauthorized) response code and the WWW-Authenticate token as part of the header. The WWW-Authenticate token has the following format:

```
WWW-Authenticate: Basic realm="Elvis Presley"
```

where Elvis Presley is the name the server has assigned to identify the protected realm. This string is actually sent as part of the HTTP header that the server sends with each of its responses, so the whole response might look like this:

```
HTTP/1.0 401 Unauthorized
Date: Tue, 12 Dec 1995 04:05:58 GMT
Server: Apache/1.0.0
WWW-Authenticate: Basic realm="Elvis Presley"
Content-type: text/html

<HEAD><TITLE>Authorization Required</TITLE></HEAD>
<BODY><H1>Authorization Required</H1>
This server could not verify that you
are authorized to access the document you
requested.  Either you supplied the wrong
credentials (e.g., bad password),
or your browser doesn't understand how to supply
the credentials required.<P></BODY>
```

The HTML included after the header is the text that will be displayed if the user is not authorized. In most installations, it is customizable.

When the browser sees this response, it will prompt the user for credentials. Figure 15.1 displays the user authentication dialog box from the Netscape browser.

**Figure 15.1:**

The user authentication dialog box in Netscape.

After the user enters the credentials, the browser sends them as part of its Authorization response in the form, *Userid:Password*, separated by a colon, and encoded with BASE64. Here's the authorization response from the Netscape browser for the preceding user-ID and password:

```
GET /cgibook/chap06/excl HTTP/1.0
Connection: Keep-Alive
User-Agent: Mozilla/2.0b3 (Win95; I)
Host: luna.bearnet.com:8080
Accept: image/gif, image/x-xbitmap, image/jpeg, image/
➥pjpeg, */*
Authorization: Basic SmltbXkgSG9mZmE6YWJjZGVmZ2hpams=
```

If the credentials supplied are acceptable to the server, it will respond with the requested data; if not, it will respond with 401 (Unauthorized) again, just as in the initial challenge. This enables users to keep trying in case they have inaccurately typed their user-ID or password. Of course, this indefinitely repeatable exchange also enables a user to keep trying password after password in a surreptitious attempt to determine someone else's credentials—it's definitely a double-edged sword.

# A Basic Authorization Example

Sometimes you might want users to be able to register with your server for access without having to wait for a system administrator to get around to entering his or her user-ID and password into the password file with htpasswd. Also, some system administrators would rather not have access to the passwords of all their users, and thus would prefer that the users enter the password themselves.

With this in mind, this section presents an example of a program that creates the entries in the password file based on input from an HTML form.

First, you'll need a form for the user to fill out. The following form asks for the user-ID and password; you might also want to get a street address, e-mail address, and other user- or application-specific information.

**Listing 15.7    auth.html**

```
<HTML>
<HEAD>
<TITLE>Basic Authentication Example</TITLE>
</HEAD>
<BODY>
<H1>Basic Authorization Example</H1>
<HR>

Please enter the Username and Password you wish to use.<p>

<FORM METHOD="POST" ACTION="addpasswd.pl">

<TABLE>
  <TR>
    <TD>Enter a Username:<BR>
```

```
      <INPUT TYPE="text" NAME="UserID" SIZE=10 MAXLENGTH=10>
   <td width=10>
     <td>Enter a Password:<br>
        <INPUT TYPE="PASSWORD" NAME="UserPass" SIZE=10
➡MAXLENGTH=10>
   <TR>
     <TD COLSPAN=3>
       <INPUT TYPE="SUBMIT" VALUE="  Let's Go!  ">
</TABLE>

</BODY>
</HTML>
```

Please note that the password from this form will be transmitted "in the clear"—that is, without any encryption or obfuscation of any sort. So if security is important (and you're using Basic Authentication anyway), you will want to enter the passwords in such a manner that they are not transmitted over the Internet at all (for example, enter the passwords with the `htpasswd` program and read them to your users over the telephone).

This form uses the `POST` method for submitting the form because the `GET` method transmits form contents as a part of the URL, making the password visible on the URL line of the user's browser. With the `POST` method, however, the form contents are passed to the server as part of the request header, thereby obscuring the contents from the view of a casual observer.

The CGI program that receives the password can then create the password file. Listing 15.8 is an example, in Perl, of how to do that with Microsoft's IIS server.

**Listing 15.8    addpasswd.pl.cgi**

```
# addpasswd.pl.cgi -- Add Password Program
#            for HTTP Basic Authorization
#
```

*continues*

**Listing 15.8    Continued**

```perl
# (c) 1995-96 William E. Weinman
#

# the password file
$Passwords = "/ cgidir/htpasswd";
# the temporary work file
$TempPass = "/cgidir/ptmp";

# 64-byte salt for crypt
@saltset = ('a' .. 'z', 'A' .. 'Z', '0' .. '9', '.', '/');

# content-type for html
$content="text/html";

# where to go when we're done
$doneurl="/home/index.html";

# post method variables
$ct = $ENV{"CONTENT_TYPE"};
$cl = $ENV{"CONTENT_LENGTH"};

# put the data into a variable
read(STDIN, $qs, $cl);

# split it up into an array by the '&' character
@qs = split(/&/, $qs);

foreach $i (0 .. $#qs)
  {
  # convert the plus chars to spaces
  $qs[$i] =~ s/\+/ /g;

  # convert the hex tokens to characters
  $qs[$i] =~ s/%(..)/pack("c",hex($1))/ge;

  # split into name and value
  ($name, $value) = split(/=/, $qs[$i],2);

  # create the associative element
  $qs{$name} = $value;
  }
```

```perl
# get the user name and password

$UserID    = $qs{"UserID"};
$UserPass  = $qs{"UserPass"};

$| = 1; # set stdout to flush after each write

# set the MIME type
print "Content-Type: $content\r\n";
print "\r\n";

# if the TempPass file exists, the password file is busy
if(-f $TempPass)
  {
  for($i = 0; ($i < 5) && (-f $TempPass); $i++)
    { sleep 1 }
  &BusyError if ($i == 5);
  }

# setup the html document
print qq(<html>
  <head><title>Adding Password</title></head>
  <body bgcolor="#dddddd">
  <h1>Adding Password</h1>);

# uncomment this to display all the variables
# print "All Variables:<br>\n";
# foreach $n (keys %ENV) { print "<tt>$n: $ENV{$n}</tt><br>\n"
}

# create the salt for crypt
# basically, that means come up with a couple of very
# unique bytes
#
($p1, $p2) = unpack("C2", $UserName);
$now = time;
$week = $now / (60*60*24*7) + $p1 + $p2;
$salt = $saltset[$week % 64] . $caltoot[$now % 64];

$cryptpass = crypt($UserPass, $salt);
```

*continues*

**Listing 15.8    Continued**

```perl
# build an associative array of the password file
open (PASS, "<$Passwords");
$umask = umask(0);
open (TMP, ">$TempPass");
umask($umask);
while(<PASS>)
  {
  chop;
  print TMP "$_\n";
  ($tname, $tpass) = split(':');
  $tapass{$tname} = $tpass;
  }
close(PASS);

unless($tapass{$UserID})
  {
  print qq(Adding $UserID to the password file.<p>
          Press <a href="$doneurl">here</a> to
          continue.<br>\n);

  printf (TMP "%s:%s\n", $UserID, $cryptpass);
  close TMP;
  rename($TempPass, $Passwords);
  # system "mv", $TempPass, $Passwords;
  }
else
  {
  print qq($UserID is already registered here. Send email to
➡the
          <a href="mailto:WebMaster\@bearnet.com">WebMaster</
➡a>
          if you need to change your password.<br>\n);
  close TMP;
  unlink $TempPass;
  }

print "<hr><tt>&copy;</tt> <small> 1995 William E. Weinman</
➡small><br>";
print "</body></html>\n";
```

```
sub BusyError
{
print qq[<html>
  <head><title>File Busy Error</title></head>
  <body bgcolor="#dddddd">
  <h1>Error: File Busy</h1>
  <p>The password file is busy ($i), please try again later.
  <p>If this condition persists, please contact the
  <a href="mailto:webmaster\@yourserver">webmaster</a>.
  </body></html>
  ];

exit 0;
}
```

The Perl code takes advantage of some of Perl's unique features, such as the `while(<PASS>)` loop to read the password file, and the `unless` construct to make the conditional code more clear. Also notice that you can use any character to quote a string with `print`—I often use parentheses [for example, qq(<text>)] to quote text for HTML, because it enables me to use standard double-quotes in the string without bothering to escape them.

One of the major reasons that large sites use Basic Authentication is for the client-state information that it provides. When Basic Authentication is in use, the USER_ID variable becomes available. The USER_ID variable allows a site to know which particular user is requesting any given CGI program. This can be very useful when your application requires interaction with the user, an otherwise difficult task given HTTP's connectionless transport model.

# A Form-Processing Example That Sends E-Mail

This section presents a typical application of CGI—sending e-mail to a mailbox. The application uses a form interface for a user to enter a message. For security reasons, the user is *not* allowed to enter the e-mail address of the recipient. In this case, it is hard-coded in the program. If you want to use this program for more than one recipient, you could add a lookup function to find the e-mail address.

For security reasons, it is also important that nothing from the HTML is used on the command line that gets passed to the Perl `system()` function. Keep in mind that the HTML file is not secure, and can be duplicated and changed on a user's system. When you pass anything from a form response, or even a hidden field, to a shell command line, it exposes your system to attack.

Listing 15.9 is an HTML file that presents a form to the user for sending e-mail via CGI.

You will need a mail transport agent software such as POSTMAIL and an SMTP server for this program to work. POSTMAIL can be downloaded from `http://www.software.com`. An evaluation copy of a SMTP server for NT can be downloaded from `http://www.metainfo.com`.

### Listing 15.9  email.html—A Form for Sending E-Mail via CGI

```html
<html>
<head>
<title>Email Bill</title>
</head>
<body bgcolor="#e0e0e0">

<h1>Email Bill</h1>
<hr>

<form action="/home/mailit.pl " method=post>

<p>Please enter your name:<br>
<input type=text name=name size=60>

<p>Please enter your email address:<br>
<input type=text name=from size=60>

<p>Please enter the subject of your message:<br>
<input type=text name=subject size=60>
```

```
<p>Please enter your message:<br>
<textarea name=body rows=15 cols=64>
</textarea>

<p>
<input type=submit value="Send It!">
<input type=reset value="Clear">

</form>

<hr>
</body>
</html>
```

Figure 15.2 is a Netscape screen showing the form from listing 15.9 being filled in.

**Figure 15.2:**

The Email Bill form in Netscape.

The Perl program in listing 15.10 is the CGI program that actually sends the e-mail. It uses all the techniques discussed in this chapter to receive input from the server, and return a confirmation display to the user. It uses Perl's `system()` function to call the *POSTMAIL* mail delivery agent on the IIS server.

**Listing 15.10    mailit.pl.cgi—Send E-Mail to a Pre-Defined Address**

```
# Filename: mailit.pl
# (c) 1996 William E. Weinman
#
# a generic example of a cgi program that sends
# the response to a form encapsulated in an
# email message to a pre-determined address
#

# your email address goes here (please don't use mine!)
$emailto = "wew\@bearnet.com";
$webmaster = "webmaster\@bearnet.com";

# Send the MIME header
print "Content-type: text/html\r\n\r\n";

print qq(
<html><head><title>Form Response</title></head>
<body bgcolor="#e0e0e0">);


$ct = $ENV{"CONTENT_TYPE"};
$cl = $ENV{"CONTENT_LENGTH"};

# check the content-type for validity
if($ct ne "application/x-www-form-urlencoded")
  {
  print "I don't understand content-type: $ct\n";
  exit 1;
  }

# put the data into a variable
read(STDIN, $qs, $cl);

# split it up into an array by the '&' character
```

```
@qs = split(/&/,$qs);

foreach $i (0 .. $#qs)
  {
  # convert the plus chars to spaces
  $qs[$i] =~ s/\+/ /g;

  # convert the hex tokens to characters
  $qs[$i] =~ s/%(..)/pack("c",hex($1))/ge;

  # split into name and value
  ($name, $value) = split(/=/,$qs[$i],2);

  # create the associative element
  $qs{$name} = $value;
  }

print qq(
<h1>Form Response</h1>

<p>The following information is being forwarded by e-mail:

<p>
Remote Host: <tt>$ENV{"REMOTE_HOST"}</tt><br>
Remote Addr: <tt>$ENV{"REMOTE_ADDR"}</tt><br>
User Agent:  <tt>$ENV{"HTTP_USER_AGENT"}</tt><br>
From: <tt>$qs{"name"} &lt;$qs{"from"}&gt;</tt><br>
Subject: <tt>$qs{"subject"} [Via Form]</tt><br>

<p>Message follows:
<pre>$qs{"body"}</pre>
\n);

# Make sure you have write permission set for /cgimail!!
open(MAIL, "¦ /cgimail/postmail -t -f'$webmaster'");

# These lines must be terminated with CR-LF pairs!
print(MAIL "From: $qs{name} <$qs{from}>\r\n");
print(MAIL "X-WWW-Form: $ENV{SCRIPT_NAME}\r\n");
print(MAIL "Reply-to: $qs{name} <$qs{from}>\r\n");
```

*continues*

**Listing 15.10 Continued**

```
print(MAIL "To: $emailto\r\n");
print(MAIL "Subject: $qs{subject} [Via Form]\r\n\r\n");

print MAIL qq(
Remote Host: $ENV{"REMOTE_HOST"}
Remote Addr: $ENV{"REMOTE_ADDR"}
User Agent:  $ENV{"HTTP_USER_AGENT"}
From: $qs{"name"} <$qs{"from"}>

Message follows:
$qs{"body"}

);

close(MAIL);
```

Figure 15.3 is a Netscape screen showing the output of the CGI program in listing 15.10. This screen shows the user that what they have entered in the form is being e-mailed to the recipient.

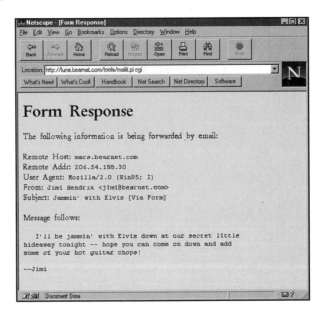

**Figure 15.3:**

Response to the e-mail form.

Listing 15.11 shows the complete e-mail message as it is received in the recipient's mailbox.

**Listing 15.11    mailit.pl.cgi—Send E-Mail to a Pre-Defined Address**

```
Return-Path: webmaster@bearnet.com
Received: (from nobody@localhost) by luna.bearnet.com (8.6.12/
➥luna) id QAA08485; Thu, 15 Feb 1996 16:49:46 -0600
Date: Thu, 15 Feb 1996 16:49:46 -0600
Message-Id: <199602152249.QAA08485@luna.bearnet.com>
From: Jimi Hendrix <jimi@bearnet.com>
X-WWW-Form: /tools/mailit.pl
Reply-to: Jimi Hendrix <jimi@bearnet.com>
To: wew@bearnet.com
Subject: Jammin' with Elvis [Via Form]
X-UIDL: 824424783.000

Remote Host: mars.bearnet.com
Remote Addr: 206.54.188.30
User Agent:  Mozilla/2.0 (Win95; I)
From: Jimi Hendrix <jimi@bearnet.com>

Message follows:

    I'll be jammin' with Elvis down at our secret little
hideaway tonight -- hope you can come on down and add
some of your hot guitar chops!

--Jimi
```

This section has presented a small CGI program that uses all the techniques discussed so far in this chapter. It is useful as a real-world working application that demonstrates the use of CGI, and can be easily expanded to provide more functionality.

The next section presents a more complex form of CGI, called *Non-Parsed Header CGI.* This form of CGI bypasses the server and sends HTTP responses directly to the client, for cases where the server does not have the flexibility to perform the desired action.

# Non-Parsed Header CGI

When a normal CGI program responds with output to the standard out stream, the server intercepts the stream and incorporates it with standard HTTP to the client. There are situations, however, where the standard responses aren't sufficient to perform the necessary functions. Non-Parsed Header (NPH) CGI is designed to handle those situations.

Most servers implement a special way of calling a CGI program that does not intercept the header, called NPH-CGI. On most servers, it is invoked when the CGI program is in a file that starts with the letters, "`nph-`" (e.g., `nph-myprogram.cgi`). If this doesn't work on your server, talk to your system administrator or consult the server documentation to find out how to run NPH-CGI on your system.

When you write an NPH-CGI program, you need to provide a valid HTTP response in your header. This next section discusses what is required by the HTTP specification to form a valid header.

# An Introduction to HTTP

*HyperText Transfer Protocol* (HTTP) is the protocol used by Web servers to negotiate the flow of data between the server and the client. The HTTP protocol defines a set of messages that fall into two categories: "request" messages from the client, and "response" messages from the server.

Request messages are sent by the client to the server to request data. This is the basic format for an HTTP request message:

```
<method> URI <HTTP-version>
```

A typical request might look like this:

```
GET /cgibook/chap01/index.html HTTP/1.0
```

The server then sends a response to the client in the following form:

```
<response-header>
<data>
```

The first part of the response is the *response header*. It begins with a *status line* that contains the version of HTTP being used, a *status code,* and a *reason phrase.* The status line is followed by a series of MIME-formatted header lines that describe the details of the response.

The most common response status code that you will send is "200", which essentially means, "Okay, here's the data you requested." The other response codes defined in HTTP/1.0 are listed in table 15.3. For full definitions and usage guidelines, see the HTTP Internet Draft referenced previously.

### Table 15.3    HTTP Response Status Codes

| Status Code | Reason Phrase |
| --- | --- |
| **Informational 1xx** | |
| Undefined in HTTP/1.0 | |
| **Successful 2xx** | |
| 200 | OK |
| 201 | Created |
| 202 | Accepted |
| 204 | No Content |
| **Redirection 3xx** | |
| 300 | Multiple Choices |
| 301 | Moved Permanently |
| 302 | Moved Temporarily |
| 304 | Not Modified |

*continues*

**Table 15.3  Continued**

| Status Code | Reason Phrase |
|---|---|
| **Client Error 4xx** | |
| 400 | Bad Request |
| 401 | Unauthorized |
| 403 | Forbidden |
| 404 | Not Found |
| **Server Error 5xx** | |
| 500 | Internal Server Error |
| 501 | Not Implemented |
| 502 | Bad Gateway |
| 503 | Service Unavailable |

The response header is always followed by a blank line to indicate that the header is finished. If there is a body of data associated with the response, it follows the blank line.

A response to the preceding request might look like this:

```
HTTP/1.0 200 OK
Date: Mon, 22 Jan 1996 17:52:11 GMT
Server: Microsoft-IIS-W/2.0
Content-type: text/html

<html>
<head>
<title>Chapter 1 &#183; "Hello, World!"</title>
</head>
<BODY bgcolor="#dddddd">

   . . . document body . . .

</body>
</html>
```

It is important to note that newlines in HTTP messages are represented by both a carriage-return (0D*hex*) *and* a linefeed (0A*hex*). Some systems —including Unix systems and some software on Macs and PCs—do not normally use both characters in their line endings. Many servers and clients will go ahead and recognize line endings that are either a single carriage-return or a single linefeed; in fact, the current HTTP specification encourages them to do so. Some clients don't recognize these line endings, however, and it's not required of them to do so.

Just make sure to end your lines with both characters, in the correct order, and your code will work with more clients without problem.

It is beyond the scope of this chapter to present the definitions of all the possible fields in an HTTP transaction. You will get what you need to know here, but for all the gory details of HTTP, you can get a copy of the Internet draft that describes it at `ftp://ftp.internic.net/internet-drafts/draft-ietf-http-v10-spec-04.txt`.

The point to remember is that the server sends the client a stream of characters that represent the different elements of the response. If you know the format of what an HTTP server sends, you can mimic its protocol and send customized responses to handle specific circumstances not otherwise supported by the server.

Normally, when you run a CGI program, the server will intercept the MIME header and simply incorporate its elements into the overall header that it sends to the client. You don't want this to happen if you're generating your own responses—you'll need a way of bypassing the server altogether. This is what NPH-CGI is for.

# Coding a Non-Parsed Header CGI Program

Keep in mind that when you write an NPH-CGI program, you need to provide a valid HTTP response in your header. Listing 15.12 is a skeleton NPH-CGI program that does that in Perl. The technique should be obvious enough to see how to implement it in other languages.

**Listing 15.12   A Skeleton NPH-CGI Program**

```
# nph-skel.pl.cgi
#
# Hello World in NPH-CGI
#
# (c) 1996 William E. Weinman

$HttpHeader = "HTTP/1.0 200 OK";
$ContentType = "Content-type: text/html";

print "$HttpHeader\r\n";      # note the \r\n sequence!
print "$ContentType\r\n\r\n";

print "<http><head><title>NPH-CGI Hello World</title></
➥head>\n";
print "<body><h1>Hello, World!</h1></body></html>\n"
```

It really is that simple. Just make sure that you send the response header before anything else, that your newlines are carriage-return/linefeed pairs, and that the last line of the header has two newlines after it.

Now that you know how to do this, you're probably saying, "Well that's cool, but what do I do with it?"

I'm glad you asked.

## Server-Push Animation

The most popular technique for creating inline graphic animations on a Web page is called *server-push*. In a nutshell, this technique uses an NPH-CGI program to push successive "frames" of an animation from the server to the client, one after the other, without waiting for subsequent requests from the client.

Server-push animation works with the special MIME-type, "multipart/x-mixed-replace". The "multipart" content type is a method of encapsulating several entities (which the MIME specification calls "body parts") in the body of one message. The "x-mixed-replace" subtype is an invention of Netscape's (also supported by a number of other browsers) that allows each encapsulated entity to replace the previous one on a dynamic page.

The main part of the document is called a *container,* because it is used to hold the contents of the subordinate entities. The container document uses boundary strings to delimit the individual entities so that they can be extracted by the client.

The correct syntax for the container's "Content-type:" declaration is as follows:

```
Content-type: multipart/x-mixed-replace;boundary="random-
➥string"
```

The boundary string is used with two leading dash characters (e.g., --random-string) to introduce the MIME header of each subordinate entity; and with two leading *and* two trailing dashes to terminate the entire container (e.g., --random-string--). Listing 15.13 is an example of how a server-push stream should look.

## Listing 15.13    A Server-Push Stream Example

```
HTTP/1.0 200 OK
Content-type: multipart/x-mixed-replace;boundary="foo"

--foo
Content-type: text/plain

Text string 1.

--foo

Content-type: text/plain

Text string 2.

--foo
```

*continues*

**Listing 15.13   Continued**

```
Content-type: text/plain

Text string 3.

--foo
Content-type: text/plain

Text string 4.

--foo--
```

The boundary string, with its leading and trailing double-dashes, must be on a line by itself set off from the rest of the stream by carriage-return/linefeed pairs. The client software will expect this, and it is required by the RFC 1591 MIME specification. In other words, the preceding example would be coded with a string like this:

```
print "\r\n--foo\r\n"
```

and

```
print "\r\n--foo--\r\n"
```

The string used for the boundary needs to be some string that is not likely to be found in the encapsulated entities, to avoid having the entities inadvertently split up. This is not a likely problem with graphics files, of course, but you need to watch out for it—especially if your graphics files have comment blocks in them.

Now, with all this background information, you're probably anxious to see it all come together. The next section presents a full working example of server-push.

Although it is currently optional, it is a good idea to also include a Content-Length header in your contained entities. Future versions of HTTP might require this in some circumstances, and it gives some browsers enough information today to display a progress indicator as it downloads each part of the animation.

# A Complete Server-Push Example

The NPH-CGI program in this section reads a list of individual GIF files and pushes them out to the client using server-push.

Listing 15.14 is a Perl program that reads a list of filenames from a text file and sends them as parts in a multipart MIME stream, as documented earlier in this chapter.

**Listing 15.14    A Generic Server-Push Animation Program in Perl**

```
# nph-push.pl
#
# (c) 1996 William E. Weinman
#
# Generic CGI Push Animation
#

# response header stuff
$httpokay = "HTTP/1.0 200 Okay";
$ct = "Content-type:";
$cl = "Content-length:";
$boundary = "foo";
$ctmixed = "$ct multipart/x-mixed-replace;
➥boundary=$boundary";
$ctgif = "$ct image/gif";

# the list of files to animate
$listfile = "animate.lst";

# delaytime can in seconds (can be fractional)
$delaytime = 1.5;
```

*continues*

**Listing 15.14 Continued**

```perl
$| = 1; # force a flush after each print

# read the list
open(LISTFILE, "<$listfile");
@infiles = <LISTFILE>; # is perl suave, or what?
close(LISTFILE);

# send the main http response header
print "$httpokay\n";
print "$ctmixed\n\n";

# main loop
foreach $i (@infiles)
  {
  chop $i; # lose the trailing '\n'
  $clsz = &filesize($i);
  # inside boundaries have a leading '--'
  print "\n--$boundary\n";
  if ($sleepokay)
    {
    # this is perl's famous less-than-one-second sleep trick!
;^)
    select(undef, undef, undef, $delaytime);
    }
  else
    { $sleepokay = 1;}
  # uncomment this to send the filename--useful for
  # debugging, harmless to the browser, and a bad
  # idea for production use, because it gives a potential
  # intruder useful information.
  #
  # print "X-Filename $i\n";

  # the content-length header may be required by HTTP 1.1,
  # it's optional in HTTP 1.0, but some browsers will
  # use it to display progress to the user if you send it.
  print "$cl $clsz\n";
  print "$ctgif\n\n";
```

```
    # now send the GIF, keeping it open for a minimum
    # amount of time.
    open (INFILE, "<$i");
    sysread(INFILE, $buffer, $clsz);
    close(INFILE);
    syswrite(STDOUT, $buffer, $clsz);
    }

# the trailing boundary with both '--' indicators
print "\n--$boundary--\n";

# this is here because it was ugly up there.
sub filesize
{
($dev, $ino, $mode, $nlink, $uid, $gid, $rdev, $size,
    $atime, $mtime, $ctime, $blksize, $blocks) = stat($_[0]);

return $size
}
```

There are couple of things worth noting in the Perl source code for this example. One is the assignment, "`$¦ = 1;`", near the top of the program. This is the Perlism for flushing an output stream buffer after each write to it. It ensures that all the bytes are sent at the time that they are intended to, keeping your output smooth.

Another note about the Perl code: notice the line " `select(undef, undef, undef, $delaytime);`". This is Perlish for a sleep with sub-second resolution. It's ugly, but it works well, and there's nothing like it in C. `sleep` usually works only on one-second boundaries, so a command like `sleep 1` will sleep for an unpredictable amount of time between zero and one second.

One last technique worth noting is the line for reading the file-name list into an array, "`@infiles = <LISTFILE>;`". That in itself is enough reason to learn a new language!

This chapter has covered a lot of ground. In it you have learned the basic requirements of a CGI program, the meanings of all the different components, definitions of all the standard CGI variables, and some specific techniques for getting reliable results from CGI. Although this chapter is not designed to provide all the details of CGI, you now have the tools necessary to create CGI programs of your own.

If you would like to learn more about CGI, the author has written a book that covers the subject in far greater detail. *The CGI Book* (New Riders Publishing, ISBN 1-56205-571-2) is a complete reference and programming guide for CGI with chapters on processing forms, understanding URLs, imagemaps, user authentication, cookies, server-side includes, animation, e-mail, and CGI security.

# Chapter 16

# Database Interfaces

This chapter focuses on exactly what a database interface, often called a gateway, can and cannot do to help you access a database. It is important to know the potential of a tool before you start to use it in order to set realistic expectations for you and your application users.

These are the main topics covered in this chapter:

➤ What do interfaces and gateways do?

➤ Using a database over a network

➤ Using a database interface

➤ Using commercial products

➤ Using freeware or shareware gateways

➤ Supporting software needed

Please note that there could be some confusing terminology. The software provided by a database vendor to access the database is called an interface. The gateway that connects the Web to your database interface software can also be called an interface. Some gateways require a database-specific module to talk to a database, and the module can be called an interface.

In this chapter, the term *interface* refers to the provided database software, the term *gateway* refers to Web/database connection software, and specific gateway modules are identified as they are used in the gateway software. The common gateway interface provided by HTML is referred to simply as CGI. Hopefully the diagram in figure 16.1 will help eliminate most of the confusion.

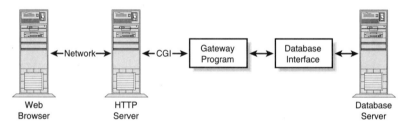

**Figure 16.1:**

An overview of the pieces required to access a database from the Web.

## Retrieving Database Information

When someone uses a Web browser to access a database, there are several components involved in passing the user query to the database and getting back the results. The action happens as follows:

1. The user calls a gateway program using CGI, usually by clicking on a hyperlink or pressing a button in the Web browser.

2. The Web browser collects the information entered by the user to send to the CGI program.

3. The browser then contacts the HTTP server on the machine where the CGI program resides, asking the server to find the CGI program and pass it the information.

4. The HTTP server checks to see if the requesting machine is allowed to access the CGI program.

5. If the user is allowed access, the HTTP server locates the gateway program and passes the Web browser information to the gateway. Steps 1–5 are shown in figure 16.2.

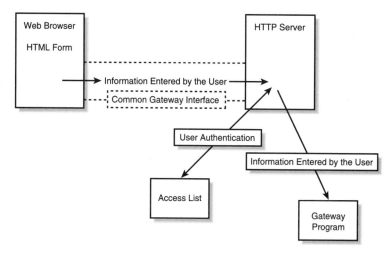

**Figure 16.2:**

Calling a CGI program from a Web browser.

6. The gateway program is executed.

7. First, the gateway processes the passed-in information into a format the database understands.

8. Next, the gateway uses the database module to pass the database query to the database interface.

9. The database interface parses the database query for accuracy.

10. If the interface finds a syntax error in the query, an error message is passed back to the gateway program.

11. The error message is sent to the HTTP server, which sends it back to the Web browser for display to the user, and the process stops here. Steps 6–11 are shown in figure 16.3.

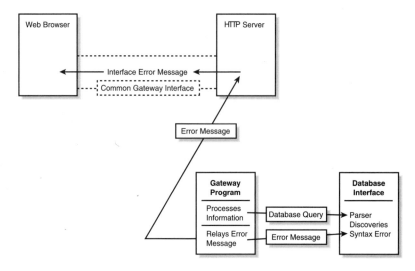

**Figure 16.3:**

Sending back an error message.

12. If there is no error, the database interface sends the query to the database.

13. The database performs the query and passes back any results to the gateway program, through the database interface.

14. The gateway program formats the results and sends them back through the CGI to the server for relay to the Web browser.

15. The Web browser displays the results. Steps 12–15 are shown in figure 16.4.

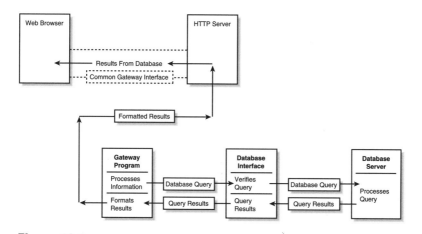

## Figure 16.4:

Sending back formatted database query results.

Despite how the process might sound, it works very smoothly. In many cases, the database module and database interface are integral parts of the gateway software. The module might be a Perl library of subroutines that is parsed as part of the Perl gateway program, or the interface might be a C library that is compiled or linked into an executable gateway program. Although the database module or interface is necessary to provide database connectivity, it does not necessarily exist as a separate program.

If you plan to connect your database to the Web, no matter which gateway product you use—freeware or commercial—most of them will use CGI to send data back and forth between the Web browser and database. Which operating system you use will determine exactly how that is done.

To access a database server running on a Unix platform, for example, there are several options. Freeware and shareware gateways abound for Unix platforms. If you plan to design your own, Perl is a good choice if your database has a command-line interface that will accept commands via standard input. If the added capabilities provided by an API or 4GL are what is needed, using C/C++ for your gateway is a good way to go. If you would rather buy a commercial product, you can find one to support most commercial databases.

For PC or Macintosh platforms, options are more limited because these platforms do not provide the programming freedom present under a Unix operating system. Most databases for these platforms require a proprietary interface that does not provide any way to access the database externally, or they use the *Open Database Connectivity* (ODBC) standard API for database access. Shareware products are rare for these platforms, but several commercial products have arisen to meet the need for Web/ database connectivity.

# What Do Interfaces and Gateways Do?

Simply put, *interfaces* provide a method to interact with a database. SQL commands that create tables; insert, update, and delete data; return query results; and so on, are passed to the database engine for processing, and the results are passed back. Database vendors can provide interfaces of varying sophistication to meet your needs.

*Gateways* receive data passed from a Web browser through an HTTP server and convert it into a form the database can understand. The converted data is passed to the database interface and the database executes it. The database results, if any, are returned to the gateway program, which converts the results so the Web browser can display it. The converted results are passed back to the Web browser and are displayed.

A gateway cannot work alone. Database engines are not simple programs, and they require special interface software to talk to the outside world. The gateway requires some sort of channel to talk to the database. This channel is provided by the database interface, which is special software provided by the database vendor. The gateway talks to the interface, which talks to the database.

Exactly how this process works depends on the capabilities of the target database and the type of gateway you use. There are three methods for a Web server to talk to a database engine:

➤ Using a database without networking capabilities

➤ Using a database with networking capabilities

➤ Using third-party networking software

The main consideration in each method is which software is used to handle the network connections for database access from remote computers.

# Using a Database Over a Network

Why is it so important to use a network connection? Would it not be easier to have the users on the same machine as the database? Although it would be easier, if the database is relatively large and the number of users is high, performance becomes a big issue. A database server likes to have the total resources of the host computer to itself.

If the database front end is a GUI application, GUIs require a lot of resources such as memory and CPU time. Database performance is directly related to the amount of memory and CPU time the database engine has access to. GUI applications and database servers do not share resources nicely. Some database engines actually "lock" large portions of memory for their exclusive use, preventing any other programs from using the locked memory. This practically requires the database front end applications to run on another machine to give the GUI applications and the database the computer resources they need.

When the database access applications are moved to other machines, this requires some way to access a database across a network. The database queries submitted to the database and the results obtained are passed across the network. This requires software dedicated to handling the information traveling from computer to computer.

## Using a Database without Networking Capabilities

In some cases, a database will not have client/server capabilities. A database may be able to handle multiple users at once, but only if the users are on the same machine the database server resides on. Some database vendors offer networking capabilities as an added feature and charge a client licensing fee for every machine that has network access to the database.

In this case, running an HTTP server on the same machine as the database server can alleviate the problem, provided the server machine can handle the double load. As detailed in figure 16.5, this method relies on the Web client and server to provide the networking capabilities.

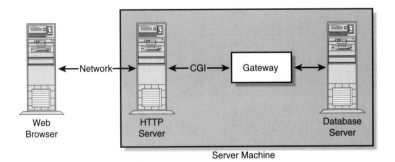

**Figure 16.5:**
Using a database with no networking support.

This method is about as simple as it gets. The HTTP server, CGI programs, and database server all exist on the same machine, giving CGI programs direct access to whatever database interface program you want to use. Database queries and results returned from the database don't travel over the network back and forth to CGI programs, so response time is as good as it can be.

However, this method assumes the Web browsers accessing the data are running on remote machines. If the database is of medium to large size and there are many users, it is definitely *not* a good idea to have the database server, HTTP server, and multiple Web browsers all running on the same machine. This can bring even a powerful machine to its knees.

If you expect a lot of visitors to a Web site, or you have a large amount of data to put on the Web, you will probably end up dedicating a machine to be your server. Most large databases are on a dedicated machine anyway, so if your server can handle the extra HTTP server load, this is the best way to go in most cases.

Even if there currently are machines on your network with client licenses to remotely access the database, the simplicity of this method appeals to a lot of system administrators.

# Using a Database with Networking Capabilities

If the target database comes with built-in network capabilities or you have purchased at least one license for remote access, this gives the option of running the HTTP server on a remote machine and accessing the database using the database network software.

Using a database with existing network support presents several options (see fig. 16.6). If the data can be broken into several distinct types, it is a good idea to use a separate HTTP server for each type of data, and even to run each HTTP server on a different machine, if you have the capacity. This reduces the load caused by the HTTP servers and could also reduce bottlenecks on a single node of the network, if the database server machine can serve multiple subnets.

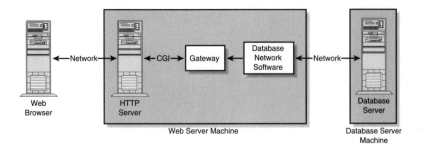

**Figure 16.6:**

Using a database with networking support.

With this method, the CGI programs are located on the same machine as the HTTP server. Many DBAs prefer to have a dedicated machine for the database server to eliminate potential problems with unruly software and to protect their data as much as possible. This method would appeal to them because it moves the HTTP server and CGI programs off the database server machine.

Just remember the database software responsible for network support must be installed on every machine that has access to the database. As mentioned before, this can be expensive due to per-machine licensing fees.

This method also works well if you have more than one database server. A single HTTP server can access multiple database machines through CGI programs, as shown in figure 16.7.

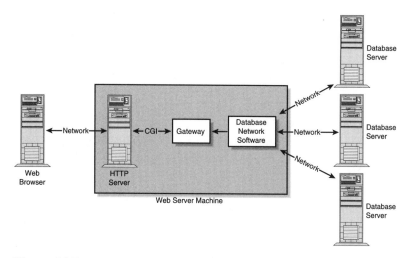

**Figure 16.7:**

Using a Web server to access multiple database servers.

If you can use multiple database servers to lighten the load on any one database, performance can increase dramatically. However, this is only a factor with truly large databases. In most cases, a single database server will handle the load.

# Using Third-Party Networking Software

Another way to access a database from a Web server is to use third-party networking software, or even to develop your own. Using software that supports several different databases can offer you the flexibility of talking to databases from different vendors on different kinds of machines (see fig. 16.8).

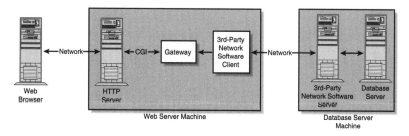

**Figure 16.8:**

Using third-party networking software.

The third-party software must be able to accept database queries from a CGI program on the same machine, pass it over the network to the other half of the network software, submit the query to the database, get the results, and pass the results back over the network and hand them to the CGI program.

In some ways, this functionality is redundant when you consider an HTTP server will do most of what the third-party software does. If you need a way to handle requests for multiple databases, however, using customized networking software as a traffic cop might be the way to go.

As an additional step, the networking software can also be used as database translation software. Database queries can be boiled down to a single set of functions and then no matter what kind of database is used, the programs look the same by using a generic programming interface.

If the networking software is combined with a generic database API, this enables programmers using a single programming interface to submit queries to databases of different kinds. The network/API software translates the queries into database-specific syntax, sends the query over the network to the selected database, and formats the results for relay back to the requesting program.

## Using a Database Interface

To use a Web/database gateway, it is necessary to know what kind of interface the database provides. Whether the most simplistic command-line interface or the most sophisticated programming API, the database has to provide some way to get to the data.

The capabilities of your database interface determine the sophistication of your database application. If you choose to use a command-line interface for its simplicity, your application will be limited in what it can do. Command-line interfaces do not allow you to nest database queries or format the database results.

If you choose to use a programming API, on the other hand, your application can do anything the database is able to do, but you will be required to learn how to use the API in your application. The features needed by your database application will determine the interface you use.

Using a database interface requires the user to learn at least a little of the database query language provided by the database vendor. In most cases the language is some flavor of the Structured Query Language (SQL). SQL is a standard query language, but most database vendors have added non-standard extensions to SQL that take advantage of specific features their database offers. This means if you learn SQL for one database, moving to another database can require learning a slightly different syntax or losing some functionality and gaining others.

# Using the SQL Language

Although a discussion of the SQL database language is beyond the scope of this book, a brief overview is helpful for understanding some of the examples used in this and other chapters. For more information on SQL, look for New Riders' book, *MSCE Training Guide*, in the Fall of 1996.

SQL (pronounced *sequel*) is used to interact with the database. SQL gives you a way to talk to the database and tell it what to do with your data. There are a host of standard SQL commands, and many databases have their own extensions that differ from other databases, but you can manage almost any database with just the following six SQL commands:

1. **CREATE** creates a new database. Other things can be created, such as tables, indexes, and views. The CREATE command registers a new database with the database server so that new data can be stored.

2. **DROP** destroys a database or elements of it, such as tables, indexes, and views. Once something has been dropped, it cannot be recovered.

3. **SELECT** retrieves selected data out of the database.

4. **INSERT** puts data into the database.

5. **UPDATE** changes data that already exists in the database.

6. **DELETE** removes data from the database.

Each of these commands takes parameters that detail how they behave. As an example, DELETE can be used to remove a single record from the database, or every record in the database. As you can tell, SQL is a powerful language, but can do terrible things to a database in the wrong hands.

For this reason, many database gateways are limited to using the SELECT statement only. This eliminates the possibility of a careless user deleting your database. Gateway products that offer full functionality should also provide some sort of security mechanism to limit who can use commands other than SELECT.

## The Command-Line Interface

The command-line interface is the most common and easiest method to use, but it also provides the fewest features. In its simplest form, a command-line interface gives you the ability to enter database query commands and submit them to the database. The results are displayed on-screen, which can be a problem if the results are bigger than your screen.

Following is a representative sample of a command-line interface. The interface shown is *msql*, provided by the shareware database Mini SQL. The database "customer" has already been created, and the command-line interface is being used to create the "customer_info" table.

### Listing 16.1

```
lightspeed:~/msql/bin$ msql customer

Welcome to the MiniSQL monitor.  Type \h for help.
```

```
mSQL > \h


MiniSQL Help!

The following commands are available :-

        \q       Quit
        \g       Go (Send query to database)
        \e       Edit (Edit previous query)
        \p       Print (Print the query buffer)

mSQL > CREATE TABLE customer_info (
    ->    cust_id int primary key,
    ->    first_name char(32),
    ->    last_name char(32),
    ->    middle_name char(32),
    ->    titles char(32),
    ->    address_line1 char(40),
    ->    address_line2 char(40),
    ->    city char(32),
    ->    state char(2),
    ->    zip_code char(10)
    -> )
    -> \g

Query OK.


mSQL > \q
Bye!

lightspeed:~/msql/bin$
```

SQL commands are typed at the prompt, then \p tells msql to echo the query, and \g tells msql to submit the query to the database. \q quits from the interface, and \e invokes a text editor to enable you make changes to the last command you typed. After you edit your command, you leave the editor and the new command is displayed on the command line, ready to be sent to the database.

Command-line interfaces are commonly used by database administration (DBA) personnel to do routine database administration, such as creating new database tables, inserting a few rows of data, or executing simple queries to get data out of the database. Command-line interfaces are easy to use over a modem line or through a telnet session because they are text-based and require no GUI software, which makes them fast and efficient to use.

Command-line interfaces provided by other databases will differ slightly, but the functionality is the same. You can enter SQL commands, submit them to the database, and use some kind of editor to edit the last command.

Products such as Informix Software's dbaccess take the command-line interface one step further by giving the user a menu-driven interface. Actions are selected from a menu at the top of the screen, which can lead to another submenu of choices or can execute a command. If you prefer the typical text editor to submit SQL commands, there is a menu option to use an editor and create commands for submission to the database. Informix's upgrade to dbaccess called *isql* adds more menu items and form capabilities. Users can create forms for any database table that makes queries, inserts, updates, and deletes much easier than using SQL commands.

Command-line interfaces also have the capability of accepting bulk queries from standard input and emitting the results to standard output. A gateway can make use of this type of database interface by submitting queries via standard input and capturing the results. The query results can be posted as-is to the Web browser, or some minimal amount of processing can be done to format them.

The following is a source code listing of the command file "do_table.sql." Do_table.sql does exactly the same thing as the CREATE command entered in msql from the command line. In addition, it adds a record to the table. (The small arrows indicate the code really exists on a single line.)

**Listing 16.2**

```
# Command file for Mini SQL
#
# Command: msql customer < do_table.sql

CREATE TABLE customer_info (
  cust_id int primary key,
  first_name char(32),
  last_name char(32),
  middle_name char(32),
  titles char(32),
  address_line1 char(40),
  address_line2 char(40),
  city char(32),
  state char(2),
  zip_code char(10)
) \p\g

INSERT INTO customer_info VALUES( 1, 'Jeffrey', 'Rowe',
➥'Paul', Â'Webmaster', '1234 Webster Way', NULL,
➥'Spiderville', 'VA', Â'123-456-7890')
\p\g
```

A command file is submitted to msql using standard input with this command:

```
msql dbname < do_table.sql
```

*Dbname* is the name of the database the command file should be run against. This command takes the contents of do_table.sql and submits them to the msql interface using standard input. msql reads the commands as if they had been typed on the command line and executes them, one by one.

The results of the command file are printed to standard output as shown here:

**Listing 16.3**

```
lightspeed:~/msql/bin$ msql customer < do_table.sql

Welcome to the miniSQL monitor.  Type \h for help.

mSQL >      ->      ->      ->      ->      ->      ->      ->      ->
Query buffer
— — — — — —

CREATE TABLE customer_info (
  cust_id int primary key,
  first_name char(32),
  last_name char(32),
  middle_name char(32),
  titles char(32),
  address_line1 char(40),
  address_line2 char(40),
  city char(32),
  state char(2),
  zip_code char(10)
)
[continue]
    ->

Query OK.

mSQL >      ->      ->      ->
Query buffer
— — — — — —
INSERT INTO customer_info VALUES( 1, 'Jeffrey', 'Rowe',
➥'Paul',  'Webmaster', '1234 Webster Way', NULL,
➥'Spiderville', 'VA', '123-456-7890')

[continue]
    ->
```

```
Query OK.

mSQL >        ->
Bye!


lightspeed:~/msql/bin$
```

The command-line interface works well as a fast, cheap method of accessing a database from the Web. The biggest drawback is the limited ability to format the results for display. Results are returned as a block of text, and, unless the gateway program knows the format, there is little that can be done other than removing leading or trailing lines. Other methods are more complicated, but offer greater flexibility.

# Using API Interfaces

Another useful method for accessing a database is to use an application programming interface (API) provided by the database vendor. An *API* is a library of functions that programmers use to write database access programs. In most cases the API recognizes the same SQL statements used by the command-line interface.

The library can be linked into a custom database program to provide direct access to the database. Queries can be constructed ahead of time and presented to the user in a list, or on-the-fly as the program runs, building a query that depends on user input. APIs usually provide access to the data at a lower level than the command-line interface, which makes interface programs using an API faster than submitting bulk transactions through the command-line interface.

Many APIs also contain an extremely useful feature called a cursor. A *cursor* is a data structure that can be used in a program to capture multiple rows of data to be processed one at a time. This enables the programmer to format each row of output, stop processing after a specified number of rows, allow user input as the data is displayed, and so forth. This is distinctly more user-friendly than having to deal with query results as a block of text like the command-line interface gives you.

API programming for different databases works much the same way. A connection is opened to the database engine and a process handle is returned. The *handle* is what identifies a connection to a particular database. Multiple connections can be maintained, and each will have a unique handle.

After the connection is made, queries can be constructed and passed to the database as character strings using a query function. If the query fails, an error code is returned. If the query is successful, another function call can be made to store the returned results in a cursor. Other function calls are used to step through the cursor or to access a particular record directly. After a program has finished processing the data, a function is called to free the memory associated with the cursor, and the database connection is closed.

The following program, msql_api.c, is a simple database access program that uses the Mini SQL API to access data in the customer database, using the customer_info table. The program passes a query string to the database and prints out the results by using a cursor.

### Listing 16.4

```
/*
 * msql_api.c - a sample application for using the Mini SQL
 * programming API.
 */

#include <stdio.h>
#include <stdlib.h>

/* Needed for the msql API functions and datatypes. */
#include <msql.h>

void main()
{
  m_result *msql_data;  /* an msql cursor for returned data */
```

```
  m_row msql_row;        /* a row of data returned from a query
*/
  m_field *msql_field;  /* a structure of info about a field*/
int result;            /* result returned from function call*/
int socket;            /* socket descriptor for db connection */
int numrows;           /* number of rows returned from query */
int numfields;         /* number of fields in a row of data*/
int i,j;               /* loop counters */

  /* Connect to the database and report an error if necessary */
  result = msqlConnect("lightspeed.beowulf.com");

  if ( result == -1 ) {
    fprintf(stderr, "Unable to connect to database.\n");
    fprintf(stderr, "  %s\n", msqlErrMsg);
    exit;
  }

  /* If successful, save the socket descriptor for future use */
  socket = result;

  /* Select the database to query and report any error */
  result = msqlSelectDB(socket, "customer");

  if ( result == -1 ) {
    fprintf(stderr, "Unable to find database customer.\n");
    fprintf(stderr, "  %s\n", msqlErrMsg);
    exit;
  }

  /* Send a query to the database */
  result = msqlQuery(socket, "select * from customer_info");

  if ( result == -1 ) {
    fprintf(stderr, "Error querying database.\n");
    fprintf(stderr, "  %s\n", msqlErrMsg);
    exit;
  }
```

*continues*

**Listing 16.4    Continued**

```c
/* Store the results, if any, in a cursor */
msql_data = msqlStoreResult();

/* Get the number of rows and fields returned */
numrows = msqlNumRows(msql_data);
numfields = msqlNumFields(msql_data);

/* Process each row, field by field */
for (i=0; i<numrows; i++)
{
  fprintf(stdout, "\n");

  /* Get a row of data */
  msql_row = msqlFetchRow(msql_data);

  for (j=0; j<numfields; j++)
  {
    /* Get information about a field */
    msql_field = msqlFetchField(msql_data);

    /* Print the field name */
    fprintf(stdout, "%15.15s:", msql_field->name);

    /* Determine the type of data in the field and print it
    */
    switch (msql_field->type)
    {
      case CHAR_TYPE:
        fprintf(stdout, "%s\n", msql_row[j]);
      break;
      case INT_TYPE:
        fprintf(stdout, "%d\n", atoi(msql_row[j]));
      break;
      case REAL_TYPE:
        fprintf(stdout, "%f\n", atof(msql_row[j]));
      break;
    }
  }
}
```

```
    fprintf(stdout, "\n");

    /* Free the memory associated with the cursor */
    msqlFreeResult(msql_data);

    /* Close the connection to the database */
    msqlClose(socket);
}
```

When msql_api is run, it displays the record you entered into the database from your command file in the previous section.

**Listing 16.5**

```
lightspeed:~/msql/bin/programs$ msql_api

        cust_id:1
     first_name:Jeffrey
      last_name:Rowe
    middle_name:Paul
         titles:Webmaster
  address_line1:1234 Webster Way
  address_line2:
           city:Spiderville
          state:VA
       zip_code:12345-6789

lightspeed:~/msql/bin/programs$
```

Some APIs offer a more complicated data structure than the cursor called a descriptor. A *descriptor* is a complicated beast that contains all kinds of information about the data, including the data type, field name, field size, and other pertinent information. Using descriptors, a programmer can query a database without knowing anything about what kind of data will be returned. By using the descriptor information, the data can be identified and processed accordingly.

A lot of databases now offer APIs based on the Open DataBase Connectivity (ODBC) standard. ODBC is important because it is a *standard,* which means an API that declares itself ODBC-compliant must meet certain conditions in relation to how it works. If an API truly meets ODBC standards, programs written to access one database using ODBC should be able to access any other database using the same function calls. This greatly simplifies the task of interacting with multiple databases from different vendors.

# Using Commercial Products

There is an old adage that states, "You get what you pay for." This is true among database interfaces as well. Commercial products offer many user-friendly features that make building applications faster and easier, but they don't come cheap.

There are commercial products for constructing database front-end applications, and products are appearing that do the same for constructing gateway programs to use with CGI.

## The GUI Interface

These days most users expect some kind of GUI when they use database applications. Using a mouse and text fields, push-buttons, and menus is far easier than learning SQL and figuring out the underlying structure of the database you want to use so you can reference tables and fields directly.

The same thing applies to designing and constructing a database interface. Database application programmers are used for delving deeply into the database documentation and reading between the lines to figure out how to create database access programs. If GUI tools are available to simplify the process, the programmer's productivity can increase manyfold.

The GUI interface is nice, but GUI-based interfaces have to be developed by programmers who understand the operating system, who know how to incorporate the database API functions with the GUI code, and who know how to develop a new GUI for every different computer that will be used to access the database.

A programmer might know one or two operating systems, but it is rare for any one programmer to know all flavors of UNIX, MS Windows, OS/2, and the Macintosh operating system well enough to develop applications under them all. Database vendors have begun to address this cross-platform support issue with builder tools that help programmers port applications to different operating systems.

# Builder Tools

To combat the time and expense of developing custom database applications, some database vendors have introduced builder tools that try to automate the development process. By providing users with a selection of controls and text entry fields, prototypes and full-blown applications can be constructed in a fraction of the time it would take to complete a custom application.

In many cases, builder tools can create applications that are more fully integrated with the underlying database functionality, allowing programmers to more fully use the features of a particular database. This locks you into a proprietary scheme that the database vendor controls, but it can maximize the usefulness of your database interface applications.

An ideal product would depict database elements in a visual manner. Table and field names are provided in pull-down menus and forms can be constructed by selecting the tables and fields you want on the screen. Controls such as buttons or scroll bars are selected from a palette and placed on the form, resizing them as needed. After the GUI is constructed, the underlying code is written using a proprietary programming language dedicated to database access.

Some builder tools provide cross-platform support. Some provide more features than others. All of them are relatively expensive and are probably worth more than gold if you need a full-featured database front end constructed by next Tuesday, and you don't want (or can't afford) to hire a cadre of programmers.

# Using Freeware or Shareware Gateways

If you want to establish a Web presence with limited funds, the freeware/shareware route probably appeals to you. Some of the gateway products in this category are free to educational or research organizations, but charge a fee for commercial use. The fee is generally far less than most commercial products.

Shareware products appeal to programmers who like to get their hands into the guts of an application, or to organizations with only a small amount of data that doesn't justify a large, commercial database.

Most shareware products are simple, straightforward implementations with limited features and support. They do the job without a lot of fanfare, and most are stable and do what they are supposed to do. By using shareware products, a Webmaster can build a substantial Web site that offers full database access, at a minimum of expense.

## Source Code

One of the big attractions of shareware to some programmers is the source code. Many shareware products come complete with the source code used to construct the database interface. In some cases, such as Perl or shell scripts, this is inevitable because the source code is compiled at runtime. In other cases, the C source code is provided for users to compile their own version of a program to run on whatever hardware they use. This can eliminate dependency on vendors to fix bugs in their code, but it also requires more knowledge and programming skill on the user's part.

The availability of the source code allows programmers to customize an application for their particular needs. Most shareware is distributed under the Free Software Foundation's GNU software license, which allows modifications as long as the original copyrights and author names are retained in the source code.

# Software Support

Many of the available shareware products are actively supported by the author(s). A polite e-mail message generally produces a timely response. Some products have mailing lists where users exchange bug fixes and ideas on how to best use the software. The Internet is an unending fountain of user experiences, and chances are that someone else has had your problems or questions and an answer is only a few keystrokes away. The shareware concept reflects Internet philosophy at its best.

# Supporting Software Needed

To use or develop an interface, you will need some sort of supporting software. Even if the interface is a Unix shell script, the shell software must be present on the machine. Other types of interfaces require specific software to run, or to provide functionality that allows database access. Some of the different kinds of supporting software are listed here, but there are others.

## Compilers

A compiler is the most hardware-dependent software there is. If an interface comes with source code that needs to be compiled to run on a specific machine, you will have to have a compiler that matches the language in which the source code is written. If your machine does not have a compiler, there are versions of *Gnu C compilers* (gcc) for virtually every hardware platform, including PCs and Macs.

In addition to standard compilers, some commercial products have their own compiler of sorts. As an example, Informix Software, Inc. has a product called ESQL/C for use with Informix databases. ESQL/C enables database application programmers to create C programs that incorporate database features into their programs. Features such as imbedded SQL statements, cursors, and descriptors can be included without using API function calls.

Programs are written predominantly in C, with language extensions provided by ESQL/C also included in the code. Programs are preprocessed by the ESQL/C compiler, which converts ESQL/C language extensions into C. A normal compiler turns the resultant C code into executable programs. This process is shown in figure 16.9. Source code using ESQL/C is usually easier to read and maintain than code using API function calls. There are also versions of ESQL for COBOL, Ada, and other languages.

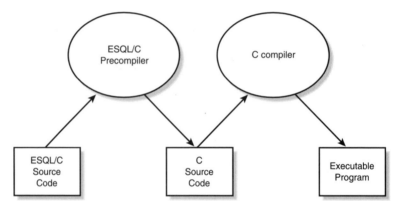

**Figure 16.9:**

Using a database precompiler.

## Libraries

Naturally, if you plan to use an API to access a database, the API must be on the system where you do development work. In most cases, the API is provided as a C library file that is linked into your code as it is compiled.

For example, Sybase, Inc. offers an API library called DB-Library as part of their Open Client product. DB-Library is exactly what the name implies: a library of function calls for accessing a Sybase database engine.

Using a library enables programmers to develop multiple database applications using a single set of function calls, and enforces programming techniques common to all applications. This makes it much easier for database application developers to read and maintain code they had no part in writing.

# Perl Extensions for Database Interfaces

As mentioned before, one of the most useful programming languages for database access via CGI programs is Perl. By itself, Perl cannot easily access a database, but combined with a compiler or API from a specific database, Perl can make CGI programming a breeze.

There are a lot of products available on the Internet that combine Perl and other database products. IsqlPerl uses Perl libraries and the ESQL/C compiler from Informix to create a database access language for Informix databases. SybPerl does the same with Perl and DB-Library for Sybase databases. OraPerl is used with Oracle databases, pgPerl with Postgres, IngPerl with Ingres, and MsqlPerl with Mini SQL. The list goes on. Chances are if you have a database, there is a Perl-based language to support it.

In addition to Perl programs based on specific database products, there are a host of ancillary Perl programs to make life easier for programmers. Steven Brenner's cgi-lib.pl is one of these. Perl programmers are a vocal and prolific lot, and it is a good bet there are Perl programs already written that will solve database access problems you might be having.

Now that you know what database interfaces do, you are better prepared to explore the issues involved in choosing an interface product.

# Chapter 17

# Introduction to Database Connectivity with Microsoft SQL Server and Oracle CGI Scripting

The introduction of Mosaic as a World Wide Web (WWW) navigation tool has resulted in an explosive growth of users and data on the Internet. Things that used to take considerable time and expertise to do, such as finding out which hotels are in a city or which houses are for sale, can now be accomplished with a click of a hypertext link. This explosive growth has not gone unnoticed by those wanting to get their information to the general public. Companies, universities, organizations, and individuals are discovering that the Web is an extremely convenient and powerful tool for making information about that organization available to a global audience.

One of the most difficult jobs for a Web site maintainer or developer in WWW publishing is keeping information in documents current. Many Web sites can consist of thousands of documents, each with information that may be duplicated elsewhere. When the information changes it can be quite a challange to ensure that that change is reflected everywhere. This is where the power of a database can greatly simplify the task of maintaining the data. Integrating Microsoft SQL Server or an Oracle database into Microsoft's Internet Information Server can simplify information maintenance, capture and process data from the users, and help provide a more dynamic and interesting Web site.

Because most companies already manage information in one or more large databases, integrating existing data into a Web server may take less time than most realize. Although database and Web integration is still a relatively new process, it is simple enough to accomplish a great deal.

There are currently several "gateways" and tools that aid in developing WWW sites using SQL Server or Oracle. However, it is important to understand the underlying mechanism by which most of these gateways work. This chapter gives a brief overview of Web and Web architecture to assure an understanding of the material that follows. Following the overview is a discussion on how to connect IIS to Microsoft's SQL Server using Internet Database Connector (IDC) and Open Database Connectivity (ODBC). IIS sites with an Oracle server can benefit from the next section on CGI scripting with Oraperl. Perl and Oracle are used to process the form and communicate with each other as needed. To illustrate the points being discussed, a database consisting of one table of employee information is used. After you have an understanding of the architecture and mechanism, you will be better equipped to evaluate and choose among the various options and tools available.

# Web and Web Server Architecture

When you push a hypertext link or enter a Uniform Resource
Locator (URL) in a Web browser, your browser sends a message
to the Web server that is referenced by that URL. When the Web
server receives the request, it is sent to the appropriate process; in
many cases, a HyperText Transfer Protocol (HTTP) server. The
HTTP server then takes this request and decides how to handle it.
Usually, the outcome is to find a specific file on the Web server
and return it to the browser.

For example, the following URL causes the Web browser to
contact the host computer, bristol.onramp.net, to issue an HTTP
request for the document index.html:

**http://bristol.onramp.net:80/index.html**

Instead of simply retrieving a file, you can also ask the server to
run an application for you. The application that is executed as a
result of the request (whether it is a POST or a GET request) is
called a CGI script or application. CGI stands for Common
Gateway Interface and has a set of standard mechanisms for
getting incoming data and returning the results. It is via the CGI
script that you can connect to an Oracle database. An overview of
CGI is given in a later section of this chapter. The whole process is
shown in the flowchart in figure 17.1.

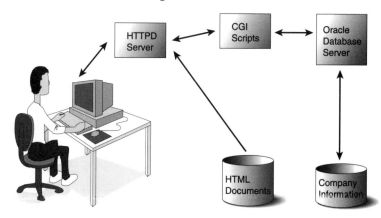

**Figure 17.1:**

The major pieces of Web architecture, and the communication flow to an
HTTP server.

In HTML, there are two different methods used to invoke an application:

➤ **GET.** Uses a format similar to all hypertext URLs. For example, the following URL utilizes the GET method to run the application called getdata.cgi on the host computer bristol.onramp.net.

http://bristol.onramp.net:80/cgi-bin/getdata.cgi

➤ **POST.** This method is most often used in *forms*, another document style, discussed in the next sections, that enables push buttons, edit fields, selection lists, and other mechanisms to be used to create a form.

This method of calling applications works well when you want to call an application via a hypertext link. There may be a limit to the amount of data that can be passed using this method. The HTML specification supports another method called POST. Both the GET and POST methods will be discussed at greater length later in the chapter.

## Forms Overview

Before you can get into how CGI scripts process data, you need to cover some basic form information because the output of a form is usually the input to a CGI script.

Forms can greatly simplify the task of collecting data from the end user. Using editable fields, selection lists, radio or push buttons, and so on, a FORM can be built that captures data from the end user in a convenient fashion. When the user has filled out the form, the data is sent to your Web server for processing via a CGI script or application. Figure 17.2 shows a basic form.

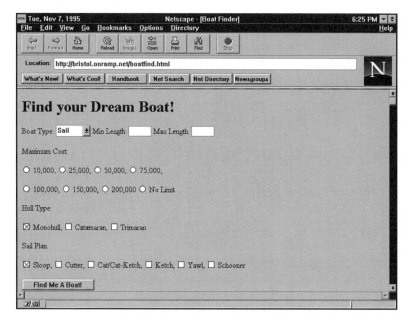

**Figure 17.2:**

A basic form and input types.

# Basic Form Types

There are many basic types (or HTML tags) that are used in form processing. This chapter works with only a subset of these, the form type and four variations of the input type: text, radio buttons, submit, and reset. There are many other types available but they are beyond the scope and intent of this chapter.

➤ Form

➤ Text

➤ Radio button

➤ Reset

➤ Submit

## The Form Tag Type

The first is the form tag itself:

```
<FORM ACTION="http://bristol.onramp.net/cgi-bin/
putinfo.cgi" METHOD=POST>
```

The form tag specifies the address of the CGI application to be run and the method for passing the form data to that application. In this example, the application is putinfo.cgi and is being called using the POST method. The form is terminated with a </FORM> tag.

## The Input Tag

The input tag identifies the HTML element as an input type. This is the main tag used in forms processing and has many variations. Some input tags allow text entry and some allow list item sections. A subset of these input tags, including text, radio buttons, submit, and reset, are described in the following sections.

### The Text Input Type

The text input type enables users to enter data into a text field. The format is:

```
<INPUT NAME="name" TYPE="TEXT" SIZE="20">
```

This results in a 20 character editable field on the form. It is also possible to set the maximum allowed characters by specifying the MAXLENGTH tag. Also, if you want a default value to appear, the VALUE="" attribute can be used. For example, to limit the above to 20 characters with a default of NONE, the following tag can be used:

```
<INPUT NAME="name" TYPE="TEXT" SIZE=20 MAXLENGTH=20
VALUE="Michael">
```

## The Radio Button Input Type

The radio button allows only one of a set of choices to be selected. For example, to indicate a salary range, the following definitions could be used:

```
<INPUT TYPE="RADIO" NAME="salary" VALUE="10000" CHECKED>
<INPUT TYPE="RADIO" NAME="salary" VALUE="25000" >
<INPUT TYPE="RADIO" NAME="salary" VALUE="50000" >
<INPUT TYPE="RADIO" NAME="salary" VALUE="75000" >
<INPUT TYPE="RADIO" NAME="salary" VALUE="100000" >
```

Note that in the case of the radio button, the name is the same for all the buttons. This is very important because the name defines a group of items associated with this set of buttons. Only one button with the name "salary" could be selected at any one time. Another set of buttons would require a different group name.

## The Submit Input Type

When the SUBMIT button is pressed, the data will be sent to the application indicated in the FORM tag. This is a very simple construct with only a VALUE tag. This value will also be displayed on the button.

```
<INPUT TYPE="SUBMIT" VALUE="Submit Form">
```

Some browsers will now pass the value of the button on to the CGI application, but this is a fairly recent addition and cannot be counted on for all browsers. Until this is fully supported, it is not possible to have several buttons indicating different actions.

## The Reset Input Type

There is one other button that is allowed: the reset button. For example, the following definition will reset all the values to their default value.

```
<INPUT TYPE="RESET" VALUE="Reset Form">
```

# Calling the CGI Script from a Form

As I previously mentioned, there are currently two methods to call CGI applications: one is the GET method and one is the POST method.

Calling an application directly from an URL always uses the GET method by default. Using the <FORM> tag; however, you can specify the method using the "METHOD =" tag. The downside of the GET method is that any arguments that are to be sent to the CGI application are sent in the QUERY_STRING environment variable. The reason this is undesirable is that many systems limit the amount of data that can be stored in an environment variable. On some systems this limit is as low as 1,024 characters. While this seems sufficient, on a complex form it is easy to exceed this limit. By specifying METHOD=POST on the form, the arguments are passed as *standard input* (stdin) of the CGI application, which eliminates any limit on the amount of data that can be passed to the CGI applicaiton.

# Argument Lists

Browsers process forms and pass the data input by the user to the application defined by the "ACTION" keyword in the form as an argument list. You can take advantage of knowing the format of this argument list to pass any additional information your CGI scripts need to run.

## Argument Lists with Name Value Pairs

Whether the POST or GET method is used, the argument list can be the same and consist of name=value pairs. Fortunately, if you rely on a form to call the CGI application, the browser constructs the argument list. If you are calling the application directly from an URL, you'll need to construct the argument list yourself. The format of the argument list follows:

```
?name=value&name=value&name=value
```

This format will need to be added to the application referenced by the hypertext link. For example, to pass the first and last name values to an application you would use the following definition:

```
<A HREF="http://bristol.onramp.net/cgi-bin/
getinfo.cgi?firstname=Michael&lastname=Marolda"> Info
about Michael Marolda</A>
```

An important note is that if the value contains blanks, the convention is to replace the blanks with a "+" sign. To pass an address with one attribute/value pair would then look like:

```
<A HREF="http://bristol.onramp.net/cgi-bin/
getinfo.cgi?street=727+Wandering+Way"> Michael's ad-
dress</A>
```

If you were passing this information from a form, this argument list would be constructed for you from the name and value parameters. The HTML:

```
<INPUT TYPE="RADIO" NAME="salary" VALUE="10000" CHECKED>
```

would result in the argument list:

```
?salary=10000
```

and would be passed to the script defined bt the ACTION keyword at:

```
http://bristol.onramp.net/cgi-bin/getinfo.cgi
```

# Passing Arguments Via the PATH_INFO Environment Variable

When a CGI script is called, the browser may pass additional environment information as well as the data that was entered. An alternative method to passing arguments via name value pairs is to use the PATH_INFO environment variable. The difference in format to cause the browser to load information in the

PATH_INFO variable is that the arguments are simply appended to the application as if you were extending the path, or location, of the script. For example, to send the first name and last name to a script using the PATH_INFO technique you could use:

```
<A HREF="http://bristol.onramp.net/cgi-bin/getinfo.cgi/
Michael/Marolda"> Info about Michael Marolda</A>
```

The PATH_INFO environment variable would contain "Michael/Marolda."

The advantage of using the PATH_INFO environment variable is that it is a very simple format. The disadvantage is that the application must decode a single string into multiple arguments, depending entirely on the postion of the data within the string to define the content of an argument. This might be difficult to maintain when more than a couple of arguemtns are passed to the CGI script.

# CGI Overview

Once you've created a simple form, you'll need to create an application to process the data. This application is commonly referred to as a CGI application (or script in many cases). Most HTTPD implementations will have a default location to put these applications. Like the documents, this location will be referenced as a relative location off the server root. For example, if the server root is:

c:\winnt\system32\inetsrv then the CGI applications can reside at:

```
c:\winnt\system32\inetsrv\cgi-bin
```

and can be referenced as:

```
http://your.machine.name/cgi-bin/yourapp.cgi
```

A CGI application can be written in any language that can process stdin and stdout, and can reference environment variables. Visual Basic and NT batch scripts can be used as well as lower-level languages such as C and C++. One of the most popular languages used in CGI application development is the PERL programming language. PERL is a very powerful language and has been ported to the Windows NT environment. Because PERL is often called a *scripting language*, many people refer to CGI applications as CGI scripts. The latter part of this chapter will focus on using PERL and its cousin Oraperl to write CGI applications.

# Connecting Microsoft SQL Server to Internet Information Server

Windows NT and IIS are fast becoming the preferred Web platform on the Internet. With Microsoft SQL Server and Internet Information Server, it is now possible to build an industrial Web site on the NT platform that is capable of storing and retrieving massive amounts of data. The seamless integration of the two products and the inclusion of intuitive graphical tools makes this a top-notch choice for anyone building a commercial Web site.

Figure 17.3 refers to the sequence of events when a Web browser performs a database query to IIS. For instance, a user visits an electronic shopping mall on the Web to gather information on a particular product. The user types in a product name on an HTML form and clicks the "Submit info" button. The browser then initiates the URL containing the Internet Database Connector that contains the appropriate SQL commands. The IDC file then sends the SQL information to the ODBC driver which communicates with the SQL Server Database. On the return trip, the IDC file receives the response data from the SQL Server via the ODBC driver. The IDC file then sends the data to the HTML template form (.HTX file) which generates to the user an HTML page containing the product information.

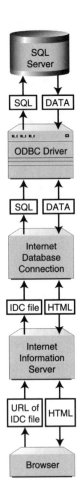

**Figure 17.3:**

Database queries to IIS.

# Open DataBase Connectivity (ODBC)

ODBC is an application programming interface designed by Microsoft to solve the problem of having to create different programs to access different databases. Given the fact that each database contains different data formats and data access rules, a programmer in the old days would have to create as many programs as there were databases.

ODBC solves this dilemma by specifying a standard interface that can interact with any database. The only requirement is that the database vendor must provide an ODBC driver. The philosophy behind ODBC is that there should be a clear separation between the database and the application. Programmers should not have to learn about the intricacies of a database in order to access it. This layer of abstraction enables the programmer to create applications rapidly and with greater reliability.

# Connecting IIS to SQL Server in Four Basic Steps

Creating database connectivity between the SQL Server and IIS can be accomplished in four basic steps as follows:

1. Install and Configure ODBC drivers for Internet Information Server

2. Develop HTML pages to start the querying process

3. Create IDC files to convert HTML query to SQL

4. Develop HTX files to convert SQL responses into HTML

## Step 1: Installing and Configuring ODBC Drivers for Internet Information Server

ODBC version 2.5 is required for communication with Internet Information Server as a result of its support for System Data Source Names (DSN). You may have already installed the ODBC drivers during your installation of IIS. If not, see your IIS documentation for installing ODBC drivers and System DSN.

## Step 2: Developing HTML Pages to Start the Querying Process

An initial HTML page is needed to call the IDC file. In the following example, when the user clicks on the "Click me to see sales items!!" button, the HTML code launches the URL (/scripts/catalog.idc) containing the IDC file.

```
HOME.HTML
<HTML>
<head>
<title>Happy Joy Joy Co.</title>
</head>
<body>
<h1 align=center>Products Catalog</h1>
<form method="post" action="/scripts/catalog.idc"
<input type="submit" value="Click me to see sales
↪items!!">
</form>
</body>
</HTML>
```

## Step 3: Creating IDC Files to Convert HTML Query to SQL

The IDC file contains SQL commands used to interact with the ODBC data source via the Httpodbc.dll on the Internet Information Server. The required parameters for the IDC file are Datasource, Template, and SQLStatement. The sample.idc file shown in the following text logs the user sa on to the SQL Server and performs a SELECT statement resulting in the retrieval of the following columns (product, price, quantity) of data. The results are then sent to the sample.htx template file via the Httpodic.dll.

**sample.idc**

Datasource: JoyJoy

User name: sa

Template: sample.htx

Required Parameters:

SQL Statement:

+SELECT product,price,quantity

+FROM pubs.dbo.joy

# The Components of an IDC File Are Explained in General Terms in the Following:

➤ DataSource: The name of the ODBC datasource defined in the ODBC applet under the Control Panel.

➤ User name: The user name required to log on to the SQL Server database.

➤ Template: Indicates the .HTX template file needed to interpret and display SQL queries and results.

➤ RequiredParameters: The IDC file cannot execute unless the parameters that follow are separated by a comma and contain values.

➤ SQLStatement: The SQL statements that you want to execute. Each line after the SQLStatement must start with a plus sign. Parameter values in SQL statements must be enclosed by percent signs.

## Step 4: Developing HTX Files to Convert SQL Responses into HTML

The HTX file is a template that accepts the SQL data from the IDC file and generates the output in HTML to the user. It contains extensions known as IDC tags, which are specific only to HTX documents and thus not part of standard HTML. The Sample.htx file produces a listing of all products with prices and quantity on hand by accessing the pubs.dbo.joy database. The <%begindetail%> and <%enddetail%> are IDC tags that specify where the return results should be displayed. By default, query results are returned in a row format. To return results in a column format, use <%%> to enclose the selected fields. In Sample.htx, <%product%>, <%price%>, and <%quantity%> are columns that are returned from the query.

**Sample.htx**

```
<HTML>
<head>
<title>Happy JoyJoy Product List</title>
</head>
<h1 align=center>JoyJoy Product Listing</h1>
<hr>
<p><b><%product%></b></p>
<i>Price</i>:<%price%><br>
<i>Quantity<i>:<%quantity%><br>
<hr>
<%enddetail%>
</HTML>
```

# Perl and Oraperl Overview

One of the more powerful features that people have added to Perl is the capability to interface with external relational database management systems (RDBMSs). Unfortunately, the Application Programmers Interface (API) into each database package has mimicked the "C" API for that package. Because the "C" API for Oracle is different from the "C" API for Sybase, and so on, each Perl interface is different for each underlying RDBMS. This situation is changing with the release of Perl 5.0. For that release, a common database API has been specified for all underlying RDBMSs. It will be a challenge to the implementors to add the support for the desired RDBMS and conform to the now standard API.

Oraperl 2.03 for Windows NT is supported only on Perl 4.036 for NT. Perl 4 is available in the Windows NT Resource Kit. You can get Oraperl from ftp://ftp.bf.rmit.edu.au/pub/Oracle/OS/MS/NT/ntoraperl.zip. It should be noted that the author regards the port as a "hack." The program was intended to be a stopgap measure until Perl 5 was released. Oraperl 2.03 for Windows NT is not supported by Oracle or Microsoft and should be used with extreme caution. As an alternative, you can also access any Oracle server via the Internet Database Connector and the appropriate ODBC drivers.

Because many of these implementations are still under development, this chapter will focus on the current Perl 4.036 Oraperl interface to the Oracle RDBMS. A comparison of the two interfaces will be discussed later.

There are only eight functions that are really required to access an Oracle database via Oraperl.

➤ ora_login

➤ ora_open

➤ ora_bind

➤ ora_fetch

➤ ora_close

➤ ora_commit

➤ ora_rollback

➤ ora_logoff

A quick overview of these functions follows.

## ora_login

The call to ora_login makes the connection to the database. The format is:

```
$dba = &ora_login($database, $user, $password);
```

ora_login requires the database name (oracle SID) to connect to the Oracle userid and the Oracle password. A handle to an open database is returned. This handle will be used in subsequent calls to the database.

## ora_open

The call to ora_open will open a cursor for a given SQL statement. The format is:

```
$csr = &ora_open($dba,$statement);
```

ora_open uses the handle returned from ora_login and creates a cursor for the specified SQL statement. The SQL statement can be any valid Oracle SQL statement and can use placeholders for bind variables. Examples are:

```
$csr = &ora_open($dba,"select firstname from employee
where id=1234");
```

or using a bind variable:

```
$csr = &ora_open($dba,"select firstname from employee
where id=:1");
```

An insert would look like:

```
$csr = &ora_open($dba,"insert into employee
(id,firstname) values(:1,:2)");
```

Whenever bind variables are used, a call to ora_bind will also be necessary.

## ora_bind

If the call to ora_open used bind variables, it will be necessary to call ora_bind to indicate what values to use. The format for ora_bind is:

```
$numrows = &ora_bind($csr, $var1, $var2, ..., $varN);
```

ora_bind takes the handle to the cursor returned by ora_open and the Perl variables that hold the data corresponding to the place-holders in the SQL statement. For updates and deletes, the value returned by ora_bind is the number of rows that were affected by the statement, while statements that affect no rows return the string "OK". An example of using bind with an insert would be:

```
$csr = &ora_open($dba,"insert into employee
➥(id,firstname,lastname) values(:1,:2,:3)";
$numrows = &ora_bind($csr,1,"Michael", "Marolda");
```

## ora_fetch

If the cursor returned by ora_open is for a select statement,
ora_fetch is used to retrieve the data associated with the results
for the select statement. The format is:

```
@data = &ora_fetch($csr);
```

The only argument to ora_fetch is the handle to the open cursor.
ora_fetch returns an array of values corresponding to the attribute names listed in the select statement. When the fetch gets
to the end of the data in the results set, an undefined value is
returned. An example that would return all the customers in a
database would be:

```
$csr = &ora_open($dba,"select id, firstname from
➥employee");
while (($id, $firstname) = &ora_fetch($csr)){
       print "Customer id = $id, Customer name =
➥$firstname\n";
}
```

ora_fetch can also be used in a scalar context and the number of
fields in the query is returned. Using the above example:

```
$nfields = &ora_fetch($csr);
```

would return 2.

## ora_close

In order to close and release any resources for a cursor, you
should make a call to ora_close. The format is:

```
&ora_close($csr);
```

## ora_commit

A call to ora_commit will commit any changes made to the
database since the last commit or rollback. The format is:

```
&ora_commit($dba);
```

## ora_rollback

Calling_ora_rollback will roll back any changes made to the database since the last commit. The format is:

```
&ora_rollback($dba);
```

## ora_logoff

Finally, ora_logoff is used to free all resources associated with an open connection to a database. The format is:

```
&ora_logoff($dba);
```

For a more detailed explanation of the above (and other) Oraperl calls, please refer to the Oraperl man pages included in its release.

"Man" pages is Unix-speak for manual pages—documentation.

# Error Handling

Oraperl functions, like most other Perl functions, can be tested directly for error or success. Oraperl also maintains a global variable, $ora_errstr, that contains the last error number and string. If you want to simply log the error to the HTTPD error log, you can use a technique like the following:

```
$csr = &ora_open($dba,"select id, firstname from
➥employee") ¦¦ die $ora_errstr;
```

A technique that I like to employ is to use a subroutine to print the error message to the Web browser and to the error log. To aid in debugging, I also include the Perl variable LINE and FILE in the error message. Finally, I use the ctime.pl library to indicate when the error occurred. This changes the error handling to the following:

```
$csr = &ora_open($dba,"select id, firstname from
➥employee") ¦¦ &dodie ($ora_errstr, __LINE__, __FILE__);
```

The dodie subroutine used in the previous line is fairly simple
and creates the string that is printed both to STDOUT (for the
Web browser) and to STDERR (which is automatically logged to
the NCSA error_log file). The following is the code to implement
this routine:

```perl
require "ctime.pl";

sub dodie
{
    local ($errstr, $errline, $file) = @_;
    $diedate = &ctime(time);
    print "Died in $file:$errline - $errstr at
    ➡$diedate<P>\n";
    die "died in $file:$errline - $errstr at $diedate";
}

1;
```

## Environment Variables in CGI Applications

Because most CGI applications are spawned using the environment for the user "nobody," you may need to set the standard
environment variables in the CGI application. The environment
variables that most commonly need to be set to run Oracle are
these:

```
$ORACLE_SID - set to your database name;
$ORACLE_HOME - set to the home directory for the ORACLE
➡installation;
$TWO_TASK - set to your SQL*Net connection string.
```

These variables can be set using the setenv Perl call:

```perl
$ENV{'ORACLE_SID'} = "www";
$ENV{'ORACLE_HOME'} = "/home/dba/oracle/product/7.1.3";
$ENV{'TWO_TASK'} = "bristol"; # SQL*Net V2
```

Additionally, your CGI application can obtain extra information via the environment variables. Some of the environment variables that may be availible to you are:

➤ **SERVER_SOFTWARE.** Tells you which HTTP server you're running.

➤ **SERVER_NAME.** The host name of the computer the server is running on.

➤ **REQUEST_METHOD.** The method used to call the script (GET or POST).

➤ **PATH_INFO.** Additonal path information appended to the CGI script.

➤ **SCRIPT_NAME.** The CGI script that was referenced.

➤ **QUERY_STRING.** Contains the argument list when the calling method is GET.

➤ **REMOTE_HOST.** The host name of the computer running the Web browser.

➤ **REMOTE_ADDR.** The host address of the computer running the Web browser.

➤ **REMOTE_USER.** Contains the userid of the person using the WWW browser.

➤ **CONTENT_LENGTH.** The length of the string found in QUERY_STRING.

➤ **HTTP_USER_AGENT.** The name of the browser being used.

Note that not all browsers pass all information. Some environment variables, such as REMOTE_USER, are only passed if the remote server is running an identification program (such as IDENTD) or if the user has entered an id that may be required as part of HTTPD authorization.

# Getting the Input

There are two ways for your CGI application to get the input data depending on how it was passed. In the case of the GET method, the data is contained in the QUERY_STRING environment variable. The length of the argument list is contained in the environment variable CONTENT_LENGTH. The method can be determined by querying the REQUEST_METHOD environment variable. The following retrieves the argument list into a Perl variable.

```
if ($ENV{'REQUEST_METHOD'} eq "GET") {
    $arglist = $ENV{'QUERY_STRING'};
}
```

Using the POST method results in the argument list being passed as STDIN (the default input device). To retrieve the argument list when the argument list is sent via the POST method, the following code segment could be used.

```
if ($ENV{'REQUEST_METHOD'} eq "POST") {
    for ($i=0;$i = $ENV{'CONTENT_LENGTH'};$i++) {
        $arglist .= getc;  # getc retrieves the next
        character  # from STDIN.
    }
}
```

In either case, you end up with a variable $arglist that contains the argument list passed from the Web browser.

# Parsing the Input

While it is nice to have the argument list available in a single variable, it is not very convenient. A better method in Perl would be to parse the string into an associative array of name value pairs. A library, CGILIB, written by Steven E. Brenner does just that.

Following is the Steven Brenner cgi-lib:

The following is the source for Steve Brenner's cgi-lib.pl. This source can also be obtained via:

**http://www.bio.cam.ac.uk/web/form.html**

```
#!/usr/local/bin/perl -- -*- C -*-

# Perl Routines to Manipulate CGI input
# S.E.Brenner@bioc.cam.ac.uk
# $Header: /cys/people/brenner/http/cgi-bin/RCS/cgi-
➥lib.pl,v 1.8 1995/04/07 21:35:29 brenner Exp $
#
# Copyright 1994 Steven E. Brenner
# Unpublished work.
# Permission granted to use and modify this library so
long as the copyright above is maintained, modifications
are documented, and credit is given for any use of the
library.
#
# Thanks are due to many people for reporting bugs and
suggestions especially Meng Weng Wong, Maki Watanabe, Bo
Frese Rasmussen, Andrew Dalke, Mark-Jason Dominus and
Dave Dittrich.

# For more information, see:
#     http://www.bio.cam.ac.uk/web/form.html
#     http://www.seas.upenn.edu/~mengwong/forms/

# Minimalist http form and script (http://
  www. bio.cam.ac.uk/web/minimal.cgi):
#
# require "cgi-lib.pl";
# if (&ReadParse(*input)) {
#     print &PrintHeader, &PrintVariables(%input);
# } else {
```

```
#   print &PrintHeader,'<form><input type="submit">Data:
➥<input name="myfield">';
#}

# ReadParse
# Reads in GET or POST data, converts it to unescaped
text, and puts one key=value in each member of the list
"@in"

# Also creates key/value pairs in %in, using '\0' to
separate multiple selections

# Returns TRUE if there was input, FALSE if there was no
input UNDEF may be used in the future to indicate some
failure.

# Now that cgi scripts can be put in the normal file
space, it is useful to combine both the form and the
script in one place.  If no parameters are given (i.e.,
ReadParse returns FALSE), then a form could be output.

# If a variable-glob parameter (e.g., *cgi_input) is
passed to ReadParse, information is stored there, rather
than in $in, @in, and %in.

sub ReadParse {
  local (*in) = @_ if @_;
  local ($i, $key, $val);

  # Read in text
  if (&MethGet) {
    $in = $ENV{'QUERY_STRING'};
  } elsif ($ENV{'REQUEST_METHOD'} eq "POST") {
    read(STDIN,$in,$ENV{'CONTENT_LENGTH'});
  }

  @in = split(/&/,$in);
```

*continues*

```perl
    foreach $i (0 .. $#in) {
      # Convert plus's to spaces
      $in[$i] =~ s/\+/ /g;


# Split into key and value.
      ($key, $val) = split(/=/,$in[$i],2); # splits on the
      first =.

      # Convert %XX from hex numbers to alphanumeric
      $key =~ s/%(..)/pack("c",hex($1))/ge;
      $val =~ s/%(..)/pack("c",hex($1))/ge;

      # Associate key and value
      $in{$key} .= "\0" if (defined($in{$key})); # \0 is
➥the multiple separator
      $in{$key} .= $val;


    }


    return length($in);
  }



# PrintHeader
# Returns the magic line which tells WWW that we're an
  HTML document

sub PrintHeader {
    return "Content-type: text/html\n\n";
  }



# MethGet
# Return true if this cgi call was using the GET request,
  false otherwise

sub MethGet {
    return ($ENV{'REQUEST_METHOD'} eq "GET");
  }
```

```perl
# MyURL
# Returns an URL to the script
sub MyURL  {
  return  'http://' . $ENV{'SERVER_NAME'} .
➥$ENV{'SCRIPT_NAME'};
}


# CgiError
# Prints out an error message which contains
  appropriate headers,
# markup, etcetera.
# Parameters:
#  If no parameters, gives a generic error message
#  Otherwise, the first parameter will be the title and
   the rest will
#  be given as different paragraphs of the body

sub CgiError {
  local (@msg) = @_;
  local ($i,$name);

  if (!@msg) {
    $name = &MyURL;
    @msg = ("Error: script $name encountered fatal
    ➥error");
  };

  print &PrintHeader;
  print "<HTML><head><title>$msg[0]</title></head>\n";
  print "<body><h1>$msg[0]</h1>\n";
  foreach $i (1 .. $#msg) {
    print "<p>$msg[$i]</p>\n";
  }
  print "</body></html>\n";
}


# PrintVariables
# Nicely formats variables in an associative array passed
  as a parameter
# And returns the HTML string.
```

*continues*

```perl
sub PrintVariables {
  local (%in) = @_;
  local ($old, $out, $output);
  $old = $*;   $* =1;
  $output .=  "<DL COMPACT>"; foreach $key (sort
  ➥keys(%in)) {
    foreach (split("\0", $in{$key})) {
      ($out = $_) =~ s/\n/<BR>/g;
      $output .=  "<DT><B>$key</B><DD><I>$out</I><BR>";
    }
  }
  $output .=  "</DL>";
  $* = $old;

  return $output;
}


# PrintVariablesShort
# Nicely formats variables in an associative array passed
  as a parameter
# Using one line per pair (unless value is multiline)
# And returns the HTML string.


sub PrintVariablesShort {
  local (%in) = @_;
  local ($old, $out, $output);
  $old = $*;   $* =1;
  foreach $key (sort keys(%in)) {
    foreach (split("\0", $in{$key})) {
      ($out = $_) =~ s/\n/<BR>/g;
      $output .= "<B>$key</B> is <I>$out</I><BR>";
    }
  }
  $* = $old;

  return $output;
}

1; #return true
```

To see how the ReadParse script would work, consider the
following HTML form fields that would be used to input personal
information:

```
<INPUT NAME= TYPE="TEXT" "firstname" SIZE=20
VALUE="Michael">
<INPUT NAME= TYPE="TEXT" "lastname" SIZE=20
➥VALUE="Marolda">
<INPUT NAME= TYPE="TEXT" "street" SIZE=20 VALUE="727
➥Wandering Way">
<INPUT TYPE="RADIO" NAME="sex" VALUE="M", CHECKED >
```

When the SUBMIT button is pressed, the argument list is constructed for you and would look like:

```
?firstname=Michael&lastname=Marolda&street=727+Wandering+Way&sex=M
```

Using Steven's ReadParse script in cgi-lib.pl, the data could then
be referenced by name in the associative array as such:

```
$in{'firstname};  # contains the value "Michael"
$in{'lastname'}; # contains the value "Marolda"
$in{'street'};  # contains the value "727 Wandering Way"
$in{'sex'}; # contains the value "M"
```

These can be used directly in the Oraperl calls. For example, to see
all the male employees, you could bind to the variables directly:

```
$csr = &ora_open($dba,"select firstname, lastname from
➥employee where sex=:1)";
$numrows = &ora_bind($csr,$in{'sex'});
```

# Displaying the Results of a CGI Application

Displaying any data retrieved by CGI scripts is actually quite
simple. HTTP operates on the principle that it reads everything
from STDIN and writes everything to STDOUT. Therefore,

anything you print to STDOUT (which is the default) will be redirected back to the Web browser. The only additional information you would need to supply would be to print a MIME header identifying the document as an HTML document. From a CGI script, to print out a simple header, you could use the following technique:

```
print "Content-type: text/html\n\n";
print "<Title> This is the title </Title>\n";
print "<H1> This is a heading </H1>\n";
```

The output would then be formatted and displayed correctly on the user's Web browser. The additional \n isn't really necessary, but I've found that it makes resultant HTML more legible when accessed via the "View Source" option that most browsers have.

This technique can be extended for printing the results of a query. Combining the Oraperl and the printing in a single script, we get:

```
$csr = &ora_open($dba,"select firstname, lastname from
➥employee where sex=:1)";
$numrows = &ora_bind($csr,$in{'sex'});
while (($firstname, $lastname) = &ora_fetch($csr)){
    print "<B>$firstname $lastname</B>n";
}
```

# Example—A Simple Employee Database

This database is based on a very simple model and should in no way be construed to be either complete or the best way to implement this functionality. However, it is simple enough to provide a fairly complete example that demonstrates both insert and query capabilities.

In our simple employee database we'll implement three features. These are:

1. Capture some employee data.

2. Select employees via last name.

3. Select greater detail about an employee returned by the previous select.

## Data to Be Captured—The Model

The database model is a single table model that contains the necessary information. The following Oracle SQL statement is used to create the table:

```
create table employee
(
    id number,
    firstname varchar2(30),
    lastname varchar2(30),
    street varchar2(30),
    city varchar2(30),
    state varchar2(2),
    zip varchar2(17),
    sex varchar2(1),
    salary number,
    CONSTRAINT pk_employee PRIMARY KEY (id)
);
```

A sequence is also created so that we can automatically generate the employee id.

```
create sequence employee_sequence
increment by 1
start with 1000
nomaxvalue
nocycle
cache 10;
```

Also we'll populate the table with a couple of records using the following inserts via SQL*Plus (or your favorite data entry tool).

```
insert into employee
(id,firstname,lastname,street,city,state,zip,sex,salary)
values(employee_sequence.nextval,'Michael','Marolda','123
➡Somewhere Lane', 'Dallas','TX',75090,'M',13000);

insert into employee
(id,firstname,lastname,street,city,state,zip,sex,salary)
values(employee_sequence.nextval,'Jan','Murphy','123
➡Another Lane', 'Los Angeles','CA','12345','F',130000);

insert into employee
(id,firstname,lastname,street,city,state,zip,sex,salary)
values(employee_sequence.nextval,'Beverly','Chapman','123
➡Street', 'Detroit','MI','54321','F',40000);

insert into employee
(id,firstname,lastname,street,city,state,zip,sex,salary)
values(employee_sequence.nextval,'Bill','Clinton','1600
Pennsylvania Ave.',
➡'Washington','DC','11111','M',200000);
```

# First Feature—Capturing the Data

The input form we'll use will have fields for all the attributes with the exception of the id attribute. This attribute will be generated upon insert.

Our employee form uses very simple text, radio button, and submit types to implement the data capture. Also, the Netscape <CENTER> tag was used to make the form a bit more aesthetically appealing.

## The HTML Used in This Example

The HTML that produced this form was:

```
<TITLE> Employee Administration </TITLE>
<H1><CENTER> Employee Administration </CENTER></H1>
```

```
<FORM ACTION="http://bristol.onramp.net/cgi-bin/empdemo/
➥empadd.cgi" METHOD=POST>
<H2><CENTER>Add an Employee</CENTER></H2>
<PRE>
First Name: <INPUT NAME="firstname" TYPE="TEXT" SIZE=20
➥MAXLENGTH=30>
Last Name:  <INPUT NAME="lastname" TYPE="TEXT" SIZE=20
➥MAXLENGTH=30>
Address:    <INPUT NAME="street" TYPE="TEXT" SIZE=30
➥MAXLENGTH=30>
City:       <INPUT NAME="city" TYPE="TEXT" SIZE=20
➥MAXLENGTH=30>
State:      <INPUT NAME="state" TYPE="TEXT" SIZE=2
➥MAXLENGTH=2>
Zip:  <INPUT NAME="zip" TYPE="TEXT" SIZE=9 MAXLENGTH=5>
Salary:     <INPUT NAME="salary" TYPE="TEXT" SIZE=5
➥MAXLENGTH=5>
Sex:        <INPUT TYPE=radio NAME="sex" VALUE="F"
➥CHECKED> Female <INPUT TYPE=radio NAME="sex"
VALUE="M"> Male
</PRE>
<CENTER>
<INPUT TYPE=SUBMIT VALUE="Add Employee"> <INPUT
TYPE=RESET VALUE="Reset Form">
</CENTER>
</FORM>
```

When the "Add Employee" button is pushed, the CGI script at
/cgi-gin/empdemo/empadd.cgi will be called. When the "Reset
Form" button is pushed, the form will be restored to its default
values.

## CGI to Store Data

In order to store the data we'll need to put together the bits and
pieces we explored earlier. The following script takes the FORM
data and creates a record in the database for that data. Also, a
confirmation and employee id is sent back to the browser.

```
#!/usr/local/bin/oraperl

#
# Include cgi-lib parser
#

require "cgi-lib.pl";

#
# Include the error reporting script
#

require "dodie.pl";

#
# Print out the MIME Content Type
#

print STDOUT &PrintHeader();
print STDOUT "<TITLE> New Employee </TITLE>\n";

#
# Parse the input
#

do ReadParse();

#
# Set the environment variables and connect to oracle
#

$database = "www1";
$ouser = "empdemo";
$opass = "empdemo";
$ENV{'ORACLE_SID'} = "www1";
$ENV{'ORACLE_HOME'} = "/home/dba/oracle/product/7.1.3";

$dba = &ora_login($database, $ouser, $opass) || &dodie
➥($ora_errstr, __LINE__, __FILE__);

#
```

```
# Ensure all variables are filled in.
#

$errorcount = 0;
foreach $key (sort keys(%in)) {
    if (length($in{$key}) == 0) {
     print "$key must be entered!<p>\n";
     $errorcount++;
     }
}
if ($errorcount) {
    exit(0);
}


#
# Get a new employee id to be used when the data is
  inserted.
# This operation could be performed at the time the
record is inserted, but this gives us a chance to report
the employee id back to the user that added the employee.
#

$csr_empid = &ora_open($dba,"SELECT
➥EMPLOYEE_SEQUENCE.NEXTVAL FROM DUAL") ¦¦ &dodie
($ora_errstr, __LINE__, __FILE__);
($empid) = &ora_fetch($csr_empid);
&ora_close($csr_empid);


#
# Create the cursor for adding the employee. For this
example, we're going to use bind variables. One of the
advantages of using bind variables is for performance.
This is true for where clauses, updates and insert state-
ments. Oracle will store an SQL string in its shared
memory area. If another SQL statement is passed to Oracle
and it matches a previous one, no actual parsing is
```

*continues*

```
required. If you have several operations that are going
to use the same where clause but with different values,
then using a bind variable:
#     .... where name = :1;
# will result in only one statement being cached.  How-
ever, if each value is assigned in the statement:
#     .... where name = 'Mike';
#     .... where name = 'John';
# each statement must be parsed separately. Similarly, if
you will be inserting many rows, it will save quite a bit
of parse time if bind variables are used for the data
values.
#

$csr_emp = &ora_open($dba,"INSERT INTO EMPLOYEE (id,
➥firstname, lastname, street, city, state, zip, sex,
salary) VALUES(:1, :2, :3, :4, :5, :6, :7, :8, :9)") ¦¦
➥&dodie ($ora_errstr, __LINE__, __FILE__);

#
# Add the employee - bind the data.  On non-select state-
  ments, this also executes the SQL statement.
#

$numrows = &ora_bind($csr_emp, $empid, $in{'firstname'},
➥$in{'lastname'}, $in{'street'}, $in{'city'},
$in{'state'}, $in{'zip'}, $in{'sex'}, $in{'salary'}) ¦¦
➥&dodie ($ora_errstr, __LINE__, __FILE__);

#
# Tidy up and exit.
#
```

```
&ora_close($csr_emp) ¦¦ &dodie ($ora_errstr, __LINE__,
➥__FILE__);
&ora_commit($dba) ¦¦ &dodie ($ora_errstr, __LINE__,
➥__FILE__);
&ora_logoff($dba) ¦¦ &dodie ($ora_errstr, __LINE__,
➥__FILE__);

#
# It's always a good idea to give some feedback.
#

print STDOUT "<H2> $in{'firstname'} $in{'lastname'} has
➥been added as employee id $empid!</H2>\n";

#
# Add a link back to the form in case another employee is
  to be added.
#

print STDOUT "<a href=http://bristol.onramp.net/empdemo/
➥empadd.html>Add another Employee?</a>\n";

exit(0);
```

## Second Feature—Displaying the Employee List

The search forms shown in figure 17.4 will be used to search the database for an employee. The last name is used as the search field.

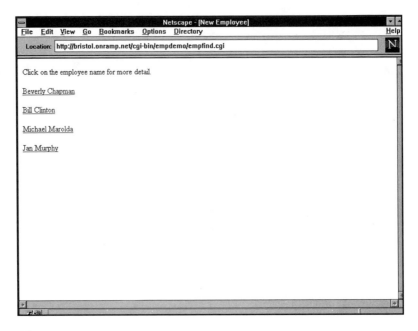

**Figure 17.4:**

The Find Employee form.

## Form

The form that we'll use is a very simple form that allows wildcard searches. For large databases, wildcard searches in Oracle may take awhile. The exception to this is when the wildcard is not the first character. In this case, and if an index exists on this field, the index can be used by Oracle's search engine. The following HTML implements our forms.

```
<TITLE> Employee Search </TITLE>
<H1> <CENTER>Employee Search</CENTER></H1>
<FORM ACTION="http://bristol.onramp.net/cgi-bin/empdemo/
➥empfind.cgi" METHOD=POST>
<H2>Find an Employee</H2>
Please enter the last name of the employee (You can use a
➥% for a wildcard):
<PRE>
```

```
Lastname: <INPUT NAME="lastname" TYPE="TEXT" SIZE=25
➡MAXLENGTH=30><p>
</PRE>
<CENTER>
<INPUT TYPE=SUBMIT VALUE="Find Employee"> <INPUT
➡TYPE=RESET VALUE="Reset Form">
</CENTER>
</FORM>
```

## CGI to Find a List of Employees

Unlike the previous CGI script, this script performs a SELECT
instead of an INSERT. Because we allowed wildcard searches (and
because there may be more than one employee with the same last
name), we need to be able to handle multiple returned records.
The simplest way will be to list all the employees that were found
by the search and tag those employees with a reference to another CGI script that gets the employee detail.

```
#!/usr/local/bin/oraperl


#
# Include cgi-lib parser
#


require "cgi-lib.pl";


#
# Include the error reporting script
#


require "dodie.pl";


#
# Print out the MIME Content Type and title.
#


print STDOUT &PrintHeader();
```

*continues*

```
print STDOUT "<TITLE> New Employee </TITLE>\n";

#
# Parse the input
#

do ReadParse();

#
# Set the environment variables and connect to oracle
#

$database = "www1";
$ouser = "empdemo";
$opass = "empdemo";
$ENV{'ORACLE_SID'} = "www1";
$ENV{'ORACLE_HOME'} = "/home/dba/oracle/product/7.1.3";

$dba = &ora_login($database, $ouser, $opass) ¦¦ &dodie
➥($ora_errstr, __LINE__, __FILE__);

#
# Find an employee or employees - create appropriate SQL
  and the cursor.
# This time we'll expand the search criteria into the
$select varaible.
# If the user had entered a M%, then the $select variable
  would contain:
#
# "select firstname,lastname,id from employee where
lastname like '%M'
# order by lastname"
#

$select = "select firstname,lastname,id from employee
➥where lastname like '%";
$select .= $in{'lastname'};
$select .= "' order by lastname";
```

```
$csr_emp = &ora_open($dba,$select) ¦¦ &dodie
➥($ora_errstr, __LINE__, __FILE__);


#
# Fetch all the data that matches.  Because this is
likely to return more than one result, this fetch will
operate within a "while" loop.
# One other feature we should have (but don't) is de-
  tecting and reporting back that no matches were found.
#

print STDOUT "Click on the employee name for more
➥detail.<p>\n";
while (($firstname,$lastname,$id) = &ora_fetch($csr_emp))
{

#
# We'll generate a hypertext link to call another cgi
  application which will get more detail about an
  individual.  Note that we have to use the "GET" method
when referencing a CGI application from a hypertext link.
#
    print STDOUT "<a href=\"http://bristol.onramp.net/
cgi-bin/empdemo/empget.cgi?id=$id\"> $firstname
$lastname</a><p>\n";

}
#
# Tidy up and exit.
#

&ora_close($csr_emp) ¦¦ &dodie ($ora_errstr, __LINE__,
➥__FILE__);
&ora_logoff($dba) ¦¦ &dodie ($ora_errstr, __LINE__,
➥__FILE__);
exit(0);
```

When the above script is executed with the value M%, the following HTML would be created:

```
<TITLE> New Employee </TITLE>
Click on the employee name for more detail.<p>
<a href="http://bristol.onramp.net/cgi-bin/empdemo/
➥empget.cgi?id=1011"> Michael Marolda</a><p>
<a href="http://bristol.onramp.net/cgi-bin/empdemo/
➥empget.cgi?id=1012"> Jan Murphy</a><p>
```

And you should see the results shown in figure 17.5.

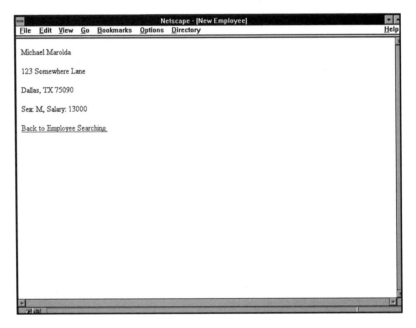

**Figure 17.5:**
The employee search results.

# Third Feature—Getting Employee Detail

This script takes the reference created by the Find Employees CGI script and in turn goes to the database and gets greater detail about that employee.

```
#!/usr/local/bin/oraperl

#
# Include cgi-lib parser
#

require "cgi-lib.pl";

#
# Include the error reporting script
#

require "dodie.pl";

#
# Print out the MIME Content Type and the title
#

print STDOUT &PrintHeader();
print STDOUT "<TITLE> New Employee </TITLE>\n";

#
# Parse the input.  One of the advantages of using Steve
# Brenner's cgi-lib.pl library is that it operates on data
# that is passed via either the POST or GET methods.  In
# each case, the result is an associative array containing
# either form fields or GET arguments.
#

do ReadParse();

#
# Set the environment variables and connect to oracle
#

$database = "www1";
$ouser = "empdemo";
```

*continues*

```
$opass = "empdemo";
$ENV{'ORACLE_SID'} = "www1";
$ENV{'ORACLE_HOME'} = "/home/dba/oracle/product/7.1.3";

$dba = &ora_login($database, $ouser, $opass) ¦¦ &dodie
➥($ora_errstr, __LINE__, __FILE__);

#
# Get the employee detail.  Again we'll use variable
  binding.
#

$csr_emp = &ora_open($dba,"select firstname, lastname,
➥street, city, state, zip, sex, salary from employee
➥where id = :1") ¦¦ &dodie ($ora_errstr, __LINE__,
➥__FILE__);


#
# Bind the employee id into the query.
#

$numrows = &ora_bind($csr_emp, $in{'id'}) ¦¦ &dodie
➥($ora_errstr, __LINE__, __FILE__);

#
# Fetch the detail data.  Because we're sure that the
employee id is going to be a unique value, we don't need
to use a while loop (although there would be nothing
technically wrong with doing so).
#

if
(($firstname,$lastname,$street,$city,$state,$zip,$sex,$salary)
➥= &ora_fetch($csr_emp))
{
#
# Print out the detail.  Somewhat boring in format but it
  gets the job done.
#
```

```
    print STDOUT "$firstname $lastname<p>\n";
    print STDOUT "$street<p>\n";
    print STDOUT "$city, $state $zip<p>\n";
    print STDOUT "Sex: $sex, Salary: $salary<p>\n";
}
#
# Tidy up and exit.
#

&ora_close($csr_emp) ¦¦ &dodie ($ora_errstr, __LINE__,
➥__FILE__);
&ora_logoff($dba) ¦¦ &dodie ($ora_errstr, __LINE__,
➥__FILE__);

#
# This time we're giving the end user an opportunity to
find another set of employees.  Another possibility would
be to link back to the employee list page.  This would
require us to send the original argument string that
first created the original employee list.  Because most
browsers support the previous page function, this is
probably not necessary.
#

print "<a href=\"http://bristol.onramp.net/empdemo/
➥empfind.html\">Back to Employee Searching.</a>\n";

exit(0);
```

Running this script results in figure 17.6.

**Figure 17.6:**

Employee details reached by choosing a name after the employee search is complete.

# Summary of Employee Database Example

The preceding example showed how to use Oracle to both capture data via the WWW and how to use WWW and CGI applications to query and browse an Oracle database. There are a few things that we could have done differently. For example, we could have focused more on error detection. This is especially true of the input data from the add employee form. Combining the last two CGI applications into a single form and application would have been more elegant and should be considered as a worthwhile exercise. In any case, using PERL to interface Oracle with the Web is a fairly simple operation and can provide many organizations with a cost-effective way of sharing corporate data over a variety of platforms.

# Perl 5 DBI

All of the code in this chapter used Perl V4 and the Oraperl extension. Perl V5 takes a different (and somewhat better) approach in that it now defines a standard API for all database implementations. For each database, there can be one (or more) database adapters that translate the API into the API of the desired database. At this writing, the Oracle DBI adapter is only in beta release. However, the differences between Perl 4 and Perl 5 are small enough that most of the examples can be easily converted. To illustrate the differences and similarities, the following are examples of an insert and a select using the current Oraperl and the Perl 5 DBI. This code comes from the earlier empadd CGI and emplist CGI.

Further information on the Perl 5 DBI specification can be found at:

FTP Archive: **ftp.demon.co.uk:/pub/perl/db** (read the README file)

## Example 1    Oraperl Insert

```
$dba = &ora_login($database, $ouser, $opass);

$csr_emp = &ora_open($dba,"INSERT INTO EMPLOYEE (id,
➥firstname, lastname, street, city, state, zip, sex, salary)
➥VALUES(:1, :2, :3, :4, :5, :6, :7, :8, :9)");

$numrows = &ora_bind($csr_emp, $empid, $in{'firstname'},
➥$in{'lastname'}, $in{'street'}, $in{'city'}, $in{'state'},
➥$in{'zip'}, $in{'sex'}, $in{'salary'});
&ora_close($csr_emp);
&ora_commit($dba);
&ora_logoff($dba);
```

### Example 2   Oraperl Select

```
$dba = &ora_login($database, $ouser, $opass);
$csr_emp = &ora_open($dba,"select firstname, lastname, street,
➥city, state, zip, sex, salary from employee where id = :1");

$numrows = &ora_bind($csr_emp, $in{'id'});

if
(($firstname,$lastname,$street,$city,$state,$zip,$sex,$salary)
➥= &ora_fetch($csr_emp))
{
    print STDOUT "$firstname $lastname<p>\n";
    print STDOUT "$street<p>\n";
    print STDOUT "$city, $state $zip<p>\n";
    print STDOUT "Sex: $sex, Salary: $salary<p>\n";
}
&ora_close($csr_emp);
&ora_logoff($dba);
```

### Example 3   Perl 5 DBI Insert

```
$dbh = &db_connect($database, $name, $password);
$sh = &db_prepare($dbh,
     " INSERT INTO EMPLOYEE (id, firstname, lastname, street,
➥city, state, zip, sex, salary) VALUES(?, ?, ?, ?, ?, ?, ?, ?,
?)");

&db_execute(&sqlh, $empid, $in{'firstname'}, $in{'lastname'},
➥$in{'street'}, $in{'city'}, $in{'state'}, $in{'zip'},
$in{'sex'}, $in{'salary'});

&db_finish($sh);
$rc = &db_commit($dbh);
&db_disconnect($dbh);
```

**Example 4    Perl 5 DBI Select**

```
$dbh = &db_connect($database, $name, $password);

$sh = &db_prepare($dbh, " select firstname, lastname, street,
➥city, state, zip, sex, salary from employee where id = :?");
&db_execute($sh, $in{'id'}
if
➥(($firstname,$lastname,$street,$city,$state,$zip,$sex,$salary)
= &db_fetch($sh))
{
    print STDOUT "$firstname $lastname<p>\n";
    print STDOUT "$street<p>\n";
    print STDOUT "$city, $state $zip<p>\n";
    print STDOUT "Sex: $sex, Salary: $salary<p>\n";
}
&db_finish($sh);
&db_disconnect($dbh);
```

# Open Issues Concerning the Use of Databases

There are still some issues with regard to using Web browsers to interface with Oracle and other database applications. The main issue is the way the data is transmitted between client and server. Historically, there has been a fair amount of communication between the client and server. In this way, the client can verify data on a field-by-field basis, populate a pop-up selection list, or automatically calculate the values in some fields based on the data in other fields. (More information about database servers and the Web and can be found in another New Riders book, *Building Internet Database Servers with CGI,* another in the *Webmaster's* series.)

The scope of data transferred between the client and server for WWW applications is a complete page. This limits the flexibility one normally finds in many client applications. Companies such as Sun and Netscape Communications Corp. are beginning to enhance their products in ways that will bring in some of that flexibility, but, as of yet, there is no standard, de facto or otherwise, that allows the flexibility needed to develop complex data entry forms. This is why many WWW database applications tend to be browsing applications and limit data capture to the bare minimum. Whenever possible, these applications use radio buttons, select lists, and other techniques to minimize the possible human error when entering data.

Another issue is the lack of tools for developing client/server applications. This will probably not be an issue for long as it is likely that many companies will produce development systems for the Web much like they have in the past. This may be hindered somewhat by the lack of standards, but in the long run, products will be available. There are currently some products that aid in the development of WWW database applications that are in the public domain. You may want to investigate products such as ORAYWWW, GSQL, Oracle's WOW, and others to see what elements they bring to the table. In many cases, while these tools are convenient for developing one-off forms, they lack the sophistication required to develop a full-fledged application.

In general, the future looks very bright for WWW and database integration. The task is simple enough that applications can be developed without sophisticated tools, although those tools will certainly be welcome when they arrive. WWW and database integration will greatly enhance the value of corporate data and provide access to that data for many employees, customers, or other interested parties who might never have seen the data otherwise.

# Chapter 18

# ISAPI

The Internet Server Application Programming Interface (ISAPI) provides the means to extend and augment the capabilities of IIS. This chapter covers the following topics:

- ➤ Understanding the ISAPI architecture in IIS
- ➤ Writing ISAPI Extension DLLs
- ➤ Writing ISAPI Filter DLLs
- ➤ Debugging ISAPI DLLs
- ➤ ISAPI and thread-safe operations

## ISAPI Overview

The purpose of ISAPI is to provide the capability to extend the functionality of ISAPI-compliant Web servers, such as Internet Information Server. Using ISAPI to extend IIS is accomplished by encapsulating the ISAPI executable code in a Windows NT Dynamic Link Library (DLL) and providing that DLL to IIS. An ISAPI DLL is made available to IIS by placing the DLL file in an IIS

Web server that has the Execute property set. The procedure for modifying IIS Web server directory attributes is discussed in the IIS Internet Server Manager online help.

Various programming languages are available for writing ISAPI DLLs, including Perl, ISAPI Basic, and Microsoft Visual C++. Because no single programming language is ideal for every development environment, you should consider the following issues when choosing an ISAPI programming language:

➤ The skill level and proficiency of the programmer in the programming language of choice

➤ The stability of the programming language—languages such as ISAPI Basic are very new and are subject to frequent changes, whereas languages such as Perl and C++ are well-established and relatively stable

➤ Cross-platform requirements—ISAPI DLLs written in Visual C++ tend to utilize Windows-specific functions, whereas Perl applications tend to be more portable to other platforms, such as UNIX and Macintosh

A Windows Dynamic Link Library (DLL) provides a method for a process to use executable code that is not part of its own executable image. When a process uses the functions provided by a DLL, the DLL is mapped into and executes in the process's address space. A module (either an .EXE or .DLL) can load and unload the DLL executable code on an as-needed basis. A single copy of a DLL in memory may be shared by multiple processes simultaneously. Functions in a DLL may be used by applications written in different programming languages, provided each application conforms to the calling conventions of the DLL functions.

For example, suppose your company has written an e-mail program and a text editor program, both of which provide the user with a spelling checker. Implementing the spelling checker functionality in a DLL provides many benefits, including:

➤ The spelling checker code is loaded into memory only once, even if the user is using the spelling checker in both programs simultaneously

➤ You can reduce development and maintenance costs of the applications by implementing the spelling checker functions in only one place—the DLL

➤ Each application may unload the DLL from its address space when it is not being used, saving system resources such as memory

➤ You can upgrade the spelling checker DLL with an improved pattern matching algorithm, without having to redistribute the applications that use the DLL

# Integrating ISAPI DLLs with Internet Information Server

IIS provides a rich set of capabilities, such as server side includes, OLE connectivity, and the Internet Database Connector. However, it is often necessary to extend the capabilities of the server to build a superior WWW site. This can be accomplished using various methods, such as Common Gateway Interface (CGI) scripts and ISAPI DLLs; CGI scripts are discussed later in this chapter in "ISA vs CGI." Some of the various applications of ISAPI DLLs are as follows:

➤ Handle input from an HTML form

➤ Generate dynamic images such as graphs and counters

➤ Write client access information to a log file

➤ Perform extended client authentication

➤ Fetch information from a database and format it for presentation to the client

An ISAPI DLL under IIS is implemented as either an extension DLL or a filter DLL. For clarity, this chapter refers to an extension DLL as an Internet Server Application (ISA); extension DLLs are commonly called ISAs. Both ISAs and ISAPI filters are discussed in detail later in this chapter.

# Internet Server Applications

The purpose of an ISA is to extend the capabilities of IIS. ISAs are essentially applications written to perform some action in response to a user request, such as clicking on a hyperlink on an HTML page or a button on an HTML form. An ISA is invoked by the client through activating an URL like the following:

**http://www.server.com/scripts/**
**myisa.dll?Command&Arg1=Param**

Note that the client may pass arguments to the ISA, Arg1 above, using the same method used to pass arguments to a CGI script. Examples of ISA functions include:

➤ Fetching information from a database, formatting the data into HTML, and sending the data to the client

➤ Generating dynamic HTML pages based on the client connection information, such as username, IP address, or browser type

➤ Building and sending a graphical image indicating server usage statistics

➤ Creating workgroup applications such as conference room scheduling, configuration management, and network gaming

➤ Processing product orders sent via an HTML form

# ISA Architecture

The IIS Web server creates a thread in the server address space for each client connection to an ISA. Communication between IIS and an ISA is accomplished using an Extension Control Block (ECB). Each thread created by IIS for an ISA is assigned a unique ECB. The data contained in an ECB remains valid until the end of the associated transaction. The ECB is a block of memory allocated by the Web server process in the server's address space. A pointer to the appropriate ECB is passed to each ISA thread. At the end of a transaction, the associated ECB memory is deallocated by the Web server. Table 18.1 shows some of the fields contained in an ECB.

### Table 18.1   Extension Control Block Fields

| Field | Meaning |
| --- | --- |
| connID | A unique connection ID assigned by IIS |
| lpszMethod | The method by which the request was made lpszQueryString String containing the query information or arguments to the ISA |
| lpszPathInfo | Extra path information provided by the client |
| cbTotalBytes | The total number of bytes to expect from the client |
| lpszContentType | The content type of the data sent by the client |
| dwHttpStatusCode | The status of the current transaction when the request is completed |
| lpszLogData | Text to be written to the IIS server log |

Although the ISA may read any of the fields in the ECB, the ISA can only modify the dwHttpStatusCode and lpszLogData fields. Using the pointer to the ECB memory block passed to it by the Web server, the ISA should set the dwHttpStatusCode field appropriately before completing the transaction.

Each ISA DLL must define and export two entry points: **GetExtensionVersion** and **HttpExtensionProc**. IIS calls the GetExtensionVersion function when the DLL is loaded. This function provides IIS with the version number of the ISAPI specification used to build the ISA and a brief description of the ISA. IIS can use the version number returned by the GetExtensionVersion function to ensure that an ISA built with a previous or incompatible ISAPI version is not being executed by the server. Each time the ISA is requested by a client, IIS calls the HttpExtensionProc function and passes the function the ECB associated with the transaction. The HttpExtensionProc function performs all necessary actions for the ISA, including processing any parameters and sending the client the appropriate HTML data. The transaction is completed when the HttpExtensionProc function returns. Figure 18.1 shows the transaction flow through an ISA.

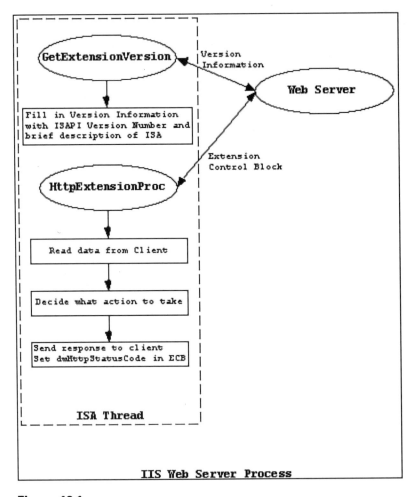

**Figure 18.1:**
ISA Transaction Flow.

Using the Microsoft Foundation Class Internet classes in Microsoft Visual C++ produces a slightly different architecture. Each MFC-based ISA defines a class derived from the MFC **CHttpServer** class. The derived class provides member functions for each command sent to the ISA via the client URL. Commands are mapped to member functions via an MFC **Parse Map**. The CHttpServer class provides a default implementation for the HttpExtensionProc function. The default implementation reads the client data and calls the appropriate ISA member function, based on the parse map. Each member function declared in the parse map must take a pointer to a **CHttpServerContext** object as its first parameter. The CHttpServerContext class not only provides a pointer to the ECB, but also provides the member functions necessary to communicate with the client. See the online Microsoft Visual C++ documentation in the Microsoft Developer Studio for more information.

# ISA vs CGI

ISAs and Common Gateway Interface (CGI) scripts are very similar in the sense that they are both executed on the server and they both communicate the results to the client. This is where the similarity ends.

CGI scripts are, in essence, executable programs. The server creates a separate process each time the CGI script is executed. In general this requires large amounts of server resources, including CPU and memory.

Because an ISA is implemented as a DLL, IIS is able to load the DLL into the IIS address space and keep it in memory. Unlike CGIs, IIS simply creates a new thread in the server's address space each time the ISA is executed. This considerably reduces the process creation, memory usage, and task switching overhead incurred versus the overhead required when executing CGI scripts. If IIS does not receive any requests for an ISA for an extended period of time, it may automatically unload the DLL to free system resources. Figure 18.2 illustrates the differences in how ISAPI DLLs and CGI scripts are executed by IIS.

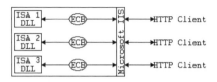

ISA 1 DLL
ISA 2 DLL
ISA 3 DLL
ECB
ECB
ECB
Microsoft IIS
HTTP Client
HTTP Client
HTTP Client
ISAPI Model
Single Server Process with Multiple Threads
CGI 1 Process
CGI 2 Process
CGI 3 Process
HTTP Server
HTTP Client
HTTP Client
HTTP Client
CGI Model
Single Server Process with Multiple CGI Processes
ISAPI Model vs CGI Model

**Figure 18.2:**
ISAPI model vs CGI model.

# Writing an ISA

The following examples are ISAs written using Microsoft Visual C++ 4.1 implementing the Microsoft Foundation Class (MFC). Note that only the relevant parts of the code are shown. Each example was created using the Visual C++ ISAPI Extension Wizard. The Wizard may be accessed in the Microsoft Developer Studio by choosing New from the File menu and selecting the Project Workspace option. Figure 18.3 shows the options available in the ISAPI Extension Wizard.

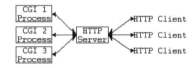

**Figure 18.3:**

Microsoft Developer Studio ISAPI Extension Wizard.

## GetServerData ISA

The GetServerData ISA shows how to use various features of the MFC Internet classes. The GetServerData ISA retrieves all of the available server variables, formats them into HTML, and streams the HTML to the client. Although this ISA is provided primarily as an introduction to writing ISAs and in general will not be used in normal Web operations, this ISA can be used for practical purposes, such as verifying IIS setup parameters (authentication method, server's IP name, and HTTP port number) and identifying which server variables are available (by parsing the ALL_HTTP variable). Figure 18.4 shows the output of the GetServerData ISA. The GetServerData ISA may be executed using an URL like the following:

**http://www.server.com/scripts/GetServerData.dll?**

Although the same functionality of the GetServerData ISA can be implemented in a CGI script, the method by which CGI scripts and ISAs access server variables is quite different. In a CGI script, each server variable is defined as an operating system environment variable. To get the value of a server variable, a CGI script uses a system service function call to get the value of the appropriate environment variable. Because ISAPI DLLs are loaded into the address space of the Web server process, the server can maintain these variables as part of the ECB passed to the ISA, as opposed to defining environment variables for each server variable. An ISA can get the value of a server variable by either calling the GetServerVariable ISAPI function or directly reading the value from the appropriate field in the ECB structure.

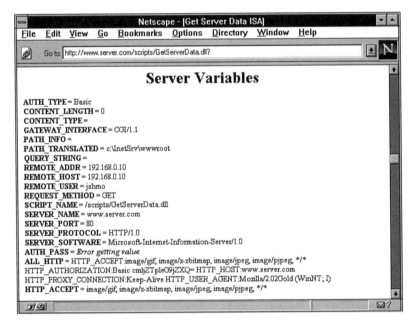

**Figure 18.4:**
GetServerData ISA Output.

The following listing shows the Visual C++ 4.1 GetServerData.cpp source code file for the GetServerData ISA.

```
// GetServerData.cpp - Implementation file for your
Internet Server
//    Get all available server information

/*
   Purpose:    This is a Microsoft Internet Information
               Server ISAPI extension (ISA). The purpose
               of this ISA is to get the server variables
               available to an ISA and send them back to
               the client as a "dynamic" HTML document.

   Parameters:
         None      Get the variables and send them
                   back to the client as a HTML
                   document.
         Default   Same as None
         Plain     Get the variables and send them
                   back to the client as plain text
                   (shows all HTML tags).

   Examples:
         http://www.server.com/scripts/GetServerData.dll?
         http://www.server.com/scripts/
➥GetServerData.dll?Default
         http://www.server.com/scripts/
➥GetServerData.dll?Plain
*/

#include <afx.h>
#include <afxwin.h>
#include <afxisapi.h>
#include "resource.h"
#include "GetServerData.h"

// Server variable names
#define NUM_VAR_NAMES 19

CHAR* szVarNames[NUM_VAR_NAMES] = {
 "AUTH_TYPE",          "CONTENT_LENGTH", "CONTENT_TYPE",
 "GATEWAY_INTERFACE", "PATH_INFO",       "PATH_TRANSLATED",
 "QUERY_STRING",       "REMOTE_ADDR",     "REMOTE_HOST",
```

*continues*

```
"REMOTE_USER",        "REQUEST_METHOD", "SCRIPT_NAME",
"SERVER_NAME",        "SERVER_PORT",    "SERVER_PROTOCOL",
"SERVER_SOFTWARE",    "AUTH_PASS",      "ALL_HTTP",
"HTTP_ACCEPT" };


/////////////////////////////////////////////////////////////
///////////////
// command-parsing map

BEGIN_PARSE_MAP(CGetServerData, CHttpServer)
  ON_PARSE_COMMAND(Default, CGetServerData, ITS_EMPTY)
 ON_PARSE_COMMAND(Plain, CGetServerData, ITS_EMPTY)
 DEFAULT_PARSE_COMMAND(Default, CGetServerData)
END_PARSE_MAP(CGetServerData)


/////////////////////////////////////////////////////////////
///////////////
// The one and only CGetServerData object

CGetServerData theExtension;


/////////////////////////////////////////////////////////////
///////////////
// CGetServerData implementation

CGetServerData::CGetServerData()
{
}


CGetServerData::~CGetServerData()
{
}

BOOL
CGetServerData::GetExtensionVersion(HSE_VERSION_INFO*
➥pVer)
{
// Call default implementation for initialization
CHttpServer::GetExtensionVersion(pVer);

// Load description string
```

```
TCHAR sz[HSE_MAX_EXT_DLL_NAME_LEN+1];
ISAPIVERIFY(::LoadString(AfxGetResourceHandle(),
                IDS_SERVER, sz,
HSE_MAX_EXT_DLL_NAME_LEN));
_tcscpy(pVer->lpszExtensionDesc, sz);
return TRUE;
}


/////////////////////////////////////////////////////////////////
///////////////
// CGetServerData command handlers

void CGetServerData::Default(CHttpServerContext* pCtxt)
{
SendData(pCtxt);
}

void CGetServerData::Plain(CHttpServerContext* pCtxt)
{
AddHeader(pCtxt, "Content-type: text/plain\r\n");
SendData(pCtxt);
}

void CGetServerData::SendData(CHttpServerContext* pCtxt)
{
CHAR szVar[1024];
DWORD dwLen = 0;

*pCtxt << "<HTML><HEAD><TITLE>Get Server Data ISA</
➥TITLE></HEAD>";
*pCtxt << "<BODY BGCOLOR=#FFFFFF>\r\n";
*pCtxt << "<CENTER><H1>Server Variables</H1></
➥CENTER><P>\r\n";

for(int i=0; i < NUM_VAR_NAMES; i++)
{
        *pCtxt << "<B>" << szVarNames[i] << "</B> = ";
        dwLen = 1024;
        if(pCtxt->GetServerVariable(szVarNames[i], szVar,
➥&dwLen))
                *pCtxt << szVar << "<BR>\r\n";
```

*continues*

```
        else
                *pCtxt << "<I><U>Error getting value</U></
I><BR>\r\n";
 }


 *pCtxt << "</BODY></HTML>\r\n";
 }
```

The **GetExtensionVersion** member function provides IIS with the appropriate version information and a short description of the ISA.

The **Plain** member function provides the capability to request a plain/text page as opposed to an HTML page; the browser will not interpret the HTML code returned by the ISA. The Plain member function sends the appropriate **Content-type** header to the browser to accomplish this. The **SendData** member function is then called to send the server variable data to the browser. The **Plain** member function may be invoked by using an URL such as the following:

**http://www.server.com/scripts/GetServerData.dll?Plain**

The **SendData** member function performs most of the work of the ISA. It retrieves the values of all the server variables, formats them, and sends them to the connected browser.

## Subscription ISA

The Subscription ISA illustrates how to use an ISA to process data from an HTML form. The data in the form is sent to the Subscription ISA DLL via an HTML POST.

This ISA could be adapted to process any type of HTML form data. Some uses of this type of ISA are as follows:

➤ Process product order requests

➤ Remote management of network servers, such as user accounts, e-mail services, WINS servers, and network shares

➤ Process user feedback information

➤ Product registration forms

The HTML form assumes that the Subscription ISA DLL is located in the /scripts IIS Web server directory. For example:

**http://www.server.com/scripts/Subscription.dll?**

The following shows both the HTML form for the Subscription ISA and the Visual C++ code for the ISA.

The following HTML form provides the input for the Subscription ISA to process.

```
<HTML><HEAD><TITLE>Subscription Application</TITLE></
HEAD>

<BODY BGCOLOR=#FFFFFF>

<CENTER><H1>Subscription Application</H1></CENTER>
<H2>Please fill out all entries:</H2>
<P>
<FORM ACTION="/scripts/Subscription.dll?ProcessNew"
➥METHOD=POST>

<TABLE>
<TR>
 <TD><B>Full Name:</B></TD>
 <TD COLSPAN=5><INPUT TYPE="text" NAME="Name" VALUE=""
➥SIZE=60 MAXLENGTH=60></TD>
</TR>
<TR>
 <TD><B>Address:</B></TD>
 <TD COLSPAN=5><INPUT TYPE="text" NAME="Address" VALUE=""
➥SIZE=60 MAXLENGTH=60></TD>
</TR>
<TR>
 <TD><B>City:</B></TD>
 <TD><INPUT TYPE="text" NAME="City" VALUE="" SIZE=30
```

*continues*

```
➡MAXLENGTH=40></TD>
 <TD><B>State:</B></TD>
 <TD><SELECT NAME="State">

<OPTION>AL<OPTION>AK<OPTION>AZ<OPTION>AR<OPTION>CA<OPTION>CO

<OPTION>CT<OPTION>DE<OPTION>DC<OPTION>FL<OPTION>GA<OPTION>HI

<OPTION>ID<OPTION>IL<OPTION>IN<OPTION>IA<OPTION>KS<OPTION>KY

<OPTION>LA<OPTION>ME<OPTION>MD<OPTION>MA<OPTION>MI<OPTION>MN

<OPTION>MS<OPTION>MO<OPTION>MT<OPTION>NE<OPTION>NV<OPTION>NH

<OPTION>NJ<OPTION>NM<OPTION>NY<OPTION>NC<OPTION>ND<OPTION>OH

<OPTION>OK<OPTION>OR<OPTION>PA<OPTION>RI<OPTION>SC<OPTION>SD

<OPTION>TN<OPTION>UT<OPTION>VT<OPTION>VA<OPTION>WA<OPTION>WV

<OPTION>WI<OPTION>WY
 </SELECT>
 <TD><B>Zip:</B></TD>
 <TD><INPUT TYPE="text" NAME="Zip" VALUE="" SIZE=10
➡MAXLENGTH=10></TD>
 </TR>
 <TR>
 <TD><B>Number of years:</B></TD>
 <TD><INPUT TYPE="text" NAME="Years" VALUE="" SIZE=5
➡MAXLENGTH=3></TD>
 </TR>
 <TR>
 <TD><BR><B>Credit Card Number:</B></TD>
 <TD><BR><INPUT TYPE="text" NAME="CardNumber" VALUE=""
➡SIZE=20 MAXLENGTH=16></TD>
 <TD><BR><B>Expires:</B></TD>
 <TD><BR><INPUT TYPE="text" NAME="Expire" VALUE="" SIZE=5
➡MAXLENGTH=5></TD>
 </TABLE>

<BR><P><BR><P><BR><P>
<CENTER>
```

```
<INPUT TYPE="submit" VALUE="Submit Subscription">
<INPUT TYPE="reset" VALUE="Reset Form">
</CENTER>

</FORM>
</BODY>
</HTML>
```

The following listing shows the Visual C++ 4.1 Subscription.cpp source code file for the Subscription ISA.

```
// Subscription.cpp - Implementation file for your
                      Internet Server
//     Subscription Processor

/*
   Purpose:      This is a Microsoft Internet Information
                 Server ISAPI extension (ISA). The purpose
                 of this ISA is to handle the input from
                 the Subscription HTML form.

   Parameters:
          None          Error
          Default       Error
          ProcessNew    Processes all of the data on the
                        form

   Examples:
          http://www.server.com/scripts/Subscription.dll?
          http://www.server.com/scripts/
➥Subscription.dll?Default
          http://www.server.com/scripts/
➥Subscription.dll?ProcessNew&

Name=jshmo&Address=home&City=Shmoville&State=SV&Zip=
➥11111&CardNumber=1234&
                 Expire=01/99&Years=1
*/
```

*continues*

```
#include <afx.h>
#include <afxwin.h>
#include <afxisapi.h>
#include "resource.h"
#include "Subscription.h"


///////////////////////////////////////////////////////////
///////////////
// command-parsing map

BEGIN_PARSE_MAP(CSubscription, CHttpServer)
 ON_PARSE_COMMAND(ProcessNew, CSubscription,
        ITS_PSTR ITS_PSTR ITS_PSTR ITS_PSTR ITS_PSTR
        ITS_PSTR ITS_PSTR ITS_I2)
 ON_PARSE_COMMAND_PARAMS(
        "Name Address City State Zip CardNumber Expire
➥Years")
 ON_PARSE_COMMAND(Default, CSubscription, ITS_EMPTY)
 DEFAULT_PARSE_COMMAND(Default, CSubscription)
END_PARSE_MAP(CSubscription)


///////////////////////////////////////////////////////////
///////////////
// The one and only CSubscription object

CSubscription theExtension;


///////////////////////////////////////////////////////////
///////////////
// CSubscription implementation

CSubscription::CSubscription()
{
}


CSubscription::~CSubscription()
{
}


BOOL CSubscription::GetExtensionVersion(HSE_VERSION_INFO*
➥pVer)
```

```
{
// Call default implementation for initialization
CHttpServer::GetExtensionVersion(pVer);

// Load description string
TCHAR sz[HSE_MAX_EXT_DLL_NAME_LEN+1];
ISAPIVERIFY(::LoadString(AfxGetResourceHandle(),
              IDS_SERVER, sz,
HSE_MAX_EXT_DLL_NAME_LEN));
_tcscpy(pVer->lpszExtensionDesc, sz);
return TRUE;
}


//////////////////////////////////////////////////////////////
///////////////
// CSubscription command handlers

LPCTSTR CSubscription::GetTitle() const
{
CString strTitle;
strTitle.LoadString(IDS_SERVER);
return (LPCTSTR)strTitle;
}

void CSubscription::Default(CHttpServerContext* pCtxt)
{
StartContent(pCtxt);
WriteTitle(pCtxt);

*pCtxt << _T("<CENTER><H1><I>Error</I></H1></
CENTER><P>\r\n");
*pCtxt << _T("All fields in the form must be filled
in.\r\n");

EndContent(pCtxt);
}

void CSubscription::ProcessNew(CHttpServerContext* pCtxt,
                       LPTSTR lpszName,
                       LPTSTR lpszAddress,
                       LPTSTR lpszCity,
```

*continues*

```
                              LPTSTR lpszState,
                              LPTSTR lpszZip,
                              LPTSTR lpszCardNumber,
                              LPTSTR lpszExpire,
                              int nNumYears)
{
BOOL bValid;

StartContent(pCtxt);
WriteTitle(pCtxt);

*pCtxt << _T("<CENTER><H1>Subscription Results</H1></
➥CENTER><P>\r\n");

// Validate the data in the form
bValid = TRUE;

// The data is valid, process the application
if(bValid)
{
        if(SendMail("Subs", lpszName, lpszAddress,
➥lpszCity, lpszState,
                         lpszZip, lpszCardNumber,
➥lpszExpire, nNumYears))
        {
                *pCtxt << _T("<H2>Thank you!</
➥H2><P>\r\n");
                *pCtxt << _T("<B>Subscription confirmed
➥for:</B><P>\r\n");
                *pCtxt << _T("<PRE><I>") << lpszName <<
➥"<BR>\r\n" <<
                         lpszAddress << "<BR>\r\n" <<
➥lpszCity << ", " <<
                         lpszState << "  " << lpszZip <<
➥"<P>\r\n";
                *pCtxt << _T("Charged to: ") <<
➥lpszCardNumber <<
                         _T(", ") << lpszExpire << _T("</
➥PRE>\r\n");
        }
        else
        {
```

```
                    *pCtxt << _T("<B>Sorry, <I>") << lpszName
<<
                    _T("</I>, an error occurred pro-
➥cessing your request.<P>");
                    *pCtxt << _T("<B>Please contact us at:</
➥B><P>\r\n") <<
                    _T("<I><A HREF=\"mailto:customer-
➥service@server.com\">") <<
                    _T("customer-service@server.com</
➥A>   or<BR>\r\n") <<
                    _T("1-800-555-1234</I>\r\n");
        }
}
else // Invalid information in the form
{
        *pCtxt << _T("<H2>Error</H2><P>\r\n");
        *pCtxt << _T("<B>Invalid information specified in
➥form.</B>\r\n");
}

EndContent(pCtxt);
}


BOOL CSubscription::SendMail( LPTSTR lpszDestination,
                    LPTSTR lpszName,
                    LPTSTR lpszAddress,
                    LPTSTR lpszCity,
                    LPTSTR lpszState,
                    LPTSTR lpszZip,
                    LPTSTR lpszCardNumber,
                    LPTSTR lpszExpire,
                    nNumYears)
{
// Write a function here to send E-mail to the address
➥specified
// in the lpszDestination parameter

return TRUE;
}
```

The **GetExtensionVersion** member function provides version information and a short description of the ISA to the server.

The **Default** member function is called if there are no commands passed to the ISA in the URL.

The **ProcessNew** member function performs most of the work of the ISA. The function has parameters that are mapped to the fields in the HTML form shown above; these parameters are also identified in the parse map. The function calls the **SendMail** function to send e-mail to the subscription department and then sends an HTML subscription confirmation notice to the client.

The **SendMail** member function is left as an exercise. It is included only to illustrate that the ISA may perform any actions necessary before concluding the transaction.

# ISAPI Filters

An ISAPI filter, like an ISA, is a Windows DLL. As opposed to an ISA, which processes Web server commands specified in an URL, an ISAPI filter modifies the way in which the Web server processes internal server events. Internal server events include writing to the server log file, translating an URL to a physical path, and authenticating connecting users. ISAPI filters are not explicitly invoked by using an URL; ISAPI filters are invoked by the server, possibly in response to an URL request. For example, an ISAPI filter could be invoked by the Web server if the user requests a document using an URL such as the following:

**http://www.server.com/Default.htm**

Processing this request may cause IIS to write an entry to the IIS log file. An ISAPI filter can be installed to handle writes to the IIS log file, in which case the filter can be invoked by the server. This is discussed in more detail in "CustomLog Filter" later in this chapter.

All ISAPI filter DLLs are loaded by IIS when the WWW Publishing Service is started. When an ISAPI filter is loaded by IIS, the filter provides IIS with a list of events. The filter may be executed by IIS each time an event on the list occurs.

The following lists some of the applications for ISAPI filters:

➤ Modifying the IIS log to contain the HTTP agent name

➤ Creating custom client authentication schemes

➤ Tracking which URLs receive the most requests

➤ Providing data encryption and secure port communications

➤ Providing custom URL mapping based on the user credentials and if the client is connecting on a secure port

## ISAPI Filter Architecture

Each ISAPI filter DLL must define and export two functions: **GetFilterVersion** and **HttpFilterProc**. When IIS loads the filter DLL, the GetFilterVersion function is called. Each time an event occurs that is associated with one or more filters, IIS determines which filter(s) to call based on the priority of the filters. If two filters have the same priority, IIS will invoke the filter that appears first in the registry (see "Installing an ISAPI Filter" later in this chapter for more information on the Windows NT registry).

Multiple ISAPI filters can be installed simultaneously for the same event. IIS must decide not only which filters to execute for each event, but also the order in which the filters should be executed.

The GetFilterVersion function for each filter is executed when the filter is loaded. This function provides IIS with the list of server events the filter will respond to. IIS uses this list from each installed filter DLL to determine which filters to execute when a specific server event occurs.

The GetFilterVersion function also specifies the priority of the filter. IIS uses this priority to determine the order in which filters for a specific server event are executed. If two or more filters are installed for the same event and each filter has specified the same priority, there is a tie. IIS

*continues*

breaks the tie by using the order, from left to right, in which the filters are specified in the NT Registry (see "Installing an ISAPI Filter" later in this chapter).

## GetFilterVersion Function

The GetFilterVersion function identifies the ISAPI version used to build the DLL. This function also informs IIS about the priority of the filter, the events to send to the filter, and the ports on which the filter should be notified. Typically a filter will request to be notified not only for the event(s) that define the application (for example LOG, URL_MAP, etc.), but also for the END_OF_NET_SESSION event. The END_OF_NET_SESSION event notifies the filter that the transaction with the client is over, providing the filter thread an opportunity to perform any cleanup before terminating, such as memory deallocation and file closing.

In the GetFilterVersion function, the specified list of server events should contain only the events that the filter will process and respond to. Invoking a filter for extraneous events incurs unnecessary overhead on the server, thus reducing the overall performance of the system.

## HttpFilterProc Function

The HttpFilterProc function is the entry point to the filter for processing a requested event. The function is passed a **HTTP_FILTER_CONTEXT** structure, which specifies the event type and port type. The HttpFilterProc function determines the type of event that occurred and performs all steps necessary to process the event. The HTTP_FILTER_CONTEXT structure also contains a pointer that can be assigned by the filter to memory allocated by the filter. This pointer is guaranteed to be valid until the end of the client transaction and may be used by the filter to store state information for the transaction.

Using the Microsoft Foundation Class Internet classes in Microsoft Visual C++ produces a slightly different architecture. Each MFC-based ISAPI filter defines a class derived from the MFC **CHttpFilter** class. The implementation of the derived class provides a GetFilterVersion member function. The CHttpFilter class provides default member functions for each of the filter events. The derived class may override these member functions to handle each event specified by the filter in the GetFilterVersion function. The event handler member functions are called by the HttpFilterProc function defined in the CHttpFilter derived class. Each event handler member function must take a pointer to a **CHttpFilterContext** object as its first parameter. The CHttpFilterContext class not only provides the data items in the HTTP_FILTER_CONTEXT structure, but also provides member functions for communicating with the client, retrieving server variable values, and allocating memory. Other parameters to the event handler functions depend on the event to which the function applies. See the online Microsoft Visual C++ documentation in the Microsoft Developer Studio for more information.

# ISAPI Filter Events

The following table identifies the events an ISAPI filter might process. A filter may specify multiple events in the GetFilterVersion function when the filter is loaded by the server. When an event occurs and the filter is invoked by IIS, the event type is identified in the HTTP_FILTER_CONTEXT structure passed to the HttpFilterProc function.

**Table 18.2   ISAPI Filter Events**

| Event | Purpose |
| --- | --- |
| SF_NOTIFY_AUTHENTICATION | A client's credentials, username, and password need to be authenticated |
| SF_NOTIFY_END_OF_NET_SESSION | The client transaction is ending |
| SF_NOTIFY_LOG | IIS is about to write an entry into the log file |
| SF_NOTIFY_NONSECURE_PORT | Only notify for client connections over a nonsecure port |
| SF_NOTIFY_PREPROC_HEADERS | IIS has preprocessed the client request headers |
| SF_NOTIFY_READ_RAW_DATA | Filter sees all data, including headers and data |

*continues*

**Table 18.2   Continued**

| Event | Purpose |
| --- | --- |
| SF_NOTIFY_SECURE_PORT | Only notify for client connections over a secure port |
| SF_NOTIFY_SEND_RAW_DATA | IIS needs to send data to the client, not including header data |
| SF_NOTIFY_URL_MAP | The server needs an URL to be mapped to a physical path |

Multiple filters, each handling the same events, can be installed simultaneously. Each filter may or may not be invoked by the server. After processing an event, a filter may notify the server that the event has been handled sufficiently and that no other filters for that event should be invoked. A filter may also decide that it does not need to process this particular occurrence of the event and can notify the server that the next filter in line should be invoked. The following example illustrates when a filter may decide not to process a particular instance of an event:

Suppose a filter is installed that processes AUTHENTICATION events, for which the filter must either allow or deny access to the server by the requesting user. The purpose of this specific filter DLL is to authenticate users who have access to sensitive information. If the specified user does have access to the sensitive information, the username and password can be authenticated by the filter, at which time the filter can either allow or deny access to the server. If the filter is invoked for a username that does not have access to sensitive information, the filter should notify the server to invoke the next AUTHENTICATION filter in line, thereby maintaining the integrity of all other installed AUTHENTICATION filters.

## Installing an ISAPI Filter

Installation of an ISAPI filter requires moving the filter DLL file to a directory that has the Execute property set and notifying IIS of the filter. To set the Execute property on an IIS Web server directory, use the IIS Internet Service Manager to modify the

Directory attributes in the WWW Publishing Service. To notify IIS to load the filter, the following value in the Window NT Registry needs to be modified using the Windows NT Registry Editor, regedt32.exe:

**HKEY_LOCAL_MACHINE\SYSTEM\CurrentControlSet\Service\ W3SVC\ Parameters\Filter DLLs**

This value is a comma-delineated list. The list identifies all of the filter DLLs that are loaded when the WWW Publishing Service starts. The list contains the full physical path to each installed filter DLL.

The order in which IIS invokes filters for a specific event is partially determined by the order of the filter DLLs in the registry key. If two filters have the same priority, IIS will invoke the filter that appears first, reading left to right, in the *Filter DLLs* registry key.

Although the following procedure does not modify any Windows NT system parameters, incorrect modifications of the registry may cause Windows NT to crash and can cause Windows NT to fail to boot correctly. Make sure you have recently created an Emergency Repair Disk; refer to the rdisk.exe utility for more information.

1. Stop the IIS WWW Publishing Service using the Internet Service Manager

2. Start the Windows NT Registry Editor, regedt32.exe, on the IIS server machine

3. Choose HKEY_LOCAL_MACHINE on Local Machine from the **W**indow menu

4. Choose Tree **a**nd Data from the **V**iew menu

5. Navigate to the SYSTEM\CurrentControlSet\Services\ W3SVC\Paramters key

6. Select the Filter DLLs entry from the value list

7. Choose **S**tring... from the **E**dit menu

8. Using arrow keys, move to the position in the comma separated list where the filter should be placed. Enter the full path to the ISAPI filter DLL file, adding a comma if necessary

9. Choose E<u>x</u>it from the <u>R</u>egistry menu

10. Start the IIS WWW Server service using the Internet Service Manager

The ISAPI filter is now installed. Use the Event Viewer, eventvwr.exe, to ensure no IIS errors occurred loading the filter DLL. If the filter installation is successful, no entries related to the filter will be placed into the Event Log.

# Writing an ISAPI Filter

The following ISAPI filter examples were written using Microsoft Visual C++ 4.1 implementing the Microsoft Foundation Class (MFC). Note that only the relevant parts of the code are shown. The examples were created using the Visual C++ ISAPI Extension Wizard that can be accessed in the Microsoft Developer Studio by choosing <u>N</u>ew from the <u>F</u>ile menu and selecting the Project Workspace option.

## URLRedirect Filter

This example is provided primarily to introduce the structure and implementation of a basic ISAPI filter. The URLRedirect filter provides the capability to map URLs to different files. One use for this functionality is to map an URL, the target for which is temporarily unavailable, to an HTML file notifying the user to try again later. Using this method, none of the HTML files that contain the invalid link need to be modified. When the URL target becomes available, simply remove the associated entry from the URLRedirect filter data file; the URLRedirect data file is discussed later in this section. For example, if a client requested the following URL:

**http://www.server.com/Default.htm**

this filter could map that URL to the following file:

**c:\InetSrv\wwwroot\NewDefault.htm**

Another application of this type of filter is to map all client requests of a specific directory to a certain file. For example, you may want to map all requests of the *Download* directory to an HTML file telling the client that the files have moved to *Software/ Download* and that the user should update any bookmarks.

The following listings show the Microsoft Visual C++ 4.1 URLRedirect.h and URLRedirect.cpp source code files for the URLRedirect.dll ISAPI filter. The URLRedirect filter reads a data file to identify URLs that should be mapped to new files. The full path to the data file is specified in the URLRedirect.cpp source code file as:

**c:\InetSrv\scripts\URLRedirect.dat**

Each entry in the data file contains the URL and the physical path to the file the URL should be mapped to. Each entry must be on a separate line and the URL and physical path must be separated by a comma. The following is a sample data file entry:

**/Default.htm,c:\InetSrv\wwwroot\NewDefault.htm**

The following file shows the URLRedirect.h include file for the filter:

```
// URLRedirect.h - Include file for your Internet Server
//    URLRedirect


class CURLRedirect : public CHttpFilter
{
private:
 CMapStringToString m_mapOldToNew;

public:
```

*continues*

```
CURLRedirect();
~CURLRedirect();

BOOL GetFilterVersion(PHTTP_FILTER_VERSION pVer);

DWORD OnUrlMap(CHttpFilterContext* pCtxt,
        PHTTP_FILTER_URL_MAP pMapInfo);
DWORD OnEndOfNetSession(CHttpFilterContext* pCtxt);
};
```

The following file shows the URLRedirect.cpp source file for the filter:

```
// URLRedirect.cpp - Implementation file for your
                     Internet Server
//     URLRedirect

/*
   Purpose:       This is a Microsoft Internet Information
                  Server ISAPI filter. The purpose of this
                  filter is to handle mapping certain URLs
                  to physical file locations. The URLs to
                  map are identified in the URLRedirect.dat
                  file.

   Note: The URLRedirect.dat file is assumed to be in
         c:\InetSrv\scripts\URLRedirect.dat
*/

#include <afx.h>
#include <afxwin.h>
#include <afxisapi.h>
#include <fstream.h>
#include <string.h>
#include "resource.h"
#include "URLRedirect.h"


///////////////////////////////////////////////////////////
//////////////
```

```
// The one and only CURLRedirect object

CURLRedirect theFilter;

/////////////////////////////////////////////////////////////
///////////////
// CURLRedirect implementation

CURLRedirect::CURLRedirect()
{
ifstream ifs;
CHAR szBuffer[2048];
LPSTR lpszTemp;

// Load the URL redirection data file
ifs.open("c:\\InetSrv\\scripts\\URLRedirect.dat",
➥ios::in¦ios::nocreate);
if(ifs.is_open())
{
        while(1)
        {
                ifs.getline(szBuffer, 2048, '\n');
                if(ifs.eof())
                        break;
                if(szBuffer[0] == '\0')
                        continue;
                lpszTemp = strchr(szBuffer, ',');
                if(lpszTemp == NULL)
                        continue;
                *lpszTemp = '\0';
                m_mapOldToNew.SetAt(_strupr(szBuffer),
➥lpszTemp+1);
        }
        ifs.close();
}
}

CURLRedirect::~CURLRedirect()
{
// Remove all of the mappings read from the data file
m_mapOldToNew.RemoveAll();
```

*continues*

```
}

BOOL CURLRedirect::GetFilterVersion(PHTTP_FILTER_VERSION
➥pVer)
{
 // Call default implementation for initialization
 CHttpFilter::GetFilterVersion(pVer);

 // Clear the flags set by base class
 pVer->dwFlags &= ~SF_NOTIFY_ORDER_MASK;

 // Set the flags we are interested in
 pVer->dwFlags |= SF_NOTIFY_ORDER_LOW |
➥SF_NOTIFY_NONSECURE_PORT | SF_NOTIFY_URL_MAP
                 | SF_NOTIFY_END_OF_NET_SESSION;

 // Load description string
 TCHAR sz[SF_MAX_FILTER_DESC_LEN+1];
 ISAPIVERIFY(::LoadString(AfxGetResourceHandle(),
               IDS_FILTER, sz, SF_MAX_FILTER_DESC_LEN));
 _tcscpy(pVer->lpszFilterDesc, sz);
 return TRUE;
}

DWORD CURLRedirect::OnUrlMap(CHttpFilterContext* pCtxt,
PHTTP_FILTER_URL_MAP pMapInfo)
{
CString strNew;
CHAR szURL[1024];

 // Convert the URL requested by the client to upper case
 lstrcpy(szURL, pMapInfo->pszURL);
 _strupr(szURL);

 // Check to see if we have mapped the specified URL to a
 // new file
 if(m_mapOldToNew.Lookup(szURL, strNew))
 {
         // A mapping was found, return the mapped
➥filename to the
         // server
```

```
        lstrcpy(pMapInfo->pszPhysicalPath, strNew);
        return SF_STATUS_REQ_HANDLED_NOTIFICATION;
}


// No redirection mapping was found, let the server do it
return SF_STATUS_REQ_NEXT_NOTIFICATION;
}

DWORD CURLRedirect::OnEndOfNetSession(CHttpFilterContext*
➥pCtxt)
{
// TODO: React to this notification accordingly and
// return the appropriate status code
return SF_STATUS_REQ_NEXT_NOTIFICATION;
}
```

The **CURLRedirect** constructor loads the entries from the URLRedirect.dat file into memory.

The **~CURLRedirect** destructor removes all of the entries from the m_mapOldToNew member variable before the filter DLL is unloaded.

The **GetFilterVersion** member function notifies the server that the filter is low priority, should be notified on *only* nonsecure ports, and should be called on both the **URL_MAP** event and the **END_OF_NET_SESSION** event.

The **OnUrlMap** member function is called when the IIS Web server is about to map an URL to a physical file path. The function checks the URL against the entries that were specified in the URLRedirect.dat file. If a match is found, the filter provides the server with the filename specified in the URLRedirect.dat file. If a match is found, the filter returns the value **SF_STATUS_REQ_HANDLED_NOTIFICATION**, notifying the server that the filter has handled the URL mapping and that no other filters should be called. If no match is found, the filter returns the value **SF_STATUS_REQ_NEXT_NOTIFICATION**, enabling any other URL mapping filters to be called.

## CustomLog Filter

Often it is desirable to compute statistics on which types of browsers clients are using to connect to the Web server. This type of information can provide Web designers, especially intranet Web designers, with the means to customize and enhance a site using a specific technology. For example, if an intranet Web designer knows that 80 percent of the visitors to a site are using a browser that supports Java, the Web designer can safely start deploying Java-based pages on the site.

Another application for modifying the log file format is to add the username to each entry in the log file. Any information available to the filter at runtime, including all server variables, may be added to log file entries by the filter. Additionally, unwanted components of log file entries, such as the Win32 status code, may be deleted from each entry in the log file by a filter.

IIS does not provide the client browser type in the default IIS log file format. The CustomLog filter illustrates how to modify the entries made in the IIS log file to add the client browser type to each entry. Adding the client browser type is accomplished by parsing the HTTP_ALL server variable for an HTTP_USER_AGENT entry. If the entry is found, the client browser type is extracted and appended to the log entry. If the HTTP_USER_AGENT entry is not found, the string "—unknown—" is appended to the log entry. The example uses the **AllocMem** function to allocate memory for log entry data. Although this is an acceptable method and is often the easiest to implement, due to the resource overhead associated with AllocMem, it may not be optimal for all filter applications. The attraction to the AllocMem function is that the memory is automatically deallocated when the client transaction is terminated.

This example assumes that IIS is writing log entries to a file. If IIS is writing log entries to an ODBC data source, another column needs to be added to the IIS log database table. The new column must be the last column in the table and must be a character field large enough to handle the text for the HTTP user agent name.

The following shows a typical entry in the IIS log file, without the custom log filter installed:

**192.168.0.10, jshmo, 6/23/96, 20:13:24, W3SVC, WWW-SERVER, 192.168.0.11, 90, 213, 4445, 200, 0, GET, /Default.htm, -,**

The following shows an IIS log entry with the custom log filter installed:

**192.168.0.10, jshmo, 6/23/96, 20:23:04, W3SVC, WWW-SERVER, 192.168.0.11, 60, 231, 4445, 200, 0, GET, /Default.htm, -, Mozilla/2.02Gold (WinNT; I),**

The following listing shows the Microsoft Visual C++ 4.1 CustomLog.cpp source code file for the CustomLog.dll ISAPI filter.

```
// CustomLog.cpp - Implementation file for your Internet
                  Server
//    Custom Log File Format

/*
   Purpose:    This is a Microsoft Internet Information
               Server
        ISAPI filter. The purpose of this filter is to
        append the HTTP User Agent name to the end
        of each server log entry.
*/

#include <afx.h>
#include <afxwin.h>
#include <afxisapi.h>
#include "resource.h"
#include "CustomLog.h"


/////////////////////////////////////////////////////////////
///////////////
// The one and only CCustomLog object
```

*continues*

```
CCustomLog theFilter;

////////////////////////////////////////////////////////////
//////////////
// CCustomLog implementation

CCustomLog::CCustomLog()
{
}

CCustomLog::~CCustomLog()
{
}

BOOL CCustomLog::GetFilterVersion(PHTTP_FILTER_VERSION
➥pVer)
{
// Call default implementation for initialization
CHttpFilter::GetFilterVersion(pVer);

// Clear the flags set by base class
pVer->dwFlags &= ~SF_NOTIFY_ORDER_MASK;

// Set the flags we are interested in
pVer->dwFlags |= SF_NOTIFY_ORDER_LOW |
➥SF_NOTIFY_SECURE_PORT |
SF_NOTIFY_NONSECURE_PORT
                        | SF_NOTIFY_LOG |
➥SF_NOTIFY_END_OF_NET_SESSION;

// Load description string
TCHAR sz[SF_MAX_FILTER_DESC_LEN+1];
ISAPIVERIFY(::LoadString(AfxGetResourceHandle(),
             IDS_FILTER, sz, SF_MAX_FILTER_DESC_LEN));
_tcscpy(pVer->lpszFilterDesc, sz);
return TRUE;
}

DWORD CCustomLog::OnLog(CHttpFilterContext* pCtxt,
➥PHTTP_FILTER_LOG pLog)
{
DWORD dwLen;
```

```
CHAR szAllHttp[1024];
CHAR szAgent[1024];

// Get the User Agent name from the server variables
dwLen = 1024;
pCtxt->GetServerVariable("ALL_HTTP", szAllHttp, &dwLen);
LPSTR lpszTemp = strstr(szAllHttp, "USER_AGENT:");
if(lpszTemp != NULL)
{
        lpszTemp += 11;
        if(strchr(lpszTemp, ','))
                *(strchr(lpszTemp, ',')) = '\0';
        if(strchr(lpszTemp, 0x0A))
                *(strchr(lpszTemp, 0x0A)) = '\0';
        lstrcpy(szAgent, lpszTemp);
}
else
        lstrcpy(szAgent, "—unknown—");

// Allocate memory for the new log entry
// Note: This memory is automatically deallocated when
//       the client transaction is completed
dwLen = lstrlen(pLog->pszParameters);
if(dwLen == 0)
        dwLen = 1;
dwLen += lstrlen(szAgent) + 3;
pCtxt->m_pFC->pFilterContext = pCtxt->AllocMem(dwLen, 0);

// Append the User Agent to the log entry
lpszTemp = (LPSTR)(pCtxt->m_pFC->pFilterContext);
wsprintf(lpszTemp, "%s, %s",
        pLog->pszParameters[0]=='\0'?"-":pLog-
➥>pszParameters,
        szAgent);
pLog->pszParameters = lpszTemp;

return SF_STATUS_REQ_NEXT_NOTIFICATION;
}


DWORD CCustomLog::OnEndOfNetSession(CHttpFilterContext*
➥pCtxt)
```

*continues*

```
{
// TODO: React to this notification accordingly and
// return the appropriate status code
return SF_STATUS_REQ_NEXT_NOTIFICATION;
}
```

The **GetFilterVersion** member function notifies the server that the filter is low priority, should be notified on both secure and nonsecure ports, and should be called on both the **LOG** event and the **END_OF_NET_SESSION** event.

The **OnLog** member function is called by the HttpFilterProc function when the IIS Web server is about to write an entry into the IIS log file. The function attempts to determine the name of the client's HTTP agent. The function then appends this name to the end of the **Parameters** log file entry. The function then returns the value **SF_STATUS_REQ_NEXT_NOTIFICATION**, enabling any other log filters to be called.

To test the CustomLog filter, use a Web browser to connect to the IIS Web server. Inspect the IIS log file to ensure the filter is appending the client user agent name to each entry. To view the IIS log file, it may be necessary to first use the IIS Internet Service Manager to stop the IIS WWW Service.

This example assumes not only that IIS is writing a log file, but also that log file entries are written to a file and not an ODBC data source. Using the IIS Internet Server Manager, check the properties of the Web Publishing Service to ensure that IIS is writing a log file.

This example will still function correctly if IIS is writing log entries to an ODBC data source. However, a modification is required to the table in the ODBC data source being used for IIS log entries. An additional column must be appended to the table. The column must be a character column wide enough to hold the browser name written by the CustomLog filter, usually a field 255 characters wide is sufficient. The ODBC driver will, in general, truncate any browser names specified by the filter longer than 255 characters.

If IIS is writing log entries to a file, the path to the file is specified in the properties of the Web Publishing Service using the IIS Internet Service Manager. The file may be viewed while the Web server is running, but the file may not contain all of the entries; there may be pending writes to the file. If IIS is writing log entries to an ODBC data source, you can use an ODBC query tool, such as Microsoft Query, to view the log entries.

# Thread Safety

Both ISAs and ISAPI filters are implemented as DLLs. The Web server creates a new thread in the Web server address space each time it executes an ISA or ISAPI filter. This means that a single ISAPI DLL may be executing in one or more Web server threads. Because ISAPI DLLs execute in the Web server address space, an application error in an ISAPI DLL can cause the Web server process to crash. When designing an ISAPI DLL, care must be taken to ensure the DLL is thread-safe. Depending on the purpose of the DLL, different methods may be employed to ensure a thread-safe design. Some of the more common methods are critical sections, semaphores, and mutexes, all of which are available under Windows NT but may not be available in your programming language of choice. Refer to your programming language documentation for information regarding thread-safe design of DLLs. If an ISAPI DLL is written in C or C++, the try/catch mechanism should be used to ensure the ISAPI DLL does not generate any fatal errors.

# Critical Sections

Critical sections are used to provide mutually exclusive access by multiple threads to a shared resource, such as a file or database handle. Only one thread at a time may own a critical section. For example, to protect a database handle from being accessed by more than one thread at a time, each thread would "enter critical section" before accessing the database handle. When the thread has finished with the database handle, the thread would "leave critical section."

A thread will wait indefinitely to "enter critical section," thus potentially blocking the thread forever if the thread that currently owns the critical section is deadlocked or has abnormally terminated.

# Semaphores

Semaphores limit the number of simultaneous accesses to a shared resource, such as a database handle. When a semaphore is created, the semaphore count is set to the specified limit. Each time a thread opens the semaphore, the semaphore's count is decremented. The semaphore can no longer be opened when the semaphore's count reaches zero. The semaphore's count is incremented when a thread releases the semaphore. For example, if you want to limit the number of simultaneous users logged into a specific database, each thread opens the semaphore before accessing the database handle and releases the semaphore when finished with the database handle. If the thread is unable to open the semaphore because the semaphore count has reached zero, the thread can wait for the semaphore to become available or the thread can fail the requested database operation.

# Mutexes

A mutex is used to synchronize access by multiple threads to a shared resource, such as a block of shared memory or a database handle. Only one thread can own a mutex at any given time. For example, to prevent two threads from using a database handle simultaneously, each thread waits to own a mutex before accessing the database handle. After accessing the database handle, the thread releases ownership of the mutex, thus allowing other waiting threads to execute.

# ISAPI DLL Application Errors

Because ISAPI DLLs execute in the same address space as IIS, if an ISAPI DLL generates any kind of application error—such as an access violation—the DLL error may cause IIS to crash. With a thread-safe design and rigorous testing, ISAPI DLL application errors should be rare, thus providing a stable IIS environment.

# Database Access and ISAs

A common function for ISAs is to interact with a database and return data to the client. Thread-safe design of the DLL is critical in this instance. When designing an ISA, take into account not only the thread-safe design of the ISA, but also the thread-safety of the database engines the ISA uses.

The JET database engine uses COM to manage database connections and is not thread-safe. Using the JET engine to connect to databases, including dBase, Visual FoxPro, and Access should be avoided if possible. Note that the DAO driver also uses COM and is not thread-safe. If it is possible, try to use a thread-safe database driver, such as the ODBC driver for Microsoft SQL Server.

# Debugging ISAPI DLLs

There are as many debugging methods as there are developers. However, some methods are more appropriate than others in certain circumstances. For example, if you have an ISA that generates HTML pages using data from a database, but the ISA is not formatting the HTML page correctly, it may be sufficient to send some HTML-formatted debug information, such as Win32 error codes, back to the browser. Sometimes, it may be necessary to debug an ISA or ISAPI filter using an interactive debugger, such as windbg or Microsoft Developer Studio. This may become necessary, for example, if your ISA cannot open a database or if your filter cannot allocate memory. Using the debugger, you can set breakpoints inside the ISAPI DLL of interest and then, using a browser if necessary, force the Web server to execute your ISAPI DLL. The following explains how to run the IIS Web server in a Microsoft Developer Studio debug session.

1. Stop all of the IIS services, including the WWW, FTP, and Gopher Publishing services using the Internet Service Manager

2. Start Developer Studio and close any open workspaces

3. Choose Open **W**orkspace from the **F**ile menu to open INETINFO.EXE, located in the IIS installation directory

4.   Choose **S**ettings from the **B**uild menu

5.   Choose the Debug tab in the Project Settings dialog box

6.   Choose General from the Categor**y** drop-down list

7.   Choose Program arg**u**ments and type **-e W3Svc**

8.   Choose Additional DLLs from the Categor**y** drop-down list

9.   Choose the Local Name box and type the full path to the ISAPI DLL of interest

10.   Choose the OK button to close the Project Settings dialog box

11.   Make sure the .PDB file is in the same directory as the ISAPI DLL of interest

12.   Start the debugging session by choosing **D**ebug from the **B**uild menu and then choosing **G**o from the **D**ebug menu

13.   Use an HTTP client such as Internet Explorer or Netscape Navigator to issue the appropriate request to the IIS session under the debugger to trigger the ISAPI DLL of interest

## Summary

Both ISAs and ISAPI filters are Windows DLLs that are executed by the Web server as a new thread in the Web server's address space. Writing an ISAPI DLL is a relatively straightforward process. There are many programming environments that support writing ISAPI DLLs, including Perl, ISAPI Basic, and Microsoft Visual C++. Regardless of the programming language you choose, using ISAPI DLLs enables you to extend the capabilities of the Web server and produce a superior Web site.

ISAs are activated through an URL sent to the server by the client. This URL could be a hyperlink on an HTML page or a button on an HTML form. The ISA's job is to process the request and respond to the client. Some of the uses for ISAs include processing HTML form data, producing dynamic HTML pages, accessing databases, and generating on-the-fly graphical images. For an ISA to function, the ISA DLL must be placed in a directory that has the Execute attribute set.

ISAPI filters are used to modify the default behavior of the Web server in response to an internal Web server event, such as writing to the IIS log file, mapping an URL to a physical path, and authenticating client connection requests. Filters must be "installed" by both placing the filter DLL in a directory that has the Execute attribute set and modifying the Windows NT registry "Filter DLLs" value.

# Index

# D

## X - Y - Z

# Check Us Out Online!

New Riders has emerged as a premier publisher of computer books for the professional computer user. Focusing on CAD/graphics/multimedia, communications/internetworking, and networking/operating systems, New Riders continues to provide expert advice on high-end topics and software.

Check out the online version of *New Riders' Official World Wide Yellow Pages, 1996 Edition* for the most engaging, entertaining, and informative sites on the Web! You can even add your own site!

Brave our site for the finest collection of CAD and 3D imagery produced today. Professionals from all over the world contribute to our gallery, which features new designs every month.

From Novell to Microsoft, New Riders publishes the training guides you need to attain your certification. Visit our site and try your hand at the CNE Endeavor, a test engine created by VFX Technologies, Inc. that enables you to measure what you know—and what you don't!

## http://www.mcp.com/newriders

# WANT MORE INFORMATION?

## CHECK OUT THESE RELATED TOPICS OR SEE YOUR LOCAL BOOKSTORE

**CAD and 3D Studio**

As the number one CAD publisher in the world, and as a Registered Publisher of Autodesk, New Riders Publishing provides unequaled content on this complex topic. Industry-leading products include AutoCAD and 3D Studio.

**Networking**

As the leading Novell NetWare publisher, New Riders Publishing delivers cutting-edge products for network professionals. We publish books for all levels of users, from those wanting to gain NetWare Certification, to those administering or installing a network. Leading books in this category include *Inside NetWare 3.12*, *CNE Training Guide: Managing NetWare Systems*, *Inside TCP/IP*, and *NetWare: The Professional Reference*.

**Graphics**

New Riders provides readers with the most comprehensive product tutorials and references available for the graphics market. Best-sellers include *Inside CorelDRAW! 5*, *Inside Photoshop 3*, and *Adobe Photoshop NOW!*

**Internet and Communications**

As one of the fastest growing publishers in the communications market, New Riders provides unparalleled information and detail on this ever-changing topic area. We publish international best-sellers such as *New Riders' Official Internet Yellow Pages, 2nd Edition*, a directory of over 10,000 listings of Internet sites and resources from around the world, and *Riding the Internet Highway, Deluxe Edition*.

**Operating Systems**

Expanding off our expertise in technical markets, and driven by the needs of the computing and business professional, New Riders offers comprehensive references for experienced and advanced users of today's most popular operating systems, including *Understanding Windows 95*, *Inside Unix*, *Inside Windows 3.11 Platinum Edition*, *Inside OS/2 Warp Version 3*, and *Inside MS-DOS 6.22*.

**Other Markets**

Professionals looking to increase productivity and maximize the potential of their software and hardware should spend time discovering our line of products for Word, Excel, and Lotus 1-2-3. These titles include *Inside Word 6 for Windows*, *Inside Excel 5 for Windows*, *Inside 1-2-3 Release 5*, and *Inside WordPerfect for Windows*.

Orders/Customer Service **1-800-653-6156**     Source Code **NRP95**

**New Riders Publishing**   201 West 103rd Street ◆ Indianapolis, Indiana 46290  USA

# REGISTRATION CARD

## Unlocking Internet Information Server

Name _____ Title _____

Company _____ Type of business _____

Address _____

City/State/ZIP _____

Have you used these types of books before? ☐ yes ☐ no

If yes, which ones? _____

_____

How many computer books do you purchase each year? ☐ 1–5 ☐ 6 or more

How did you learn about this book? _____

Where did you purchase this book? _____

Which applications do you currently use? _____

_____

Which computer magazines do you subscribe to? _____

_____

What trade shows do you attend? _____

_____

Comments: _____

_____

_____

Would you like to be placed on our preferred mailing list? ☐ yes ☐ no

☐ **I would like to see my name in print!** You may use my name and quote me in future New Riders products and promotions. My daytime phone number is: _____

**New Riders Publishing**   201 West 103rd Street ◆ Indianapolis, Indiana 46290  USA

Fax to  **317-581-4670**

Fold Here

- - - - - - - - - - - - - - - - - - - - - - - - - - - - - - - - - - - - - - - - - - - - - - - - - - - -

## BUSINESS REPLY MAIL

**FIRST-CLASS MAIL PERMIT NO. 9918 INDIANAPOLIS IN**

POSTAGE WILL BE PAID BY THE ADDRESSEE

**NEW RIDERS PUBLISHING**
**201 W 103RD ST**
**INDIANAPOLIS IN 46290-9058**

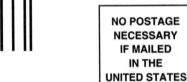